JAPAN IN THE MUROMACHI AGE

JAPAN
IN THE
MUROMACHI AGE

Edited by
JOHN W. HALL
TOYODA TAKESHI

With a new foreword by
PAUL VARLEY

East Asia Program
Cornell University
Ithaca, New York 14853

The Cornell East Asia Series is published by the Cornell University East Asia Program (distinct from Cornell University Press). We publish reasonably-priced books on a variety of scholarly topics relating to East Asia as a service to the academic community and the general public. Standing orders, which provide for automatic billing and shipping of each title in the series upon publication, are accepted.

If after review by internal and external readers a manuscript is accepted for publication, it is published on the basis of camera-ready copy provided by the volume author. Each author is thus responsible for any necessary copy-editing and for manuscript formatting. Address submission inquiries to CEAS Editorial Board, East Asia Program, Cornell University, Ithaca, New York 14853-7601.

Reprint edition first published by East Asia Program, Cornell University, 2001. The first edition of this book was sponsored by the joint Committee on Japanese Studies of the Social Science Research Council and American Council of Learned Societies (1967-96), and published by the University of California Press, Berkeley, 1977 (ISBN 0-520-02888-0 cloth, 0-520-03214-4 paper). Reprinted by permission of the Social Science Research Council.

Number 109 in the Cornell East Asia Series
Copyright © 2001 Betty Bolce Hall and Yoshiko Toyoda. All rights reserved
ISSN 1050-2955
ISBN 1-885445-09-1 pb
Library of Congress Card Number: 00-107789

15 14 13 12 11 10 09 08 07 06 05 04 03 02 01   9 8 7 6 5 4 3 2 1

CONTRIBUTORS
AND COLLABORATORS

Akamatsu Toshihide
George Elison
Kenneth A. Grossberg
John W. Hall
Hayashiya Tatsusaburō
Itō Teiji
Kawai Masaharu
Donald Keene
Cornelius J. Kiley
Kuwayama Kōnen
Miyagawa Mitsuru
V. Dixon Morris

Nagahara Keiji
Paul Novograd
John M. Rosenfield
Barbara Ruch
Robert Sakai
Satō Shin'ichi
Sugiyama Hiroshi
Tanaka Takeo
Toyoda Takeshi
H. Paul Varley
Stanley Weinstein
Kozo Yamamura

Philip Yampolsky

Editorial Assistants

Richard Staubitz   Kanai Madoka

CONTENTS

ILLUSTRATIONS

FOREWORD to the CORNELL EDITION

James Murdoch's *A History of Japan,* written between 1903 and 1917 and published in the early 1920s, was the first major history of Japan in English. Now, after nearly eighty years in print, it remains, in three volumes and 2138 pages (covering the period from early times to the Meiji Restoration of 1868), by far the longest English-language account we have of Japan's past. Brimming with detail, it takes us on a leisurely journey through the Japanese centuries. But one period of Japanese history gets startlingly short shrift: the first two centuries of Muromachi, 1336 to 1543, to which Murdoch allots only 74 pages. By contrast, he devotes a separate chapter of 39 pages just to Minamoto no Yoritomo (1147–99), founder of the Kamakura shogunate, 150 pages to the Kamakura period (not including the Yoritomo chapter), and 425 pages to the years from the introduction of guns to Japan by the Portuguese in 1543[1] to the Battle of Sekigahara in 1600. Obviously one should not judge the quality of the coverage of a topic or period in a book of history simply by the number of pages given to it. But the disparity in space allotted by Murdoch to the Muromachi period, on the one hand, and to the rest of Japan's medieval age, on the other, is striking, and certainly suggests a deliberate slighting of Muromachi.

Murdoch was an ardent adherent to the "great man" school of history, and a reading of his *History* reveals that he found little greatness in Muromachi's cast of leading characters. Here, for example, is his assessment of Ashikaga Takauji (1305–58), founder of the Muromachi shogunate: "[W]hat did Takauji originate? Absolutely nothing—except perhaps a new line of Shōguns, who, with one or two exceptions perhaps, were remarkable for nothing so much as for lack of fibre and gross incapacity . . . Takauji may indeed have been the greatest man of his time; but that is not saying very much, for the middle of the fourteenth century in Japan was the golden age, not merely of turncoats, but of mediocrities."[2]

The second major history of Japan in English was George Sansom's *Japan, A Short Cultural History,* first published in 1931. Although much shorter than Murdoch's three-volume blockbuster, it also is markedly neglectful of the

---

1. Murdoch gives 1542 as the date for the introduction of guns by the Portuguese. This is based on European records. Japanese records say 1543, and are more likely to be correct.

2. James Murdoch. *A History of Japan.* Volume 1. London: Routledge & Kegan Paul, 1949. P. 580.

Muromachi period. Thus, of its 540 pages (from earliest times to the beginning of the nineteenth century), only sixty deal with Muromachi. The century from the Ōnin War (1467–77) to the rise of Oda Nobunaga (1534–82) in the 1560s is covered in a mere three pages. Admittedly, Sansom's main concern in *Japan* is with culture, by which he means primarily religion, literature, the theater, thought, and the visual and plastic arts. But he also devotes considerable space to political, institutional, and even economic developments. His account of the founding of the Kamakura shogunate, for example, occupies some twenty pages. In view of this, a discussion of, say, the Sengoku *daimyō* and their domains would have fit nicely into the book, and would have eased the reader's sense that a century of history is largely missing from *Japan*.

Certainly Sansom does not share Murdoch's extremely negative view of Muromachi as "an era of . . . unceasing turmoil and . . . chronic misery and destitution."[3] On the contrary, after acknowledging the "confusion and turmoil of the Muromachi period," he observes that: "It was an age of ferment, but not of decay, for during the whole of the fourteenth and fifteenth centuries new institutions were developing out of the old and moving towards a maturer feudalism than that of Kamakura."[4]

Although neglectful of Muromachi in *Japan*, Sansom turned his considerable talents as an historian to that period in his post-World War II *A History of Japan, 1334–1615*, which is volume two of a three-volume history from early times until the Meiji Restoration. Fully three-quarters of *Japan, 1334–1615* is devoted to Muromachi, beginning with an entire chapter on Ashikaga Takauji and his role in restoring a semblance of order to the central provinces amid the tide of regionalism that engulfed Japan after the overthrow of the Kamakura shogunate. Having dealt mainly with cultural developments in his earlier *Japan*, Sansom concerns himself largely with political, institutional, social, and economic history in *Japan, 1334–1615*. Here, for the first time in English, is a balanced, comprehensive account of the Muromachi period from those historical perspectives. Now forty years old, *Japan, 1334–1615* is still the most detailed study we have of the Muromachi centuries.

In the very same year, 1961, that Sansom published *Japan, 1334–1615*, John Whitney Hall wrote "Foundations of the Modern Japanese Daimyo" for the *Journal of Asian Studies*.[5] Although short (only twelve pages), this article

---

3. *Ibid.*, p. 634. Murdoch asserts at the same time that Muromachi was "the golden age of Japanese pictorial art," but has little to say about the subject.

4. G.B. Sansom. *Japan, A Short Cultural History*. New York: Appleton-Century-Crofts, 1962. P. 362.

5. This article has been reprinted in Hall and M.B. Jansen, eds. *Studies in the Institutional History of Early Modern Japan*. Princeton: Princeton University Press, 1968.

was of seminal importance for at least two reasons (apart from its intrinsic value as a study of history). First, it marked the expansion of Hall's scholarly interests from the Tokugawa period back to the medieval age (and earlier). Second, it signaled, as we can see in retrospect, the assumption by Hall, already one of the leaders in Tokugawa research, of leadership also in the fields of Muromachi and Unification (Nobunaga and Hideyoshi) studies. This leadership led, among other things, to the organization of the two binational (Japanese-American) conferences whose papers were published in *Japan in the Muromachi Age* (1977) and *Japan Before Tokugawa* (1981). But long before the appearance of these conference volumes Hall had published *Government and Local Power in Japan, 500–1700* (1966), a work widely regarded as marking a coming-of-age in the study of the institutional and social history of pre-Tokugawa Japan based on extensive use of primary documents and awareness of the latest findings and theories of Japanese historians.

Murdoch and other scholars may, in earlier years, have viewed the Muromachi period as a dark, disordered age not worth the attention that other periods of Japanese history deserve, periods when "the important people lived and important things happened." But even a casual examination of what came after Muromachi—Unification and the great peace of Tokugawa—reveals that these stages in the progress of Japanese history would not have been possible without the major developments of Muromachi. Indeed, Muromachi prefigured Unification and Tokugawa in almost every important way, albeit on a lesser and sometimes severely fragmented scale. Unification and Tokugawa were based, for example, on two great building blocks, the daimyo domain *(han)* and the self-managing peasant village *(mura),* both of which were among the many achievements of Muromachi institutional history. Socially, the separation of warriors and peasants *(heinō bunri),* finally implemented by Hideyoshi on a country-wide scale, was the culmination of a powerful current emanating from the Sengoku or late Muromachi age. And the system of alternate attendance *(sankin kōtai),* which shaped the course of Tokugawa history in so many ways, was formulated from Muromachi practices dating back to the third Ashikaga shogun, Yoshimitsu (1358–1408), who, while dominating the shogunate in the last decades of the fourteenth century and the opening years of the fifteenth, required all the *shugo daimyō* to reside primarily in Kyoto. Many other examples of Muromachi precedents for Unification and Tokugawa policies could be cited, but the above will suffice to underscore the vital importance of understanding Muromachi before taking up the study of the three centuries (and more) that followed.

All historians, starting with Murdoch, have recognized the cultural brilliance of the Muromachi period. But until relatively recently their focus has been mostly on Muromachi's elite culture, including the *nō* theater, linked verse poetry *(renga)*, monochrome ink painting *(sumie)*, landscape gardening, and the tea ceremony *(chanoyu)*. As John Hall discusses in his excellent introduction to *Japan in the Muromachi Age*, one of the distinctive features of the 1973 Muromachi conference in Kyoto that led to this volume was its inquiry not only into the elite culture but also into the rich—but even then not extensively studied—field of popular culture. In discussing these contrasting cultural fields, some participants at the conference preferred the terms "great" and "little" to "elite" and "popular." But I was struck by the distinction one of the Japanese participants drew between what he called Muromachi's *yūgen* culture and its *hi-yūgen* (non-*yūgen*) culture.

This distinction is important because it directs attention to what, in my opinion, are the basic, unifying principles of Japan's elite cultural tradition: its aesthetics. There are values, such as naturalness, perishability, simplicity, suggestion, and irregularity, that are traceable back to earliest times and that have served to shape Japanese aesthetics through the centuries and to give continuity and coherence to them in a way that enables one readily to see the aesthetic connections between, say, the arts of the Heian period and those of Muromachi. *Yūgen* (mystery and depth), associated especially with the *nō* theater, was one of the major aesthetic achievements of Muromachi; so also were *sabi* (loneliness) and *wabi* (austerity, deprivation). If we use "*yūgen*" as an inclusive term to represent the aesthetically-structured world of Muromachi elite culture, then "*hi-yūgen*" becomes a useful term to alert us to the fact that there was another realm of culture, popular culture, that was not necessarily governed by classical aesthetics and hence had an originality and vitality quite its own.

Another of the Japanese participants at the 1973 conference used the metaphors of "mountains" *(yama)* and "valleys" *(tani)* to offer a revisionist view of the periodization of Muromachi cultural history. He observed that historians had traditionally regarded the Kitayama (late fourteenth century, early fifteenth century) and Higashiyama (late fifteenth century) epochs as great cultural "mountains," befitting their names. Focusing their studies on these mountains, historians had relatively ignored what came between and after as though they were "valleys" that produced little of cultural importance. Yet, as this participant pointed out, periodizing Muromachi cultural history into mountains and valleys is extremely misleading. Some historians have expressed astonishment that a disordered, troubled age like Muromachi could have given rise to even two epochs of such astonishing cultural flourishing as Kitayama and Higashiyama. But the truth is that culture and the arts flourished uninterruptedly throughout Muromachi and hence the terms

Kitayama and Higashiyama themselves should probably be abandoned as outdated concepts.

The *nō* theater, because of the creative brilliance of Kan'ami (1333–84) and especially Zeami (1363–1443), was largely a Kitayama phenomenon. But all the other major arts of the Muromachi period—linked verse, monochrome ink painting, landscape gardening, the tea ceremony—developed over periods that spanned much or most of the Muromachi years. The tea ceremony, which in many ways epitomized Muromachi cultural brilliance because it brought so many arts and crafts together, is an excellent case in point. With its origins in the late fourteenth century, it gradually developed during the fifteenth century as an "elegant" pursuit, only to shift radically in character during the sixteenth century and reach a high point of aesthetic and cultural achievement as *wabicha* (tea based on the *wabi* aesthetic) under Sen no Rikyū (1522–91) during the age of Unification (the Azuchi-Momoyama cultural epoch).

The major political periods in premodern Japanese history from at least the eighth century on are almost all designated by the locations of their effective governments.[6] Thus we have Nara (710–84), Heian (794–1185), Kamakura (1185–1333), Muromachi (1336–1573),[7] and Edo (1600–1868). (Muromachi and Edo are also alternatively known as the Ashikaga and Tokugawa periods after their ruling warrior houses.) The only one of these periods whose traditional dates are seriously questioned is Muromachi, which has two subperiods—the age of War Between the Courts (Nanboku-chō, 1336–92) and Sengoku (1467 or 1478–1568)— that some historians believe should be recognized as separate, major periods. My feeling is that, inasmuch as the names for the major periods are based on political history and specifically on the locations of effective governments, the Nanboku-chō age should not be separated from Muromachi. To do so would be tantamount to the "decapitation" of Muromachi, since the basic structure of the Muromachi shogunate was evolved during the span 1336–92. On the other hand, it might be conceptually helpful and also more logical to separate Sengoku from Muromachi, preferably with a beginning date of 1478, the year after the Ōnin War, and a terminal date, as recognized by most scholars, of 1568, when Nobunaga entered Kyoto and began the process of Unification.

I offer two principal reasons for recognizing Sengoku as a separate, major period in premodern Japanese history. First, referring again to the fact that most of the major periods are identified by the location of their effective

---

6. An exception is what I have labeled the age of Unification of Nobunaga and Hideyoshi. In fact, there is no standard political designation for this age, although it is known in cultural history as the Azuchi-Momoyama epoch.

7. Muromachi is a section of northeastern Kyoto where the Ashikaga established their shogunate.

governments, the Muromachi shogunate ceased to be an effective government after the Ōnin War. During the Sengoku age the "effective government" became a congeries of governments: those of the Sengoku *daimyō*. Secondly, Kyoto no longer held center stage in Japanese history after the Ōnin War (and for the duration of the Sengoku age). Surely one of the most distinctive features of the Muromachi period was the centrality—indeed, geographic dominance—of Kyoto and its environs in nearly all aspects of Muromachi life, political, social, economic, and cultural. Sengoku, which witnessed the development of new towns and even burgeoning cities in the castle towns (*jōkamachi*) of the Sengoku *daimyō*, set the stage for the remarkable urbanization of Japan from the late sixteenth century that insured that no city would again attain the dominance Kyoto had enjoyed in earlier Muromachi times.

The organizers of the 1973 Muromachi conference at least tacitly endorsed the idea of separating Sengoku from Muromachi by restricting the coverage of most of its papers to the period up to the Ōnin War. In the words of John Hall, writing about the published results of the conference: "The essays in [*Japan in the Muromachi Age*] have not attempted to concentrate systematically upon the post-Ōnin century of Muromachi history." In fact, Hall and others working with the Joint Committee on Japanese Studies of the American Council of Learned Societies and the Social Science Research Council were already planning a separate conference on the Sengoku age. This conference, also a binational, Japanese-American undertaking, was held on Maui, Hawaii in 1977. Although originally called the "Conference on Sengoku Japan," it dealt with the period from roughly 1500 until 1650, a unit of time that included much of Sengoku, the age of Unification, and the critical first half-century of the Tokugawa period.

The 1973 conference was truly a watershed event in the study of the Muromachi period in this country. Bringing together an exceptionally large number of Japanese and American participants (twenty-five), it produced eighteen essays for publication in *Japan in the Muromachi Age*. These essays range over nearly every major aspect of Muromachi—political, institutional, social, and economic history, foreign relations, literature, painting, architecture, and Buddhism. Few other books in English can compete with it for breadth of coverage of a major period in premodern Japanese history. It is a great boon for the field of Japanese studies in general to have it once again in print.

Paul Varley

PREFACE

This volume is the outcome of a binational conference held in the summer of 1973 in Kyoto, Japan. The "Conference on Japan in the Muromachi Age" was one of a set of five academic gatherings planned under the auspices of the Joint Committee on Japanese Studies of the American Council of Learned Societies and the Social Science Research Council. Funds for the conference series were provided by the Ford Foundation in a grant to the SSRC in 1969.

As with any group activity of this sort, the Conference on Japan in the Muromachi Age could not have taken place were it not for the cooperative labor of a great many individuals. The original planning was done by a committee consisting of Robert Brower, University of Michigan; Marius B. Jansen, Princeton University; William H. McCullough, University of California, Berkeley; John Rosenfield, Harvard University; H. Paul Varley, Columbia University; Stanley Weinstein, Yale University; and the present writer. To this group were added three Japanese members— Akamatsu Toshihide, Ōtani University; Hayashiya Tatsusaburō, Kyoto University; and Toyoda Takeshi, Hōsei University.

During 1970 the planning committee helped to define the nature of the conference, select topics for papers, and identify possible paper writers and other participants. As plans became more concrete, it became evident that strong direction was needed in Japan as well as the United States. Professor Toyoda provided that direction, and it was largely due to his efforts that the full cooperation of so many leading Japanese scholars was obtained. As a result he was asked to serve as joint chairman of the conference. In the spring of 1972 Professor Toyoda came to Yale University where final arrangements were made for holding the conference in Kyoto.

In the final year of preparation of the conference the planners were faced with a critical problem. With the unexpected devaluation of the dollar, expenses in Japan were raised by a third. Additional funds were needed, and it was decided to raise money in Japan to cover the deficit. Again Professor Toyoda gave his time and energy to the search for funds. He was joined by Mr. Tanabe Tatsurō of the International House of Japan, whose knowledge of foundation sources in Tokyo proved invaluable. In Kyoto, Professor Akamatsu interested the Abbot of Kinkakuji in contributing toward the conference, while the authorities of Sōkokuji were induced to offer the temple's Great Hall free of charge. The Japan

Foundation, the Mitsubishi Foundation, the Yoshida International Education Fund, and the Ishibashi Foundation also contributed toward the conference.

Fund raising activities and the difficulty of coordinating the work of paper writers and collaborators urged the necessity of setting up an administrative center in Japan. Mr. Matsumoto Shigeharu of International House kindly offered the services of his staff and permitted the use of International House as the business office for the conference.

As the time for the conference approached, other persons were called upon for further contributions. Professors Sugiyama and Kanai of the University of Tokyo Historiographical Institute helped with program scheduling and the preparation of Japanese texts and résumés. Professors Akamatsu and Hayashiya arranged for a variety of special events in Kyoto. Mr. Matsushita, director of the Kyoto National Museum, made special additions to the Museum's current display to include works of special significance for the conference. Finally Professor Atsuta of Kobe University superintended the assembling of conference facilities and organized a group of Kyoto University students to serve as aides.

The conference took place August 27 through September 1, 1973. It was attended by the following Americans: George Elison, Colby College; Kenneth A. Grossberg, Princeton University; John W. Hall, Yale University; Marius B. Jansen, Princeton University; Donald Keene, Columbia University; Cornelius J. Kiley, Villanova University; V. Dixon Morris, University of Hawaii; Paul Novograd, Columbia University; John Rosenfield, Harvard University; Barbara Ruch, University of Pennsylvania; Robert K. Sakai, University of Hawaii; Stanley Weinstein, Yale University; H. Paul Varley, Columbia University; Kozo Yamamura, University of Washington; Philip Yampolsky, Columbia University.

The Japanese participants were Akamatsu Toshihide, Ōtani University (Professor Emeritus, Kyoto University); Akiyama Terukazu, Tokyo University; Fujii Manabu, Kyoto Furitsu University; Haga Kōshirō, Daitō Bunka Gakuin; Hayashiya Tatsusaburō, Kyoto University; Imaeda Aishin, Tokyo University; Itō Teiji, Kōgakuin University; Kanai Madoka, Tokyo University; Kawai Masaharu, Hiroshima University; Kitagawa Tadahiko, Tenri University; Konishi Jin'ichi, Tokyo Kyōiku University; Kuwayama Kōnen, Tokyo University, Miyagawa Mitsuru, Osaka Kyōiku University; Murai Yasuhiko, Kyoto Joshi University; Nagahara Keiji, Hitotsubashi University; Satō Shin'ichi, Nagoya University; Shigemori Mirei, Kyoto; Sugiyama Hiroshi, Tokyo University; Tanaka Takeo, Tokyo University; Toyoda Takeshi, Hōsei University (Professor Emeritus, Tohoku University).

While not all participants are represented as authors of papers or as collaborators, all had a part in making the conference a success. In five days of serious discussion each paper was subjected to thorough analysis. Each emerged the better as a result. All conference participants are thanked for their contribution to this published product.

Finally, the editors wish to thank the staff of the SSRC, particularly John Campbell, David Sills, and Susan Pharr, for their sympathetic administrative support thoughout the long period of preparation for the conference and the even longer period of editorial work required to bring the conference papers into publishable form. They wish to acknowledge as well the valuable services rendered by Richard Staubitz and Kanai Madoka who, as Editorial Assistants, helped shape the conference papers into coherent form. Our special respect goes to Adrienne Suddard who with patience and skill brought order and polish to the final manuscript. Emiko Staubitz is thanked for preparing the glossary and index; Robert L. Williams for his mapwork and drawings. Finally, the following students in the Yale Graduate School assisted in the proofreading: Keiko Itō, Lee M. Sands, Sheldon Garon, Susan Cowell, Amy Plaut Gassman, and James L. McClain.

JOHN WHITNEY HALL
Yale University

INTRODUCTION
The Muromachi Age in Japanese History

JOHN W. HALL

Significant reinterpretations of major portions of a nation's history occur periodically as historians combine new findings with new approaches or as they pursue their inquiry with different conceptions of the nature of the historical process. It was the good fortune of the participants in the Conference on Japan in the Muromachi Age to be witness to such a major reinterpretation. The history of Japan has passed through a number of phases of interpretation during the last century. An early reliance on the "great man" interpretation has given way to more impersonal analyses of social and political processes. A common preoccupation with "cultural history" has broken down into a series of specialized approaches: economic, social, intellectual, or religious. Japanese history has been looked at through the eyes of Toynbee and Marx, and its meaning contrasted to the import of European and Chinese history. Through such processes Japan's history has acquired its currently accepted contours and its assumed place within the larger context of world history.

It is natural that historians working outside Japan should differ from Japanese historians both in their knowledge of Japanese history and their evaluation of its significance in a broader world context. Few scholars not born to the Japanese language can claim the capacity to deal easily and creatively with Japanese historical materials; few scholars outside Japan can acquire the same familiarity with the voluminous literature of a given field of Japanese historical study as can their Japanese counterparts. Thus there is a natural lag in the dissemination of the latest findings and interpretations from out of the body of professional Japanese historians to the community of professional historians outside Japan and beyond them to the foreign reading public. This is not to say that advances in the study of Japanese history can be made only in Japan by Japanese scholars. But the process of study and restudy by non-Japanese is obviously more laborious, and interpretations are less easily reviewed or revised within the smaller circle of specialists who exist outside Japan.

In recent years, the general outline of Japan's modern history has been

1

absorbed into the consciousness of the world at large. Japan's dramatic entry into the mainstream of modern world events has forced a recognition of the strength of Japan's historical momentum and has urged comparisons between the revolutionary process in Japan and in other parts of the world. The result has been a natural concentration of attention on nineteenth- and twentieth-century Japanese history. Thus the great body of foreign scholarship on Japan has been focused upon the late Tokugawa period, the Meiji Restoration of 1868, and the subsequent century of modern development. Earlier periods have been left to the occasional generalist or to specialists in literature, art, and religious studies. It is naturally in these earlier periods that the lag between the work by Japanese historians and the interpretations held outside Japan has been most pronounced.

Among the most neglected and misunderstood chapters in Japanese history has been the Muromachi era which encompassed the fourteenth and fifteenth centuries. The neglect has been characteristic not only of foreign scholars but of Japanese as well. A primary reason for this was that the Muromachi age has been looked upon until now chiefly as a time of transition, an interlude between a more important classical era, as epitomized in the Heian period, and a more vigorous early modern age, as exemplified in the Tokugawa period. The Muromachi age, for all its cultural brilliance, has been regarded as a time of political weakness and institutional decay.

Although cultural historians have long recognized the Muromachi age as a time of important achievements in the arts, they did not until recently attempt to link these achievements to any durable changes in the structure of government or in the social conditions of the country. To many writers, in fact, the cultural flowering of the Muromachi period seemed fortuitous, the result of a successful but ephemeral effort by a newly emergent military aristocracy to emulate the classical style of life of the court nobility. Furthermore, since so much of Kyoto and its elite society was presumed destroyed in the Ōnin War (1467–1477), it was assumed that there was little significant continuity between what transpired before and after the great Ōnin watershed. Some historians have gone so far as to claim that nothing which happened prior to the Ōnin War could be considered relevant to modern Japan.

Once historians began to play down the significance of the Muromachi age, neglect tended to cumulate. Because few scholars interested themselves in Muromachi history, the period was generally inadequately treated in the standard history books. This poor treatment, in turn, was interpreted as reflecting the inherent opaqueness of the period itself. It has long been assumed that materials did not exist which would permit an adequate reconstruction of basic Muromachi institutions.

This view of the Muromachi age has come under increasing attack in recent decades, chiefly from among Japanese historians. Through diligent search these scholars have uncovered source materials which have opened up to full investigation most aspects of the period. New studies of the Muromachi shogunate and its sources of power, of the shugo houses and their local sources of support, of village and city organization, have revealed that important changes in political and social organization were taking place and that these were having profound effects upon Japan's institutional development. Studies of Muromachi patronage patterns have helped to link these political and social developments with the cultural achievements of the age and with the changing life styles of the elite and the masses.

As more has been learned about the Muromachi age, historians have begun to change their views regarding its place within the sweep of Japanese history. It has long been acknowledged that many of the art forms and aesthetic principles which emerged in the Kitayama and Higashiyama environments became important ingredients of what is recognized today as Japan's distinctive cultural tradition. It was then, for instance, that the arts of nō drama, monochrome painting, landscape gardening, tea ceremony, and renga poetry were perfected. Now historians are showing us that in the spheres of political organization and social behavior as well, the Muromachi age gave rise to new patterns which likewise became important elements in a distinctly Japanese political and social tradition. Thus the Muromachi era is being looked upon as a seminal period of institutional and cultural change, a time during which many of the dominant traditions of political organization and religious and artistic expression which were to persist until modern times took shape.

This new insight into the Muromachi age is not yet widely disseminated and has been confined largely to the circle of pioneer Japanese historians who are still breaking new ground in their studies of the period. In recent years, however, enough persons outside Japan have begun to work in the field of medieval Japanese studies to make possible a worthwhile exchange between Japanese and foreign specialists. As a consequence it became both feasible and attractive to consider the holding of an academic conference on Japan in the Muromachi age as a way to give more recognition and currency to the work of contemporary scholars in the field and also to stimulate further interest in the study of medieval Japan outside Japan, particularly in the United States. Thus it came about that in 1969, as part of the program of the newly established Joint Committee on Japanese

Studies of the Social Science Research Council and the American Council on Learned Societies, the Conference on Japan in the Muromachi Age was given a place along with four other conferences devoted to certain aspects of contemporary Japanese development.

The conference took place from August 27 through September 1, 1973 in Kyoto, the seat of the Muromachi shogunate, in the main hall of Sōkokuji, the temple most closely identified with that government. Tables and chairs arranged on the tatami of the great hall, along with four welcome electric fans, were the only concessions made to the temple architecture whose style had been set in the Muromachi age some five centuries before. Japanese was used as the language of the conference, and for five days some thirty-five scholars, Japanese and American, shared their views on the Muromachi age, discussing the fourteen papers which had been distributed for the occasion. The results were both informative and dramatic.

The drama of the conference unfolded at several levels. There was, first, the excitement which came from the realization that Japanese and American scholars could communicate fully and with relative ease on such subjects as professionally demanding as the structure of Japan's medieval government or economy, popular Buddhist religious sects, or the aesthetics of linked-verse poetry. The American scholars, used to working with Japanese, were not surprised at the possibility of private communication with Japanese scholars, but many of them experienced for the first time the thrill of discovering the possibility of holding the attention of a conference assemblage consisting in large part of outstanding Japanese specialists.

The drama was played out at another level, in which scholars from differing disciplines and unfamiliar to each other, sat around the same table and shared their ideas. On the American side this had a double meaning. Most American specialists in the medieval Japanese field came from environments in which they were forced to work in isolation even when attached to a major university. The feeling of strength in numbers, the sense that a new field of Japanese studies was coming into its own, was strongly shared by the American participants. For the Japanese the experience was probably less explicit. Yet among them too the realization that theories and interpretations could be shared between the several fields of literature, art, architecture, or social organization proved stimulating.

It is not for an American observer to comment on what the Japanese scholars, either individually or collectively, learned or newly discovered about Muromachi history as a result of the conference. On the American side the experience was vastly enlightening. For them a whole era of

Japanese history, until then partially or imperfectly understood, was brought to life and given new meaning. As noted above, the still common view of the Muromachi period as carried in the historical surveys written in English was that of an age in which a brilliant culture was somewhat mysteriously supported on the weakest of political foundations and throughout long periods of incessant warfare. Muromachi culture defined in terms of *nō* and of Zen temples, Sung-style monochrome painting and austere stone gardens, was commonly explained as the product of a combination of energy provided by the new military aristocracy and the artistic talents and sensibilities of the old court nobility. Nurtured in the great monasteries which surrounded the city of Kyoto, this culture was presumed to have survived only partially and precariously the political disintegration which followed the Ōnin War. Not until the peace imposed by the Tokugawa shogunate at the start of the seventeenth century did the Japanese regain the capacity to take an interest in cultural pastimes. Meanwhile, by the end of the seventeenth century, a culture of the "common people" had begun to blossom in the great cities of Kyoto, Osaka, and Edo. In the common view this popular culture was made to appear suddenly and spontaneously, the product of a new urban social group which had only recently made its appearance in the centers of Tokugawa political power.

This interpretation left much of the period between the fourteenth and seventeenth centuries in Japan subject to puzzling contradictions. If the culture of the Muromachi age was chiefly the product of aristocratic patronage, and if that patronage is believed to have been destroyed in the Ōnin war or in the century of civil struggle which followed, then how does one account for the strong continuity of the several aesthetic traditions which were defined during the Muromachi age? If the only aspect of Muromachi culture worthy of note was the work of the elite levels of society, then how is one to account for the appearance in such mature form of a popular urban culture during the late seventeenth century? If Kyoto is thought to have been destroyed during the Ōnin War and the aristocracy totally impoverished, then what accounts for the glowing descriptions of sixteenth-century Kyoto by the Jesuit missionaries who saw it as a city of great beauty with well kept streets and splendid palaces?

To be sure the answers to these historiographical contradictions have been given by specialists in Muromachi history for some time, but the new insights have not as yet had their effect upon the general literature. Nor has there as yet been a fully coordinated attack upon the interpretive problems presented by the Muromachi period. Thus the greatest single contribution of the conference on Muromachi Japan was that it brought together from a variety of disciplines confirming evidence that the Muromachi period must be significantly reconsidered.

The most generally applicable of the new ideas which emerged from the conference was the conclusion that historians have tended to overplay the element of decay and have too often looked upon signs of institutional change as evidence of chaos. In survey histories the court nobility is commonly killed off several times over only to be discovered as having survived into the seventeenth century. Kyoto is described as a city in ruins many times over, but little is said of the energy of the people who rebuilt the city into the form so admired by its sixteenth-century European visitors. Although historians have recognized the evidence of economic growth, they have seen it almost as a contradictory element, something to set against the picture of political decay. They have given little thought to the possibility that such growth might be related to fundamental changes in the popular substructure of Japanese society.

The conference papers and attendant discussions emphasized over and over again the strong and vigorous continuities in both the elite and popular levels of society, of the "great" and "little" traditions, throughout the war-filled fifteenth and sixteenth centuries. They emphasized particularly the vigorous new developments in popular culture—the formation of an urban society with its attendant literature, arts, and religious practices. They revealed that Muromachi culture was not simply an upper class affair. They showed that the origins of the popular culture of the Edo period could in many instances be traced back to the Muromachi age.

Discovery of a "popular element" in Muromachi life led to another interpretation of general applicability. No matter what aspect of Muromachi history one might choose to explore, one was sure to discover new complexities and new dimensions which made old simplistic interpretations untenable. Muromachi life was many-faced and many-leveled. It was much richer in variety than had been imagined. For every genre of artistic or literary expression, there were both elite and popular manifestations. The monochrome ink paintings appreciated by the upper class could be matched by popular pictorial art directed at people on all levels of society to illustrate religious sermons or to tell entertaining stories. The rigorous life of monastic training in some Zen monasteries could be contrasted with the freer style of religious movements which appealed to the elite as well as the unlettered masses. Exquisitely refined nō was not the only dramatic form worthy of note in an age that produced the comical kyōgen, popular ballad singers, and itinerant dramatic performers. Just as political historians had discovered the vigorous activities of local gentry and village leaders below the level of the elite figures who alone had seemed worthy of attention by medieval historical chroniclers, so in the cultural sphere new strength and creative capacity was now recognized at the popular level.

To some extent, of course, this recognition came not from any new discovery of the popular level of Muromachi culture but rather from a new willingness to find the popular culture worthy of attention. This change of view followed from the realization that without the prior Muromachi development, the later Edo flowering could not have happened when it did. It also resulted from a realization that many of the elements of the Muromachi "great tradition," which are considered particularly new, should be attributed less to the creative work of aristocratic artists than to the adoption by the elite of elements from the "little tradition." Men of humble origins were intimately involved in the perfection of such genre as *nō*, poetry, gardens, architecture, and certain styles of painting. This affirmation of a vigorous popular base to Muromachi culture served not only to draw attention to a neglected dimension of the age, it forced historians to realize that they had looked upon the Muromachi age in too narrow a fashion. In fact, for nearly every aspect of higher culture, popular elements lay close to the surface or closely related, much as kyōgen was to nō.

Out of these new discoveries emerged an appreciation of the need for a major rethinking of the periodization of the Muromachi period. Traditionally the Muromachi age has been described from the center outward as a time of political weakness. The first shogun, Ashikaga Takauji, seemed incapable of establishing firm central control. Although Takauji's grandson, the third shogun Yoshimitsu, managed to unite the country briefly and to play for a time the role of absolute hegemon, his successors proved ineffective. The sixth shogun, Yoshinori, was assassinated by one of his own vassals. The eighth shogun, Yoshimasa, retreated to his villa while the great lords of the land fought out their quarrels in the streets of Kyoto. After the Ōnin War the shogunate, according to the traditional interpretation, was powerless, and Japan entered its century of "a country at war."

The conference forced a reconsideration of this periodization. Although there can be no question that Yoshimitsu brought the Muromachi shogunate to its early peak of power, bakufu strength lasted well beyond his death in 1408 into the time of Yoshinori (1429-1442). Yoshimasa's rule (1443-1490), though marred by the Ōnin War, did not mark the absolute end of the bakufu's power. Neither politically nor culturally can the period after the end of the Ōnin War in 1477 be dismissed simply as a time of warfare and chaos. The Ashikaga shogunate continued to play an important role in the politics and the economic affairs of the capital area, while throughout Japan the sixteenth century witnessed the most dramatic development of popular culture and new social and economic institutions at the local level.

These, then, were the main overall results of the conference's assessment of the Muromachi period—a new discovery of continuity and vigor in political and social institutions, a new-found popular element which demanded respect, and as a result a new periodization. Together these discoveries seemed to confirm the opinions of the conference participants that the Muromachi age must be considered one of the seminal periods in Japanese history. In one way or another all the essays presented in this volume elaborate these themes.

A meeting as thoroughly binational as the Conference on Japan in the Muromachi Age can hardly fail to have had its moments of drama and emotion. On the part of the Japanese, perhaps the first such moment came with the realization that the Americans not only talked their language but did so sometimes with style and wit. For the Americans the moment of greatest nervousness came at that point in the evening reception at Kyoto University when it became apparent that in true Japanese style each would be expected to sing or in some way perform in answer to the well-polished performances of their Japanese hosts. For all alike the high point of the conference came on the third day when Professor Weinstein, speaking about the development of popular religious beliefs, uttered the name of Nichiren. At that very moment a deafening crash of lightning plunged the great hall of Sōkokuji in darkness. Some attendants brought out altar candles to illuminate the continuing discussion. For the next half hour the flicker of candlelight played upon the conference table while torrential rains poured off the massive roof of the great hall. Between enveloping rain and candlelight the conference participants were drawn into a unity of mood and objective of unusual intensity.

PART ONE
Time and Place

1

Muromachi Japan: A Note on Periodization

In Japanese historical periodization the years from roughly the middle of the fourteenth century to the middle of the sixteenth century are referred to as either the Ashikaga or the Muromachi age. The first name derives from the house of Ashikaga which held the office of shogun from 1338 to 1573. The second derives from the location in Kyoto of the primary shogunal headquarters. Present-day historians prefer to use the term Muromachi, since it has a broader connotation and is less associated with the strictly political and elite aspects of the period. The name Muromachi evokes, in other words, not only the political struggles which swirled about the Ashikaga shoguns and the great regional lords, but also the many cultural and religious achievements of the period and the widespread social changes evident in both town and village.

But, despite the tendency to play down the importance of the ruling family, it is still the events in the political realm which must provide the main points of reference for the historian's sense of the internal divisions within the Muromachi age as a whole. A brief summary of the political history of the Muromachi period centering on the Ashikaga house will serve, therefore, to make explicit the periodization which is implicit in the essays which follow.

The Ashikaga house was descended from the same Seiwa branch of the Minamoto clan as was the shogunal house of the preceding Kamakura period. As one of the important supports of the Kamakura shogunate, the Ashikaga house held the military governorships of Kazusa and Mikawa provinces, while cadet branches—among them the Shiba, Niki, Hosokawa, Hatakeyama, Imagawa, and Isshiki houses—extended the family influence over these and other provinces of the northeast. In the warfare which attended Emperor Go-Daigo's attempt between 1331 and 1336 to destroy the Kamakura shogunate and bring a return to direct imperial rule, Takauji, head of the Ashikaga house, first aided in the destruction of

11

the Kamakura shogunate and then ousted Go-Daigo from Kyoto. In 1338, having set up a puppet emperor, Takauji established a new military government in Kyoto with himself as shogun. During the next two centuries, fifteen members of the Ashikaga house served in that office.

Shogun	In Office		Shogun	In Office
Takauji, 1305–1358	1338–1358		Yoshihisa, 1465–1489	1473–1489
Yoshiakira, 1330–1367	1358–1367		Yoshitane, 1466–1523	1490–1493, 1508–1521
Yoshimitsu, 1358–1408	1368–1395		Yoshizumi, 1480–1511	1494–1508
Yoshimochi, 1385–1428	1394–1423, 1425–1428		Yoshiharu, 1511–1550	1521–1546
Yoshikazu, 1407–1425	1423–1425		Yoshiteru, 1536–1565	1546–1565
Yoshinori, 1394–1441	1428–1441		Yoshihide, 1540–1568	1565–1568
Yoshikatsu, 1434–1443	1441–1443		Yoshiaki, 1537–1597	1568–1573
Yoshimasa, 1436–1490	1443–1473			

Typical of so many dynastic histories, the history of the Ashikaga house records vigorous military and political leadership in the early years with a tendency to lose national influence in later generations. During an early formative period, the first shogun Takauji and his brother Tadayoshi established the shogunate and fought for its security. But they left to the second shogun, Yoshiakira, a still precarious hegemony. The emperor Go-Daigo and his successors managed to keep alive a court in exile in defiance of the Kyoto-based court from which the Ashikaga shogunate derived its legitimacy, and this provided a rallying point for continued opposition to the Ashikaga house. Many historians, in fact, consider the period from 1336 to 1392, during which the two rival imperial courts remained in conflict, as a separable epoch in Japan's history to which they assign the name "Nambokuchō Jidai," i.e., the Era of the Northern and Southern Courts.

It fell to the lot of the third shogun, Yoshimitsu, to consolidate the power of the Ashikaga shogunate by bringing to an end the division of the imperial line and by tightening Ashikaga control over the great regional lords, the *shugo-daimyō*. The brief period from 1392, when the north-south court rivalry was resolved, to Yoshimitsu's death in 1408 is consequently regarded as the high point of Ashikaga power and influence. These years are generally referred to as the Kitayama epoch, a term which derives from the location of the villa built in the suburbs of Kyoto by Yoshimitsu in his later years. Kitayama therefore stands for both the political ascendancy of the Ashikaga house and for the first burst of cultural florescence brought about by Yoshimitsu's lavish patronage of the arts.

It has been presumed that Ashikaga fortunes declined rapidly after Yoshimitsu's death, a definite turning point coming in 1441 when the shogun Yoshinori was assassinated by one of his own vassals. This episode, the so-called "Kakitsu affair," has been given new meaning in the work of recent Japanese historians, and this is reflected in the essays which follow. Yoshinori is now looked upon as the shogun who came closest to converting the Ashikaga shogunate (the Muromachi *bakufu*) into a "feudal monarchy." But his assassination brought to an abrupt end this trend toward centralization of power. Thereafter the Ashikaga house reverted to its role of feudal hegemon. As keeper of the balance of power among competing regional lords, the political importance of the shogun was reduced. But the Ashikaga house retained sufficient power to feature in yet another era of high cultural achievement. This occurred during the later years of the eighth shogun Yoshimasa's life, particularly from his retirement in 1473 to his death in 1490, during which time he acted as patron of the arts from his villa set in the Higashiyama district of Kyoto. It is to these years that the name Higashiyama has been applied.

Although recent historical interpretations have done a good deal to discount the significance of the Ōnin War which ravaged the capital from 1467 to 1477, the Ōnin years still must be regarded as marking a major turning point in Japan's political history. The essays which follow suggest that the war itself did not critically determine the subsequent course of history. Yet the "late Muromachi" period clearly constitutes a distinct and separable epoch. Whether the period from 1477 to 1573 is conceived of separately under the name "Sengoku" (the Warring States Period) or is thought of simply as the "late Muromachi era" is not of great importance. The years after 1477 evoke for most scholars an entirely different range of problems and questions from those of the previous century and a half. The political historian turns from an interest in the Ashikaga house to studies of the struggles for power among the regional lords, or between them and newly emergent groups in villages and towns. The social historian turns from preoccupation with elite levels of society to a concern for developments among the peasantry and townsmen. The cultural historian sees as the significant features of this period the spread of popular religious beliefs and organizations and of literary and artistic genres of popular appeal.

The essays in this book have not attempted to concentrate systematically upon the post-Ōnin century of Muromachi history. But they all, to some extent, lead up to it and offer interpretations which suggest that post-Ōnin developments should be looked upon as continuations of trends identifiable in the first half of the Muromachi age. Beyond 1477, however, the historian is given no clear landmarks for purposes of periodization. The arrival of Portuguese ships and Jesuit missionaries after 1543, which might serve as such a landmark, may be an event of importance from the point of view of world history, but Japan's first encounter with the West was of little fundamental significance for the political, social, economic, or even religious development of sixteenth-century Japan. Sengoku Japan, a time of immense social and cultural change, remains largely uncharted and historiographically undifferentiated.

2

Kyoto in the Muromachi Age

HAYASHIYA TATSUSABURŌ
with George Elison

Although the history of Japan during the Muromachi era rightly embraces all that happened throughout the country from the Kantō provinces in the northeast to Kyushu in the southwest, much of the significant activity of the period took place in and around the great city of Kyoto. From its founding in 794 as Heian Kyō, Kyoto was the city of the emperor and the court nobility. Its political importance was partially eclipsed by Kamakura during the period of the first shogunate, but it continued to serve as the cultural and economic center of the country throughout the twelfth and thirteenth centuries. With the establishment of the Ashikaga shogunate in Kyoto in 1338, the city again became the undisputed center of national politics. Kyoto was the stage upon which much of the action described in the succeeding essays took place, and the changing look of Kyoto, both in physical form and human organization, illustrates many of the fundamental changes which affected all of Japan during the Muromachi era.

THE EMERGENCE OF MEDIEVAL KYOTO

The city known as Heian Kyō came to an end together with the Heian period. The great fire which swept the capital in the fourth month of Angen 3 (1177) reduced most of the city to ashes, sparing neither the imperial palace nor the great hall of state (Daigoku-den) which was the imperial government's ultimate architectural symbol. The great hall was destined never to be rebuilt. Even though the era name was changed after this calamity to Chishō (Continuing Tranquillity) in the hopes of ensuring a brighter future, the new era and its successors saw only new turbulence and warfare as the Gempei War (1180–1185) swept the land.[1]

1. For a brief summary of the disturbances of the Chishō years and the several stages of the Gempei War, see Hayashiya Tatsusaburō, "Chūsei shi gaisetsu," in *Iwanami kōza: Nihon rekishi* (Tokyo, 1962), 5: 13–16.

With the collapse of the old order, Heian Kyō also lost its authority. The city's very name—Capital of Peace and Tranquillity—went out of use, to be replaced by the term Kyoto.

The new political order which Minamoto Yoritomo established in 1185 was directed not from imperial Kyoto but from provincial Kamakura. To be sure, the imperial court remained in Kyoto; for a time it retained considerable vigor and even repaired its capacity for political maneuvers. But the shogunate had by far the greater power, a fact proved conclusively in 1221 when the Retired Emperor Go-Toba initiated an armed confrontation with Kamakura only to be forced to capitulate within one month. The so-called Jōkyū Disturbance rang down the curtain on Kyoto as the main stage of national affairs; and it stayed down for a century. Kamakura was clearly the seat of effective authority, and it made sure that its presence was felt directly in Kyoto. In Rokuhara resided the shogunate's powerful agents, the Rokuhara Tandai, who kept their eyes upon a restive court. The resulting dualism remolded the character and physical shape of Kyoto.

The medieval character of Kyoto was revealed clearly in the city's transformation into a primary religious center. Heian Buddhism had assumed for itself the role of the nation's protector and stressed the interdependence between Buddha's law and the imperial sway. Yet the main Tendai and Shingon establishments were set down some distance from the capital. With the appearance of new, more popularly oriented faith sects, such as Jōdo and Nichiren, and the strongly patronized Zen sects, particularly Rinzai, this condition changed. Except for Zen, the new religious orders were less immediately tied to the state or the aristocracy. Rather they directed themselves to the salvation of the individual and were meant for the sake of the populace at large. Their headquarters were either in Kyoto or in the city's immediate environs. Kyoto was thereby being transformed into a religious center in the true sense of the phrase, a characteristic the city was destined to retain into modern times.

Another major characteristic of medieval Kyoto is revealed in the city's growth as a primary commercial center. The increase in agricultural productivity which occurred during the middle and late Kamakura period was accompanied by the commercialization of the surplus product. Kyoto's emergence as a commercial city was a phenomenon of the Muromachi era, but the origins can be seen in the inqreased circulation of money during the previous age. The growth of commerce and the rise of new religions were not discrete phenomena. Commerce spread along routes frequented by adherents of the new faiths; religion was transmitted along routes which merchants had pioneered. Kyoto became the major crossroads of this interrelated network and was nourished by expanding contacts with the provinces.

These changes in Kyoto's basic character were reflected in the city's physical shape. The Heian capital had been laid out along a north-south axis and divided into left (or eastern) and right (or western) halves named Sakyō and Ukyō. When, during the Heian period the city spread across the Kamo River to the east, the same axis prevailed; Kyō, to the west of the river, and Shirakawa, to the east, were ranged alongside each other. In the Kamakura period, however, the city gradually oriented along an east-west axis, dividing into upper (northern) and lower (southern) halves. Eventually the distinction would assume a formal character, so that Kyoto in the Muromachi period was conceived of officially as consisting of northern and southern halves: Kamigyō and Shimogyō. The notion took root during the Nambokuchō period, and as it did so the rebirth of Kyoto began.

THE MUROMACHI RESTORATION OF THE CAPITAL

During the period of warfare between the Northern and Southern Courts, Kyoto was restored to its position as political capital of the country, thereby regaining the national prominence it had lost to Kamakura. But the political center of the city was no longer the palace of the emperor as had been the case in the Heian period. Rather, although the Kamakura regime had been brought down in the name of the emperor, the city owed its prestige to a Kamakura general, Ashikaga Takauji, who first helped and then thwarted Emperor Go-Daigo's attempt at an imperial restoration. Following his military victories, Takauji decided to abandon Kamakura and relocate the military headquarters. After careful consideration, he chose Kyoto, and the seat of authority was returned to the city of the emperor.[2]

The actual political significance of this move in the long run was to be diminished by the fact that the Ashikaga shogunate never succeeded in extending completely its control throughout the country. But the cultural significance of the move was epochal. The patronage of the Ashikaga shoguns, most notably Yoshimitsu and Yoshimasa, contributed significantly to the emergence of those distinctive styles in the arts which we as-

---

2. That Takauji gave substantial weight to this problem is evident in the fact that his own *Kemmu shikimoku* (Kemmu injunctions) of 1336 begins with the question whether or not to move the bakufu from Kamakura; Satō Shin'ichi and Ikeuchi Yoshisuke, eds., *Chūsei hōsei shiryōshū* (Tokyo, 1957), 2: 3. Cf. Hayashiya Tatsusaburō, *Nambokuchō*, in *Sōgen shinsho*, 4 (Osaka, 1967): 82.

sociate with the Muromachi period. Of course, the role of host to the Ashikaga regime was not an unmixed blessing. The regime's vicissitudes could not but affect Kyoto, and the decline of the shogunate's political fortunes, which were already well advanced by the middle of the fifteenth century, attracted disasters upon the capital. Paradoxically, it was the experience of those disasters—in particular the Ōnin War of 1467–1477—that helped strengthen the city's capacity to exist on its own terms. Amidst war, fire, and pillage a new solidarity was achieved by the townspeople, and a new communal life came into being.

Why did Ashikaga Takauji settle on Kyoto for the location of his bakufu? Part of the answer lay in his perception of regional differences within Japan. In the long and narrow Japanese archipelago, conditions differed greatly between the eastern and western parts of the country. The modes of life were not the same, and there grew up a contrasting sense of values: in the eastern part of the country the emphasis was on land and rice, in the western part on trade and cash; in the east the horse was the principal means of transportation, in the west the boat predominated; the east had always, and not without justification, been deemed more primitive, while the west was the cultural center of the country. Takauji's decision to move the bakufu from the east to the west surely was influenced by such considerations. It is highly likely that Takauji had decided early on that he would no longer depend solely upon land and proprietary domains as his base of power. Rather he would encourage the expansion of trade with China and put his emphasis on the commercial economy. His decision was undoubtedly influenced both by political and economic considerations.

The establishment of the Ashikaga shogunate in Kyoto was accompanied by other new developments. Throughout the Kamakura period there had been no set place for the imperial palace, and the sovereigns moved from one "private residence" (sato dairi) to another. During the imperial schism of Nambokuchō, the Northern Court was settled in a permanent location in Kyoto (although Go-Daigo and his successors in the Southern Court were forced to wander through the mountains of Yoshino). The site which Takauji picked for his protégé, Emperor Kōmyō, was in Tsuchimikado Higashi no Tōin. The emperor moved to his new palace in 1337, thereby establishing it as the sato dairi of his own lineage.[3] After the two branches of the imperial house were reconciled in 1392, this site attained the official status of "palace" (gosho) which has been associated with it ever since. Although fire has destroyed the buildings many times over, and the dimensions of the palace have changed over the centuries,

3. On the Tsuchimikado Gosho, see Kyōto Shi, ed., Kyōto no rekishi (Tokyo, 1967), 3: 42–44.

and the appearance of the surrounding grounds has undergone many changes, there has been no major shift in the location of the Kyoto Gosho. The Tsuchimikado Gosho did not compare in size, impressiveness, or public function with the great imperial palace of Heian Kyō. Nor was it representative of the architectural monuments of the Muromachi period as was Kyoto's other gosho, the shogun's residence.[4] When Yoshimitsu's Palace of Flowers (Hana no Gosho) was completed, the headquarters of the military aristocracy and the court of the imperial aristocracy reached toward each other across Karasuma-dōri in Kamigyō. This physical proximity symbolized the close tie between the court and the military which was responsible for the initial development of Kyoto in the Muromachi period. Perhaps a third element ought to be added to the symbol: the great Zen monastery of Sōkokuji, founded by Yoshimitsu and located only two avenues to the east of the Hana no Gosho to serve as the family temple of the Ashikaga house. This triad—imperial, military, and Buddhist—defined quite well the character of Kamigyō, the Upper Capital, which even in the post-Muromachi period would be known as the city's aristocratic quarter.

When it was completed in 1381, the Hana no Gosho boasted not only its famous profusion of flowers but also a size twice that of the emperor's palace, a clear sign of the actual balance of power in the capital. The gardens were laid out, and the residential complex built, according to the classic architectural principles of the imperial aristocracy. Although this adherence to classical forms may not reveal Yoshimitsu's actual mode of government, it surely does reveal his monarchal pretensions. It was not merely sedulous attention to courtly precedent that made him construct his palace that way. Yoshimitsu was not satisfied to rank at the apex of the military hierarchy and its power structure; he wished to demonstrate also that he was at least the peer of the *kuge*. He was both shogun and the bearer of exalted court ranks and titles. The elegance of his palace had to be no less than imperial. The Hana no Gosho was the perfect physical sign that he had amalgamated the imperial style and prestige with his own, thereby fulfilling his ardent desire for distinction.

If Kamigyō was the aristocratic quarter, then Shimogyō, the Lower Capital, was the domain of the townsmen. Its northern border changed from time to time but was generally held to be Nijō-dōri. Between the two parts of the city were open spaces where no people resided; as the place name Yanagi no Bamba indicates, there was room enough for riding grounds. Shimogyō centered on Shijō-dōri, and the area to the south of

4. For a list of Takauji's Kyoto residences, see *Kyōto no rekishi*, 3: 386–387; for a description of Yoshimitsu's Palace of Flowers, ibid., 3: 387–389.

that street was the earliest to develop commercially. This area became known as the Old Quarter, Furumachi, the kernel out of which the townsmen's world of Kyoto sprouted and grew.

The area of Shirakawa to the east of the Kamo River gradually declined in importance after the abolition of the office of the In (the office of the Retired Emperor). Thereafter until the Ōnin War it appears that the entire area of Shirakawa reverted to farmland. In contrast, Toba to the south prospered, albeit under a new name. Kusatsu, as this area came to be known, became the bustling riverport of Kyoto. Boats coming from the Inland Sea unloaded their goods here, which were then transported by carters and packhorse-drivers into the city itself. Farther to the southeast, Uji, which had flourished even in the earlier periods, gained additional renown as a tea-producing center during the Muromachi period.

Off to the northwest, Saga, a terminus for lumber and other products brought from the mountainous provinces to the north, also attained new prosperity as a riverport when Ashikaga Takauji built there the great Zen monastery Tenryūji in order to solace the spirit of his adversary Go-Daigo. The surroundings of the Tenryūji became a center of usury, the home grounds of the moneylenders known as the *Saga dosō*. Buddhist halls of prayer coexisted with a goodly number of sake breweries and counting houses.

THE WORLD OF PRESTIGE

The representative architectural monuments of the Muromachi military aristocracy are the Golden Pavilion and the Silver Pavilion. The former stands for a period when the Ashikaga shogunate was at its zenith; the latter dates from when the bakufu was sliding irretrievably toward its nadir. The first edifice is located in the hills north of the city, and the second in the hills which flank Kyoto on the east. Those two locations—Kitayama and Higashiyama—have given their names to the two epochs of cultural history which define and express the Muromachi period's distinctive aesthetic qualities.

The age of Kitayama is associated primarily with Ashikaga Yoshimitsu but may be extended to 1441 when Yoshinori, the last strong Ashikaga shogun, was murdered. The Higashiyama period is limited to the half century between the succession of Yoshimasa, the eighth shogun, in 1443 and his death in 1490.[5] Cultural historians have found no convenient label to

5. Hayashiya Tatsusaburō, "Higashiyama bunka," in *Iwanami kōza: Nihon rekishi* (Tokyo, 1963), 7: 305. On the Higashiyama epoch within the context of the development of a national culture in medieval Japan, see also my "Chūsei ni okeru toshi to nōson no bunka," in *Koten bunka no sōzō* (Tokyo, 1958), pp. 268–270.

The Golden Pavilion (Kinkakuji). Courtesy of the Consulate General of Japan, N.Y.

affix to the eighty-three years following Yoshimasa, known as the Sengoku period. Japan was a country at war, and war and culture seem incompatible concepts. But despite these apparent contradictions, there was a systematic progression of cultural developments throughout the Muromachi period, and it is possible to see a continuous line connecting the seventeenth century with the fourteenth, leading from Kitayama to Momoyama.[6]

The Golden Pavilion of Kitayama is the memorial of that eventful last decade of the fourteenth century when Ashikaga Yoshimitsu, who presided over the settlement of the imperial schism, sought to extend and further refine his claims to political paramountcy. In the eclectic style of this building we find yet another reflection of Yoshimitsu's complex personality. Situated by design at the focal point of the garden was the Shariden or Reliquary, now known as the Kinkaku or Golden Pavilion. The first of its three stories was built in the residential style of the imperial aristocracy; the second and third epitomize the architecture of a Zen temple patronized by military aristocrats. Moreover, its location on a pond and its brilliant golden color are Pure Land conventions. Thus we find in the Golden Pavilion a synthesis of aristocratic (imperial and military) and Buddhist (Zen and Amidist) styles. Yoshimitsu had comprehensive tastes and sweeping ambitions. If ever architecture reproduced a style of government, then the Kinkaku was such an edifice: it was the ideal image of the transcendent bakufu of Yoshimitsu's day.

The second of the two monuments, the Silver Pavilion, was built by Ashikaga Yoshimasa with reference to the model of the Golden Pavilion. In contrast to its model, the Silver Pavilion is not refulgent with glory. Rather, it represents an aesthetic equipoise to political decline. The hillside villa of which it is a part was laid out on top of the ruins of a temple destroyed in the Ōnin War, the Jōdoji, which itself tells a good part of the story of this shogunal abode.[7] Yoshimasa had abandoned the rank of shogun in the middle of the great war. When work on the Higashiyama villa began in 1482, his son and successor Yoshihisa supposedly cautioned him against any further withdrawal from the world of affairs. We are told that Yoshimasa's response was: "The daimyo do as they please and do not follow orders. That means there can be no government."[8] He seems from the start to have envisioned his new residence as a place of repose. He

6. Hayashiya Tatsusaburō, *Machishū: Kyōto ni okeru "shimin" keisei shi* (Tokyo, 1964), in *Chūkō Shinsho*, 59: 112–115, provides a basic schema of this continuity.
7. On the Higashiyama villa, see *Kyōto no rekishi*, 3: 401–408.
8. *Daijōin jisha zōjiki* (Tokyo, 1933), 7: 398, entry dated Bummei 14(1482)/5/16. Yoshimasa expressed identical sentiments in a letter apparently addressed to Konoe Masaie and dated [Bummei 8(1476)]3/7; reproduced in *Kyōto no rekishi*, 3: 360.

The Silver Pavilion (Ginkakuji). Courtesy of the Consulate General of Japan, N.Y.

supervised the construction in person, and his last years were entirely
devoted to this project. He died on the site in 1490, the year after the Kan-
nondō, which we know better as the Ginkaku, was built. His plan to
sheathe the pavilion in silver (as the Kinkaku was sheathed in gold) was
not realized.[9]

The Golden Pavilion is all the more brilliant because the sunlight pours
unimpeded upon the foothills of Kitayama. The Silver Pavilion seems to
be always in the shadows; the sun is obstructed by the trajectory of the
Eastern Hills. The wheel of fortune had rotated, and Yoshimasa's public
role was far humbler than Yoshimitsu's. Their architectural monuments
reflect not only their personalities but also the political and cultural conditions of their times. Between Kitayama and Higashiyama the Ashikaga
shoguns had defined a world of prestige to which the military aristocracy
might aspire. Although Kyoto itself inevitably lost its concentration of
political power, the city never lost its capacity to inspire emulation among
the prestigious and powerful, whether in Kyoto or in the provinces.

In their provincial domains, the shugo addressed themselves not only to
the problems of wealth and power but also to those of cultural prestige,
and they transplanted Higashiyama culture to their own castle towns.[10]
The best illustration of this search for an unassailable cachet of prestige is
the remarkable proliferation of provincial cities which might be called
"Little Kyotos," such as Yamaguchi in Suō Province or East Takayama in
Hida. These cities became, in effect, Kyoto's provincial extensions and indicated the degree to which Muromachi culture had diffused throughout
the country. The first characteristic of such cities was the similarity of the
natural surroundings. Each had to have its own "Mount Hiei" and its
own "Eastern Hills"; a "Kamogawa" flowing through the city precincts
made the prerequisite of a beautiful mountain-and-river setting complete.
The second requirement was a certain cultural environment: Kyoto's famous monuments were imitated, and the Gion Shrine and the Inari
Shrine were copied. Third was the cities' political role. Just as Kyoto was
ideally the locus of authority over the entire country, so were these towns
the centers of rule over provincial domains; they were traditionally the
seats of provincial civil or military governors. It was not absolutely necessary to fulfill all three of the requirements, but they had to be met more or
less if the city was to qualify as a Little Kyoto.

9. A brief account of the artistic components of life in the Higashiyama epoch is given in
Hayashiya Tatsusaburō, *Nihon: rekishi to bunka* (Tokyo, 1967), 2: 24–28. For a more detailed discussion, see *Kyōto no rekishi*, 3: 453–480.
10. On the culture of the regional domains (*ryōkoku bunka*) and its relation to the "Little Kyoto"
syndrome, see *Kyōto no rekishi*, 3: 663–675; also Hayashiya, *Nihon: rekishi to bunka*, 2: 45–46,
94–95.

We may say that the Little Kyoto phenomenon occurred because historical conditions favored it. If the geographical conditions proved unfavorable, if the stage setting for a Little Kyoto was incomplete, the provincial lord could at least console himself with a pictorial representation of the capital's varied scene. Richly decorated screens depicting the panorama of the capital and its outskirts (*Rakuchū-Rakugai-zu byōbu*) were produced in considerable numbers during the sixteenth century, some by outstanding artists such as Tosa Mitsunobu and Kanō Eitoku.[11] They were in even greater demand in the provinces than in the capital itself and were used to embellish the residences of the lords of the domains. Throughout a century of war and shifts of fortune, Kyoto retained its powers of attraction as the country's cultural center.

THE WORLD OF "VIRTUE"

It would be a mistake, however, to concentrate overly on the rise and fall of the Ashikaga shogunate as explanation of Kyoto's changing fortunes. The splendors of Muromachi were related equally to the increasing economic power of the city's mercantile elite. In reviewing the social history of the Muromachi period, we cannot stress too heavily the importance of the *dosō* ("warehouse keepers" who served also as moneylenders) and the economic power they represented. Yoshimasa did not create the Higashiyama style by himself. Nor was an undifferentiated mass such as "the peasantry" or "the townspeople" directly responsible for the cultural product of that epoch. Rather it was the rich merchants of Kyoto that provided the wherewithal for the magnificent Higashiyama culture.[12]

Seen in this light, the age of Higashiyama achieves a special significance in the history of the city of Kyoto. The townsmen had had almost no influence on the preceding Kitayama culture; for that matter, their social organization was still at a rudimentary stage in Yoshimitsu's time. In the Higashiyama epoch, however, Kyoto's urban society underwent a metamorphosis: the townsmen emerged as holders of considerable economic power because the wealthy dosō had joined them. But also the merchants, by virtue of their close contact with the political leaders of the Higashiyama cultural scene, became participants in a sophisticated cultural life of their own. The imports from China which gladdened the

11. The courtier Sanjōnishi Sanetaka mentions that Tosa Mitsunobu was in early 1507 painting a screen depicting Kyoto for the Asakura family of Echizen; *Sanetaka-kō ki* (Tokyo, 1935), 4: 675, entry dated Eishō 3/12/22.
12. Hayashiya Tatsusaburō, "Higashiyama jidai to minshū no seikatsu," in *Chūsei bunka no kichō* (Tokyo, 1963), p. 242.

heart of the Lord of Higashiyama—the paintings, the pottery, and all those precious things called *karamomo*—passed through the hands of merchants engaged in the Ming trade before they reached Yoshimasa. In the process, these óbjects enriched the lives and entered the culture of the townspeople. Yoshimasa's indispensable arbiters of taste, the men who judged and professionally appraised his imported art objects and who defined the elegant disciplines of tea and of flower arrangement, were most often of low birth, like Ikenobō Senkei and Murata Jukō. Such men in turn brought these arts to the city populace, transfusing them into the cultural and social lifeblood of Kyoto.[13] In this way the townspeople gained an appreciation of the artistic elements of Higashiyama culture, a process which made possible the birth of an autogenous urban culture.

But the townspeople approached the arts quite differently from the way the aristocracy did. Theirs was not the world of political or social prestige but rather of profit and practicality. The splendors of Muromachi were related intimately with the increasing economic power of the moneylenders. The new intimately with the increasing economic power of the moneylenders. The new nurtured by human requirements. Painting developed within the framework of *fusuma-e* (the *fusuma* is a room divider); ceramics were appreciated in the form of daily implements, of teabowls and of flower vases. Art was esteemed for its utility; at the very least, it ceased being idealized and became something possessed of an extremely practical design.

This tendency to put high value on utility had its political parallel in the manifestation of *tokusei*, or "virtuous rule." The original meaning of the phrase derives from the Confucian ideal of benevolent rule, the universal norm of politics. In the usage current from the end of the Kamakura period, the idea of tokusei assumed a very particular meaning. After the Einin Tokusei Edict (1297), *toku* for "virtue" and *toku* for "profit" were interchangeable, so that "virtuous rule" may be understood as "profitable rule." The Einin Edict, which had the highly utilitarian effect of wiping out debts, was meant to succor the Kamakura shogunate's housemen who had fallen into severe financial straits in the aftermath of the Mongol invasions. The Ashikaga shogunate's tokusei were of a somewhat different sort and were used either to help bakufu finances or to pacify peasant confederations (*do-ikki*). When the populace demanded remissions, the shogunate responded by passing tokusei edicts. Eventually the shogunate became parasitically attached to this "profitable rule" by way of scheming for profits. Yoshimasa alone ordered tokusei some thirteen times. That

13. See Hayashiya Tatsusaburō, *Kabuki izen* (Tokyo, 1954), in *Iwanami shinsho*, 184: 127–144; also idem, *Kyōto* (Tokyo, 1967), pp. 166–169. On the arts of the "Ami," see also "Kinsei no taidō," in *Koten bunka no sōzō* (Tokyo, 1959), pp. 291–295.

may have been the peak of this utilitarian practice, but it was not the end. The bakufu continued to proclaim tokusei until its last days.

If the shogunate as well as certain segments of the populace profited from tokusei, then who was hurt when debts were canceled? We note that the rich were in the Muromachi period called *utoku* or *utokunin* (possessors of virtue), but in this context to possess "virtue" did not mean to do good but to be well-to-do. Special efforts to find out who these individuals were and register them for the purposes of taxation may be seen in the sources as early as 1304, when the Tōdaiji instructed several of its proprietaries to enroll the rich on lists called *utoku kyōmyō*. The Ashikaga shogunate, whose immediate domains were neither extensive nor secure enough to provide a solid financial base, derived a substantial portion of its income from the utoku, on whom it levied special taxes called *utoku-sen*. Indeed, the financiers of Kyoto, the dosō and the rich sake brewers, became the most dependable source of income for the bakufu. This fact was especially apparent in the days of Yoshimasa, whose life of luxury was made possible mainly by the close links which tied him to the usurers. Yoshinori demanded twelve special levies *(kurayaku)* in one year; Yoshimasa turned to them as often as nine times in one month! To be sure, the chronicler is apt to be exaggerating, but it is clear that as the fifteenth century progressed the shogunate's financial position deteriorated until it became in effect a debtor of the dosō.

Throughout the Muromachi period the practical-minded world of the utokunin was gradually taking shape. We shall call it the world of "virtue." Yet profit was never absent from the minds of its participants. Even those who practiced artistic endeavors such as poetry composition or the tea ceremony sought to put their proficiency to some sort of practical use and profit, so that we find emphasis placed on the "virtues" of poetry *(katoku)* or of tea *(chatoku)*. This practical orientation was the spirit which underlay the cultural climate of the *machishū*. It led away from the medieval world of religion toward a more secular conception.

MACHI STRUCTURE AND MACHISHŪ CULTURE

The great war of Ōnin completed the transformation of Kyoto. Physically, the city was reduced to ashes as armies which at one time numbered 160,000 on one side and 90,000 on the other fought there for control, although effective countermarches were carried on only for the first two years; after that military activity subsided to swirls of depredation within and without the city. Warfare in the city slowly died out when there was nothing left to loot. Practically all the cultural monuments of the Heian period were destroyed by the marauding soldiery, as were the newer parts of the city which had grown up since the Nambokuchō period. In this conflagration the Ashikaga shogunate's authority over Kyoto collapsed. But the city as a social and cultural organism was not destroyed. The townspeople—machishū—took their turn upon the stage of history as masters of the city.

The term *machi* was extremely important in the history of Kyoto in the Muromachi period.[14] It did not simply describe a topographical entity but expressed also a social concept. A machi, aside from being a row of houses, was also a communal aggregate composed of the households facing each other from the two sides of a street. To this nucleus was linked adjoining machi, so that machi associations (*kumi*) came into existence. These *machi-kumi* formed the cellular structure of the city's living organism.

Such associations are attested to in contemporary sources from 1401 onward. In 1401, Ashikaga Yoshimitsu gave to the priests of Rokkakudō in Shimogyō the authority over what was called the "Sanjō-omote sō-yonchō-machi."[15] The phrase clearly connotes that the four-block-strip along Sanjō avenue comprised a social unit and, above all, that the proximate location of the houses across from each other was the binding factor. A new and, in the social sense, more readily manageable machi structure had developed which transcended the classical pattern of one *chō* square blocks, the smallest administrative subdivisions of Heian Kyō.

The people living in the same machi acted as members of a communal body—responsible for fire and crime prevention and mutual protection—and were jointly liable. Even by the first half of the fifteenth century we find them on occasions supplementing, if not supplanting, official law enforcement agencies. Although their self-assertion was by no means aggressive, the essentials of the machi structure were laid down in this early period as a sense of solidarity began to develop among the machi populace. The seeds of autonomy were present, merely awaiting the appointed historical season.

The proper conditions for the emergence of a limited form of self-government were created by the Kakitsu disturbance in 1441. In the aftermath of the shogun Yoshinori's assassination, Kyoto was subjected to increasing assaults from the outside, and the machi organizations had to assume functions beyond those of internal security. Thus attacks on the merchant moneylenders within the city by rural confederations (*do-ikki*)

14. For further discussion of the origins of the machi structure and of the Kyoto townspeople's community, see Hayashiya Tatsusaburō, "Machishū no seiritsu," in *Chūsei bunka no kichō*, pp. 189–214; and idem, *Machishū*, pp. 83–109.
15. "Yasutomi ki," Ōei 8(1401)/5/28, in *Zōho shiryō taisei*, 37 (Kyoto, 1965), 1: 4. Cf. *Kyōto no rekishi*, 3: 84.

and bands of peasants and packhorse drivers brought various defense measures mutually undertaken by the machi and the dosō.

Peasant revolts were not simply a rural problem. Kyoto inevitably was involved because the city's usurers were reaping immense profits from the countryside by means of rice hoarding and manipulation of prices. Although the rich pawnbrokers and sake brewers bore the brunt of peasant retaliation for such exploitation, all who lived in the same machi suffered. Moreover, the dosō were indispensable financial agents even for humble shopkeepers and common artisans. Hence the urban populace of Kyoto could not ally themselves with their rural counterparts. Instead, the townspeople strove to strengthen the cohesiveness of their own communal organizations in the face of peasant vehemence.

When the Kakitsu disturbance temporarily disoriented the bakufu, the dosō were stripped of protection. Less than a month after the shogun's murder, troops from the shogunate guard were looting warehouses; less than two months after that, the full force of the do-ikki had burst upon the city. The dosō sent for help to the shogun's deputy, the kanrei Hosokawa Mochiyuki, paving the way with one million in copper cash. When the chief shogunal administrator issued orders to quell the tumults, he found none among the shogun's provincial lords willing to enforce them. Only the issuance of a tokusei edict, the very first granted by the Muromachi bakufu, staved off the total destruction of the city's storehouses.[16]

This event, known as the Kakitsu rebellion, was but the prelude to a riotous crescendo. In 1447 the do-ikki forces pillaged Ōmiya Shichijō; in 1454 and again in 1457 they scourged the dosō in various parts of the city.[17] The climax of this series was the uprising in 1462, doubly calamitous because it followed so soon after the horrors of the famine of 1460–61. No less than thirty machi were destroyed by fire before the peasants could be chased out of Kyoto.[18]

As a result of these peasant uprisings and the Ōnin War which began five years later, the bonds between the common townspeople and the dosō were drawn tighter, making possible a more forceful reaction against the common peril. For instance, in 1486 we find armed machishū members taking the field against a rural league encamped within Kyoto in the Tōji temple precincts.[19] By the beginning of the sixteenth century, the

16. On the Kakitsu ikki and the ensuing tokusei edict, see *Kyōto no rekishi*, 3: 300–303.

17. "Yasutomi ki," Bun'an 4(1447)/7/9, in *Zōho shiryō taisei*, 38, 2: 193; and ibid., Kyōtoku 3(1454)/9/8 and 11, in *Zōho shiryō taisei*, 40, 4: 89, 91. Cf. *Kyōto no rekishi*, 3: 303–304.

18. *Daijōin jisha zōjiki* (Tokyo, 1932), 3: 207, entry dated Kanshō 3(1462)/9/21. On the Kanshō famine, see *Kyōto no rekishi*, 3: 107–114.

19. On the absorption of the dosō into the machi structure, see Hayashiya, *Machishū*, pp. 102–104.

townspeople's armed strength had developed to such an extent that they could energetically confront the recurrent do-ikki and also assume some of the garrisoning responsibilities which the shogunate could no longer shoulder. As the traditional power structure splintered, the townspeople had to fend for themselves. Under the circumstances which prevailed after the Ōnin War, the division between ordinary shopkeepers or artisans and the "possessors of virtue" was bridged completely.

A new element in the machi structure was that aristocrats who had been ruined in the Ōnin War were now included in the coalition. Thus there was a further transformation of the character of the machi. The machi first embraced the holders of economic power, the dosō, and then incorporated the possessors of cultural accomplishment, the old kuge aristocracy. Here was created an extraordinary symbiosis.

Many of the old imperial aristocracy had fled Kyoto during the worst of the Ōnin War. But afterward, longing for the cosmopolitan attractions of the capital and aware of their slipping hold on their provincial properties, the kuge returned. By the first decades of the sixteenth century, for example, the machi of Kamigyō had a number of bankrupt nobles—nobles who may have boasted ancient pedigrees but who, in their reduced circumstances, had become indistinguishable from the plebeians in whose midst they lived. Kuge had become identified with their machi.[20]

In the parlance of the day, the people of the machi were called machishū and were commonly labeled by the name of the place where they resided, for example "Muromachi-shū" or "Nijō-shū." It would be a mistake, however, to view the machishū as a distinct class, such as the chōnin constituted in later periods. Rather, the machishū were local collective bodies, and that is their salient characteristic. In other words they were not a class; they were a community. Nevertheless, the emergence of the machishū was a preliminary stage in the creation of a strong townsman class.

KYOTO UNDER MACHISHŪ LEADERSHIP

In due course the machi structure developed to the point where townsmen representatives (sōdai) were in effect exercising the functions of city government. The townspeople's autonomy began in the 1490s and peaked in the decade of the 1530s. It was by no means easily gained or maintained, and it ended in 1568 when a new type of warlord, Oda Nobunaga, occupied the city. Machishū autonomy, in other words, derived from the Sengoku condition of political fragmentation. The townspeople of Kyoto saw in the endemic civil wars of the period an opportunity

20. *Machishū*, pp. 106–109; "Machishū no seiritsu," pp. 203–205.

for themselves. In the ebb and flow of military struggle during this period the autonomy of the machishū was frequently reinforced. This was especially true in the four-year period beginning in 1532, the time of the *Hokke ikki* when the machishū controlled Kyoto in the name of the Lotus sect. The Lotus confederation and its organizational effects constitute the climatic phase in the history of the machishū.

The Lotus sect, introduced into Kyoto in 1294, was an important ingredient in the townsmen's lives.[21] The townspeople of Kyoto had been little touched by the classical and esoteric sects of Japanese Buddhism but were deeply influenced by the sects that developed out of the "Kamakura Reformation," most notably by the Hokke, or Lotus, sect founded by Nichiren. Zen, which had many followers among the military aristocracy, was embraced also by those townsmen of substance, particularly the dosō, who desired to emulate the life style and aesthetic standards of the samurai notables with whom they consorted. But although rich merchants may have appreciated the values of Zen, the common people of sixteenth-century Kyoto held to the more comfortable and practical teachings of the Lotus sect.

The first convert is said to have been a carpenter, and the first patron a sake brewer. In the Muromachi period, rich merchants continued their financial support, and artisans their spiritual allegiance. Although aggressive missionary methods no doubt had much to do with its success, the sect's wide acceptance by the townsmen was due above all to the inherent appeal of its message. The Lotus sect represented an unusually practical and this-worldly form of Buddhism. It asserted that there is profit in the present world and that comfort in this life is attainable by anyone who trusts in the power of prayer and perseveres in religious practice. It was a view strongly attractive to a busy and profit-seeking urban population.[22]

The extent of acceptance of the Lotus sect by the machishū was reflected in the distribution of Buddhist temples within the city proper. The major temples of the other sects—except Sōkokuji at the northern and Tōji at the southern edge of town—were all located in the outskirts of Kyoto, away from its daily life. In contrast, there were no less than twenty-one Nichiren temple strongholds inside Kyoto, of which thirteen were in Shimogyō.[23] Several boasted truly imposing edifices and occupied vast grounds, being surrounded with moats and earthen embankments for

21. For further discussion of the townsmen's religion and the Hokke ikki, see Hayashiya, *Machishū*, pp. 144–158; for a more extensive treatment of the Nichiren sect and the Ji sect, *Kyōto no rekishi*, 3: 134–158; and for an elaborate consideration of the Hokke ikki, ibid., 3: 540–568.
22. This point is made by Toyoda Takeshi in his seminal article, "Chūsei no toshi to shūkyō," *Bunka* (September 1948), restored 1.1 [12.134]: 58.
23. The locations of all but four of the twenty-one are established in *Kyōto no rekishi*, 3: 542.

protection. In effect, some of the main temples of the Lotus sect presented the appearance and possessed the character of fortresses. They could serve as rallying points for the townspeople in times of crisis, as they did during the period of the Hokke ikki.

The force which set off the Hokke ikki did not come from among the townsmen and Lotus sectarians. Rather it occurred in response to the challenge presented from the partisans of another powerful Buddhist organization, the True Pure Land or Ikkō sect, which dominated the countryside around Kyoto. The two sects were composed of antipodal elements: the Ikkō sect drew its believers from among peasants; the Hokke sect depended upon townsmen. It was the basic incompatibility of the aims and interests of the urban and rural sectors of Muromachi society which set the two Buddhist sects on a collision course.

Fighting between the Hokke and Ikkō partisans erupted in the summer of 1532 when Ikkō sect forces, under the leadership of its pontiff Shōnyo, attacked Kenponji, one of the major centers of the Hokke sect, in the port city of Sakai. Following their successful siege of Kenponji, the Ikkō forces turned on Nara, burnt Kōfukuji, and ransacked the Kasuga shrine. The news of these attacks caused considerable apprehension in Kyoto, particularly since it was rumored that the Ikkō forces intended to turn on the capital next.

Just as they had done in the mid-fifteenth century to protect themselves from peasant ikki incursions into the capital, the townspeople of Kyoto banded together to meet the challenge, and for weeks there was intense agitation as armed processions of militants numbering in the thousands paraded through the streets of Kyoto under the banner of Nichiren chanting the invocation of the Lotus sutra. The Lotus sect's twenty-one major temples were at the forefront of this activity, and their priests and adherents were the confederation's main constituents. Although a number of unattached warriors and arms-bearing village chiefs from suburban areas joined in, the mass of the Hokke ikki was made up of machishū. At the apex of the league's structure were the rich dosō of Kyoto, who on occasion took an active part in its military campaigns.[24]

After initial setbacks, the Hokke partisans took the offensive at the end of 1532, continuing into 1533 when they joined forces with Hosokawa Harumoto, military strongman of the capital area, in an attempt to destroy the Ishiyama Honganji, headquarters of the Ikkō sect, in Osaka. Although this fortress proved impregnable, a rapprochement was worked out, thereby ending the Hokke ikki's involvement in large-scale offensive campaigns. Thereafter, the Lotus sect forces limited themselves to defen-

24. Ibid., 3: 554.

sive activities, such as fending off peasant uprisings and fortifying the town against potential attacks. In 1534 the situation seemed to stabilize. The shogun Ashikaga Yoshiharu came back to the city which he had fled in 1528, and the capital seemingly returned to normalcy. There followed two deceptively calm years.

The trouble was that the Nichiren adherents had been altogether too successful in filling the vacuum of authority within the city and had thereby aroused the jealousy and threatened the vested interests of certain established powers. The refusal to pay rents, a common complaint according to the records of the day, and the development of autonomous governing structures among the machishū obviously threatened feudal interests. Moreover, the spirit of political autonomy was conjoined with an intolerant spirit of religious righteousness. This overt sectarianism was felt particularly by the established religious institutions, which were offended both by the erosion of their proprietary rights within the capital and by the disdain which the Lotus sect offered them on doctrinal grounds.

Reacting most violently to this dual challenge were the monks of the Tendai establishment on Mt. Hiei. After securing the neutrality of the Hokke ikki's erstwhile allies, such as Hosokawa Harumoto, and the financial assistance of their enemies, such as the Ishiyama Honganji, armies mobilized by the Hiei priests attacked Kyoto at the end of the seventh month of 1536 and destroyed the Hokke headquarters at Honkokuji. The Hokke ikki collapsed. All twenty-one major temples of the Lotus sect were in ashes. Shimogyō was destroyed entirely; Kamigyō suffered less because the invaders spared the areas around the bakufu and the imperial palace. The machishū had resisted valiantly and their sacrifices were great, but within the capital the power of the Nichiren sect was broken.

On the surface, the conflict of 1536 appears as a religious dispute. But the event's true significance transcends the sectarian dimension. It was a clash between the vestiges of the old order, actively represented by Mt. Hiei, and the newly emergent autonomous force of the townspeople, who fought under the sign of Nichiren. The machishū had taken administration of their city into their own hands; for a period of four years they had ruled Kyoto. In the end, they were defeated, and much of their city lay in ruins. But the communal structures which they had consolidated over the years of crisis survived.

Six months after the defeat of the Lotus confederation we find five representatives of the machishū of Shimogyō appearing at the shogun's residence bearing gifts and greetings. Each of the five spoke for a machi association—the Nakagumi, Nishigumi, Tatsumigumi, Ushitoragumi, and Manachō-han-gumi. This occasion is noteworthy, because it marks the first time that the existence of machigumi are fully attested to in written sources.[25] Although we do not find machigumi again mentioned by name until the mid-sixteenth century, there is evidence that such communal structures had developed beyond the machi level and spanned the entire city by 1539; the townsmen's organization had expanded into a network which grouped the machi into interconnected chains. The Hokke ikki no doubt hastened the emergence of these machigumi, but it would not be correct to say that it generated them. Rather, they were the matured forms of a process of social development spanning more than a century. Thus the Hokke ikki was in more than one way an epochal event in the history of Kyoto. During it, the townspeople's solidarity reached its height. After it, there occurred a parting of the ways among the machishū.

THE EARLY MODERN TRANSFORMATION

Having weathered the disorders of the Sengoku period, Kyoto stood at yet another crossroads when Oda Nobunaga made his triumphal entry into the city in 1568. At first, Nobunaga posed as protector of the traditional principles of legitimacy. He installed Ashikaga Yoshiaki as shogun and built for him an exquisite residence. He also restored the emperor's dilapidated palace to respectability, if not splendor. But the restoration of the old order was not Nobunaga's objective. By 1573 his differences with Yoshiaki had become both apparent and irreconcilable. This conflict had most unfortunate results for the capital, in particular for its "aristocratic" quarter, Kamigyō. Nobunaga applied the technique of massive intimidation against the shogun and the city to gain submission to his new order, methodically burning down some ninety villages around the city's periphery. In the face of this threat Shimogyō submitted fully and thus prevented its destruction. Kamigyō, perhaps as a warning to others, was burnt, pillaged, and almost totally destroyed. The Jesuit missionary Luis Frois, who had joined the fleeing throngs, was told that six or seven thousand houses went up in flames and that not a single one of Kamigyō's rich storehouses escaped looting and burning. The Ashikaga bakufu was thus brought to its end. Kyoto was deserted by its shogun, and for the last time the presence of a military hegemon had invited destruction upon the city.

The new order which emerged was not Oda Nobunaga's, despite his original triumphs. Nobunaga was destined to spend his days shuttling between east and west in the pursuit of his avowed aim "to overspread the empire with military might" (tenka fubu). When he met his tragic end in

25. "Nentō gohairei sanpu ranshō no hikae," cited in Kyōto no rekishi, 3: 566.

the Honnōji Affair of 1582, the task of reunifying Japan was taken up by Toyotomi Hideyoshi. The last stage of the unification process saw Kyoto once again the focus of political attention. Under Hideyoshi the city was to be refashioned into the strongpoint of military domination over the entire country. Such a plan meant the demise of medieval Kyoto.[26]

In 1590 Hideyoshi began his new plan for Kyoto with an order to rearrange the machi layout. Since the days of Heian Kyō, the basic pattern had been that of blocks one *chō* square. Hideyoshi sliced these open from north to south, creating a new pattern of oblongs. His second major step was to concentrate the city's religious establishments in Tera-machi and Tera no Uchi, areas set apart specifically for that purpose. By this measure he intended to demonstrate firmly that the new secular power would henceforth prevail over religious authority, the relic of the medieval world. Hideyoshi especially wanted to discipline the main temples of the Hokke sect, those old centers of machishū spiritual life and resistance. Finally, Hideyoshi decreed the construction of an earthen wall, the Odoi, about the circumference of Kyoto, and he limited the avenues of traffic with the outside to the customary seven exits. These measures were parts of a plan to turn Kyoto into a fortress city. The focal point of the new *jōkamachi* (castle town) was to be the castle known as the Juraku no Tei, into which the Imperial Regent, Grand Chancellor, and Hideyoshi had officially moved in 1587.

In the Heian period, Kyoto had boasted a great castle gate, Rashōmon, but it had remained an unfortified city, without a wall, until Hideyoshi girdled the city with ramparts. The creation of special temple areas was also of significance for the city's fortification: in case of attack, Teramachi and Tera no Uchi formed outer defense perimeters. Hideyoshi's other city planning measure, the rearrangement of the machi, progressed in areas such as Rokuchō-machi between the imperial palace and the Juraku no Tei, where the people were evicted and the space utilized for daimyo mansions and samurai residences. But the plan did not penetrate the area around Shijō Muromachi, the old quarter of Shimogyō.

Hideyoshi's attempts to refashion Kyoto did not in the end succeed. The reasons may have been the townspeople's resistance, as well as his own change of mind. The Juraku no Tei was torn down in 1595 as a consequence of the disgrace and execution of Hidetsugu, Hideyoshi's putative successor, to whom it had been presented. With the destruction of the city's central castle, the existence of its circumferential wall became

---

26. On Hideyoshi's policy toward Kyoto and its traces even today in the city, see Hayashiya, *Kyōto*, pp. 183-190; for an extensive treatment of the problem, see *Kyōto no rekishi*, 4 (pt. 3): 227-349, particularly 286-320.

meaningless, and the Odoi was abandoned. Hideyoshi instead rebuilt the Kyoto suburb of Fushimi into a model castle town. Thus Kyoto escaped the full brunt of urban renewal until the advent of yet another military hegemon, Tokugawa Ieyasu. Yet even then it retained many of its Muromachi attributes. For while the Tokugawa placed a castle and military garrison in the midst of the city, Kyoto remained largely a community of court nobles, priests, and townspeople.

PART TWO
Political Organization

3

The Muromachi Power Structure

JOHN W. HALL

From the writings of George Sansom, for whom Ashikaga government meant the personal qualities and idiosyncrasies of the shoguns and the leading provincial lords, we have come a long way toward a better understanding of the politics of the Muromachi period. What was once a barely credible history of erratic and arbitrary acts by power-hungry rulers or of unprincipled treachery by "turncoat" vassals now takes on new logic and meaning when interpreted in terms of conflicting power structures and clashing political interests at the national and local levels. Above all, we are brought to a realization that the Muromachi bakufu did not exist in a vacuum. It was forced to respond continuously to changing conditions at the national level among the Ashikaga family, the imperial court, and the competing members of the Ashikaga military elite; and at the local level between regional lords and their vassals or between local military proprietors and the underlying village society. As an organ of national government, the shogunate was a product of the interaction between Sansom's "great men" and the more basic forces of change which operated at each level of society during the fourteenth, fifteenth, and sixteenth centuries.

Strictly with respect to the shogunate itself, there have been four lines of inquiry which have helped in recent years to better explain Muromachi politics. The first has been the effort to describe and assess the sources of the shogun's income and, by inference, his power. It has come as a surprise that, unlike the shogun of the Edo period, the Ashikaga house did not base its position upon the possession of an overwhelmingly large land base. In fact, attempts to identify the estates upon which the shogun relied have yielded only inconclusive information. The Ashikaga *goryō*, or private estates, in the early fifteenth century appear to have consisted of only thirty-five proprietorships located in the provinces of Shimotsuke, Kazusa, Sagami, Mikawa, Yamashiro, Tamba, and Mimasaka. And no clear indication exists of the size or nature of income derived from these holdings.

Although the head of the Ashikaga house during the Kamakura period had been shugo of Mikawa and Kazusa, the shogun in Ashikaga times was shugo of no province, unless one can count the home province Yamashiro, which was administered for the bakufu through the head of the Board of Retainers (*samuraidokoro*). From time to time other provinces were declared "shogunal provinces" (*goryōkoku*), among them Aki, Harima, and Chikuzen. But these too were placed under the administrative control of non-Ashikaga shugo.

The conclusion reached is that the "power" of the shogun rested primarily on the network of family and feudal relationships which Takauji and his successors managed to put together. In other words, power was more a matter of personal and family connections than of property. No study has yet described in simple form the power structure of the *sōryō* system (the extended family network) of the Ashikaga house, and we are only now beginning to learn about the size and nature of the large number of hereditary vassals (*hikan*) who were attached to the Ashikaga shogun. Another area which has recently opened up is the study of the shogunal military guard (the *hōkōshū*). These guards, drawn from nonheir members of the shogun's vassal houses (in the main from non-kin-related, i.e., *tozama*, houses) served as yet another network of personal relationships upon which the shogun could rely. Yet they at no time constituted a force of sufficient proportions to allow the shogun to assert a private hegemony over his shugo subordinates. From what little we know about the guardsmen, at any given time they numbered fewer than 350 men.

From the economic point of view, even though landholdings themselves seem a less important element in the shogun's power base, it has now become clear that there were certain residual national powers of taxation upon which the shogun, and to some extent the shugo, could rely. The extent to which the province-wide unit tax (*tansen*) and the authority to exercise "half share" (*hanzei*) rights over estate holdings contributed directly to the shogun's treasury has yet to be made explicit. What is clear is that the military aristocracy of the Ashikaga period was riding on top of certain fundamental changes in the system of land tenure and taxation, a condition only partially suggested by what is commonly called the transition from the estate (*shōen*) to a fief (*chigyō*) system. The subject is pursued below in the essay by Professor Miyagawa.

Scholars have been more successful in their analysis of the manner in which the shogunate came to put increasing reliance on the commercial wealth of the city of Kyoto and its environs. During the last century of its existence, it is clear that, although the economic base of the shogunate steadily narrowed, a sophisticated relationship had been worked out between the shogun's house and the commercial establishments of the city which included elements of tax farming as well as methods of profiting from foreign trade. We are left to ask the question whether the Ashikaga shogunate was indeed showing the way to the kind of alliance between feudal and commercial interests which played such an important part in the creation of the castle-town system of the Edo period.

If overwhelming military and economic power was not the base upon which the Ashikaga shoguns rested their supremacy, what of their role as national heads of state? The second line of recent inquiry into the shogunate is concerned with the problem of the shogun's legitimacy and the concepts of rulership which the Ashikaga shoguns developed. The older view that intrigue and balance-of-power politics was all that kept the shogun's head above the waves of anarchy is clearly inadequate. Yoshimitsu's apparent efforts to embrace, if not displace, the imperial house and his seemingly irresponsible act of accepting investiture as "King of Japan" by the Chinese emperor are now permitted to take on more rational significance. Was Yoshimitsu trying for a legitimate status of "monarch" for himself and his successors? Did in fact some of these successors, Yoshinori and Yoshimasa in particular, conceive of themselves as monarchs?

During the Ashikaga regime the post of shogun did acquire nearly all the powers later exercised by the Tokugawa shogun: disposition of rewards and punishments, the levy of various duties and services, the right to approve imperial succession and to judge disputes among military houses, control of the city of Kyoto, and authority over Japan's foreign relations. The shogun was in fact serving as the national head of state under an umbrella of legitimacy provided by an emperor whom he in effect controlled. But an explicit effort to give formal shape and philosophical support to a new concept of monarchy did not materialize. The fact that such an effort failed is as significant as the effort itself. Since the suggestion that there was a conscious push toward the status of monarch by the Ashikaga shoguns has not been fully pursued, the reasons for its failure have been given even less attention. But the failure of the shogun to maintain a position of absolute command over the great military houses and the inability of the shogun to develop a bureaucracy fully responsive to his will are matters of record.

A third line of inquiry which serves to pull together these aspects of Ashikaga politics has been the study of the bureaucratic organs of the bakufu itself. The papers by Professors Satō and Kuwayama which follow reflect the efforts of scholars in recent years to analyze the bakufu from a functional point of view as a power structure. The three-phased develop-

ment of bakufu organization which these scholars describe helps immensely to explain the political history of the time. As a result of their work we
can see how, under the first five shoguns, there was a parallel effort to
build up both the feudal and the monarchal organs of administrative control. The post of deputy shojun (*kanrei*) takes on new significance when the
kanrei is seen not only as the prime officer (and hence prime supporter) of
the shojun but also as the mediator between the shugo and the tendency
toward despotism shown by such shojuns as Yoshimitsu and Yoshinori. It
is noteworthy that the Ashikaga shofunate reached the zenith of its power
at a time when the allegiance of the shugo was given as much to the idea of
the valance of power, as symbolized by the shogun's council of senior
vassals, as to the shogun himself. Yoshinori's attempts to enhance
shogunal power by the use of a personal bureaucracy ended predictably in
his assissination by one of his own senior vassals. The Ashikaga shogunate
never achieved an administration capable of governing the entire nation. It
could not in the end do more than serve as a symbol of legitimacy for what
can be called the "shugo system," in other words for the collectivity of
shugo who competed for power in the provinces.

In the final analysis, then, an understanding of the power structure of
the Ashikaga shogunate must involve a fourth line of inquiry, namely, a
study of the relationships between shogun and shugo and between shugo
and the provinces. The subject has been explored in several of its parts,
as in the essay by Professor Kawai. But it has yet to be described in
its national totality. As Kawai points out, the nature of shogun-shugo
relations was not uniform throughout the Ashikaga period. The early
period of adjustment through warfare to an uneasy balance of power was
succeeded by the era of Yoshimitsu when the shugo of all provinces except
those in the Kantō and Kyushu built their residences in Kyoto. In this way
they participated in a sort of early version of *sankin-kōtai*, the system
whereby the Tokugawa shoguns obliged their vassals to reside in Edo in
alternate years. This was also the time of the successful functioning of the
system of kanrei rotation and the periodic holding of shugo councils
(*yoriai*) for policy decisions. It was as much the effort of the shogun to
dominate this balance of power as it was the growth of independent shugo
ambitions that destroyed the Muromachi political system. By the time of
the Ōnin War, when the shugo-shogun alliance had begun to come apart,
a new stage in the relationship of bakufu to shugo had been reached; but
at the same time the nature of the shugo themselves had begun to change.
By this time the full force of the changes in the countryside which gave rise
to new and more locally entrenched regional lords had begun to be felt. As
explained by Professor Miyagawa, the chigyō system of landholding now

displaced the old shōen system and, as Professor Nagahara's paper illustrates, partially independent village communities had begun to make their appearance in the countryside. The warfare of the early sixteenth century had a very different meaning from that of the fourteenth century, and the new provincial lords, the Sengoku daimyo, who played Kyoto politics were of a quite different category from the earlier shugo. Many, in fact, were upstarts, like the Mōri, who had only recently gained possession of such legitimizing titles as shugo or *shugodai* (deputy shugo). After the Ōnin War, Kyoto and the provinces, to a large extent, went their own separate ways.

As the focus of political attention in the sixteenth century moved away from the capital to the provinces, there to witness the great territorial daimyo of the Sengoku age in the making, it is of considerable surprise to note that Kyoto continued to thrive as a cultural and commercial center if no longer as a center of political influence. It is for this reason that, despite the mortal weakening of the office of shogun, the story of the bakufu cannot end here. A powerless but symbolically significant Ashikaga shogun, a moderate affluence based on the continuing alliance between shogun and commercial houses, a bakufu still functioning as the keeper of peace in Kyoto, survived into the mid-sixteenth century, not to be displaced until overwhelmed by the new order represented by the great warlord, Oda Nobunaga.

4

The Ashikaga Shogun and the Muromachi Bakufu Administration

SATŌ SHIN'ICHI
with John W. Hall

The government of the Ashikaga shogun took its initial shape between the years 1338 and 1392, that is, between the time when Takauji assumed the post of shogun and Yoshimitsu managed to bring to an end the separate existence of the Southern Court. For that reason Muromachi government generally is described from the way it looked in the later years of Yoshimitsu's rule. Perhaps the outstanding feature of the Ashikaga system of government was that, except in the purely administrative offices of the bakufu, the shogun's regional vassals served both as high officials of government and as local military governors (shugo). The central organs of the bakufu thus inevitably responded to the competition for power among these regional lords. As a national leader, therefore, the Ashikaga shogun was essentially a hegemon placed over a coalition of shugo houses. Outside of the capital it was the shugo who "governed the country" in the name of the shogun.

By 1392 the Ashikaga shogun could claim a relatively secure authority over a coalition of shugo houses numbering some twenty members who among them held jurisdiction over the forty-five provinces of central Japan. Shugo of the ten eastern provinces were made accountable to the shogunal headquarters at Kamakura. Those of the eleven Kyushu provinces were placed under the rather uncertain authority of one of their number who was appointed the shogun's deputy for the region. Shugo of the central bloc of provinces were obliged to take up residence in Kyoto so as to be available for shogunal service. Their provincial affairs were consequently delegated to locally resident retainers who served as deputy shugo (*shugodai*).

The bakufu as central administration developed along two lines. Serving the external affairs of the shogunate were several important offices each headed by a ranking shugo. Chief among these was the *kanrei*, or

45

SHUGO under the ASHIKAGA SHOGUNATE c.1370

Shugo related by blood to the Ashikaga

Ashikaga

Utsunomiya

Satake

Chiba

Uesugi

Yūki

Uesugi

Takeda

Imagawa

Momonoi

Kyōgoku

Nitta

Yoshimi

Toki

Togashi

Hatakeyama

Yamana

Toshiki

Sasaki

Nitta

Akamatsu

Noro

Kōrokuji

Yamana

Hatakeyama

Hosokawa

Sasaki

Takeda

Shibukawa

Ōuchi

Kōno

Shōni

Shibukawa

Imagawa

Ōtomo

Aso

Shimazu

deputy shogun, who presided over the council of chief vassals known as the *yoriai*. The *samurai-dokoro*, or Board of Retainers, through its chief officer, the *shoshi*, represented the shogun's authority in military and law enforcement matters. Among the regional authorities the *Kantō kanrei*, or governor general of Kantō at Kamakura, was of sufficient importance that the post was initially assigned to a branch of the Ashikaga house. Other regional offices were established in the far north (Oshū) and south (Kyūshū). For his central administration the shogun relied on a personal guard force and a group of offices staffed by hereditary administrative specialists. These handled such matters as tax collection, adjudication of land disputes, and the promulgation of shogunal orders and decisions. Figure 1 presents a simplified chart of Muromachi government as it appeared in Yoshimitsu's day.

While corresponding to the common manner in which Muromachi government is described in standard treatments of the subject, this chart is inadequate for two reasons. It is obviously oversimplified, and it gives no hint of the dynamic functional changes which affected the bakufu during the first century and a half of Ashikaga rule. Although the political history of the Muromachi period gives evidence of the changing balance of power between shogun and vassal shugo, changes in the structure of Muromachi bakufu organization and in the relationship between shogunal power and the bakufu administration are yet to be explored. This essay will suggest an approach to the problem.

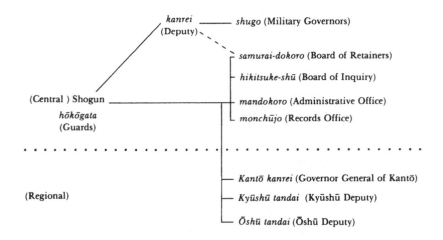

FIGURE 1. Organization of the Muromachi Shogunate, ca. 1392

It is useful to think of bakufu administrative organization as undergoing three phases of evolution, each representing a different configuration in the relationship between the shogun, his administration, and his chief vassals. The outstanding feature of the Muromachi bakufu organization in its early formative period was the fact that the shogun Takauji and his brother Tadayoshi shared political power, each accountable for a different set of political functions. Takauji, as shogun, preferred to play the political role of chief of the country's military houses *(buke no tōryō)*, assuming the power of command over the *bushi* as their overlord. As a consequence, Takauji exerted direct control over those organs within the bakufu by which political-military authority was exercised, such as the *samurai-dokoro* (Board of Retainers) and the *onshō-kata* (Office of Rewards) through which military vassals were rewarded for military service.

The shogun's brother Tadayoshi was placed in charge of the more "bureaucratic" organs of government. Under his superintendence, for instance, were such judicial organs as the *hikitsuke-kata* (Board of Inquiry) and *monchūjo* (Records Office). Through these he exercised judicial control over the landholdings of the military aristocracy. As such he represented the more monarchal tendencies within the Ashikaga government by contrast to the more feudal aspects which were his brother's concern. This two-headed administrative arrangement was clearly unstable and eventually led to the clash between the two brothers which ended in 1352 with Tadayoshi's death by poisoning. Thus, almost before the bakufu had established itself, it faced a crisis of near fatal proportions.

The important post of kanrei (deputy shogun) was created as a means of surmounting this problem of the bifurcated administration. The kanrei, which under Takauji had been a fairly minor bureaucratic post, was converted into a prime officer whose function it was to serve as a unifying force between the two separate lines of administrative control, feudal and bureaucratic. The kanrei was now appointed from among the most powerful of the shogun's vassals, namely, members of the Ashikaga inner circle who were also shugo of several provinces. Historically three such families were called upon to supply kanrei: the Shiba, Hosokawa, and Hatakeyama.

In addition to the enhancement of the office of kanrei, a council of senior vassals *(jūshin-kaigi)* was also created. It was comprised of the heads of the above three houses joined by a number of additional influential vassals and became an organ for public discussion and consensus decision on important political matters. The council of senior vassals served a dual purpose: not only did it assist the shogun and kanrei in the formulation and enforcement of bakufu policy but also it constituted a means for limiting the concentration of power in the hands of the shogun and kanrei. This arrangement characterized the second phase in the evolution of bakufu political organization, a phase which corresponded roughly to the shogunal reigns of Yoshimitsu, Yoshimochi, and Yoshikatsu.

The shogun Yoshinori, however, adopted a new approach to government by personally involving himself in judicial and policy-making matters. This action had a decisive effect upon the balance of power around the shogun. Under the system inaugurated by Yoshinori, the shogun directly superintended the *bugyōnin-shū* (Corps of Aministrators) and through them attempted to monopolize the formation of bakufu policy and its enforcement. The result was a radical change in the influence of the post of kanrei. In the previous phase, the kanrei had served as the chief coordinating agent among the several organs of the bakufu administration and as the voice of policy concensus among the shogun's vassals. With the emergence of the bugyōnin-shū, the political status of the kanrei and the influence of the council of senior vassals were both diminished. It was this circumstance which characterized the third phase of bakufu political organization, a phase which was still in its formative stage under the shogun Yoshimasa and reached maturity after the Ōnin War.

During the third stage of bakufu organization the shogun came to rely increasingly on a group of families hereditarily associated with shogunal administration. Though the Ashikaga house itself increasingly lost effective political power, these families managed to maintain the shogun as an institution for nearly a century after the Ōnin War. Not only were the officers who comprised the then active organs of bakufu government drawn exclusively from a limited group of families, these officers continued to serve in their posts unaffected by changes in political conditions or by personnel changes among shogun, kanrei, and other upper-level wielders of political influence. This was true for the bugyōnin who ran the *mandokoro* (Administration Office) and other similar offices. It was also true of the military families who comprised the shogunal guards. It was this "heredification" of the lower levels of bakufu administration that ultimately gave the shogunate its great staying power, albeit over an ever diminishing sphere of influence.

The *hōkōgata* were corps of bodyguard officers serving under the shogun's direct command. The guardsmen normally lived in Kyoto and stood watch in rotation at the shogun's palace. Fortunately we are able to determine the nature and composition of the several guard groups from guard rosters *(goban chō)* which remain for the 1440s, the 1450s, and the year 1487. From these three sets of rosters we are able to conclude that throughout the period covered by these documents the guards were organized in the same five corps (i.e., the *go ban)* and that the personnel composition of the several corps remained roughly the same in terms of the houses from which they were drawn.[1] Thus for the period of roughly half a century on either side of the Ōnin War, the structure of the guard groups and the families from which the guards were recruited underwent almost no change.

The same was also true of the composition of the samurai-dokoro which was in charge of the enforcement of justice and police protection in the city of Kyoto. As is commonly known, the *shoshi* (who served as chief officer) was, from at least the time of Yoshimitsu, selected from among four houses which ranked next to the three kanrei houses in prestige among the shugo. These were the Yamana, Akamatsu, Isshiki, and Kyōgoku. It was also the practice that one of the retainers of the shoshi would be designated as deputy-shoshi (i.e., *shoshi-dai*). His job was to assist the shoshi and to take charge of the administration of the city of Kyoto. In later years, however, clerks known as *yori'udo* (i.e., bugyōnin specialized in legal administration) took over the management of the samurai-dokoro using subofficials known as *zōshiki* who were given the job of inspection and prosecution. Again we find that both the yori'udo and the zōshiki were appointed from certain prescribed houses. In other words, despite changes in the political conditions of the bakufu, despite changes at the level of shoshi and shoshi-dai, the samurai-dokoro was run on a normal, day-to-day basis by a predetermined group of officials. As the following essay by Professor Kuwayama describes in greater detail, the same also became true of the mandokoro.

Not only did the lower levels of bakufu officialdom become hereditarily fixed, the hereditary officials found ways of protecting themselves from their competitors, whether within or without the shogunate. Among the various groups of hereditary officials who staffed the organs of bakufu administration, particularly among those who were of the same socio-official status (*mibun*), there developed a strong sense of solidarity and group identity. For instance, the guardsmen as a collective group, particularly those who belonged to the same guard group, exhibited a strong spirit of solidarity in the face of opposition. The bugyōnin also banded together in confronting other status groups within the administration. This feeling of identity among groups of officials was so strong that on occasion they even rejected the commands of their superiors. In other words, there came a

1. For an analysis of the problem of dating the three groups of *goban-chō* records, see Fukuda Toyohiko, "Muromachi bakufu no 'hōkōshū': goban-chō no sakusei nendai wo chūshin to shite," *Nihon rekishi* no. 274 (1971). Also, on the dating of the establishment of the *hōkōgata*, I have surmised that the guards were created during the time of Yoshimitsu; see my "Muromachi bakufu ron," in *Iwanami kōza: Nihon rekishi* (Tokyo, 1963), 3. Fukuda, in the above cited article, puts it in the time of Yoshinori.

time in the history of the bakufu when lateral ties binding particular functional or status groups together became conspicuously stronger than the vertical authority ties between higher and lower levels of the administration. A good illustration of this tendency is found in the incident in 1485 when the bugyōnin and the guardsmen confronted each other. The incident began when one or two bugyōnin and hōkōshū quarreled over a matter of seating order at the shogun's palace. Soon the bugyōnin and hōkōshū were divided into opposing camps. The hōkōshū refused to abide by a restraining order from the shogun Yoshihisa. The bugyōnin, sixty strong, countered by threatening as a group to take the tonsure. Eventually the matter was settled amicably but not before a considerable polarization had taken place.

The third phase of bakufu organization was characterized by the two features of hereditary holding of office and group monopoly of certain functions around the shogun. There are obviously a number of reasons why this should have happened. The bugyōnin, for example, were officials who commanded a skill in writing which the general run of bushi at that time lacked; they also had administrative skills and special legal knowledge which could be applied to judicial cases. Because they monopolized such technical skills and information, they were indispensable to the administrative functioning of the bakufu. That a group of this sort should seek to oppose the wielders of actual political power is not a phenomenon confined to this particular age or situation: it is a feature common to most dynastic administrations. It was also natural in the case of groups like the bugyōnin that possession of a certain background and social status would constitute a necessary criterion for membership in the group. Furthermore, given that membership was also expected to bring certain material and intangible benefits, the group tended to become a closed unit. Muromachi society contained many such groups—merchant guilds, religious communes, and peasant villages for instance—in which group exclusiveness and communal solidarity served as protective devices. The above merely reveals that these tendencies, observable more generally throughout Muromachi society, had exerted their influence on bakufu administration as well.

Although the hereditary holding of certain offices within the bakufu gave stability to the shogunate and helped to extend its life, this tendency exerted a dramatic influence upon the powers of the shogun and upon the political process between the Muromachi bakufu, the shogun, and the great territorial lords. Looking back to the start of the third phase, it will be recalled that the rise of the bugyōnin had resulted from the shogun's effort to increase his personal power in relation to the kanrei. Yoshinori

SATŌ SHIN'ICHI at top right.

had tried to assert direct control over the several organs of the bakufu administration and thereby make the bakufu responsive to his personal rule. From the administrative point of view the succeeding shogun managed to achieve more direct control over bakufu administration, but the result in terms of power politics (i.e., the shogun's ability to influence the shugo) was to weaken almost to a point of impotence the shogun himself. The system which characterized the second phase of bakufu political organization, whereby the kanrei worked through the council of senior vassals, served both to support the shogun and to check the exercise of excessive power by him, thereby making shogunal rule acceptable to the shugo. The kanrei and the council members were able to mediate between the shogun and the various organs of bakufu administration, and between the shogun and the rest of the bushi class. As long as he remained a symbol of concensus policy among the great regional houses, the shogun could exert a critical influence upon the nation.

After shogunal attempts to curtail the powers of the kanrei failed and as the offices of the shogun's central administration became increasingly hereditary within a narrow group of retainers, the shogun, particularly after the Ōnin War, found himself cut off from the collective support of his shugo coalition. No longer disposed to serve merely as a mediator and supporter, the kanrei reduced the shogun to a puppet. By the end of the fifteenth century the office of kanrei, now almost exclusively the possession of the Hosokawa house, had replaced the shogun as the most powerful political office in Kyoto. The shogun, supported by his hereditary guards and administrators, continued as an honored institution but without the national influence to which earlier shogun had aspired.

5

The Bugyōnin System:
A Closer Look

KUWAYAMA KŌNEN
with John W. Hall

In the preceding essay, Professor Satō has described in general terms the several stages of evolution through which Muromachi bakufu political organization passed. According to his analysis, the primary characteristic of the last phase was the increasingly prominent role played by hereditary guardsmen as military and police officials and by hereditary officials known as *bugyōnin* in the civil bureaucracy. This phase of the bakufu's civil administration is best identified as the period of the "bugyōnin system." This essay will look more closely at the bugyōnin phenomenon in an effort to determine the origin and the manner in which these officials consolidated their position within the bakufu regime.

The group of officials with which we are concerned were referred to variously as *bugyōnin* (a term which can be translated literally as administrators), *bugyōshū* (corps of administrators), and *yuhitsushū* (corps of secretaries). It is the latter alternative designation that most clearly indicates their administrative functions. All told, the administrative corps consisted of about sixty individuals. Although the term *bugyōshū* referred to this entire group of special administrative officials, there were naturally rank and status distinctions among them. The two chief distinctions were between the ranks of *shiki-hyōjōshū* (counselors) and *hikitsukeshū* (adjudicators). Both terms derived from administrative functions which had once been performed within the Kamakura bakufu. Even though these functions had been discontinued, the terms for them had been retained as designations for certain rank categories among the Ashikaga shogun's retainers. Moreover, between these rank categories and certain offices within the Muromachi government a practice of rank-to-office equivalence came into being very much along lines which had characterized the early imperial system of administration. For instance, it was customary for a person attaining the rank of *shiki-hyōjōshū* to resign the post of deputy chief

54 KUWAYAMA KŌNEN

(*shitsuji-dai*) of the *mandokoro*. Thus we surmise that this particular post was normally filled by someone with the lower rank of *hikitsukeshū*.

Material for the identification of the bugyōshū group of families is provided by a class of documents known as "administrative directives" (*bugyōnin-hōsho*). By analyzing these documents, together with other writings and records, it is possible to draw up a roster of bugyōshū members for the Muromachi period, with but a few chronological gaps.[1] As a result we can determine that, after the mid-fifteenth century, the bugyōshū was drawn mainly from the following families: Inō, Saitō, Sei, Jibu, Matsuda, Suwa, Nakazawa, and Fuse. The common factor which distinguished these families was that they all were from lines which had served the previous Kamakura bakufu as administrators.[2] In other words, the corps of administrators of the Muromachi age was drawn exclusively from families which, since the time of the Kamakura bakufu, had specialized in the handling of administrative functions within the bakufu. We can think of the bugyōshū as a group of families who monopolized certain administrative skills and who controlled certain information such as knowledge of previous administrative practices. As specialists in "good precedents" and "respected usages," these families performed an important function in medieval politics and were respected accordingly.

Despite the clear indication that the Ashikaga bugyōnin were inherited from the previous Kamakura administration, their activities did not become particularly noticeable in the Ashikaga government records until rather late—not, in fact, until about the middle of the fifteenth century, or at the time of the sixth shogun, Yoshinori. Bugyōnin documents assumed their classical form in the period on either side of the Ōnin War. For that reason it is best to take the period around Ōnin and Bummei (roughly the 1460s through the 1480s) as the basis for an analysis of the bugyōnin phenomenon.

The administrative structure of the Muromachi shogunate was in principle based on that of the Kamakura shogunate. Consequently, the Ashikaga shoguns retained such organs as the *samurai-dokoro* (Board of Retainers), the *mandokoro* (Administrative Office), and the *monchūjo* (Records Office) which had been the most important offices of the Kamakura bakufu. They also created several organs centering on the *hikitsuke-kata* (Board of Inquiry), which was responsible for handling legal suits. Through the work of Satō Shin'ichi we can construct the or-

1. For a list of *bugyōnin*, see for example *Kadokawa Nihonshi jiten* (Tokyo, 1966), appendixes, pp. 996–1001.
2. Satō Shin'ichi, "Muromachi bakufu kaisōki no kansei taikei," in *Chūsei no hō to kokka*, ed. Ishimoda Shō and Satō Shin'ichi (Tokyo, 1960), p. 488.

ganizational chart shown in figure 1 depicting Muromachi bakufu administration in the early years.[3]

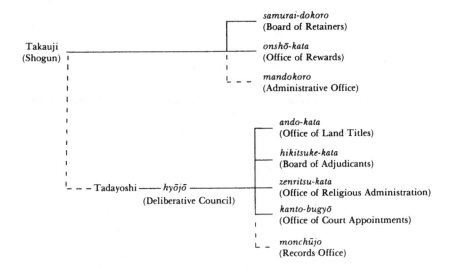

FIGURE 1. Muromachi Bakufu Organization, ca. 1350

Despite the retention of office nomenclature from the Kamakura period, however, the functions assigned to these offices under the Ashikaga shogun frequently differed considerably from what they had once been. For instance, in the Kamakura bakufu the organs which had developed to take charge of public governmental affairs were separated under two different functions: *hyōjō* (administrative) and *hikitsuke* (judicial). In the early Muromachi bakufu the hikitsuke-kata took over both these functions under the command of Tadayoshi. Following the deaths of Tadayoshi and Takauji the hikitsuke-kata were reorganized several times, but in 1379, when Shiba Yoshimasa became kanrei and the so-called "kanrei system" was established, the hikitsuke-kata's functions were absorbed under the kanrei.[4]

3. Ibid.
4. *Nihon no rekishi*, 9, *Nambokuchō no dōran*, ed. Satō Shin'ichi (Tokyo, 1965), p. 343.

In the Ashikaga shogunate one of the first notable changes to affect the samurai-dokoro was that it was charged with protection of the capital. In this capacity it absorbed the remaining powers of the Office of Capital Police (the *kebiishi-chō*) which had served as the police force of the imperial bureaucracy. The senior officer of the samurai-dokoro, the shoshi, served concurrently as the shugo of the home province of Yamashiro. Along with such police powers, the office also acquired authority over litigation in the city of Kyoto (its judicial actions were known as *samurai-dokoro-sata*).[5] The samurai-dokoro was quite active in the years up to the Ōnin era, but there is almost no record thereafter of its activities. After the Ōnin War, in fact, there are almost no remaining documents which can be identified with the samurai-dokoro, so that we are probably correct in surmising that it had by that time totally lost its significance.[6]

The monchūjo, which had been the prime judicial body in Kamakura times, also had its function changed under the Ashikaga shogun. It became what has been referred to as a "documents center for military houses" (*buke no kirokusho*), its purpose being simply to preserve land records.[7]

In this fashion, the various offices which had had their origin in the Kamakura bakufu had each undergone drastic change, both in function and influence, by the latter half of the fifteenth century. The only bureau which showed any vitality was the mandokoro (Administrative Office).[8] The mandokoro had originally handled the shogunal household administration along with exercising what was known as administrative decisions (*mandokoro-sata*). Under the Kamakura bakufu judicial system these included the general business of legal decisions in the field of property and dealt with such matters as loans, debts, sales, and purchases.

The chief officer of the mandokoro, called the *shitsuji*, was appointed hereditarily from members of the Ise family. Little is known about the history of the Ise family during the Kamakura period except that they appear to have been hereditary vassals (*fudai no hikan*) of the Ashikaga house. From the Nambokuchō era onward the Ise house held a position of influence in the Muromachi bakufu, one reason being that it had become responsible for the early upbringing and training of the shogun's children.

5. Satō Shin'ichi, "Muromachi bakufu ron," in *Iwanami kōza: Nihon rekishi* (Tokyo, 1963), 3.

6. Haga Norihiko, "Muromachi bakufu samurai-dokoro tōnin bunin enkaku koshō-kō," in *Tōkyō Daigaku kiyō: Bungakubu-hen*, 16 (1962); idem, "Muromachi bakufu samurai-dokoro kō," in *Hakusan shigaku*, 10 (1964), continued in *Chūsei no mado*, 13 (1963); idem, "Muromachi bakufu shoki kendan shōkō," in *Nihon shakai keizaishi kenkyū: Chūsei hen* (Tokyo, 1967).

7. There are those who attribute a greater role to the *kirokusho*; see, for example, Kasamatsu Hiroshi, "Muromachi bakufu soshō seido 'iken' no kōsatsu," *Shigaku zasshi* 69.4 (1959): 27.

8. Kuwayama Kōnen, "Chūki ni okeru Muromachi bakufu mandokoro no kōsei to kinō," in *Nihon shakai keizaishi kenkyū: Chūsei hen* (Tokyo, 1967).

In a document entitled the *Busei kihan* we find the statement, "The *shitsuji-dai* has assumed the affairs of state instead of the shitsuji." The post of shitsuji-dai (i. e., deputy chief) referred to was the officer in charge of the group of yori'udo (clerks) who comprised the working membership of the mandokoro. The post was considered especially important, and appointments were made to it from among members of the bugyōshū who held the rank of hikitsuke-shū, purportedly on the basis of "ability and experience." The clerks, numbering some twenty members in all, were all members of the bugyōshū. From the available information on personnel changes, it appears that from three to five among the clerks were designated hikitsuke-shū.[9]

Another important officer of the mandokoro was the mandokoro-dai, a post held in hereditary succession by the Ninagawa family. The mandokoro-dai should not be thought of as a working member of the bureau. Rather, as a retainer of the Ise house, which served as chief of the bureau, he functioned on behalf of the Ise family. As the mandokoro gained in importance within the bakufu structure, the position of the Ninagawa house also rose in importance.

It can be seen that the composition of the mandokoro rested on a delicate balance between families such as the Ise and their retainers, the Ninagawa, who sought to enhance their status by virtue of their special relationship to the shogun and the yori'udo families, which since the Kamakura period had traditionally been eligible to become shitsuji-dai of the office (see figure 2).

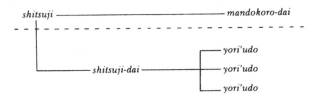

FIGURE 2. Muromachi Bakufu Mandokoro, ca. 1450

The personnel divisions were both political and functional. The shitsuji—mandokoro-dai axis, for example, handled the household affairs of the shogun, while the shitsuji-dai—yori'udo axis assumed the more public judicial functions of the office. For this purpose the latter group maintained its own deliberative council, which could meet independently and without the attendance of the shitsuji. The mandokoro council, com-

9. *Ninagawa monjo*, vol. 14 (documents in the Naikaku Bunko, now located in the Kokuritsu Kobunshokan).

posed of the shitsuji-dai and the yori'udo, conducted meetings known as *naidan*. In an age when administrative and judicial affairs were not yet thought of as separate matters, the deliberative council came to handle both types of problems.

The results of the council meetings were transmitted in documents called *bugyōnin-hōsho*, or administrative directives. It is these documents, a number of which remain to this day, that reveal the full scope of the powers and functions of the later mandokoro. In these documents the administrative decisions are no longer confined to the sale and purchase of property or to matters of loans and debts, which had been the main business of the mandokoro during the Kamakura period. Muromachi period directives encompass adjudication between high-ranked claimants which obviously had once been within the sphere of competence of the samurai-dokoro. Clearly at some point in time, still not reliably determined but probably about the beginning of Ōnin (1467), the mandokoro had absorbed the functions of the samurai-dokoro. The hikitsuke-kata, who had once served as the judicial organ of the shogunate, had already been abolished, and the monchūjo (Records Office) no longer exerted any influence. Thus it is clear that by this time the mandokoro had become the only bakufu office with any real function and authority. It is this situation which typified the stage of bakufu organization under which the bugyōnin system became ascendant.

As must already be evident, the rise of the mandokoro and the ascendancy of the bugyōnin did not come about suddenly. By studying the documents which emanated from this office, however, we can get some sense of how and when it arrived at its position of preeminence within the bakufu bureaucracy.

The deliberative decisions of the mandokoro were expressed in directives *(bugyōnin-hōsho)*. Characteristic of these documents was the fact that they were signed jointly by more than one officer.[10] The standard directive ended with the statement, "Having received the shogun's command we so order." After this was affixed the date, and in the same line one signature. In the next line came another signature or sometimes two. The bugyō who signed in the same line as the date was the one who served as duty officer at the time. Those who signed below him did so as countersigners. Only for matters of major importance did the shitsuji himself affix his signature, and it was then that two countersignatures would appear.

The first question to be answered is when it was that this type of docu-

---

10. Satō Shin'ichi, *Komonjogaku nyūmon* (Tokyo, 1971), p. 166.

ment came into use. Because of the scarcity of available evidence a
definitive answer cannot be given. But a number of points can be made.
First, examples of the documentary form in question can be found dating
from the 1380s to the 1420s. As a case in point there are the relatively early
documents dated 1382/10/18 found in the "Tōji hyakugō monjo" collection, which are orders giving exemptions from the special national tax
(tansen) then being collected to pay for the imperial succession ceremony.
Since these documents all deal with nationally imposed taxes or state services (kokuyaku) they cannot be looked upon as being of a routine variety.

Second, administrative directives first began to deal with matters other
than tansen and kokuyaku during the 1430s, and this became a common
occurrence from about the 1440s.

Third, during the first part of the fifteenth century, the kind of subject
matter which was later handled by administrative directives was apparently dealt with in a document (actually a series of two documents)
known as the gohan-migyōsho and the Muromachi shōgunke migyōsho (i.e., the
shogun's personally signed order and the kanrei's order based upon it.)

Finally, the use of the gohan-migyōsho together with the Muromachi
shōgunke migyōsho, appears to have varied inversely with the growing use
of the bugyōnin-hōsho. The 1471 document of the former kind is undoubtedly one of the last of its type.

From this inquiry into documentary forms it is clear that, if we exclude
the examples dealing with unusual matters such as the tansen and
kokuyaku, a definite break in pattern occurred on either side of the period
from about Eikyō (1429) to Bummei (1469). Before Eikyō it was the
gohan-migyōsho followed by the order in the name of the kanrei which
transmitted the shogunal will; after Bummei it was the administrative
directive issued under the authority of the bugyōnin that served this purpose. We can conclude then that it is with the end of the Yoshimitsu-
Yoshimochi era and the beginning of the Yoshinori era that the new
documentary form came into use.

What political circumstances can be identified behind this change in
documentary style? As already suggested, the answer is to be found in the
character of the new shogun. Because Yoshimochi died without leaving an
heir, it became necessary to select a new shogun from among existing eligible members of the Ashikaga family. Yoshinori, who previously had
entered the priesthood, was selected by lot by the Ashikaga retainers. After
becoming shogun, Yoshinori left his tranquil monastic existence to live out
a life that would be full of turmoil and culminate in his assassination in the
so-called "Kakitsu Affair." Yoshinori's personal qualities alone make him

an interesting historical personage,[11] but more to the topic at hand is the fact that he apparently made a definite change in the Muromachi administrative system, which under Yoshimitsu and Yoshimochi had centered on the kanrei. Professor Satō has identified the phase of bakufu organization under Yoshimitsu and Yoshimochi as the era of the "kanrei system." It is this period which is generally considered the high point of the Muromachi bakufu's effectiveness as a national government. According to Satō's view the newly established post of kanrei combined the powers of its predecessor, the shitsuji (i.e., the shogun's private secretary), and that of *hikitsuke-tōnin* (i.e., head of the Board of Adjudicants). As such the kanrei served as the public manifestation of the shogun's office. Because studies of the kanrei system have not progressed very far, a great many points involving the actual details of what happened in the bakufu after Yoshinori's appointment must await further study. But it does appear that Yoshinori, shortly after his appointment as shogun, revived the then defunct *hyōjō* (Deliberative Council) and the attendant process of adjudication (hikitsuke), thereby attempting to check the power of the kanrei. The contemporary monk Mansai of Daigoji Sambōin wrote at the time: "Wishing to rule justly so as not to arouse general complaint, the shogun sought to revive the hyōjōshū and the office of hikitsuke-tōnin."[12] It is quite apparent that the cause for "general complaint" was the feeling that too much power was being concentrated in the hands of the kanrei. Events do not reveal any specific occurrence which might have stimulated this negative view of the kanrei, but it is reasonable to suppose that Yoshinori's attempt to curtail the kanrei's power, and coincidentally to enhance the position of the shogun, was an early indication of the autocratic tendency which he later displayed.

As it turned out, the old administrative organs were not revived. Rather a new deliberative-adjudicative procedure made its appearance at about this time known as the shogunal hearing *(gozen-sata)* and the presentation of the brief *(iken)*.[13] Under the new procedures, deliberations were conducted in the shogun's presence *(gozen)*. On these occasions, briefs, or *ikenjo*, were presented which laid out the details of investigations conducted

11. Satō Shin'ichi, "Ashikaga Yoshinori shiritsu ki no bakufu seiji," in *Hōsei shigaku* 20 (1968); Saiki Kazuma, "Kyōfu no yo: Kakitsu no hen no haikei," in *Senran to jimbutsu*, ed. Takayanagi Mitsutoshi Hakushi Shōju Kinenkai (Tokyo, 1968).

12. "Mansai Jugō nikki," item for Shōchō 1(1428)/5/26, in *Kyōto Teikoku Daigaku Bunka Daigaku sōsho* (Kyoto, 1918-20).

13. Ishii Ryōsuke, *Chūsei buke fudōsan soshōhō no kenkyū* (Tokyo, 1938); Kasamatsu, "Muromachi bakufu soshō seido 'iken' no kōsatsu."

by the bugyōshū together with citations of relevant precedents. These briefs became the basis for the shogun's decisions. How this new system differed from that for handling administrative and judicial rulings under the kanrei system is unclear, since we do not know precisely what the kanrei's involvement in the decision-making process was or what the role of the bugyōshū was at the time. We cannot imagine, of course, that under the kanrei system the bugyōshū were totally excluded from the decision-making process. But we can readily imagine that, with the introduction of the practice of presenting briefs before the shogun, the initiative powers of the bugyōshū were greatly increased.

We can conclude then that, as the shogun and his hereditary administrators began to handle administrative matters, and as the relative influence of the kanrei within the bakufu bureaucracy began to decline, the manner in which the shogun's wishes were transmitted and the documentary style of this transmission changed. This would account for the shift from the use of the gohan-migyōsho together with the kanrei's order to the use of the administrative directive (bugyōnin-hōsho).

From the institutional point of view these documentary changes reflect the rise of the mandokoro and its absorption of the functions of other administrative organs. The bugyōshū which came to the fore at this juncture did so by increasing its capacity to influence policy through the presentation of briefs to the shogun. This trend, which had its beginnings under Yoshinori, came into its own during the first decades after Yoshimasa became shogun, that is, during the middle of the fifteenth century. I have proposed therefore that we call the period in bakufu organizational history distinguished by this administrative system—it comes to an end only with the destruction of the Muromachi bakufu—as the era of the "bugyōnin system."

In conclusion I should like to offer some comments on the significance of the bugyōnin system and to point out a number of questions concerning it which remain for future study.

First, the bugyōnin system exerted a conservative influence on bakufu policy, one which sought to preserve "the system" against change. The bugyōshū were specialists in legal matters. They preserved documents and records from the past and were learned in the laws and regulations of the old imperial system. To settle any legal question, they would draw the needed precedents from the documentation they controlled and would expound upon the relevant legal principles. Naturally, because of this legalistic approach, such persons would try to make decisions on the basis of legal usage and interpretation. Rather than matching new circumstances with new laws, the bugyōshū tended to make deductions from existing law even if they had to twist the interpretation to do so.[14]

Another reason for the conservatism of this system had to do with the sources of economic support upon which the hereditary administrators relied. Although we must infer from limited historical evidence, it appears that the bugyōnin, like most of the civil aristocracy, were supported by relatively meager land tenures.[15] Such tenures became increasingly insecure as the Muromachi period wore on. To overcome this insecurity, the bugyōshū developed other sources of income by making arrangements with powerful temples and shrines, such as the Sammon (i.e., the Enryakuji of Mt. Hiei, Tōji, Kōfukuji, Kitano-sha, and Sumiyoshi-sha, which commonly sought representation in the shogun's government. As a result, they acquired what might be called retainerships from these institutions.[16] A bugyōnin, by agreeing to serve as spokesman for a given wealthy religious institution, would assume responsibility to represent the interests of that institution, in any suit that might be brought before the mandokoro. For this the bugyōnin would receive a regular source of income. Thus, while at first glance it might appear that the bugyōnin were relying on precedent and on the correct application of law in making their judgments, it is probable that the influence they exerted in the bakufu tended to favor the great temples and shrines and the existing order. How this conservative tendency came into being and was allowed to grow within the bakufu is as yet little understood. The problem remains, in fact, one of the main questions requiring further study.

But the issue is more complicated than appears at first glance. For, though there is no doubt about the conservative nature of the bugyōnin system as it came to dominate the bakufu political process, the system was not begun for conservative reasons. The shogun Yoshinori, who initiated the system, clearly had in mind to use the legalistic specialization of the bugyōshū as a means of enhancing the authority of the shogun. In an age that respected tradition, the capacity to handle complex bureaucratic procedures by reference to old usages and precedents was a valuable political device. And Yoshinori used this device for his own advantage. An important question that needs further study, therefore, is how the

14. This is Kasamatsu's conclusion from his study of the "iken" system.

15. Kuwayama Kōnen, "Muromachi bakufu keizai no kōzō," in *Nihon keizaishi taikei*, vol. 2, *Chūsei* (Tokyo, 1965).

16. From the document "Muromachi bakufu shobugyō shidai" we learn that in addition there were bugyō attached to Jingū (Ise) and Hachiman (Iwashimizu) shrines and Tōdaiji, Onjōji, and Omuro (Ninnaji) temples.

bugyōnin system acquired its own momentum and increased its hold over the bakufu and even the shogun.

Finally, the fact that the bugyōnin system survived to the final days of the Muromachi bakufu needs explanation. It is generally assumed that the historical significance of the Muromachi bakufu ended with the Ōnin War. Yet in both name and actuality the bakufu lasted a century longer. It would seem that we have tended to kill off the bakufu before its time. A further inquiry into the functioning of the bugyōnin system beyond the Ōnin War might well serve as a means of getting at the nature of the bakufu in its final century.

6

Shogun and Shugo: The Provincial Aspects of Muromachi Politics

KAWAI MASAHARU

with Kenneth A. Grossberg

Muromachi government has been defined as a coalition between the shogun and the most powerful of his provincially based vassals, the shugo. By the Muromachi period the provinces of Japan were no longer capable of being administered by bureaucratically assigned governors accountable to a central authority, as they in theory were under the imperial system. Each province consisted of a patchwork of holdings by semi-independent local proprietors (now increasingly referred to as *kokujin,* or "men of the province") and of estates belonging to religious institutions or to absentee noble proprietors residing in the capital. It is over these provinces that the shogun assigned his chief vassals as shugo, a term which may be translated roughly as "military governor."

It was characteristic of the shugo that, while they were individually the most powerful military figures of the country, they were nonetheless not all-powerful in the provinces over which they were placed. The lands which they directly controlled rarely amounted to more than a fraction of the total territory in any one province. Moreover, within the provinces it was possible for kokujin to maintain direct ties of allegiance to the shogun over the heads of the shugo. The shugo's position in a province was as dependent upon the allegiance of local "men of the province" as the shogun's national position was upon the support of his vassal shugo. Any inquiry into the relationship between shogun and shugo thus requires an understanding of the interaction of two sets of political relationships: those at the center between shogun and shugo and those in the provinces between shugo and kokujin.

The main phases of the shogun-shugo relationship coincide closely to those noted in the preceding essays with respect to bakufu political organization. Active shugo participation in bakufu politics as a group supporting the primacy of the Ashikaga house can be said to have reached its

A more detailed treatment of some of the subjects reviewed in this essay may be found in Kawai Masaharu, *Chūsei buke shakai no kenkyū* (Tokyo, 1973).

zenith during the Ōei-Eikyō era (ca. 1394–1440). In the years when the Muromachi bakufu was at the height of its power, the shugo played an important supportive role in central government affairs. Conversely the bakufu gave support to the shugo in their efforts to set down secure provincial roots. But after 1441, when the bakufu's role as national hegemon began to weaken, the heavy involvement of the shugo in the life of the capital proved to be to their disadvantage. Increasingly, shugo were forced to compete with groups of local lords who took advantage of their proximity to the local agrarian base to undercut shugo authority.

Most shugo houses of importance in the early Muromachi period failed to meet the challenge of local competition in the years after the Ōnin War. Only in exceptional cases did a shugo construct a local power base firm enough to withstand the pressures of kokujin competition and thus retain the status of domainal lord into the Sengoku period. By and large the lords of the Sengoku age, the so-called sengoku-daimyo, came from the ranks of the newly risen kokujin. Thus, paralleling the process of bakufu transformation described in the previous essays, the provinces also underwent a change in the pattern of local rule in which the shugo system of the early Muromachi period was ultimately superseded by the daimyo system of the Sengoku age. The century following the Ōnin War witnessed the emergence of genuinely automonous regional hegemons, the sengoku-daimyo, who had little inclination to recognize the authority of the shogun except when it suited their purpose.

THE MUROMACHI BAKUFU AND THE SHUGO HOUSES

During the first phase of bakufu-shugo relations, when widespread fighting was occasioned by the division of the imperial line into the Northern and Southern Courts, shogunal policy toward the shugo was subject to frequent changes. Despite the admonition contained in the basic Ashikaga code, the *Kemmu-shikomoku*, that shugo should be appointed on the basis of ability to govern, not as a reward for military assistance, the shogun violated his own principle by using shugo appointments as a means of winning powerful local families to his side. Often the shogun simply assigned to the most powerful family within a province the office of shugo over that province. Moreover in the early years, while fighting continued, the shogun was not in a position to restrain the shugo as though they were his appointed officials, and he could do little to prevent them from extending their local powers in a variety of ways. During this first phase shugo began to acquire local proprietary bases by which they converted themselves from the bureaucratic status of military governor, as the

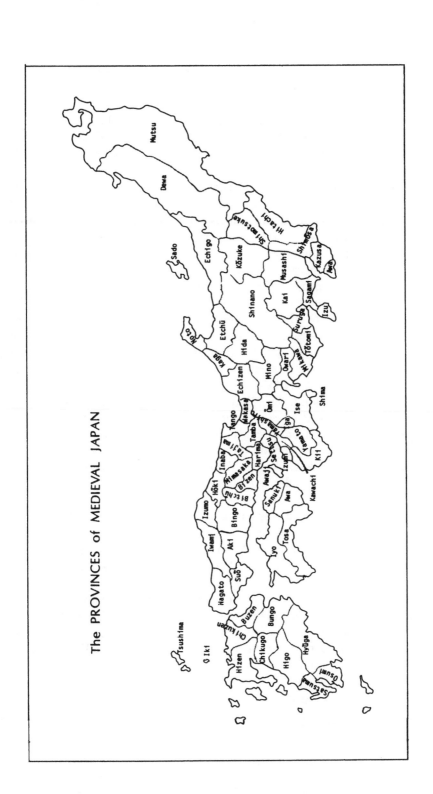

The PROVINCES of MEDIEVAL JAPAN

term shugo implied, into true regional lords to which the term daimyo, or magnate, is more aptly applied.

The second phase of the bakufu's development, roughly from 1392 to 1441, brought the apogee in the shogun-shugo relationship. As the several shugo continued to extend their powers over their assigned provinces, they found the backing of the bakufu advantageous and even necessary, while the bakufu grew in national influence to the point that it could oblige most shugo to take up residence in the shogun's capital of Kyoto.

With the exception of the ten Kantō provinces, which had been placed under the jurisdiction of the Kamakura Headquarters, and the eleven Kyushu provinces, which were superintended by the Kyushu Deputy, the shugo of the remaining forty-five provinces all built official residences in Kyoto during this period. Sinc as many as seven of these were shugo of more than two provinces, the actual number of shugo residing in Kyoto did not exceed twenty-one or twenty-two. The Governor General of the Kantō at Kamakura (the *Kamakura Kubō*) retained a considerable degree of autonomy vis-à-vis the shogun because of the historical status of Kamakura as the original site of the bakufu and because of his personal importance as a cadet member of the Ashikaga house. Thus the Kamakura Kubō required the shugo of the provinces under his authority to reside in Kamakura. The Kyushu Deputy, on the other hand, being simply an appointed officer of the bakufu, did not wield comparable regional influence. Consequently the various Kyushu shugo did not hesitate to contact the shogun directly. Kyushu shugo, such as Shimazu Motohisa and Ōtomo Chikayo, although not required to do so, built mansions in Kyoto and regularized relations with the bakufu.

Each of the shugo was, of course, accompanied by a full retinue of vassals, relatives, household servants, and others amounting to several hundred persons. The shogun freely availed himself of the labor forces which the shugo brought with them. When Yoshinori undertook the renovation of the shogun's Muromachi residence, he commanded various daimyo to supply, among other things, quantities of large rocks needed for the garden. It is recorded that the labor force contributed by the Hosokawa house amounted to 3,000 men, and by the Akamatsu house 2,800 men.[1] Not only shugo but lesser provincial proprietors, who were not required to reside in Kyoto, spent a good deal of time there and even built and maintained residences within the city.[2]

Although compulsory shugo residence in the capital was not a part of written statute law, as it would be when Edo succeeded Kyoto, in actual

1. "Manzai Jugō nikki," Eikyō 1/10/23, in *Zoku gunsho ruijū* (Tokyo, 1928); "Kammon gyoki," Eikyō 3/11/4, ibid.
2. "Manzai Jugō nikki," Ōei 32/5/21.

practice it was rigorously adhered to. To return to one's province without the express permission of the shogun was regarded as a rebellious act tantamount to treason; and this regulation, which seems to have been established during the last years of Yoshimitsu's rule, was strictly enforced by Yoshimochi and Yoshinori. Shugo often petitioned the shogun many times without receiving permission to take leave.[3] Because of this situation, shugo sometimes enlisted the aid of intermediaries close to the shogun to plead their case for them. For example, in 1418 Akamatsu Mitsusuke, shugo of the three provinces of Harima, Bizen, and Mimasaka, had Gakuin Ekatsu, the chief priest of the Rokuon-in of the Sōkokuji, request permission for him to return to the provinces. The request was denied, and Gakuin's role in the affair became one of the reasons why he was reprimanded by the shogun and eventually forced to leave Kyoto.[4]

In most cases, the primary reason for a shugo's eagerness to return to the provinces was the desire to ensure his control over, and especially the flow of income from, his territories. But this in itself was not considered by the shogun a legitimate excuse for wanting to leave the capital. Permission to return to the countryside was easily obtained only in times of crisis, when the shugo were called upon to subdue an enemy of the bakufu within provinces under their jurisdiction or in neighboring territories. Ōuchi Moriharu, for example, the shugo of Suō, Nagato, Chikuzen, and Buzen, was allowed to return to western Japan in 1425 specifically to chastise the Ōtomo and Shōni houses, who were illegally seizing lands in Chikuzen and Buzen. Likewise the shugo of Ise, Toki Mochiyori, received permission in 1428 to remain in Ise in order to help suppress remnants of the Southern Court's guerrilla forces. In the same year Imagawa Norimasa, shugo of Suruga, was permitted to leave the capital to prepare his forces for a punitive expedition against the rebellious governor of Kantō, Ashikaga Mochiuji. But even for such an emergency, permission was granted only after careful deliberation by the bakufu. In the case of Hosokawa Mochiharu, shugo of part of Iyo province in Shikoku, shogunal permission to return to Shikoku was given in order to chastise two local kokujin. Yet, it was the considered opinion of some within the bakufu council that a shugo should not have been permitted to return to his province simply to punish some of his own men.[5]

During the uncertainty of the first phase of bakufu administration, when revolt threatened to break out at any time, the compulsory residence of shugo in Kyoto was used as a security device, providing the shogun with

3. Ibid., Eikyō 1/2/28.
4. "Kammon gyoki," Ōei 25/3/18.
5. "Manzai Jugō nikki," Eikyō 3/9/28.

hostages as a guarantee of loyalty. Among the shugo assembled in Kyoto were some, such as Yamana Tokihiro and Ōuchi Moriharu, who had at least once in the past raised the standard of rebellion against the bakufu. When men of this sort obtained permission to leave Kyoto temporarily, they were required to leave a suitable hostage behind in the capital to ensure that they would engage in no mischief during their absence. Thus the bakufu forced Ōuchi Moriharu to appoint his son as his representative in Kyoto when he left for the provinces.[6]

Yet the routine settling of shugo in the capital should not be construed simply as the result of bakufu coercion. There were obvious incentives: the opportunity to participate in the politics of the central government, the chance to share in commercial profits available in Kyoto, and the possibility of enjoying the refined culture of the capital. In explaining the centralizing tendencies of the second phase of bakufu rule we need to examine more carefully these political, economic, and cultural incentives.

In the bakufu's formative period the shogun had ruled by personal decree with the help of his personal corps of administrators, but with the establishment of the kanrei system the shogun's personal leadership was subordinated to a consultative council of the important shugo, the yoriai. Shugo thus actively contributed to bakufu decision-making. Policy concerning important problems—e.g., the handling of the rebellious governor of Kantō or the treatment of the Southern Court—was decided only after consultation with the assembled shugo.

With the adoption of the shugo council system, the scope of government expanded, although the main actors were limited to seven or eight families. These included the "three kanrei houses" (Shiba, Hosokawa, Hatakeyama) and a few other powerful shugo, such as the Yamana, Akamatsu, Ōuchi, Isshiki, and Imagawa. As bakufu elder statesmen (*shukurō*), these families were regarded as representing shugo opinion in Kyoto, while the kanrei acted as political mediator and coordinator for all of them. At this time the kanrei was more of a spokesman for the collective will of the shugo assembled in Kyoto than he was an instrument for strengthening shogunal authority. This became evident in 1434 when the shogun Yoshinori was thwarted in his desire to attack the monasteries of Mt. Hiei by the unanimous opposition of the kanrei and the shugo, who threatened to put their own mansions to the torch and disperse to the countryside if he persisted in such a course.[7] Thus the relatively smooth course of bakufu administration from the 1390s through the 1430s was due to the vitality of the kanrei system, which encouraged positive participation by the shugo in the central government.

6. Ibid., Eikyō 2/12/17.   7. "Kammon gyoki," Eikyō 6/12/10.

From the economic standpoint, residence in Kyoto enabled the shugo to take advantage of newly developed sources of commercial capital. By the late Kamakura period Kyoto was already flourishing as a vigorous commercial community, and in fact one of the reasons why the Ashikaga established their bakufu in Kyoto was to gain control of what had become Japan's prime center of economic growth. Within the city a class of wealthy merchants known as *dosō* (usually described as pawnbrokers) had grown up by this time. The dosō maintained close ties with certain religious establishments of the capital and members of the court aristocracy for whom they performed a number of services including the collection and delivery of taxes and the sale of goods derived from distant estates. The bakufu was able to intrude upon this relationship by imposing a tax on the dosō in 1393.[8] During the next few decades the bakufu intensified its efforts to exploit the commercial wealth of Kyoto, and the shugo appear to have followed suit. Although there exist records for only two or three examples of shugo dealings with individual Kyoto dosō, the practice must have been widespread. Shugo also engaged the services of both Kyoto and provincial merchants in trading ventures with China and Korea.

As the prime symbols of new wealth and status in the society of the capital,[9] the shugo were often called upon by the shogun to contribute large sums of money to defray expenses for special celebrations or for repair of palaces and religious structures, and they met these demands with little apparent trouble. In 1416, for example, to pay for rebuilding the retired emperor's palace which had been destroyed by fire, the shugo were ordered to collect a tax from their provinces. Since funds were needed immediately, a flat tax of 100 strings of cash *(kanmon)* was assessed upon the shugo houses for each of their assigned provinces.[10] To pay for moving the shogun back into the newly renovated Muromachi palace in 1431, the shugo were saddled collectively with an assessment of 10,000 strings, which they apportioned among themselves in the following manner: the shugo assembled at the kanrei's residence decided that the seven shugo houses which held three or four provinces would each pay 1,000 kanmon, and the fifteen remaining shugo who held only one province would each contribute 200 kanmon.[11] In addition to such exactions, the shogun would from time to time call on the shugo at their mansions, and the lavish entertainment required for such occasions could run to as much as 400 kan-

8. Satō Shin'ichi and ·Ikeuchi Yoshisuke, eds., *Chūsei hōsei shiryōshū* (Tokyo, 1969), vol. 2, *Tsuikahō*, arts. 146–150.

9. "Kammon gyoki," Ōei 31/4/21.   10. Ibid., Ōei 23/6/5.

11. "Manzai Jugō nikki," Eikyō 3/9/3.

mon.[12] It is reasonable to conclude that shugo who could survive such onerous financial burdens must have been men of considerable wealth.

From the cultural point of view, residence in Kyoto was attractive to the shugo because it enabled them to enjoy refinements which they could not find in the provinces. By association with the court aristocracy, the shugo gained access to the classical culture of the imperial court; through friendship with the priests of the Zen monasteries which surrounded the city, they became privy to the much admired Chinese civilization. The shugo competed with each other in literary and cultural pursuits, hosting poetry salons at their mansions and building pavilions in the Zen style within their residential compounds for purposes of meditation or entertainment. In the high culture of the capital the shogun's Muromachi palace occupied a special place, providing the focus for various cultural activities. It acted as the cultural salon for the shugo, many of whom were men of high literary and cultural attainments as well as powerful political figures—Hosokawa Yoriyuki, Hosokawa Yorimoto and Mitsumoto, Shiba Yoshimasa and Yoshishige, Hatakeyama Mitsuie and Mitsunori, Yamana Tokihiro, Akamatsu Mitsusuke, Ōuchi Yoshihiro and Moriharu, Imagawa Ryōshun, Imagawa Norimasa, Kyōgoku Takauji, and Rokkaku Ujiyori, for example.

Professor Satō has already noted that a consequence of Yoshinori's despotic behavior was the deterioration of the kanrei-yoriai system. Yoshinori's highhanded acts included the execution of shugo and the pitting of one against another in order to bend them to his will. He caused the death of Isshiki Yoshitsura of Wakasa and Toki Michiyori of Ise. In numerous cases he ousted incumbent heads of shugo houses and granted the headship rights (*sōryōshiki*) to other members of the family, thereby confusing the shugo inheritance structure. Even the kanrei were not immune: Yoshinori banished Hatakeyama Mochikuni, the legitimate successor to Hatakeyama Mitsuie, and gave the office to a younger brother instead. Again in the case of Akamatsu Mitsusuke and his son Sukeyasu, Yoshinori proposed to take the provinces of Harima and Mimasaka away from them. It was this act which incited the two Akamatsu leaders to his murder. A period of reaction followed Yoshinori's assassination, as dispossessed shugo such as Hatakeyama Mochikuni and Togashi Yasutaka rushed to regain their former positions. The ensuing internecine struggles split shugo houses into factions supporting either the former or incumbent shugo and further weakened the cohesion of the shugo coalition which had given stability to the country.

During the first half of shogun Yoshimasa's rule, up to the outbreak of

12. "Kammon gyoki," Eikyō 2/12/20.

the Ōnin War, two of the three shugo houses which traditionally rotated in the office of kanrei ceased to exercise that function. The Shiba house was the first to succumb, and factional struggles among the Hatakeyama eventually left the Hosokawa as the sole family capable of serving as kanrei. This of course meant that the primary function of a rotating kanrei-ship, that of official mediator for the shugo, ceased to be performed. The resultant strife between shugo houses became an increasingly conspicuous aspect of Kyoto politics.

At the same time, the shugo houses were gradually losing control over their provinces—either to their deputies, the *shugodai,* or to other provincial vassals. Enforced residence in Kyoto was the main reason for this loss of effective command at the local level. As already noted, one of the reasons why shugo wanted to return to their home provinces was to prevent such an eventuality. The predicament which Kyoto-based shugo faced can be seen in the case of Shiba Yoshiatsu, who was ostensibly shugo over Echizen, Owari, and Tōtōmi, but whose vassals, the Kai, Oda, and Asakura, seized actual control, even to the point of jeopardizing his very economic existence. Yoshiatsu returned to Echizen in 1428 to try to regain command of his sources of income but failed in the effort.

Increasingly the shugo who remained in Kyoto lost wealth as well as political power to their provincially based vassals. When in 1465 Kyōgoku Mochikiyo, shugo of Izumo and northern Ōmi and head of the important bakufu office, the *samurai-dokoro* (Board of Retainers), stopped receiving dues from some of his territories, he granted the lands to his vassal Taga Takatada, then serving as deputy chief of the Board of Retainers. Having thus given up his proprietor's claims over these lands, he managed to recover a portion of the former dues via his subordinate.[13]

As the shugo council system gradually disintegrated, the shogun was forced to turn to other sources for support. One such source was the private guardsmen, the *hōkōshū.* This group had been brought into being by Yorimitsu as special bodyguard officers and by Yoshimasa's time had become fully established. Their political influence had grown correspondingly. In fact, throughout the Ōnin War the bakufu was able to maintain a position of strict neutrality precisely because of the support of the five guard groups. In addition to families such as the Ise, who were original vassals of the Ashikaga house, guardsmen were drawn from junior branches of shugo houses and from kokujin-class proprietors who came to reside in Kyoto, such as the Kobayakawa of Aki. With the backing of the guardsmen, the bakufu managed to retain a modicum of influence or at

13. "Inryōken nichi-roku," Kanshō 6/5/3, in *Dai Nihon Bukkyō zensho,* 151 vols. (Tokyo, 1913–22).

least independence. When Yoshimasa's successor Yoshitane fell from
power in 1493 as a result of Hosokawa Masamoto's coup d'etat, the guard
groups fell apart, and the bakufu became a government in name only. The
territorial lords freely ignored the bakufu and concentrated their energies
entirely on managing their own territories or invading their neighbors'. It
was this condition that characterized the Sengoku period.

THE GROWTH OF THE SHUGO "PROVINCIAL DOMAIN" SYSTEM AND ITS LIMITATIONS

During the first phase of Muromachi bakufu development
the shugo had begun the process of converting kokujin families within
their assigned provinces into private vassals, although this was not as yet
based on a thoroughgoing lord-vassal relationship involving the lord's
enfeoffment of the vassal. Early Muromachi institutions of proprietorship
and land tenure were so varied and complex that no simple system of
dominance by shugo over province was possible. As we shall see, few indeed were the shugo houses which managed to come through the disintegration of the shugo system after the middle of the fifteenth century to
emerge as true domainal lords in the feudal sense.

From the outset, the shugo were given certain powers and advantages
by the bakufu which permitted them to extend their control over local
military landholders and religious organizations. For instance, the shugo
were given the authority to dispatch agents to supervise land transfers or
adjudicate land disputes on behalf of the bakufu; they were given the right
to grant lands confiscated in wartime as rewards (onshō) to bushi within
their provinces; and they were permitted through the hanzei tax provisions
to grant half of the land dues on shōen estates within their jurisdiction
belonging to the court nobility or religious centers to their military supporters as a source of "military provisions." In this way, the shugo were
able to organize powerful warrior leaders (kokujin-class bushi) within
their provinces into bands of personal subordinates (hikan).

The shugo also served as military governors over the provinces, representing the authority of the bakufu, collecting province-wide taxes on
behalf of the shogun, and even exacting general taxes and levies in their
own right for presumed national purposes. These activities accelerated the
decline of the old estate system and the extension of shugo land and
military control at the local level. Successful shugo were able to convert the
provinces over which they were placed into what historians have called
"provincial domains" (ryōkoku). The process varied radically from region
to region, and at no time did shugo obtain the kind of unitary proprietary

control over their territories that the later daimyo managed to do. There were, in other words, limitations to the process. The shugo domains differed considerably from each other depending on the nature of the shugo house and the structure of local kokujin interests. This can be demonstrated in the following case studies of shugo politics in four provinces of western Japan: Aki, where the shugo failed to establish personal control over any significant portion of the local gentry; Bingo, in which a partial *ryōkoku* structure was fashioned; and Suō and Nagato, two provinces which exhibited all of the traits of an effective and vigorous provincial domain.

Aki Province

The Takeda house, whose original base was the province of Kai in eastern Japan, became shugo of Aki during the Kamakura period. In the warfare which brought the Kamakura bakufu to an end, Takeda Nobutake declared himself for Ashikaga Takauji. Thus, when his elder son Nobushige became shugo of Kai, his younger son Ujinobu was given the province of Aki and governed there for about thirty years as a loyal appointee of the Muromachi bakufu. As shugo he frequently awarded lands in fief to his supporters in the province—among them the Kumagai, the Kikkawa, and the Terahara—and a feudal type lord-vassal relationship developed between these families and Ujinobu. This process was cut short in 1371 when the bakufu abruptly named Imagawa Ryōshun, at the time the Kyushu Tandai, as shugo of Aki. From then on, the Ashikaga avoided entrusting the province they considered so politically and strategically important to them to the governorship of non-kin-related houses like the Takeda. Instead they alternately appointed Ashikaga cadet families such as the Hosokawa, Shibukawa, and Yamana to the post of shugo of Aki, and finally simply declared Aki a part of the shogun's private domain (*goryōsho*).

During the twenty-odd years Imagawa Ryōshun was nominally shugo of Aki, Ōuchi Yoshihiro, shugo of neighboring Suō, gradually extended his influence into the province, freely making grants of land to local families in an attempt to bind them to him as loyal vassals. In 1392 Ryōshun was relieved of the Aki shugoship, which then was given to the kanrei Hosokawa Yoriyuki,[14] who was in turn replaced by Shibukawa Mitsuyori. After only a few years Mitsuyori was succeeded, in 1403, by Yamana Mitsuuji, who received orders from the shogun to consolidate

---

14. *Mōrike monjo*, no. 1334, in Tōkyō Daigaku Shiryō Hensanjo, *Dai Nihon komonjo, iewake monjo* (Tokyo, 1904–).

control over the kokujin of the area. These local families, however, formed alliances (*ikki*) and resisted. Forced to admit defeat, Mitsuuji was stripped of his shugoship in 1406.

The Aki kokujin, under the leadership of the Mōri family, continued to resist central control and remained organized as a local confederation. After Mitsuuji's failure to reexert central control, the role of the shugo of Aki became largely that of mediator between the increasingly independent kokujin ikki and the bakufu. This was especially true after Aki was designated a shogunal province.

At one time or another Yamashiro, Harima, Aki, and Chikuzen provinces were all designated goryōkoku. It is no coincidence that they all lie in western Japan in a line stretching from Kyoto to Kyushu: the shogunal house was particularly concerned with strengthening its influence in this region. How shogunal control over such provinces differed from shogunal control over those placed under the common variety of shugo is not fully apparent. Shugo were appointed over them but these appointees appear to have been more directly accountable to the shogun. Also within these provinces certain lands were reserved for payment of dues to the shogun. The imposition of these dues was not designed simply to strengthen the shogun's financial position: the political objective of extending the shogun's personal rule into the various provinces was equally important. In other words, the shogun was anxious to acquire direct powers of overlordship over kokujin vassals in these provinces.

Aki serves to illustrate the shogun's attempt to encourage kokujin vassals at the expense of a shugo's provincial power. In 1431, for example, the shugo of Aki, Yamana Tokihiro, was ordered by the shogun Yoshinori to undertake a military mission against the Ōtomo of Kyushu. Tokihiro ordered the kokujin in Aki to proceed to the Kyushu battlefront, but they failed to respond. Although Tokihiro was a respected leader at the capital and a successful governor of the province of Bingo, he seemed to be unable to establish his authority in Aki. In actuality, independent Aki kokujin such as the Takeda and Kobayakawa had been advised by the scheming shogun not to obey Tokihiro. They set out for the front only after the shogun himself had personally ordered them to do so.[15] The precocious development of Aki kokujin into independent lords can be attributed not only to the frequent rotation of shugo but also to the shogun's personal interference, which served to undermine shugo authority and thus enable the kokujin to enhance their own power.

15. "Manzai Jugō nikki," Eikyō 4/1/23.

Bingo Province

In contrast to Aki, the province of Bingo remained under the authority of a single shugo house, the Yamana, from the early years of Muromachi until 1538. Although by the end of this period the Yamana had lost most of their real power as shugo, at least until the Ōnin War they devoted a great deal of energy to strengthening their land base and vassalage system in Bingo. Yamana Tokiyoshi, father of Tokihiro, who was to become shugo of Aki, was appointed to Bingo in 1379. It was Tokihiro, however, who as shugo under three successive shoguns—Yoshimitsu, Yoshimochi, and Yoshinori—was probably most vigorous in his administration of Bingo. He was followed by Yamana Mochitoyo, who was also appointed shugo of Harima as a reward for his role in punishing the Akamatsu after the Kakitsu disturbance. Mochitoyo went on to become commander of the western army in the Ōnin War, which was ranged against the eastern forces of Hosokawa Katsumoto.

Upon becoming shugo of Bingo in 1401, Yamana Tokihiro appointed two deputies to the province as a means of implementing his command. By acting on their own authority to confirm landholdings and grant new lands as rewards, the Yamana established lord-vassal relationships with many kokujin in the province, the relationship between the Yamana and Yamanouchi-Sudō, a powerful kokujin family in northern Bingo, being a case in point. When a dispute broke out in the Yamanouchi-Sudō family over claims to family property, the shugo adjudicated the matter by sending a representative into the disputed lands to carry out a survey.[16] On another occasion the Yamana granted the Yamanouchi-Sudō in perpetuity military support estates which were only supposed to be given temporarily under the hanzei provision. They also granted in fief lands which legally belonged to absentee shōen proprietors who resided in Kyoto. By means of such practices, the Yamana gained vassals in Bingo and accelerated the destruction of the shōen system.[17]

The Yamana possessed estates in Bingo which were designated "shugo lands" (*shugo ryō*).[18] But it was chiefly through the practice of tax contracts that the shugo extended economic control over the province. Although records are not complete, it is known that the Yamana house served as tax agent for the so-called "public lands" of Kawamo; served as tax trustees in Ōta-no-shō for the absentee proprietor, the great monastery of Kōyasan; and managed Tsuboo-no-shō for the Ichijō family, who were among the

---

16. *Yamanouchi-Sudōke monjo*, nos. 90, 92, in *Dai Nihon komonjo, iewake*, series 15 (Tokyo, 1940).

17. Ibid., nos. 88, 89.

18. "Manzai Jugō nikki," Eikyō 4/9/11; *Yamanouchi-Sudōke monjo*, no. 183.

high nobles around the emperor. The Yamana record of tax management
showed many instances of nonpayment and misappropriation. Ultimately
these estates were appropriated by the Yamana and given as fiefs to local
kokujin in return for pledges of allegiance.

In spite of all their efforts, Yamana rule of Bingo began to suffer
reverses from about the end of the Ōnin War, primarily as a consequence
of a family quarrel which weakened the family leadership. During the
Ōnin War, Yamana Mochitoyo gave the Bingo shugoship to his son
Koretoyo, who then joined the enemy eastern army against both his father
and younger brother Masatoyo. Presently Masatoyo began to fight with
his own son Toshitoyo. Because of this the head of the Yamana house had
to remain in Kyoto and had little opportunity to supervise affairs in Bingo.
Meanwhile the backing of the shogunate which had supported shugo
authority in Bingo weakened. The Yamana, on their own, found it increasingly difficult even to control their chief subordinates. Soon kokujin
families began to infringe on the shugo's former authority.

By 1483 the kokujin Yamanouchi-Sudō Toyonari was tax contracting
for the Yamana on the province's shogunal estates.[19] In 1490 he received
authority over the province's "public lands." In 1492 Toyonari was appointed *tansen bugyō* (collector of tansen) for all of Bingo by the Yamana,
who no longer had the ability to collect tansen levies by themselves.[20]
These were functions which normally were performed by the shugo's
deputy. But the Yamanouchi-Sudō were able to gain possession of them in
return for the cancellation of loans which they had made to both the shugo
and his deputy. Ultimately the Yamana were obliged to relinquish to the
Yamanouchi-Sudō family complete administrative authority over Bingo in
exchange for an oath of allegiance to the Yamana.[21]

Suō and Nagato Provinces

In both Suō and Nagato the Ōuchi family as shugo managed to establish
what amounted to a "shugo provincial domain." The Ōuchi did so by extending their control over the local kokujin more effectively than the
Yamana had done in either Bingo or Aki. In Suō and Nagato the kokujin
were firmly enlisted as feudal type vassals, and were even referred to as
housemen (gokenin). Again in contrast to the Yamana of Bingo, whose
strength began to wane after the Ōnin War, Ōuchi power in Suō and
Nagato grew stronger than ever during the Sengoku era. The explanation
for this can be found in the nature of the relationship which the Ōuchi
house had with the kokujin of these provinces.

The Ōuchi were, first of all, themselves originally kokujin who managed

19. *Yamanouchi-Sudōke monjo*, no. 183.   20. Ibid., nos. 156, 157, 159.
21. Ibid., nos. 134, 161, 172.

to become shugo through their own effort. From the twelfth century they had served as provincial officials under the imperial system and had become local landholders of considerable influence. The first shugo of Suō appointed by Ashikaga Takauji was Washizu Nagahiro, head of a minor Ōuchi branch family. Ōuchi Hiroyo, head of the main Ōuchi family, opposed the appointment and revolted against Takauji by joining the Southern Court cause. He proceeded to defeat the Washizu and, after declaring himself shugó of Suō, invaded neighboring Nagato and expelled its shugo. Thus by means of a *fait accompli* Hiroyo won the bakufu's grudging consent and was recognized as shugo of both Suō and Nagato, after which he promptly changed sides once more. Abandoning the Southern Court in 1363, he proceeded to Kyoto for an audience with the shogun, Yoshiakira.

His successor Ōuchi Yoshihiro proved his loyalty to the bakufu in the Kyushu and Meitoku uprisings and was rewarded with the shugoships of Iwami, Buzen, Izumi, and Kii, bringing under his sway a total of six provinces. When in his later years the shogun Yoshimitsu attempted to restrain the most powerful of his shugo, Yoshihiro became one of the main objects of shogunal enmity. Finally in 1399 Yoshihiro raised the flag of revolt against the bakufu at the town of Sakai (near present-day Osaka) and was killed in battle shortly thereafter.

It was Yoshihiro's dying wish that his younger brother Moriharu should have Suō and Nagato, but the bakufu attempted to thwart the succession by sending its military forces into those provinces. The kokujin of Suō and Nagato, however, stood by Moriharu and defeated the bakufu forces. Eventually in 1404, the bakufu, finding itself unable to have its way, recognized Ōuchi Moriharu's right and officially appointed him shugo of the two provinces.

After being confirmed as shugo, Moriharu proceeded to Kyoto and there for twenty years participated in bakufu politics until allowed to leave the capital in 1425 in order to suppress another Kyushu rebellion. As a reward for a successful campaign, he added Buzen and Chikuzen to his sphere of authority, bringing his total number of shugoships to four. His main power base, and the area where his administration developed most extensively, remained Suō and Nagato.

Moriharu utilized two stratagems to strengthen the bonds with kokujin in areas under his authority. To sever the ties which such families as the Nihō and the Naitō (which had served as direct shogunal vassals under the Kamakura bakufu) had with the Muromachi bakufu, and to make them establish direct links with the Ōuchi, Moriharu privately confirmed their landholdings, irrespective of whether these were "original possessions" (*honryō*) or lands subsequently received as fiefs (*kyūchi*). Moriharu

also appointed such families to serve as his deputies or as other local functionaries.[22] To strengthen their sense of loyalty to him individually and to
emphasize their vassal status, Moriharu made his kokujin vassals participate in ceremonies at Ōuchi family shrines and temples, such as the Hi-
gamisan Kōryūji and the Kokuseiji.[23] It was under Moriharu that we see
the beginning of the practice of referring to Ōuchi-related kokujin as
gokenin (housemen), the enforcement of loyalty oaths, and a variety of other
measures which strengthened the lord-vassal character of the kokujin relationship to the Ōuchi family.[24] It was also at this time that the Ōuchi as
shugo began to levy their own province-wide taxes and corvée requirements.

Ōuchi Mochiyo, Moriharu's successor, remained in Kyoto, where he
became one of Yoshinori's personal attendants. He was killed along with
the shogun during the Kakitsu affair. Norihiro, who followed Mochiyo,
did not go to Kyoto, but rather built his official residence in the town of
Yamaguchi in Suō. From this base he showed his independence from
bakufu interference, fighting against the kanrei Hosokawa Katsumoto and
leading his troops into Aki in 1457 in defiance of bakufu orders. In 1465,
the year of his death, Norihiro was sent by the bakufu to punish Kawano
Michiharu of Iyo province but went to his aid instead. It was Norihiro who
directed the first compilation of Ōuchi house laws, the Ōuchi-shi kakegaki,
which were designed to strengthen contact between the shugo's capital at
Yamaguchi and the outlying districts of the province. These laws
emphasized the "housemen" status of Ōuchi vassals and sought to cen-
tralize political authority in the hands of the Ōuchi. The Ōuchi provide an
unusual example of a shugo house which survived the Ōnin watershed to
attain daimyo status during the Sengoku era.

KOKUJIN IKKI AND THE RISE OF A KOKUJIN LORD

An alternate route to the creation of a daimyo domain is exemplified in the rise of the Mōri house of Aki. The Mōri, a kokujin house
based in Aki, were able to extend their position as kokujin lords by making
common cause with neighboring kokujin in confederations or leagues,
called ikki, which they eventually came to lead. The Mōri had been jitō, or
land stewards, under the Kamakura shogun. At one time they had also
held territory in Echigo and Kawachi, but in order to survive the
vicissitudes of the Nambokuchō period the main family found it necessary

---

22. Miurake monjo, pp. 283–510, in Dai Nihon komonjo, iewake, series 14 (Tokyo, 1937).
23. Kōryūji monjo and Kokuseiji monjo, both in the manuscript library of Tōkyō Daigaku Shiryō
Hensanjo.
24. "Ōuchi-shi kakegaki," art. 9.

to concentrate its attention in Aki. Although this meant that they had to forfeit their other holdings, they gradually consolidated a stable power base within Aki. In the territories they controlled, the Mōri distributed individual villages among their branch families. These families were held together by a sworn compact (*ikki*) under the leadership of the head of the main (*sōryō*) family. The resulting confederation was strong enough to defy shugo interference in local affairs even when bakufu strength was at its highest. Thus, under the protection of the compact, the Mōri were able to entrench themselves firmly as indigenous local proprietors. As small, but independent kokujin, the Mōri maintained ties with the bakufu as minor direct vassals of the shogun.

Although kokujin usually remained in the provinces, a few such as Mōri Mitsufusa and his son Hiromoto were sufficiently important to be called to Kyoto on numerous occasions, to perform military duties and to attend the shogun.[25] Among Aki's other kokujin were those such as the Kobayakawa who joined the shogun's personal guard and consequently took up more or less permanent residence in Kyoto. The relationship of kokujin like the Mōri and the Kobayakawa to the shogun had two aspects. First, by linking themselves directly to the shogun, they were able to parry shugo efforts to force them into submission. Second, by borrowing the shogun's authority when necessary, they could enhance their own capacity to counter opposition from their own branch families. For example, the Mōri narrowly averted succumbing to a revolt by their junior cadet families in 1419 when the family head, Mōri Mitsufusa, proceeded to Kyoto and obtained from the shogun Yoshimochi official confirmation of his sōryō status.[26]

The Mōri were not the only kokujin of Aki who accepted the principle of shogunal authority but did not submit voluntarily to a shugo's commands; kokujin frequently acted in concert to forestall shugo pressures. For example, when Yamana Mitsuuji was made shugo of Aki in 1403, he ordered the kokujin to present proof of rightful ownership for their landholdings and tried to seize for himself any illegally acquired lands. In response, thirty-three families, most of the Aki kokujin, organized themselves into a league. In the following year they joined forces as an ikki and resisted the Yamana.

According to an agreement drawn up at this time by the Aki kokujin confederation, disputes between two members of the league were to be judged by all the others in council. Threats against any member from an outside source were to be met with unified action by all members. Although all pledged obedience to the shogun in Kyoto, they also promised

25. *Mōrike monjo*, no. 119.   26. Ibid.

to help resist forfeiture if the bakufu without reasonable cause ordered a
member to surrender his lands. Again, in cases where they were made
subject to province-wide taxes imposed by the shogun through the shugo,
the decision on whether or not to pay such taxes was to be made after discussion among all the league members.[27] In this way decision-making
within the province passed from the shugo to the kokujin confederation.
Initially the bakufu intended to suppress the kokujin league, but in the
end it pardoned Mōri Mitsufusa and the others and made Yamana Mitsuuji relinquish the post of shugo.[28] The incident thus culminated in a victory for the ikki.

Despite the temporary character of kokujin leagues, which were generally organized to confront particular situations, there is evidence that
Aki kokujin leagues led by the Mōri continued to be active over the course
of a considerable period of time. In 1512 nine of Aki's most powerful
kokujin families, including the Mōri, Amano, Kobayakawa, and Kikkawa,
formed a confederation. They did this in reaction to the political power
vacuum created when the Ōuchi began to lose their grip in Suō and
Nagato as a result of their involvement in bakufu politics. Almost by
default, the maintenance of order in Aki province became the responsibility of the kokujin league.

The charter of this league, like that of its predecessor, consisted of five
articles with similar provisions: internal conflicts were to be settled by
deliberation among all league members; external threats were to be dealt
with by collective action; in instances where an individual kokujin had
received orders from either the shogun or a shugo, or in situations where a
member wished to petition his superior, final decision was to be made on
the basis of discussion with the other members and not by individual
choice; and a vassal of any of the member families who wished to desert
his lord would not be accepted as a vassal by any other member of the
league. In this way the kokujin lords closed ranks to prevent their own
vassals from gaining independent power and influence.

Out of this situation one kokujin, Mōri Motonari, grew to become the
most powerful daimyo in the entire region, inheriting and expanding upon
the position formerly occupied by his lord the Ōuchi. He did so by totally
annihilating in 1555 the Sue of Suō who had aspired to succeed to the
Ōuchi power. The Mōri success in this critical battle can be attributed to
the fact that the Aki kokujin individually declared themselves for Motonari. No doubt the reason they did so was the fact that the Mōri had
frequently provided leadership for ikki in the past. In other words,

27. Ibid., no. 24.   28. Ibid., nos. 38–42.

Motonari was able to exploit his family's historic leadership role within Aki province.

Nevertheless, when Motonari succeeded to the headship of the Mōri house, absolute authority over a consolidated domain had not yet been achieved. Even the Mōri vassals were not all securely reduced to the status of retainers. In 1532 thirty-two Mōri vassals had presented Motonari with an oath in which they sought a guarantee that he would not require them to give up their status as small-scale landholders, in return for which they promised to jointly undertake the repair of walls and irrigation ditches and the disciplining of traitorous vassals.[29] The practice of making Mōri vassals pledge absolute loyalty to their lord was not adopted until 1550, when Motonari faced a dangerous rebellion in his own ranks.[30] The Mōri family started from the position of one among equals as leader of a kokujin league. Gradually, by concentrating power in his own hands, the Mōri chief became the leader of a province-wide union of ikki leagues. Ultimately he was able to absorb all Aki kokujin into his band of vassals. Each of these steps advanced the Mōri along the road toward becoming a daimyo.

THE FORMATION OF THE SENGOKU-DAIMYO

By the middle of the sixteenth century the shugo had everywhere disappeared from Japan to be replaced by regional lords of the sengoku-daimyo variety. A glance at the origins of these sengoku-daimyo reveals that the large majority had emerged from the kokujin class; these were men who had held inferior positions within local administrations, such as shugodai, but who had succeeded in replacing their former shugo masters. Only in exceptional cases did shugo houses, such as the Ōuchi, transform themselves from shugo to daimyo status. This is because most shugo, being constrained to reside in Kyoto and to rely on the bakufu for their own authority, found themselves stranded after the Ōnin War when the bakufu's power declined. The only shugo of central Japan who survived the Ōnin War was the Ōuchi, and even they eventually succumbed to the Mōri. All other shugo who successfully made the transition, such as the Shimazu and Ōtomo of Kyushu, and the Imagawa and Takeda in the Kantō, were located in peripheral areas, so that they had not become involved in bakufu politics. It is informative to follow the course of Ōuchi development beyond the Ōnin War to see how this family managed to hold on in western Japan until displaced by the Mōri.

29. Ibid., no. 396.   30. Ibid., no. 401.

Unlike the other Kyoto-based shugo, the Ōuchi, even while engaged in the capital, worked strenuously to acquire a secure provincial domain and then to maintain their power over it. Thus the Ōuchi chief frequently returned to his provincial base to make his presence felt, generally on the pretext of suppressing anti-bakufu rebellions in northern Kyushu. This was especially true of Ōuchi Norihiro, who, even before the Ōnin War, established his headquarters in Yamaguchi and devoted his undivided attention to administering the Ōuchi territories. He left to his successor Masahiro a provincial lordship structure which was already highly developed, and this in turn left Masahiro free to proceed to Kyoto after the outbreak of the Ōnin War and take the leadership of the western army after the death of Yamana Mochitoyo. In 1477 Masahiro finally returned to Yamaguchi, with regrets that he had stayed away so long. No sooner had Masahiro returned to western Honshu than he launched a campaign to retake parts of northern Kyushu, which had been seized while he was in Kyoto. He also restrengthened Kagamiyama castle in Aki province as a base from which to control the kokujin of that province.[31] In order to tighten control over his vassals, he issued a myriad of laws concerning such varied aspects of government as the maintenance of peace and public order, the control of communication and traffic within his domain, and the circulation of currency.

By 1478 Masahiro's Kyushu campaigns were bearing fruit. Having defeated the Shōni, he granted the conquered areas as fiefs to Aki kokujin who had fought with him in the campaign. From that time on, the Ōuchi made a practice of granting fiefs to their kokujin supporters in areas far from their home base in order to impress on them their vassal status.[32] The Ōuchi also ruthlessly seized fiefs which they had previously confirmed and summarily granted them to someone else. In cases where vassal land rivalry was especially acute, or when discrepancies between respective claims were unusually broad, the Ōuchi would settle suits by simply confiscating the fiefs in question and putting them under direct family control.[33] Likewise, in border disputes between neighboring vassals, the Ōuchi would dispatch emissaries to carry out surveys on both sides of the argument. If it was discovered that the parties held land in excess of what had been confirmed (ando) by the Ōuchi as overlords, the surplus was confiscated.[34]

Masahiro further consolidated the retainer organization which Norihiro had originated, placing it under a unified chain of command. Gokenin

31. "Ōuchi-shi kakegaki," arts. 40–44.   32. Mōrike monjo, no. 156.
33. "Ōuchi-shi kakegaki," art. 59.   34. Ibid., art. 142.

who were most closely associated with the ruling house were obliged to reside in Yamaguchi where they could serve the Ōuchi. In 1485 this residence requirement was further strengthened when Masahiro forbade unauthorized trips out of the city, setting a fine to be exacted for each day a vassal was absent without permission.[35] The following year the ruling was once again revised: if a vassal returned to his country residence without permission for even a day he would be divested of his retainer status.[36]

Although Masahiro temporarily neglected the Ōuchi relations with the bakufu in order to concentrate on local administration, his successor Yoshioki actively participated in shogunal affairs. Intervening on behalf of the deposed shogun Ashikaga Yoshitane, he succeeded in regaining the position for him. In so doing Yoshioki gained for himself the position of deputy kanrei, and for the next eleven years he appeared as one of the central figures in Kyoto politics.

But during Yoshioki's ten-year stay in Kyoto, the tight administration which had been established by Masahiro over Ōuchi territories and vassals began to slacken, and soon the Ōuchi were confronted with rebellious kokujin in Aki and northern Kyushu and peasant revolts within their own domains. The recently returned Yoshioki once again set about regaining control of his ryōkoku, but rebellions sprang up in several areas.[37]

It was at this critical point that Ōuchi leadership faltered. Before Yoshioki could successfully pacify his territories he was succeeded in 1528 by his son, Yoshitaka. Under Yoshitaka, the Ōuchi house pursued an aggressive military policy, fighting to retain control of its territories. But much of the fighting was left to the Ōuchi's vassals, while Yoshitaka himself occupied his time in cultural pursuits in Kyoto or Yamaguchi. Yoshitaka's propensity to play the courtier led him to devote more attention to the refinement of his etiquette than to the pursuit of military advantage. As a result Sue Harukata, an Ōuchi vassal who had done much of Yoshitaka's fighting, executed a coup d'état in 1551 in which Yoshitaka was killed.

The destruction of the Ōuchi house by the Sue plunged the former Ōuchi territories into a state of great uncertainty. But the Sue, having momentarily replaced the Ōuchi as masters of western Japan, were soon obliged to compete for this position with the Mōri of Aki. In 1555, Mōri Motonari defeated the Sue in a decisive battle at Miyajima, thereby acquiring the entire Ōuchi legacy. As we have already noted, the Mōri owed

35. Ibid., art. 86.   36. Ibid., art. 103.   37. Ibid., art. 175.

their remarkably rapid growth to a series of successful alliances with the kokujin of Aki and Bingo and the subsequent conversion of these kokujin into full-fledged house vassals. After the victory at Miyajima, the Mōri tighthened military discipline and codified a set of laws to unify their control over the various bands of kokujin.[38] In this way, the Mōri had more or less succeeded in uniting the entire Chūgoku region under their rule by the time Motonari died in 1571. In the interim they had established a system of uniform land tenure, fixed a policy toward the peasants, and cemented relations with the Inland Sea merchants. In short they had constructed a full, autonomous sengoku-daimyo power base.

38. *Mōrike monjo*, .nos. 224–226.

PART THREE

Lordship and Village

In the previous essay Professor Kawai looked upon the passage from shugo to sengoku-daimyo in the provinces mainly from the perspective of the political authority structure at the national and provincial levels. As he described it, the essential factor in the transition from shugo to daimyo rule was the growth of feudal authority relations within the military class. Implicit in his analysis of the provincial struggles which led to the rise of the sengoku-daimyo was the assumption that the feudal system, in which political authority was fully coalesced with possession of property rights at the local level, was stronger than the system of shugo provincial rule that it displaced. By "shugo provincial rule," Professor Kawai had in mind a system based on three specific institutions: the bakufu-shugo political framework, the kokujin lordship system of landed proprietorship, and the sōryō system of extended family organization. Among these aspects of the displaced system of shugo provincial rule, it was the institution of kokujin lordship which in Professor Kawai's opinion served as the pivot of transition from what under the shōen system had been a vertically stratified system of land rights to the chigyō, or fief, system of land possession which characterized the later feudal domains. While the shugo had been unable to convert their provinces of assignment into unitary proprietary possessions, kokujin had managed to acquire proprietary lordships over which they held rights of land tenure and administration that were essentially feudal in nature. It was on a foundation of these kokujin lordships that the sengoku-daimyo domain came into being.

In the essay by Professor Miyagawa which follows, a closer analysis is made of the proprietary foundations upon which the sengoku-daimyo domain rested. To better understand the significance of the sengoku-daimyo as agents of a new and more effective system of local rule, Professor Miyagawa starts with an inquiry into the nature of the so-called "shugo provincial domain" and how it differed from the later daimyo domains. The marked discrepancy between the shugo's political jurisdiction and his

87

proprietary rights within a given province meant that the shugo's province of assignment was not at all a true domain in the feudal sense. In contrast, the chief characteristic of the sengoku-daimyo domain was the complete interdependence of the agricultural and military spheres brought about by the general conversion to the chigyō, or enfeoffment, system of land-holding. In addition, the sengoku-daimyo utilized a system of authority which permitted him a much stronger and more widespread assertion of control over his subordinates. This was the *yorioya-yoriko* (lord-vassal) relationship which came to replace the sōryō system as the primary method of military-political association. Finally the sengoku-daimyo developed a more systematic form of taxation through the routinization of the *tansen* (the provincial unit tax). Once levied only as an extraordinary tax for national purposes, it was assimilated by the daimyo into the annual ground rent, thereby giving a sense of public requirement to the tax demands of the sengoku lords.

If the chigyō system was at the heart of the sengoku-daimyo's acquisition of independent proprietary rights over his domain, the chigyō in turn was dependent upon a firm system of subordination between lord and cultivator. Here the critical institution was the village. Professor Miyagawa suggests in his essay that peasant resistance was the most important cause of political change in the Sengoku era. This idea is amplified by Professor Nagahara. Ideally one might imagine a trend toward increasing village autonomy as a result of peasant resistance to kokujin pressures. Yet the appearance of wealthy peasants, or *dogō* (peasant chiefs), as an intermediary class between cultivators and kokujin lords put certain restraints on any such trend. Dogō needed the protection of kokujin, who in turn needed the protection of still stronger local magnates, the daimyo. Kokujin required the services of the dogō (for military purposes) and wealth from the villages which the dogō controlled. Thus an accommodation was worked out between the kokujin holders of chigyō and the peasant chiefs of the villages which comprised the holdings. It was this accommodation which made possible the sixteenth-century withdrawal of the land-based samurai into the castle headquarters of the daimyo. Ultimately, as Professor Nagahara suggests, the daimyo by assuming the cloak of "public benefit" (*kōgi*) managed to justify political and fiscal control over a military domain in which village communities subordinated themselves as self-governing units of local control and taxation.

7

From Shōen to Chigyō: Proprietary Lordship and the Structure of Local Power

MIYAGAWA MITSURU
with Cornelius J. Kiley

THE SHUGO PROVINCIAL DOMAIN

No discussion of provincial politics of the Muromachi period can neglect the dual nature of the shugo. A shugo was the chief political authority in the province or provinces to which he was appointed, and, at the same time, he was also a lord of certain domains in the sense that *shōen* proprietors or *kokujin* were lords of domains.[1] But these domains did not correspond to the boundaries of his political authority. Thus to call the shugo's province his "domain" is a misnomer. Any use of the term *shugo-ryōkoku*, or "shugo provincial domain," must make clear that the province was by no means the shugo's full proprietary possession.[2] Provinces were controlled politically by the shugo, and the extent of this control depended in considerable degree on the size of the shugo's proprietary holdings within the province. But even the greatest of the shugo held only a fraction of any province as a lordship possession.

In the early years of the Muromachi bakufu the office of shugo was awarded only to powerful landholders, either cadet branches of the

1. In this essay I define "lordship" *(ryōshusei)* as designating a relationship of feudal superordination based on the possession of a "domain," a relationship resting ultimately on the subordination of a "serf" class whose rents and other dues belong to the lord by proprietary right. This tax nexus, then, is viewed as fundamental to the "feudal" order, but its maintenance depends on what is here defined as an "external condition" of feudalism, the power of the lord to control other essential facilities like vacant lands, water rights, and markets.

2. This observation is made in the light of the active controversy over interpretation of the nature of the shugo's provincial authority. See, for example, Satō Shin'ichi, "Shugo ryōkokusei no tenkai," in *Chūsei shakai: Shin Nihonshi taikei*, ed. Toyoda Takeshi (Tokyo, 1954); Nagahara Keiji, "Shugo ryōkokusei no tenkai," in *Nihon hōkensei seiritsushi no kenkyū* (Tokyo, 1961); Kurokawa Tadanori, "Shugo ryōkokusei to shōen taisei," *Nihonshi kenkyū* 57 (1961); Kurokawa Tadanori, "Chūsei kōki no ryōshusei ni tsuite," *Nihonshi kenkyū* 68 (1963); and Tanuma Mutsumi, "Muromachi bakufu to shugo ryōkoku," in *Kōza Nihonshi*, 3, *Hōken shakai no tenkai* (Tokyo, 1970), pp. 85–108.

Ashikaga line or unrelated magnates. Their lands were widely scattered, both within and outside their province of appointment, and in most cases the holdings outside the province were the more extensive. To take a single example, in the sixth decade of the fourteenth century, the shugo of northern Ōmi, the Kyōgoku, held jitō rights to six domains in the province, but the bulk of Kyōgoku holdings were scattered throughout distant provinces. Their holdings in Ōmi, though considerable, were but a small fraction of the domains located there. In another more extreme example, Kō no Morohide, the shugo of Yamashiro during the Ōei era (1394–1398), held domains located mostly in the Kantō and Tōkai regions; not a single one was located in Yamashiro, his appointed province.[3]

Most shugo land tenures were defined in terms of *shiki* (rights), typically *jitō-shiki* or *ryōke-shiki* in some *shō* or *gō*, although these shiki had already ceased to be what they had been in earlier ages. Shiki in the Muromachi period were not part of the vertical hierarchy of rights (i.e., *honke-shiki*, *ryōke-shiki*, *azukaridokoro-shiki*, and *jitō-shiki*), all affecting the same parcel of land, a condition which was typical of Kamakura period land tenure. Rather, each of these shiki represented an independent holding, a domain existing side by side with other domains.[4] This general state of affairs had come about during the period of the wars of the Northern and Southern Courts with the deterioration of the shōen system. As the structure of vertically stratified tenures broke down, a shiki-holder within a shō or gō generally came to enjoy complete proprietary control over his jitō or ryōke, free from superior tenures.

With holdings so widely scattered, how did the shugo exercise control over his several domains? Usually, he did so through his position as chief heir, or *sōryō*, which allowed him to act as head of an extended lineage. Shugo control over its cadet families, who were often local lords with their own holdings, was exercised through an inheritance system in which the sōryō was invested with the ultimate authority over family properties in their entirety. As head of the main lineage, the shugo generally controlled domains by awarding them to kinsmen or by appointing kinsmen as estate managers. Within the shugo's own province, however, the sōryō system of control could not be very effective because the domains so held were limited. As time passed, moreover, this control system gradually deteriorated as cadet branches became autonomous kokujin lords. This trend

3. Nagahara Keiji, "Nihon ni okeru hōken kokka no keitai," in *Kokka kenryoku no shomondai*, ed. Rekishigaku Kenkyū kai (Tokyo, 1950).
4. Miyagawa Mitsuru, "Shōensei no kaitai," in *Iwanami Kōza: Nihon rekishi* (Tokyo, 1963), *Chūsei* 3, pp. 119–162 (hereafter cited as *IKC*); Kurokawa, "Chūsei kōki no ryōshusei ni tsuite," pp. 53–63.

was especially pronounced when the branch family's holdings were distant from the shugo's province.

No shugo held more than a small fraction of the sum total of domains within his province of assignment, and it cannot be thought that he held the province as a proprietary lordship. On the contrary, the provinces controlled by the shugo consisted of small scattered domains under the proprietorship of kokujin. To put it another way, kokujin, including shugo cadets, who regarded the land as their own and extracted dues from its cultivators, represented the general type of proprietary lordship at this time. Looked at in this way the shugo within his province was himself one of the local kokujin.

Because kokujin lordship was the basis of local power, the shugo worked to expand his control of holdings in his province, thereby increasing his ability to control shōen proprietors and local kokujin from above. To accomplish this the shugo had certain advantages. Using the public backing of the bakufu, shugo were able to extend their proprietorships and link them into a system of political alliances within their provinces.

In theory, shugo were local officials appointed to each province as part of the national public administration. As the *Kemmu shikimoku* of 1336 states in Article 7: "The office of shugo has from ancient times been an office of public administration."[5] Initially, the shugo's public authority was limited to "the three great constabulary duties": the muster of capital guardsmen and jurisdiction over cases of treason and homocide. Gradually the shugo acquired more extensive powers from the bakufu, including the power to execute judgment in cases regarding land or domains, to arrest and punish those accused of unlawful harvesting, and to administer *hanzei*, a system whereby half of the income from certain estates was expropriated for military purposes. Another power, acquired through the bakufu from the imperial court, was the authority to collect *tansen*, which was originally an extraordinary levy measured in cash (*sen*) and imposed uniformly throughout each province on each *tan* (about one-third of an acre) of "public land." In exchange for assuming the burden of collecting this tax, the shugo by the middle of the fifteenth century had asserted the right to levy shugo tansen and shugo corvée in recompense for services as occasion demanded.[6]

Thus by expanding and intensifying his public administrative authority, the shugo expanded his control over his province as one component of the nationwide authority exercised by the bakufu. As such his position con-

5. "Kemmu shikimoku," in Satō Shin'ichi and Ikeuchi Yoshisuke, eds., *Chūsei hōsei shiryōshū* (hereafter cited as *CH*), 3 vols. (Tokyo, 1957–65), 2.
6. Miyagawa Mitsuru, "Nambokuchō," in *Taikō kenchi ron* (hereafter cited as *TK*), 3 vols. (Tokyo, 1959–63), 1: 94–312.

tained certain elements of political imperium as well as of personal vassalage. Within the provincial structure the shugo's authority was of course lesser in scope than the bakufu's, and the power of the shugo over his province had its limits. For example, certain shōen were by bakufu order immune from entry by the shugo of the province or his agents.

Although as a part of the nationwide authority structure the shugo gained the means of exerting considerable influence over his province of appointment, the authority which the shugo derived from the bakufu did not directly affect the area of proprietary lordship. This authority consequently cannot be viewed as feudal or proprietary. But it could become the means for preserving or expanding feudal domains. There remains, then, the question of how the shugo utilized his political and military authority to expand his proprietary holdings.

The shugo had the power to make awards of hanzei rights and used this power to make grants to his own dependent vassals. When the apparatus of the old imperial provincial office, and control of provincial domains (*kokugaryō*) along with it, fell into the shugo's hands, the accompanying lands could be granted to dependent vassals. Shōen sometimes fell under shugo receivership (*shugo-uke*), an arrangement in which the shugo took complete charge of the domain, promising the former proprietor a guaranteed annual payment. Such shōen in fact became the de facto domains of the shugo, who could appoint his vassal as deputy (*daikan*) to take control of them. All these methods were used by shugo to expand their domains in their provinces. The network of control extended by these means was to some extent feudal, since grants of domains in exchange for oaths of loyalty were the medium within which it operated.

The strength of the shugo's proprietary lordship powers over his province may be evaluated by considering the territorial extent of shugo domains in the province and the strength of the bond established between the shugo and his dependent vassals. In the first instance, the shugo strove to convert kokujin into dependent vassals by assigning them hanzei grants or lands seized from old provincial domains.[7] The extent to which this was accomplished within the shugo's province varied and is not readily ascertainable. That no province was organized as a "domain" through such means is suggested by the survival of shugo-immune shōen into the next century and the promptness with which shugo provinces generally fell apart after the Ōnin War. In no case did a shugo manage to reduce his entire province to the status of personal domain through the process of expanding his private holdings within it.

---

7. Kurokawa, "Shugo ryōkokusei to shōen taisei"; Sugiyama Hiroshi, "Shugo ryōkokusei no tenkai," in *IKC*, 3; Minegishi Sumio, "Jōshū ikki to Uesugi shi shugo ryōkoku taisei," *Rekishigaku kenkyū* 284 (1964): 26–36.

Nor was the shugo immediately successful in his attempt to reduce the
kokujin to a condition of total vassalage. His relationship with local kokujin remained extremely loose. The more stable bond as between lord and
retainer was yet to be widely attained. For example, the Yamana uprising
of 1391, and later shugo rebellions against the bakufu, were swiftly put
down because the shugo's retainers defected so readily. The weakness of
the vassalage bond was due partly to the fact that the subordinate
relationship was imposed on kokujin at the initiative of the shugo, and the
kokujin was constrained to accept it against his will. This weakness also
resulted from the fact that the kokujin who became vassals were attempting above all to preserve and expand their own proprietary holdings. And
it was these holdings that must be recognized and examined as con-
stituting the most fundamental feature of Muromachi local governance,
namely, the kokujin lordship system.

THE KOKUJIN LORDSHIP SYSTEM

The terms *kokujin* (lit., a provincial) and *kunishū* (the provin-
cials) became current in the middle of the fourteenth century when the
war between the Northern and Southern Courts was at its height. They
were general designations for local military stewards (*jitō*) or peasant
leaders (*dogō*) used to distinguish these local leaders from the shugo and
his retainers who had newly arrived in their province. But although both
proprietary lords and village leaders were indifferently called kokujin,
their modes of existence were strikingly different.[8] The village chief was an
economically independent villager, but his political status depended on his
role as a leader and representative of the village council and other peasant
associations. By contrast, the proprietary lord (*ryōshu*), though he too
might live in the village, had ceased to participate directly in rural
management. Being a lord, he was not included in rural associations, and
his status depended on his power to control, and extract dues from, the
peasantry. It is of course this latter group who are called kokujin or kokujin lords for the present discussion.

Some kokujin lords emerged from among th dogō during the wars of the
early Muromachi period, but most were the successors of Kamakura
period jitō. In the Kinai region kokujin were usually militarily weak and
their domains small.[9] The domains of the kokujin lords of the Muromachi
period differed significantly from those of the Kamakura jitō. It had been
typical of their predecessors to have holdings scattered widely over several

---

8. Tabata Yasuko,"Chūsei kōki kinai no dogō no sonzai keitai," *Nihonshi kenkyū* 82 (1966).
9. Shimada Jirō, *Nihon chūsei sonrakushi no kenkyū* (Tokyo, 1966).

provinces, except for the original ancestral holding.[10] In addition, the land rights, or shiki, of Kamakura jitō were normally part of a vertically stratified hierarchy of overlapping rights affecting the same land; proprietary autonomy was acquired only at a later time through such techniques as partition of the land (*shitajichūbun*) or jitō trusteeships (*jitō ukesho*). In contrast to this, kokujin domains were generally concentrated in the vicinity of a single ancestral domain, and kokujin tenures, although referred to as *jitō-shiki, daikan-shiki*, and the like, were not part of a stratified system of tenures but separate parcels of land existing within a shō or gō. This regional concentration and legal autonomy of domain holdings was the distinguishing characteristic of the kokujin lordship tenures.

To the extent that the kokujin acquired proprietary independence, he came into a sharper, more direct confrontation with village councils and peasant associations. And the independence he had gained from the shugo made him all the more isolated in his dealings with the local community. Ultimately, confrontations with the peasantry became the kokujin's most crucial problem. Last-ditch opposition from shōen proprietors, pressure from the shugo, and competition within the kokujin class itself all contributed to the way in which the kokujin's control of his domain developed. But the most important factor was conflict with the peasant class.

The members of the kokujin class, as is abundantly attested by surviving documents, first consolidated their original ancestral domain and then set out to expand their holdings by such measures as appropriation of peasant fields, illegal seizures, receipt of awards for military service, purchase of peasant "name fields," reclamation of new paddy fields, and the assumption of "deputy trusteeships." As the kokujin acquired housemen (*kenin*), attendants (*chūgen*), and servants (*genin*), they used these subordinates to strengthen their hold on their domains. But the most universally prevalent system of control utilized by kokujin, particularly in the early stages, was the sōryō organization.

In the sōryō system of control, the kokujin, whose domains generally included several villages within a shō or gō, distributed them, village by village, among the cadet branches of his lineage, who were thereby permanently resettled. These cadets in turn divided their assigned domains, letting out some to peasants as individual owner's rights (*myōshu-shiki*) or cultivator's rights (*saku-shiki*) and managing the remaining portion directly. In time these cadet families became leaders and representatives of the people of their village. As the sōryō, the kokujin lord, besides controlling his own inherited domain, exercised command over his dogō kinsmen and could use them both as a police or military organization against outsiders and as the means of controlling the peasants in the villages.

10. Tashiro Osamu, "Sengoku ki ni okeru ryōshusei," *Rekishi* 26 (1962).

The Kobayakawa of Aki (mentioned by Professor Kawai) are an example of a kokujin house which very early developed a proprietary domain by this method. In Numata no shinjō, one of the Kobayakawa jitō holdings, the jitō shares (i.e., stipendiary fields) were located in the villages of Kuranashi, Oda, Nashi, Ōkusa, Yoshina, Tamari, Kamiyama, Nora, Kusai, and Takasaki no ura. These jitō lands were assigned on a village basis to different cadet branches of the Kobayakawa line, and the cadet families settled in these villages and assumed their names.[11] We soon hear of the Kuranashi family, the Oda family, the Ōkusa family, the Kamiyama family, and the Nora family which, although branch families of the Kobayakawa, were also members of the villages where they managed part of their holdings personally and let out the rest to the peasants as myōshu-shiki or saku-shiki. By virtue of their original nonpeasant status, they emerged as leaders of their village communities. They became, in other words, dogō. The Kobayakawa sōryō line, acting as leader of these branches, discharged duties owed to the bakufu and dealt directly with the shugo and other kokujin. The sōryō line controlled the villages of its domain through its branch houses, and it worked to expand its domains by acquiring shiki titles within the shōen system such as general inspector (sōkengyō-shiki), clerk (kumon-shiki), and constable (sōtsuibushi-shiki), all of which gave them additional stipendiary lands.[12] They also expanded their holdings through vigorous land reclamation projects.

The kokujin class, as it developed its means of control at the local level, withdrew from personal involvement in agriculture and increasingly relied on the work of individual peasant cultivators. As the kokujin secured their control of the external conditions needed for agricultural production, such as forests, undeveloped grasslands, water rights, flood control systems, and market and transportation facilities, they were further able to strengthen their grip on the peasantry. The indispensability of water to the prevailing wet-rice agriculture needs no special explanation. Forests and open fields were sources of supply for fuel and fertilizer needed for rural production, and markets provided goods, especially iron tools and salt, that were absolute necessities of life and production for the peasantry. It is only natural that kokujin lords exerted themselves to acquire control over these facilities.

Controversies over water or open fields between kokujin or between sōryō and cadet families were frequent and were caused by the kokujin lord's attempt to acquire forests, water rights, and other requisites to his control of his domain. Facilities of this broad type were always bequeathed from sōryō to sōryō as the family's main inheritance. In the testaments of

11. Kitazume Masao, "Nambokuchō Muromachi ki ni tsuite," Rekishigaku kenkyū 246 (1960): 13–23.
12. Ibid.

kokujin there is frequent mention not only of arable fields but also of forests, meadows, irrigation water, and markets. In the case of the Kobayakawa family, we find that, whereas the domains of cadet families were mainly wet or dry rice fields, the sōryō's domain, in addition to such fields, included Numata marketplace. In the case of the Sakai family, kokujin of Taki-gun in Tamba, there remains a family settlement agreement in which the arable fields were distributed in roughly equal quantity to the next sōryō, his younger brother, and his half brothers, but mountains, forests, and watercourses were to be controlled by the sōryō.[13] The sōryō allowed the other heirs to use these other rights and properties, but only in proportion to the amount of field held. The usufruct rights in uncultivated territories, irrigation water, and markets assured the cadet houses of leadership in their villages. Because these rights were controlled by the sōryō house, the kokujin lord controlled the villages and, thereby, advanced its lordship.

The branch houses which established themselves as peasant chiefs and village leaders under the sōryō system were not always receptive to the control of the sōryō house, tending gradually to become independent of sōryō control. Some branch families such as the Kuranashi of Numata no shinjō, a branch of the Kobayakawa,[14] gained their independence, became lords in their own right, expanded their domains, produced cadet houses of their own, and, as a "great cadet family," rivaled the sōryō house. As the system of domainal control based on the sōryō institution slowly weakened, the leadership authority of the sōryō over his lineage group often passed to household chiefs (*katoku*) of each of the cadet branches, leading to a fragmentation of the older kinship organization.

To counter this tendency of cadet branches to pull away from the main line, sōryō houses resorted to a number of devices, the most notable one being abandonment of the practice of divided inheritances. Increasingly, sōryō houses, while appealing to their branches for kinship solidarity, replaced the customary divided inheritance with unigeniture through the sōryō line. With the institution of sōryō unigeniture, it became impossible for second sons to establish independent branch families, and most of them accepted support from the sōryō or katoku (i.e., household chief) in exchange for personal services. In this way, they and their descendants became the katoku's household retainers, or vassals. The testament of the kokujin Kobayakawa Shigeyoshi states, "The aforesaid domains I bequeath to my son Yoshiharu, in unrestricted possession, directing him to support his younger brother Yagorō." Likewise, Kobayakawa Naka-

13. *Sakai monjo*, Ōei 2(1425)/1/8, "Sakai Takanobu yuzurijō"; Oka Mitsuo, "Muromachi jidai Tamba Ōyama no shō shūhen no dōkō," *Keizaigaku ronsō* 11, no. 2.
14. Kitazume, "Nambokuchō Muromachi ki ni tsuite."

yoshi's testament of 1398 states, "My domains I bequeath to the household chief Hirokage, and I direct my later sons Harukage, Tarōsaburō, and Shōjumaru to render service as household retainers, ever obedient to Hirokage's commands."[15] The conversion of second sons into household retainers created the basis for the formation of a feudal hierarchy within the kokujin lordship system.

In the branch houses established prior to the change to unigenitural succession, the same practices appeared. Unigenitural household chiefs were established, and cadets were required to become their retainers. There was, nonetheless, an important difference. Because the heads of branch families had not yet attained complete political or economic independence, they had to cope with a number of difficult problems: the opposition of shōen proprietors, competition with other kokujin over vacant tracts and water resources, and, above all, the problem of retaining control over their own cadet branches, dependent vassals, peasant chiefs, and peasant associations. The countermeasure most appropriate to the preservation of smaller establishments faced with these problems was the formation of leagues or ikki. The alternative was to become the dependent vassal of a shugo or the client of a stronger sōryō house.

The kokujin ikki, as described by Professor Kawai in the previous essay, was a league of small- to medium-sized kokujin united by common interests. In it all members agreed to act in unison, in accordance with the articles of a sworn covenant. In Aki, for instance, the Akimitsu, Kamiyama, Oda, and Ōkusa houses, all cadet branches of the Kobayakawa family that had become independent kokujin, entered into ikki covenants on three separate occasions—in 1431, 1442, and 1451.[16] This type of kokujin ikki appeared in every region and represented a general trend of the times. Some examples are the "Mōri Lineage Assembly" of Aki, the "Suda League" of Kii, the "Seven Chiefs of Takashima" of Ōmi, the "Yōhoku Band" of Echigo, and the "Matsuura League" of Hizen. Participants in these ikki included nonkindred as well as kindred houses, territory being a stronger basis of affiliation than kinship. The change from the sōryō system to the kokujin ikki may therefore be seen as a movement from kinship to territoriality as a basis of political organization. The purposes of the ikki, as revealed by the written covenants, included mutual guarantees of independence in resistance both to sōryō control and to pressure from the shugo to become vassals or pay tansen taxes. In addition, an important objective of these leagues was to

15. *Kobayakawa ke monjo,* Ōei 5(1398)/5/13, "Kobayakawa Nakayoshi jihitsu yuzurijō," in *Dai Nihon komonjo, iewake monjo* (hereafter cited as *KM*), series 11.
16. *KM* 1–104, Eikyō 3(1431)/2/10, "Kobayakawa Kagetaka keiyakujō"; *KM* 2-460, Kakitsu 2(1442)/11/16, "Kobayakawa shoshike rensho keiyaku jōan"; *KM* 1-109, Hōtoku 3(1451)/9/kichijitsu, "Kobayakawa honjō shinjō ikkechū rempan keiyakujō."

combat rebellious tendencies among cadets, dependent vassals, peasant chiefs, and the peasant class beneath them. The oath of the Yōhoku Band, for instance, included reference to "the rebellious members of one another's households," and the ikki of Kobayakawa cadets referred to "the cadets and dependent vassals of our households" and declared "that the family chief will maintain individually his kindred of other houses."[17]

We may conclude, then, that the kokujin ikki was a form of counter-measure taken by the kokujin in defense of their lordships, corresponding to the *shōke ikki* or leagues of village communities. The ikki itself was a limited form of political organization. Its main purpose was to preserve the status quo; it had no potential for the formation of a more extensive feudal hierarchy. This limitation was not to be overcome until the appearance of the sengoku-daimyo.

When a kokujin became a vassal of the shugo it was, as we have seen, at the shugo's insistence. As a consequence, the bond between shugo and vassal was so unstable that at the slightest change in the shugo's fortunes the vassal would desert him. Also contributing to the fragility of the bond between shugo and vassals was the fact that kokujin lords usually became shugo vassals only as a means of preserving or expanding their own lordships. Moreover there were other alternatives to vassalage to the shugo for the small or medium kokujin lord, for he could attach himself as a dependent to a more powerful sōryō house.

Significantly, when a small kokujin became dependent on a more powerful sōryō house, this did not lead to a revival of the sōryō system but to a system of nonfamilistic feudal vassalage. When protection was requested of a powerful regional figure by an independent kokujin lord, this protection naturally had its price. For example, the Oda family of the Kobayakawa lineage, in order to resist the illegal occupation of their lands by the Hiraga and to obtain confirmation of their title, requested protection of the Kobayakawa sōryō in Numata. In return they presented to the Kobayakawa chief their domains of one-half of Tamari village.[18] Eventually, this price would take the form of vassalage on a strictly feudal basis, but this practice became universal only at a later state of development with the appearance of the sengoku-daimyo.

It is essential to bear in mind the importance of the institution of kokujin lordship within the total political system of the Muromachi period. For, although we tend to emphasize the relationship between bakufu and shugo as the backbone of the Muromachi political order, kokujin lordship was the fundamental institution upon which that order rested. To be sure,

17. Ibid.
18. *KM* 2-227, Entoku 4(1492)/4/24, "Oda Motonori keiyaku utsushi."

the bakufu frequently came to the aid of shōen proprietors, prohibiting illegal invasion and occupation of shōen lands by kokujin. Also through the
shugo it compelled kokujin to pay tansen and similar taxes. But such acts
were not a denial of the kokujin lordship system; kokujin lords were given
the same recognition and protection as shōen lords. When the shugo
sought to reduce the kokujin to vassalage, collecting tansen from them or
enforcing bakufu orders against them, this too was not a denial of kokujin
lordship. Rather the shugo in such instances were carrying out their
national administrative duties and were only secondarily attempting to expand their personal power. The shugo deputy (*shugodai*) system, too, was
merely kokujin lordship in disguised form. In fact, the enforcement of
hanzei and the designation of deputies, actually a kind of kokujin
trusteeship, was a positive contribution to the expansion of kokujin
lordships. Thus the bakufu, or the bakufu-shugo structure, must be seen
as the guarantor of kokujin lordship at the local level.

An especially important link between the bakufu and kokujin lords was
the confirmation of domains. From the very beginning the bakufu had
held the right to confirm the domains of shugo, shogunal vassals, and jitō.
By the early fifteenth century it had extended this power to include
temples, shrines, nobles, and all kokujin, whether shogunal vassals or
not.[19] In doing this the bakufu had ignored the old distinction between immune shōen and the provincial domain (*kokugaryō*), most probably in the
belief that all domains were in the last analysis public and therefore
belonged ultimately to the holder of supreme proprietary power, that is,
itself. But, however that may be, these broad powers of confirmation,
which far exceeded those held by the Kamakura bakufu, were extremely
important. To the extent that it was able to serve as the ultimate legal
power in the confirmation of domains, the Muromachi bakufu as the
national sovereign headed a feudal hierarchy comprising itself and the
shugo, kokujin, temples, shrines, and nobles whose lands it confirmed. In
principle, one might say, an early form of feudal monarchy had been
created.

Of all the types of proprietary lords organized into this hierarchy, it
must be emphasized, the central position was occupied not by the shugo,
the religious institutions, or the nobility but, rather, by the kokujin. Thus
it was essential for the bakufu, while establishing shugo as its prime agents

19. In 1350 Retired Emperor Kōgon confirmed Kuradono no shō in Settsu as a holding of
Kanroji Fujinaga. This tells us that at that time the court still had the power to confirm domains
for temples, shrines, nobles, and warriors who were not shogunal vassals. Before long, however,
this confirmation power had fallen into the hands of the bakufu. In 1384 the shogun Ashikaga
Yoshimitsu confirmed Munekiyo of the Iwashimizu Hachiman shrine in the domains left by his
elder brother Norikiyo. *Iwashimizu monjo*, Shitoku 1(1384)/7/6, in *KM*, series 4.

over the provinces, to extend into these provinces its right of direct land
confirmation. The Muromachi bakufu, in sum, erected through its powers
of confirmation over domains a power structure based on the kokujin
lordship system which underlay the more nationally visible bakufu-shugo
power structure. It was for this reason that the shugo were never able to
convert their provices of assignment into their own "provincial domains."

THE PROVINCIAL DOMAIN SYSTEM
OF THE SENGOKU-DAIMYO

The system of independent kokujin lordships began to
decline in the latter half of the fifteenth century. The year 1428 marked a
high point in the proliferation of *doikki,* peasant leagues led by those very
rural chiefs, the dogō, on whom the kokujin relied for control over the
villages. As a result of these leagues, and the numerous uprisings to which
they gave birth, the kokujin came into direct confrontation with the dogō.
Worsening conflicts, acting as a primer charge on internal dissension in
the shogunal and shugo houses, set off a nationwide explosion. The Ōnin
War which broke out in 1467 was a prime result. But the conflict was
more widespread and deeply rooted than that revealed in the fighting in
Kyoto. The disturbances of Ōnin signaled the destruction of the entire set
of interrelated institutions which had supported the Muromachi regime:
kokujin lordship, the remnants of the shōen system, and the bakufu-shugo
structure.

Under pressure from the peasants led by the dogō, the kokujin frequently failed to retain their local authority and were compelled to relinquish to
the dogō their control of forests, vacant fields, water, and the like, as well
as to recognize peasant contracts (*hyakushō uke*) over the fields which comprised their domains (see the following essay). In their attempts to
preserve their domains, weaker kokujin sought protection from the
stronger, and eventually became their vassals.[20] The basic trend was
toward the gradual disappearance of the independent kokujin lordship
and the formation of hierarchical feudal relationships between the more
powerful kokujin, the future sengoku-daimyo.

As described by Professor Kawai in the previous essay, the powerful
kokujin who became sengoku-daimyo could come from many different
backgrounds. They might be strong sōryō houses whose cadets had requested protection and been made into vassals, politically powerful men
who had been relied upon as arbitrators in disputes between kokujin, or
kokujin ikki members who had gradually come forward as outstanding

20. *KM* 2-236, Meiō 3(1494)/1/19, "Koizumi Motouji keiyaku jōan."

leaders and protectors of the league. By virtue of their superior power in the midst of continuous warfare and disorder, such men seized the right to confirm domains that had been the bakufu's prerogative. Exercising the power to confirm the domains of small and medium kokujin lords seeking aid, arbitration, or protection, these powerful figures demanded vassalage in return for protection, and thereby raised themselves to the status of regional lord. As the result of this new process of confirmation, a feudal hierarchical relationship was formed that was considerably stronger than the precarious tie between the shugo and his retainers or the sōryō and his cadets. Thus the effort of the hard-pressed kokujin class to preserve its holdings worked together with the aggrandizing effort of powerful local magnates to bring into being the true feudal domain of Japan.

Fundamental to this process were developments within the still lower peasant-leader stratum in the provinces. The dogō class, having wrested peasant trusteeships and powers of exploitation over forests, vacant lands, and water from the kokujin, had taken over control of the villages. At the same time, however, conflicts between dogō and ordinary peasants began to surface. To acquire security against such pressure from below, these dogō now approached the kokujin class and, becoming their vassals, emerged as a new class of militarized village chiefs.[21] As a consequence, a new hierarchical feudal relationship based on a guarantee of tenure was formed between the kokujin and the dogō. Because the dogō took the initiative in seeking this relationship to secure his domain, the relationship was usually considerably more stable than that between shugo and kokujin. Although these changes took place over time and assumed many forms, the result was the emergence at the beginning of the sixteenth century of a three-tiered feudal hierarchy of sengoku-daimyo, kokujin, and dogō. The provincial domain system of the sengoku-daimyo was thereby created.

The mainstay of the sengoku-daimyo's control over his domain was the chigyō system, whereby the daimyo had paramount lordship over all land in his domain including the power to confirm fiefs.[22] In the Kamakura period, the word chigyō had designated possession of land under a claim of title, and some legal protection was given to this possession. By the sixteenth century, chigyō generally meant possession at the sufferance of higher authority. Through the chigyō system, the daimyo bestowed confirmation on the "original domains" of the kokujin and dogō under his control, invested them with rights of chigyō (*chigyō ategai*), and granted confirmation of lands already in possession (*tōchigyō*).

21. Kurokawa, "Chūsei kōki no ryōshusei ni tsuite."
22. Miyagawa Mitsuru, "Sengoku daimyō ryōkokusei," in *Hōken shakai to kyōdōtai*, ed. Shimizu Morimitsu and Aida Yūji (Tokyo, 1961).

What reveals the strength of the sengoku-daimyo's political authority
over his vassals is the extent to which the daimyo could exercise control
over lands in possession (*chigyōchi*) of his vassals. Under the legal principles
then prevailing in daimyo domains, vassals were permitted generally
to sell their "original" or "ancestral" domains (*honryō*), while their right
to sell land awarded by the lord (*onkyūchi*) was denied or restricted.[23]
"Changes of possession" (*chigyōgae*) were seldom forced on the vassal by
the daimyo as was to be the case in the late sixteenth century, except in a
few cases of awarded land. Sengoku-daimyo made frequent cadastral surveys of their territories, but these were not denials of the vassals' property
rights in their chigyō lands. Rather, they were intended to consolidate the
basis on which the chigyō system could operate and to establish a standard for levies of military service, taxes, and tansen.[24] Thus there were
limits on the power the daimyo could exercise over the lands of his vassals.
The kokujin's objective in submitting to vassalage, of course, was the
retention and protection of his domain. The limitation this placed on the
daimyo's power was the distinguishing feature of the sengoku-daimyo
chigyō system.

On the basis of the chigyō system, the sengoku-daimyo maintained a
vassal organization'which was divided into two major groups. The most
important group was composed of fief holders classed variously as
hereditary retainers (*fudai*),kinsmen (*ichimon*), and outsiders (*tozama*). The
last were kokujin who had not joined the band until it had acquired unam-
biguous local preeminence. The second group was made up of the horse
guards (*umamawari*), foot soldiers (*ashigaru*), comrade clients (*yoriko dōshin*),
junior vassals (*wakatō*), dependent retainers (*hikan*), attendants (*chūgen*),
and minor attendants (*komono*). Of this group, some were direct vassals of
the daimyo, others were rear vassals whose direct ties were with upper
level retainers, but nearly all were drawn from the dogō class.[25]

A very noteworthy element in the daimyo's vassal organization was
the *yorioya-yoriko* (surrogate parent-surrogate child) relationship upon
which command authority rested. The yorioya-yoriko system allowed the
daimyo to expand the scope and efficiency of his vassal organization. The
yorioya relationship was created when the daimyo bestowed "boon land"
(*onchi*) on the dogō of the villages in his domain, thus making them his
vassals and at the same time grouping them into separate units to be

23. *CH*, 3: "Imagawa kana shikimoku" (legal formulary compiled under Imagawa Yoshimoto
circa 1553), 13; "Jinkaishū" (legal formulary compiled under Date Tanemune circa 1536), 100;
"Kōshū hatto" (legal formulary compiled under Takeda Shingen circa 1557), 12; and
"Rokkaku shikimoku" (legal formulary compiled under Rokkaku Yoshiharu and others circa
1567), 10.
24. Miyagawa, "Sengoku daimyō ryōkokusei."
25. Ibid.

assigned as military followers to upper ranking retainers. The higher ranking retainer, the yorioya, was entrusted with the daimyo's power of command over the yoriko.[26] The pseudokinship ties on which this new form of
organization was based had in all likelihood been established as a sub-
stitute for the disintegrating sōryō system. Sengoku-daimyo everywhere
employed it in the construction of powerful, large-scale vassal organizations. The position of the dogō in this organizational structure was particularly important. As vassals, they provided military service in time of
war. As cultivators in the villages where they lived, they maintained order
and collected taxes. Control of the dogō stratum became a critical factor in
the daimyo's capacity to control the general peasantry while augmenting
the military strength of his domain.

Contributing also to the strength of the sengoku-daimyo was the increased tax revenue which he could command. Access to new sources of
tax revenue was achieved when the daimyo successfully converted tansen
taxes into an annual impost and incorporated it into the annual ground
rent (nengu).[27] When the authority to impose tansen shifted from the imperial court to the bakufu, the bakufu delegated the shugo to collect it.
Eventually shugo began to levy "shugo tansen" as their own needs dictated, and, as we have seen, this tax became an important source of income for the shugo. By the latter half of the fifteenth century, shugo
tansen, which had been levied with increasing frequency, was simply incorporated into the regular annual ground rent. This procedure, in addition to increasing the revenues which could be expected from the daimyo's
domain, also served to give such taxes a more "public" quality. Thus the
process of incorporation of tansen into nengu was a distinguishing feature
of the sengoku lordship.

Tansen originally had been an extraordinary levy for national purposes,
as is shown by the statement "for construction rice for Ise shrine, a tansen
of 50 cash per tan of public field."[28] It was calculated on the amount of
"public field" in a province and levied in the name of the proprietary
sovereign of the country, either emperor or shogun. The amount of public
field was presumed to coincide with the field area recorded in provincial
registers called ōtabumi. Since the beginning of the Muromachi period the
amount of cognizable public field everywhere decreased steadily and in
some provinces ceased to exist.[29] The standard for tansen thus became a
putative, rather than an actual, amount of public land.

26. Kikuchi Takeo, "Sengoku daimyō no kenryoku kōzō," Rekishigaku kenkyū 166 (1953): 1–77.
27. Murata Shūzō, "Sengoku daimyō Mōri shi no kenryoku kōzō," Rekishigaku kenkyū 73 (1940).
28. Mōri ke monjo, in KM 1–72, "Mōri shi ikkechū ekifukōmai tansen haifu chō."
29. Momose Kesao, "Tansen kō," in Nihon shakai keizaishi kenkyū, chūsei hen, ed. Hōgetsu Keigo
Sensei Kanreki Kinenkai, 3 vols. (Tokyo, 1967), 2: 3–34.

Daimyo increasingly took advantage of the ambiguity of the public land concept to distribute the tansen burden over the entire domain. Since it was unclear which parts of his domain were public fields, the lord could distribute his entire tansen burden over his domain, because for the peasantry the whole domain was the public land of the lord.[30] This practice almost certainly resulted from measures taken on the initiative of the kokujin lords and was already common by the time the sengoku-daimyo came into their own.

In this way, tansen in the Sengoku period came generally to be levied every year, either on the public fields within domains or on domains in their entirety. The original standard for assessing tansen was inequitable in that it was based on land area alone, without regard to productivity. As nengu assessments were made on the basis of quality as well as area, the tendency was to change tansen assessments so as to be proportional to nengu assessments, thereby making the tax more equitable. The sengoku-daimyo, in a word, had come to exact a single tax, of which part was nengu and part was tansen calculated on the same basis as nengu.

In places where nengu was collected in cash, tansen would be collected in cash as well, and the combined cash figure assessed became the "cash assessment," or kandaka. This kandaka figure was used as a basis for calculating the size of chigyō grants and the consequent military service requirements exacted by daimyo in certain areas such as the Later Hōjō, Takeda, Uesugi, Date, Mōri, and Ōtomo.[31] However, in those areas where nengu was levied in rice, tansen too was calculated in terms of rice assessment. The total of nengu and tansen thus calculated became the annual "rice dues" (bummai).[32] But despite these differences in terminology and practice, it is important to recognize that the kandaka system used for chigyō lands was merely an alternative for "rice dues" and the "rice

30. "Settsu no kuni Amakawa mura mizuchō," in TK, 3. A few entries, where area alone was the basis of taxation, record tansen along with bummai.

31. Fujiki Hisashi, "Sengoku daimyō seika no shugo-shiki to tansen," ed. Tōhoku Shigakkai, Rekishi 32 (1966).

32. Ōtani monjo. An entry from a survey of Kitasakura no shō in Ōmi dated 1509 reads:

Kikuba

300 bu [5/6 of a tan]	Tansen: 179 cash; rice equivalent, 2 to 7 shō 2 gō
Rice dues [bummai]: 9 to	Dwelling house dues: 5 shō 2 gō
Remitted: 1 to 3 shō 5 gō	Fixed rice: 3 to 9 shō 1 gō
Service [kuji] rice: 5 shō	
Saemon Tarō	

It appears from this that bummai, or "rice dues," amounting to the sum of the items that follow, was actually a sort of nengu of which the older nengu, listed here as "fixed rice" (jōmai), was but a part. Tansen was converted into a rice amount and, with certain other charges, added to the "fixed rice" to produce the final rice assessment.

assessment" system; the evaluation of landholdings on a cash basis was not an essential component of sengoku-daimyo regimes. Far more important for understanding the sengoku-daimyo domain is the fact that the increased revenues of the sengoku-daimyo came from the incorporation of tansen and other such imposts in nengu.

8

Village Communities and Daimyo Power

NAGAHARA KEIJI
with Kozo Yamamura

The two and one-half centuries stretching from the era of the wars
between the Northern and Southern Courts to the Sengoku period were a
time of great institutional change in Japan. During this period the shōen
system of the imperial state structure finally came to an end, and the
political power of the nobles in the capital (that is, the shōen proprietors)
declined precipitously. Following the collapse of noble power, actual
power in the provinces was exercised first by the kokujin and then by the
sengoku-daimyo. Although historians have tended to emphasize this
momentous political upheaval, change was not limited to these political
developments. Social and economic structures too underwent important
transformations during this period, with important implications for the
exercise of political authority and power within the national structure.
Particularly significant was the emergence of the village community as an
active participant in the political struggles of the period. As Professor
Miyagawa has elaborated in the preceding essay, central to the establishment of the sengoku-daimyo domain was the process whereby the daimyo
came to terms with this new political participant and established effective
control over the land and cultivators of his domain. The purpose of this essay will be to examine the structure and function of the late medieval
village community and to analyze the role of the peasant community in the
formation of the sengoku-daimyo domain.

In medieval Japan, villages were heterogeneous in size and structural
characteristics, reflecting local geographic and historic conditions. The
most distinctive feature of the medieval village was that it formed a functional community for its peasant inhabitants. Regardless of the terminology which appears in historical records, when a group of inhabitants in
geographical proximity formed a communal structure for the purpose of
carrying out economic, social, and political functions, this was a "village
community." Thus a village community, though perhaps actually a composite of hamlets, had as its important functions to further the economic

well-being of each member of the community; to exercise the social and political functions necessary to resist the lord's authority and to improve each member's social and political status; and to defend the community against intrusion by outside powers, whether political or military.

Village communities were not, of course, autonomous in the performance of these functions or in the assurance of protection against external threats. Such functions were performed, in fact, within the context of higher authority as exercised by lord or proprietor, or of superior local power as exerted by *jitō* or *kokujin*. For example, in the use of water and commons (mountains and open fields), the lord's authority was imposed upon the village community, and some degree of restriction was placed on the freedom of use which otherwise would be limited only by self-imposed community rules. In actual fact, in any given locality the lord constantly attempted to reduce the extent of self-government within the peasant community by the imposition of his political authority. To this end, a lord might name some peasants in the upper stratum of the community to the village offices through which uses of water and commons were regulated and taxes in kind and corvee were collected. Thus lord and peasant viewed the village community from quite different perspectives as a result of the conflicting and mutually exclusive relationship between their interests, and village communities constituted arenas of conflict between them.

THE STRUCTURE AND ROLE OF
VILLAGE COMMUNITIES

Kamikuze-no-shō, a well-known shōen four kilometers southwest of Kyoto, typifies the medieval village community.[1] This shōen, which belonged to Tōji (a large temple of the Shingon sect), was a small, comparatively compact estate which encompassed precisely that geographical area occupied by a village community. The rich historical evidence preserved by the temple allows us to examine the life of the community in depth.[2]

According to the land register of 1357,[3] this shōen had 53.1 chō in paddies and 8.1 chō in uplands, a total cultivated area of 61.2 chō. This land was held, as shown in table 1, by 52 persons. It is generally supposed that

1. In using this shōen as an example it is admitted that conditions in Japan varied considerably according to region. On these regional differences, see Nagahara Keiji, "Muromachi bakufu shugo ryōgokuseika no tochiseido," *Keizaigaku kenkyū* 15 (1971).

2. Uejima Tamotsu, *Kyōkō shōen sonraku no kenkyū* (Tokyo, 1970), is a useful study in which this shōen is intensively examined.

3. *Tōji hyakugō monjo, ma,* in *Dai Nihon shiryō,* series 2 (Tokyo, 1924), 6; Kamikuze-no-shō, "Hyakushōmyō nayose-chō" (1357), ibid., series 6 (1924), 21: 635–657.

TABLE 1

Landholding Pattern
in Kamikuze-no-shō, 1357

Number of chō	Number of Landholders
Over 2	3[a]
1–2	9
0.5–1	17
Under 0.5	23

Source: Land Register of
1357.
[a] One of the three was the
shōen's administrative officer
(shōkan or kumon) who held
17.4 chō.

the labor of a nuclear family was able to cultivate one chō of land. Hence
those households holding land in excess of that amount would presumably
have a part of their holding worked by tenant cultivators or by a dependent labor force such as genin. By the same token, households with less
than half a chō could not subsist on their landholding. This meant that
they most likely became tenant cultivators or came to accept the status of
dependent laborers of large landholders in exchange for the latter's protection.[4] Although we are unable to present a definite statement on peasant
society as it related to the economic structure of Kamikuze-no-shō,[5] there
were from the economic point of view two clearly differentiated groups of
peasants: the upper who were owner-cultivators and/or landlords and the
remainder who were owner-cultivators and/or tenants. Two status terms
used to designate the members of this shōen—myōshu and hyakushō—can
be thought to correspond to the two economic groups just described.

According to a record written in 1458,[6] nearly a century later than the
land register which we have just examined, we find that the inhabitants of
this shōen were classified under two still different terms: "samurai-
equivalent status" (sauraibun), of which there were 21, and "peasant-

4. Peasants of dependent status, in the sense used here, were not persons directly under the
shōen ryōshu but persons who were economically dependent on upper class peasants and who
were required to provide taxes in kind and corvée to upper class peasants in exchange for various
economic and other assistance.
5. Uejima, Kyokō shōen sonraku no kenkyū, holds that upper class peasantry relied on lower class
genin for labor. I do not find evidence for a class division within the village; see my Nihon hōkensei
seiritsu katei no kenkyū (Tokyo, 1961).
6. Tōji monjo, 6 (1959): item 303, in Tōkyō Daigaku Shiryō Hensanjo, Dai Nihon shiryō, iewake
monjo, series 10.

equivalent status" (*jigebun*), of which there were 89. Presumably persons who performed some subordinate function for local magnates of military-aristocratic status were classified in the "samurai-equivalent status" while all others were put in the "peasant-equivalent status."

During the Muromachi period there was, as noted in the essay above, a growing tendency of peasant leaders to become *hikan* (followers or retainers) of military lords, be they shugo or kokujin. About the time the document under consideration was composed, some of the upper stratum of the peasant class began to be called *tonobara* (the lord's men) in many village communities. This term gives us a clue to the condition of the inhabitants of Kamikuze-no-shō who were listed as of "samurai-equivalent status." These landowners, although classified legally as myōshu within the shōen, had raised themselves above peasant status by becoming hikan of samurai. Table 2 shows this apparent dual class structure.

TABLE 2

Class Structure in Kamikuze-no-shō, 1458

	Status[a]		
	Economic	*Shōen*	*Sociopolitical*
Class I	Owner-cultivator and/or landlord	myōshu	Samurai-equivalent
Class II	Owner-cultivator and/or tenant	hyakushō	Peasant-equivalent

Source: *Tōji monjo*, Wo 303.
[a]The three statuses do not necessarily correspond on a one-to-one basis, and the economic status is indicative only of the general pattern.

In Kamikuze-no-shō there was one person who held by far the largest landholding, 17.4 chō, most of which was cultivated by tenant-cultivators who paid *kajishi* or rent. Such a person, by virtue of his wealth and superior status as shōen administrator, was able to acquire a position approximating that of proprietary lord. Not all village communities produced such middle-level lordships, and great variation obviously existed in the degree of political independence which such families might acquire. On the other hand, the example of Kamikuze-no-shō provides us with a common model of a three-layer village community in which resident lord, peasant leaders, and common peasantry were drawn together into a political-economic unit.

Before leaving the example of Kamikuze-no-shō, it is necessary to amplify the above example by drawing on material from other case

studies. Not apparent in Kamikuze-no-shō, but common in examples
elsewhere, were two other distinguishable classes of peasants—*mōto* and
sanjo.[7] Mōto were newcomers to a village community who had not yet
been given full-fledged status as community members: their status was
defined with respect to the community rather than to the organization of
the shōen. In contrast, sanjo were persons who had been grouped together
to perform specified work (nonagricultural corvee such as transporting or
cleaning) by the shōen proprietor: their status was defined with respect to
the shōen and consequently was looked down upon by the peasants of the
community. It is difficult to determine whether sanjo were excluded from
membership in the village community or not, or whether they enjoyed
some type of restricted privilege. We note only that there existed a class of
persons who were outside the true membership of the village community,
as exemplified in the documents pertaining to our reference community,
Kamikuze-no-shō.

ECONOMIC FUNCTIONS

Peasants in feudal society privately possessed such things as
land, agricultural implements, and draft animals and, in principle at least,
carried out independent economic activities. This does not mean that each
economic unit was self-sufficient and capable of supplying all the needs for
continuing its economic life. In Japan, unlike in Europe, the two- or three-
field system which required the communal use of land did not develop. In
this sense, a village community as such did not engage in communal activities involving production. Yet the role of community in Japan was
significant in terms of the use of commons and water, both of which were
essential to paddy cultivation and, in various economic functions, to the
lives of its inhabitants.

During the early medieval period in Japan (that is, up through the
Kamakura period), the most secure form of landownership by the peasant
was the possession of *myōden* (name land). Because myōden could be
transferred through inheritance, it differed from *isshikiden* (paddies belonging to the shōen) which could be redistributed to new cultivators by the
proprietor. To be sure even myōden were to some extent precarious holdings and subject to proprietary control. There are examples of proprietors
who redistributed myōden so as to equalize the landholdings of myōshu.
Myōden in general could not be bought or sold.[8] Also, when peasants

7. Minakami Kazuhisa, *Chūsei no shōen to shakai* (Tokyo, 1969), pp. 91–111; and Hayashiya
Tatsusaburō, *Kodai kokka no kaitai* (Tokyo, 1955), pp. 285–315.
8. On the characteristics of peasant landownership, see Nagahara Keiji, "Chūsei nōminteki
tochishoyū no seikaku," *Hitosubashi ronshū* 59, no. 3 (1968).

absconded or became bankrupt, their land and houses could be distributed by proprietors to others. (This practice was known as *rōnin
manekisue*, which literally means "inviting and setting up landless persons.")[9] Thus private ownership by peasants had not yet become uncon-
ditional in this period and lords continued to exercise their authority over
the ownership and use of land.

By the late medieval period (that is, from the establishment of the
Muromachi bakufu to the Ōnin War), the distinction between myōden
and isshikiden[10] had disappeared and land began to be bought and sold
by peasants. The practice of rōnin manekisue, which typified the exercise
of proprietary authority, also disappeared. By this period, then, peasant
tenancy of land was no longer conditional; rights enjoyed by peasants had
been significantly strengthened.

During the late medieval period, paddy land communally owned by
village communities, *sōyūden*, appeared.[11] In some instances these common
lands were considered shrineland (*shinden*) attached to the village shrine.[12]
Sōyūden was either cultivated jointly by villages or worked by tenant
cultivators, and the profit from such land was frequently used for loans to
financially hard-pressed villagers, for expenses for litigations on behalf of
the village community, or for acquiring rights to water. Thus, in contrast
to the early medieval period in which loans to the needy (*suiko*) were made
by the proprietor, such loans were by the late medieval period being made
by the village community to its members. The existence of sōyūden was
neither an indication of undeveloped private ownership nor a remnant of
the proprietary authority. Rather, it was an indication of progress toward
the attainment of private ownership by the peasantry and a degree of
political and economic independence on the part of village communities.

9. The following historical evidence is revealing on the rōnin manekisue: "When paddies are
not planted or when the yields are poor because of the absconding or death of *heimin* [com-
moners], both the *azukaridokoro* and the *jitō* must cooperate to entice and settle rōnin under their
jurisdiction following [local] customs"; from a document, *Kantō gechijō*, dated 1 March 1262, in
the possession of the Kanazawa Library and published in Seno Seiichirō, ed., *Kamakura bakufu
saikyojō* (Tokyo, 1970), pt. 1, no. 106. The fact that the disposition of the land was determined by
the azukaridokoro and jitō indicates that neither village communities nor the relatives of the
absconded peasant had any voice or claim over the land vacated by the latter.
10. The *isshikiden* was land which was directly held by the shōen ryōshu, but not assigned to any
myōshu. Cultivators of isshikiden were required to pay a higher tax than was levied on myōshu
but no corvée was required.
11. For a detailed discussion of *sōyūden*, see Ishida Yoshito, *Gōsonsei no keisei*, in *Iwanami kōza:
Nihon rekishi, Chūsei* 4 (Tokyo, 1963): 35-78.
12. That the shinden in fact had the same characteristics as sōyūden is clear from the example
of Imabori. See Kanamoto Masayuki, "Chūsei kōki ni okeru Ōmi no nōson: Tokuchinho
Imaborigō no rekishi," in *Nihon shakai keizaishi kenkyū, Chūsei-hen*, ed. Hōgetsu Keigo Sensei
Kanreki Kinenkai (Tokyo, 1967), pp. 243-304.

During the early medieval period, the shōen proprietor (or his administrator) normally coordinated peasant corvée and constructed and maintained irrigation facilities, built reservoirs, dammed rivers or streams, and constructed ditches or canals. Peasants using the water were required to pay the proprietor an *iryō* or water charge on the theory that "every drop of water belonged to the proprietor."[13] By the late medieval period, such was not the case. The construction and maintenance of reservoirs and irrigation ditches was undertaken collectively by peasants either from a single village community or from several village communities banded together as a work unit for the task. Thereafter the peasants, turning the tables, would demand that the proprietor pay a water charge.[14] Gradually, the custom of paying taxes after subtracting the water charge became well established in most shōen.

Similar changes were observed for commons (*sanya,* literally, mountains and fields). During the early medieval period, a commons was considered the property of the proprietor. Peasants were allowed to cut grass and gather firewood from the commons, but it was not a secure right. There exist for this period numerous historical records relating to disputes over rights to commons.[15] Such cases usually involved the complaint of proprietor against proprietor; very few occurred among peasants or between peasant communities. During the late medieval period, the use of commons by peasants became a right sanctioned by custom, and village communities drew up their own codes pertaining to its use. To take a random example, the village community of Imabori in Ōmi is recorded as having compiled a village code in 1448, one article of which stated that unauthorized cutting of trees from commons would be subject to fine. Such village codes were rare in the early medieval period.

13. On the *iryō,* see Hōgetsu Keigo, *Chūsei kangaishi no kenkyū* (Tokyo, 1941), pp. 106 ff.
14. Hōgetsu, *Chūsei kangaishi.* In Tōji's Kanno-shō in Yamashiro, the myōshu, who had been responsible for paying the water charges, ceased paying them. By the Ōei period (1394–1428) the ryōshu's demand for the payments was in vain. Also, in the Kamikuze-no-shō where, following custom, the ryōshu was paying 5.3 koku to the peasants, the latter demanded higher payments to cover the cost of a new reservoir. When the ryōshu refused, they withheld tax payments.
15. For example, the Imabori code of 1448 stated: "A fine of 500 mon shall be imposed on those cutting young trees . . . [and] a fine of 100 mon shall be imposed for cutting branches of mulberry trees." An article in another decree issued in Imabori in 1489 read: "In the forest belonging to the village, no one shall, without proper authorization, cut or gather trees, leaves, or branches [for fertilizer]. The villagers violating [this] shall be purged [i.e., lose the privileges accorded to the members of a village community]. If the violator is not a villager, he shall be banished." Yet another decree of Imabori issued in 1502 stated: "No one shall freely enter into common or private forest for the purpose of taking branches or leaves or earth under trees [richly fertilized]. Violators shall be fined 100 mon." From an unpublished copy version of *Imabori Hiyoshi jinja monjo* in the possession of Tōkyō Daigaku Shiryō Hensanjo.

As the peasants' rights to commons became better established and the management of commons was taken over by the village communities, it became increasingly difficult for proprietors to impose their authority on these community activities in order to safeguard their political power. Proprietors were forced to adjust to the changed political situation. At the same time, new opportunities were presented to proprietary lords for maintaining their authority if they adapted to the new situation; they could now maintain their superior authority by acting as arbitrators of disputes between village communities. As we shall see, such mutual accommodation between lord and peasantry provided the basis for the formation of the later sengoku-daimyo domain.

Although the medieval village economy was basically agricultural, this did not mean that the peasants were self-sufficient in producing all the goods necessary for cultivation and consumption. Two kinds of products could not be self-supplied by peasant families. One was those goods, such as salt and iron, which could be produced only in given regions and which had to be purchased from these regions through the agency of merchants. The other was goods whose production required highly specialized skills, such as items crafted by skilled carpenters and cabinetmakers, pottery, leather goods, dyed cloth, and "manufactured" products of wrought and cast iron.

Markets in early medieval shōen were infrequently held, often only a few times a year, and rigidly controlled by shōen administrators—a reflection of the proprietor's view that markets too were his economic property.[16] Markets, in short, had not become free arenas for trading among peasants. Also, in dealing with "manufacturers," shōen proprietors provided land, or *kyūden*, to skilled artisans who, in return, produced goods as required for the lord and for the market through which peasants acquired these goods.[17] Thus, though these artisans entered villages for the purpose of meeting the needs of the villagers, they came under the control of the proprietor.

As "manufacture" and commerce grew rapidly in the late medieval period, markets began to be held much more frequently; three to six times per month became the norm. Paralleling this development, village artisans began to produce both to meet the demand of the immediate village

---

16. A letter of transfer written by Wada Shigetsura and dated 12 August 1296 read: "Included in the transfer . . . [was] the southern section of the Nanuka market (market held on 7th, 17th, and 27th of the month) in Okuyama-shō in Echigo." Such a description infers that the ryōshu considered the market his private property; Niigata-ken Kyōiku Iinkai, ed., *Okuyama-shō shiryōshū* (Niigata, 1965), p. 104.

17. On the *kyūden* system, see Nagahara Keiji, "Shōen ryōshu keizai no kōzō," in *Nihon keizaishi taikei, Chūsei,* ed. Nagahara Keiji (Tokyo, 1965), pp. 57–102.

community and to serve newly emerging regional markets. Agricultural villages near Kyoto and Nara began to specialize in the production of various processed agricultural products.[18] Faced with these changes, proprietors of shōen gradually gave up the system of encouraging production by assigning land to artisans and turned instead to the regulation of markets through decrees (ichiba kinsei, market regulations) designed to maintain peace and order and to assure orderly trading.[19]

Thus by the late medieval age proprietors were no longer able to directly control manufacture and commerce, supplementary activities in the peasant economy, but could exert their influence only indirectly by regulating markets. This shift from direct to indirect control was analogous to the change we observed in the lord's role vis-a-vis the commons, in which the arbitration of disputes between village communities was substituted for direct control by proprietors. This change in the relationship of the proprietor to the market was clear evidence that peasants in the late medieval period could obtain, independent of the proprietor, those products which they themselves could not produce. The increase in agricultural productivity and consequent expansion of trading left little opportunity for the lord to exert his direct control over the process of production. In comparison to the earlier period in which the proprietor controlled handicraft and markets and consequently deprived village communities of their economic independence, the peasants in the late medieval period clearly enjoyed a much more advantageous position.

SOCIAL AND POLITICAL FUNCTIONS

Initially the primary function of a village community with respect to its members was economic; the economic units comprising the community—individual peasant households—were unable to sustain their economic activities without support from the larger group. By the late medieval period, proprietors had fewer opportunities to directly impose their authority over the economic functions of the village communities. As the economic circumstances of the village community changed, its raison d'être also changed and became increasingly social and political.

18. Handicrafts and premodern manufacturing were specialized, as a rule, on the village basis, i.e., village A might produce oil; B, noodles; and C, bamboo shades; Wakita Haruko, *Nihon chūsei shōgyō hattatsushi no kenkyū* (Tokyo, 1969), pp. 419–522.
19. A typical example is a decree dated 25 April 1353 pertaining to conduct at the market in Numata-no-shō in Aki. In this decree, Kobayakawa prohibited his subordinates (*hikan*), along with the residents of the Numata market, from disturbing the peace of the market. His decree clearly was issued in his role as mediator. *Kobayakawa monjo*, in *Dai Nihon komonjo, iewake monjo*, series 11, no. 25.

Peasants could raise their social and economic status only in proportion
to their ability to eliminate, through a united effort, the proprietor's power
of control over various functions of the village community. Increasingly,
villagers united themselves into village communities in order to achieve
greater social and political independence. Communal solidarity was the
means for waging war against proprietary authority. Although the social
and political potential of the village community was scarcely recognized
during the early period, it was realized during the late medieval period.

One of the most profound changes in political organization was the
transformation of the village assembly (*yoriai*) into an organ for for-
mulating and articulating the common will of the villagers. Although in-
tracommunity status distinctions such as wealth, lineage, or length of
residence in the village remained important, the yoriai was attended by
nearly all of the villagers and run by consensus. Membership in the
assembly was no longer limited to myōshu, as in earlier periods, and the
peasants (*hyakushō*) now had rights of participation and voting in the
assembly. Since decisions concerning the village community were made
through "community discussions" (*shūgi*) at the yoriai, attendance at
meetings was an important duty of village members. As the first article of
the 1448 village code of Imabori village stated: "Those who fail to come
after receiving the second notice for an assembly shall be fined 50 mon."[20]

This new sense of communal solidarity and self-government was also
reflected in the increasing use of village codes to regulate the internal
affairs of the community. By the end of the Kamakura period the practice
of using a form of sworn declaration (*kishōmon*) signed by all members of
the village when a specific matter had been agreed upon became widespread. During the fourteenth century more formalized codes were
adopted in which the customs of the village, and the rights based upon
them, were made known in the form of "notices of the hyakushō" or of
"laws of the shōen."[21] By the fifteenth century, village codes, similar in
nature to a village constitution, began to be used as the basic rules for governing such communities. In the example of Imabori, the codes covered
matters relating to the village assembly; the use of common lands, mountains, and fields and of common paddy land; the accommodation of
travelers; and matters relating to preservation of law and order within the
community.

That the late medieval village communities possessed a limited form of
self-government is evident in the village codes noted above. To get a better
sense of the degree of autonomy which such communities attained we

20. *Imabori Hiyoshi jinja monjo.*
21. Satō Kazuhiko, "Nambokuchō-ki no jinmin tōsō," *Rekishigaku kenkyū*, no. 336 (1968).

must look at the village's jurisdictional autonomy and the tax contract system. Jurisdictional autonomy involved the acquisition by the peasantry of political powers which had been exercised previously by the proprietor, such as village police powers and the right to adjudicate intravillage disputes. An example will be illustrative. During the mid-fifteenth century, Sugaura village in Ōmi—a village well known for achieving a high degree of self-government—could call itself "a juridically autonomous area," and the proprietor gave implicit recognition of this.[22] If a thief was caught in this village, for example, he was punished by the village community rather than by higher authority.[23]

In contrast, an example from the early medieval period when such autonomy had not yet developed is revealing. In 1300, the *jitō* for Yamada and Kamibefu villages in Satsuma was known to have exercised his juridical power—arresting and fining heavily—even over such minor cases as the theft of sweet potatoes, speaking ill of others, adultery by wives, the possession of hidden upland, the killing of a dog, and the like.[24] To be sure, this is an extreme example which caused conflict with the villagers. However, when this example is compared to that of Sugaura, it is evident how advantageous it was for a village community to have jurisdictional autonomy.

How many villages of the late medieval period came to enjoy jurisdictional autonomy is difficult to establish. In one example, a village called Ikaruga-no-shō demanded, in 1418, that the ryōshu, Hōryūji, meet certain conditions, including payment for water and jurisdictional autonomy. These demands, agreed upon by the village, came with a threat that if not granted the myōshu and all peasants would abandon their paddy fields and abscond.[25] For a village community to win jurisdictional autonomy, it had to be prepared to mount a fierce struggle. This village did win limited jurisdictional autonomy at the expense of the shōen ryōshu but soon had to cope with a jitō who attempted to deprive the community of its hard-won autonomy.

---

22. A posted decree *(kabegaki)* written by the Sugaura village community and dated 1568/14/12 began by stating: "No entry to the shugo; this is a community with its own rules [jikendan]." The decree was signed by 16 *otona* and 20 *naka-otona*. Shiga Daigaku Keizai-gakubu Shiryō-kan, ed., *Sugaura monjo* (Tokyo, 1967), 2, no. 925.

23. "On the matter of the thief which the shō-community reported, do punish him as befitting his crime"; ibid., 2, no. 816, "Seikurō Kenkei chūmon," item dated 1433/12/15. And, "On those matters reported from Sugaura . . . the community may mete out punishment if evidence is sufficient"; ibid., 1 (Tokyo, 1960), no. 227, "Sugaura sōshō okibumi," item dated 1461/7/13.

24. "Chinzei saikyojō," 1300/7/2, in *Yamada monjo*, included in Seno Seiichirō, ed., *Kamakura bakufu saikyojūshū*, 2, no. 13 (Tokyo, 1970).

25. "Ikaruga-no-shō hikitsuke," 1393/9/15, in Abe Takeshi and Ōta Junji, eds., *Harima-no-kuni Ikaruga-no shō shiryō* (Tokyo, 1970).

In 1506, an incident involving the abduction of a bathing peasant woman gave the jitō an opportunity to claim jurisdictional rights within the village. To prevent this jurisdictional encroachment, the village community had to seek the assistance of the civil proprietor at the cost of yielding a part of the jurisdictional autonomy which the peasants had earlier won. Clearly, the attempt to gain and maintain village jurisdictional autonomy was extremely difficult when the peasantry had to battle against such a changing combination of new and old forces—shōen proprietors, jitō, kokujin. But there is evidence that the villages near and around the capital, with their more advanced economy and peasant political consciousness, did manage to acquire varying degrees of jurisdictional autonomy during the late Muromachi period.

Another method by which the village community gained freedom from direct proprietary interference was through the practice of tax contracting. Under this arrangement a village community, either the whole village or a group of villagers, contracted with the proprietor to deliver a given amount of tax in exchange for not having their yield assessed annually by an officer of the proprietor (and possibly having their tax raised). This, in short, was a method by which the peasants attempted to limit the most important right of the proprietor, the right to tax.

Early examples of tax contracting can be found in the mid-thirteenth century.[26] However, in these instances tax contracts were made with the proprietor by a group of large myōshu and not by the village community as a whole. Such a contract with several large myōshu was not necessarily disadvantageous to the proprietor, since he could be assured that taxes would be exacted from the peasants. In contrast, a tax contract with a village community, in which all the village membership participated, signified a rise in the status of villagers other than myōshu and a retreat from the proprietor's power. Such contracts could be found only in the late medieval period.

Tax contracts with whole village communities were probably achieved with more difficulty than the right to jurisdictional autonomy. The right to tax was basic to the survival of the proprietary lords, a fact to which they were increasingly sensitive as a result of the growing pressures for self-government within village communities. Even during the fifteenth century, proprietors resisted demands for contracts with village communities as a whole by agreeing to tax contracts between themselves and only the larger myōshu. Earlier studies have failed to draw sufficient distinction between

---

26. An early (1240) example of this is a record of such a contract signed by sixteen peasants of Kubo-shō of Tōdaiji; *Kubo-shō hyakushōtō ukebumi*, 1240/5/2, copy version in the possession of the Tōkyō Daigaku Shiryō Hensanjo.

these two contractual methods, but the differences are important, and the prevalence of the latter method signifies a smaller degree of independence among the peasants than is sometimes stated.

However well the late medieval village communities succeeded in strengthening their political and social unity, there still existed economic and status differences among the villagers. Moreover, the upper stratum continually struggled to elevate itself to the status of minor proprietor by shedding restrictions imposed upon it by the community. This meant that proprietary lords could gain the support of peasant leaders by giving them special privileges, such as the tax contract, and thereby weaken community unity. An examination of surviving historical evidence reveals that most tax contracts were negotiated with the upper class peasants and not with village communities as a whole. One must be cautious, therefore, in interpreting all tax contracts as a sign of the emergence of self-governing village communities. Nonetheless, we may say that, as a general trend, the tax contracts, along with jurisdictional autonomy, indicate the growth of political power in village communities and the decline of the lord's power.

By the late medieval period peasant struggles against proprietary authority had developed into open conflicts over such issues as the reduction of taxes and corvée or the dismissal of shōen administrators who had exceeded their authority. The form of these protests varied, sometimes including litigation, petition under threat of violence (gōso), absconding, and revolt.[27]

A noteworthy development in petition was the increasing use of "letters of peasant appeal" (hyakushō mōshijō) signed by more than one peasant. An analysis of these letters of appeal reveals that signers were originally limited to the upper class within the shōen. But as time went on the signers began to include villagers who were not myōshu.[28] In Tara-no-shō of Wakasa, for example, where the shōen and the village community boundaries coincided, a letter of appeal was signed in 1334 by myōshu and others, 59 individuals in all, requesting a reduction in taxes and the dismissal of the shōen administrator.[29] The signers stated that they had participated in "communion in holy water" (ichimi shinsui) before signing, meaning that the village members had taken an oath of unity after drinking holy water from the village temple in the presence of all. No better

27. On the peasant struggles during the late medieval period, see Suzuki Ryōichi, "Junsui hōkensei seiritsu ni okeru nōmin tōsō," in Shakai kōseishi taikei (Tokyo, 1949); and Nagahara Keiji, Nihon hōkensei seiritsu katei no kenkyū (Tokyo, 1961), pp. 404–460.
28. For the significance of the appearance of hyakushō mōshijō, see Satō Kazuhiko, "Hyakushō mōshijō no seiritsu ni tsuite," in Minshūshi kenkyū, 9 (1971).
29. Tōji hyakugō monjo, 1: ha–116, in Dai Nihon komonjo, Iewake monjo, series 10.

expression of the political function of a village community can be found than this.

The significance of such letters of appeal can be seen more clearly when compared to practices in the early medieval period. Then, although the shōen proprietors in theory accepted direct petitions from peasants, as did the Kamakura bakufu, it was actually next to impossible for peasants to make accusations against jitō to the bakufu. The Kamakura bakufu in 1250 established a procedure called "commoners' litigation" (*zōnin soshō*) which ostensibly enabled peasants to bring cases directly to the bakufu, but in reality this avenue of litigation was in most instances closed to peasants simply because the peasants needed a "letter of recommendation" from the very jitō who were the object of the suits.[30] Against this background, the fact that letters of appeal by peasants began to appear frequently after the end of the thirteenth century, and that proprietors were unable to ignore them, indicates that significant changes were taking place at the local level by this time.

A more direct form of peasant appeal, *gōso*, or petitioning with the threat of violence, also came into more frequent use in the late medieval period. Villagers resorted to collective physical coercion against proprietors, generally because they had little expectation of the legal process yielding any results. An example of gōso can be found in the case of Kamikuze-no-shō. In 1437 the inhabitants of the shōen appealed for a tax reduction because of flood damage. When the proprietor granted only a small part of the reduction demanded, the shōen inhabitants marched en masse to Tōji, the proprietor, to protest. According to the records of the temple: "The myōshu and all inhabitants of the Kamikuze-no-shō came. The number approached sixty. They spent a night at the warehouse of the temple and continued to press their demand."[31] Since the number of households in the shōen at that time is estimated to have been around a hundred, it is obvious that more than half of the households sent participants in this "petition under the threat of violence." Though the leaders of this demonstration were myōshu, many others also took part, and the village assembly discussed the matter. The change from the letter of peasant appeal to such tactics shows that communal solidarity had strengthened to the point of making such action possible.

Eventually the threat of violence gave way to the actual use of violence, and this trend culminated in peasant revolts (*ikki*). Threats of violence or

30. *Kamakura bakufu tsuikahō*, no. 269, in Satō Shin'ichi and Ikeuchi Yoshisuke, eds., *Chūsei hōsei shiryōshū* (Tokyo, 1955), 1.
31. A document relating to *Eikyū 9-nen Chinju Hachimangū gusō hyōjō hikitsuke*, copy version in the possession of Tōkyō Daigaku Shiryō Hensanjo.

abandonment of land continued to be the main means of applying collective pressure on the proprietor. But in confrontations with the shugo or *dosō* (moneylenders and/or pawnbrokers), both of whom were backed by the power of the bakufu, peasants organized large-scale and regionally coordinated *do-ikki* (peasant revolts).

As peasant ikki occurred more frequently, the need to strengthen social unity within village communities increased. Some of the villages in central Japan even began to construct moats around their habitations for defense against intruders.[32] Outsiders were looked upon with suspicion, and in some instances village codes prohibited the accommodation of travelers. The fact that discriminatory attitudes became generally more pervasive among the population at large toward such groups as *sanjo, eta, hinin, kawaramono,* and *mōto* was not unrelated to this growing sense of village exclusiveness.[33]

Village unity and its external manifestation, village exclusiveness, had one effect which worked against the peasant effort to secure independence from proprietary authority. The internal unity achieved by the late medieval village communities became a major reason why village communities found it difficult to pool their forces over wider areas encompassing large numbers of villages and why they tended to remain isolated and mutually exclusive. From time to time, however, efforts to form some type of village federation across village communities were successful. The formation of such federations was clearly linked to the degree of internal social unity attained by the village communities of the region. The fact that the villages around Kyoto took joint action in large-scale do-ikki clearly demonstrates the greater sophistication of the peasantry of the central area.

CONCLUSION

How did the political functions of village communities which developed during the fifteenth century change during the sixteenth and how did this relate to the rise of the sengoku-daimyo? In answering this question, a leading scholar of the Muromachi period, Suzuki Ryōichi, has advanced the following view.[34] Paralleling the increasing intensity of peas-

32. On communities with surrounding circular moats *(kangō shūraku),* see Makino Shinnosuke, *Tochi oyobi shūrakushijō no shomondai* (Tokyo, 1938), pp. 149–203.
33. Studies on the social status of the medieval peasants made by Kuroda Toshio and Amino Yoshihiko examine this point carefully. Also, for evidence on groups which were discriminated against during the medieval period, see Buraku Mondai Kenkyūsho, ed., *Burakushi ni kansuru sōgōteki kenkyū,* 3 (Kyoto, 1962) and 4 (Kyoto, 1965), especially the summary comments in each volume by Hayashiya Tatsusaburō. On the nonexclusive aspects of shōen villages during the early medieval period, see Amino Yoshihiko, *Chūsei shōen no yōsō* (Tokyo, 1966).
34. Suzuki, "Junsui hōkensei seiritsu ni okeru nōmin tōsō."

ant struggles throughout the fifteenth century, class distinctions appeared
in village communities, with the myōshu in the upper layer growing into
minor proprietors who sided with the lord's authority and becoming, in
effect, betrayers of the peasant struggle.

Suzuki's view has long been accepted as the authoritative interpretation,
its correctness seemingly borne out by the fact that the peasant revolts in
the regions near Kyoto in the course of the fifteenth century lost the élan
they once had. However, while confirming his basic observation that the
upper layer of the peasantry became minor proprietors, thus weakening
the cohesiveness of the village communities, recent research has shown
that the peasant struggles of the sixteenth century widened in geographical
scope to include all regions of Japan and that the leadership of such revolts
in many areas began to be taken by the common peasantry (hyakushō). It
is also evident that these struggles had a real effect on the coercive power
of the daimyo and that the control exerted by the sengoku-daimyo over
peasants during the sixteenth century had certain obvious limitations.
Above all, the effective tax rates were not high. This was clearly due to the
persistent peasant resistance to tax payments, and absconding as a form of
such resistance continued to plague daimyo, who were forced to take great
pains to prevent it.[35] The fundamental problem facing the sengoku-
daimyo was the suppression of peasant resistance whether by force or
accommodation.

When examined from this perspective, it is evident that the political
functions of village communities were not as weak as Suzuki has stated.
The daimyo could not refuse to recognize certain self-governing political
functions of village communities, even though in so doing they found their
own local authority challenged. In responding to this challenge, the
daimyo took two positive steps: they attempted to integrate the various institutional arrangements for village self-government into their own system
of local administration, and they sought to strengthen their mediating role
in solving intercommunity disputes.

For example, Article 64 of the Date Law of the Domain (bunkokuhō)
called the Jinkaishū states: "In cases in which merchants of other provinces
[kuni] or travelers are robbed of their valuable possessions by mountain-
robbers, the responsibility for the crime belongs to the villages in which
such crime occurred." This clearly was an attempt by the daimyo to incor-

35. The tax levied on rice cultivators by the sengoku daimyo was about 500 mon in copper coins
per tan (or in rice about 0.5 koku out of an approximate yield of 1.2 to 1.3 koku per tan). Even
when the tansen is included, the total burden was lighter than the taxes (rice, corvée, and
various taxes in kind) levied by the shōen ryōshu. The sengoku daimyo were frequently unable
to collect all the taxes because of peasants' oppositon to the taxes or because the peasants
absconded to avoid them.

porate into the framework of his polity the villagers' right to handle their own affairs with regard to the maintenance of law and order within their own territories. Article 84 of the same law stressed that, in matters relating to the use of water by geographical units larger than a single village community, established customs would continue to be respected. In this case the daimyo merely hoped to play the mediating role in intercommunity disputes.[36] Thus, rather than impose their authority arbitrarily over the village communities which comprised their domain, the sengoku-daimyo accommodated themselves to the peasant struggle by institutionalizing into their systems of local governance the various functions which had been won by village communities in their effort to secure autonomy. In so doing the daimyo sought to legitimize themselves by acting as protectors of peasant interests.

The daimyo frequently used the phrase "public good" (*kōgi*) as a way of expressing their "ideological" claim to political authority. By stressing the public, rather than private, characteristics of their authority, the daimyo attempted to justify the use of their power. At the same time they made use of the self-governing functions of village communities, reorganizing them into systems for the maintenance of law and order and for tax collection to the benefit of the daimyo.

It was this reorganization of local administration to take account of the various functions of village self-government which laid the basis of the successful daimyo domain. But since, in reality, the daimyo sought to use the self-governing capacities of the peasantry as a means of imposing his own control over peasant communities, the process was not achieved without further conflict between peasantry and daimyo, especially in the central region around Kyoto where the political functions of village communities were most developed. The great Ikkō ikki in the Nōbi and Osaka areas were an obvious demonstration of the intensity of such conflicts. The fierce resistance mounted by the Ikkō ikki exemplified this final battle against the attempts by daimyo to reorganize and restructure the political functions of the village communities, making village autonomy subject to superior daimyo authority. Only after the late medieval village communities were subsumed under daimyo control was the Tokugawa political system made possible.

---

36. The following order issued by Miyoshi Nagayoshi is a case in point:

Recently Gunke village began to dispute with Magami village concerning the path of irrigation ditches, and litigation resulted. Though both parties could present maps indicating the path of the irrigation ditches, neither has conclusive documentary evidence to prove its case. Magami village argued that no such irrigation ditches existed in earlier times, and thus Gunke village has no right to newly construct them. However, after a careful survey made by the officials who were sent to investigate the dispute, we have come to the conclusion that Gunke village's claim is justified. It is hereby ordered that Gunke village may open new ditches, as indicated on its map, in order to obtain water.

19 May 1559   For Gunke Village   Nagayoshi

PART FOUR

Commercial Economy and Social Change

One of the most important yet least understood aspects of Muromachi Japan involves the general area of commerce, urban growth, and the status of merchants and tradesmen. The subject has been neglected by historians, for source materials are scarce and statistics are almost nonexistent. Yet it is obvious that Japan underwent in the Muromachi period a major change in the structure of its economy and in the economic and social position of nonagricultural producers. The change, moreover, was to have a lasting impact upon the country.

In a very general way it is possible to explain the nature of this change as the result of the breakup of the shōen economy. Under the shōen system all nonagricultural activities—the manufacture of luxury and special products, the construction and service trades, the exchange of goods—were presumably controlled by the shōen proprietor. Shōen economy attempted to be self-sufficient. Village smiths, thatchers, and carpenters met the needs of the farming community, while special artisans, often attached in an unfree capacity to the proprietor's family establishment, produced the goods necessary for the more complicated style of life of the aristocratic class. Such goods were as yet not freely produced for a general market nor freely traded for commercial profit.

It was during the Muromachi period that this condition underwent a fundamental transformation. As Professor Toyoda's essay demonstrates, both because of the weakening of the shōen structure (brought on by the loss of effective control over the shōen by the proprietors) and because of the new demands placed upon the economy by the regionally based military aristocracy, the trades moved out of the shadow of aristocratic control, and commerce developed as a separate activity within the national economy.

The emancipation of tradesmen, artisans, and merchants from the patrimonial control of the aristocracy was not complete during the Muromachi period. Most trading and artisan activities moved into what

125

can best be considered an intermediate status of guilds and monopoly organizations (the *za*) which depended for protection on the aristocracy and powerful religious institutions. But the za were only indirectly controlled by these politically influential or socially prestigious groups, and increasingly merchants and tradesmen gained control of their own activities. Whereas the aristocracy once lived off the production of semifree service groups, they now were obliged to tax them if they would have benefit from them.

The increased freedom gained by the nonagricultural sector of the Japanese economy had two important repercussions during the Muromachi period: the growth of towns and the attendant urban commercial society and the freeing of merchants and artisans from certain social restraints. Kyoto, of course, was the prime example of urban development, from the commercial as well as social standpoint. But Kyoto was not unique. The early Sakai, as described by Professor Morris, shows that commercial communities already had a long history of independent activity by the end of the fifteenth century.

It is significant that the Ashikaga family and its administration, the bakufu, were intimately involved both in the development of a commercial economy and in the patronage of new commercial and service groups. If on the one hand the shogun relied on the services of formerly base gardeners, actors, carpenters, and decorators, so also did the bakufu become more and more dependent on the services of commercial tax contractors and on profits from foreign trade. Government in Japan, while it remained in large part dependent on control of the land, was developing a new mercantilist dimension in alliance with the emerging urban commercial class. The bakufu's reliance on "virtuous burghers" (*utokunin*), who were both tax farmers and sources of tax revenue, transformed the sociopolitical structure of Kyoto and made of the city not only the political and cultural capital but the financial and commercial center as well.

An important aspect of Japan's commercial growth during the Muromachi period was the development of foreign trade. Professor Tanaka rightly points out that the development of such trade cannot be considered separately from the broader political meaning which foreign contact had for Japan's rulers. Desire for profit took Japanese traders into foreign waters. But in an East Asian international community in which trade was subordinated to diplomacy, such traders had to turn pirate or else subordinate themselves to elaborate official regulations. Whether in the trade with China, Korea, or Ryukyu, diplomacy had to take precedence over economics. Shogun and daimyo were essential partners for Japanese merchants.

Thus the Muromachi period witnessed not only the start of Japan's emergence as a maritime trading nation but also the beginning of a self-conscious foreign policy on the part of Japan's rulers. The epoch-making, often criticized, decision of Ashikaga Yoshimitsu to accept a tributary relationship to Ming China signaled both the assertion of a positive foreign policy on the part of the bakufu and the bakufu's usurpation from the imperial court of the right to deal with foreign heads of state. By this act, the Muromachi bakufu set the precedent for the particular balance of authority between emperor and shogun for the next four hundred and fifty years.

Yet having made these observations it is important to remember that most of the changes which attract our attention during the Muromachi period were still at the beginning of their cycle even in the early years of the sixteenth century. The continuation of the za system and the continued existence of commercial tolls and barriers meant that trade was still partially unfree. Moreover, as Professor Tanaka points out, the right to control foreign diplomacy and trade was still the private prerogative of the feudal aristocracy, a right capable of being subdivided and its parts granted to vassal lords like feudal fiefdoms. Trends begun in the Muromachi period forecast the look of Tokugawa society and economy, but they were still only trends throughout the period.

9

The Growth of
Commerce and the Trades

TOYODA TAKESHI and SUGIYAMA HIROSHI

with V. Dixon Morris

THE BAKUFU, THE DAIMYO, AND COMMERCE

It might be expected that the civil wars which attended the struggle to establish the Muromachi bakufu would have had a disruptive effect on the national economy, retarding both agricultural productivity and the growth of commerce. To the contrary, the wars which attended the destruction of the Kamakura regime were themselves a reflection of the new economic vigor and entrepreneurial drive among the provincial military aristocracy. As for the fighting, the movement of troops and their posting in distant areas stimulated rather than hindered the circulation of goods. Moreover, as the military class became increasingly removed from actual involvement in local production, merchants and artisans were given new opportunities for commercial activity. Above all, Kyoto came to enjoy a faster pace of economic activity as it became once again the seat of government and as the warrior class joined the nobility and the priesthood as members of a consuming elite. Thus the early Muromachi age in fact saw a spurt in the production of goods and the exchange of commodities, with Kyoto and the several river and seaport towns linked to it as the center of this activity.

First among the factors contributing to commercial growth was the consumer economy formed by the old civil aristocracy and religious institutions. The Northern Court, which was patronized by the Ashikaga family, had a severely limited sphere of authority; its proprietary holdings suffered from the incursions of the military class and steadily diminished in value. Nonetheless, the Ashikaga government prevented the complete eradication of the estates of the nobility and religious institutions, so that the aristocrats in the capital continued to receive substantial rents from the hinterland, at least until the time of the Ōnin War. Religious institutions, moreover, often participated directly in the management of their provincial estates, so that they, too, received a sustained income. Such rents were paid either in kind from estates close at hand or in monetary form from more distant areas. With money, the proprietors could purchase a part of the rice they needed in Kyoto itself. This development of the markets of Kyoto and, to a lesser degree, Nara as purveyors of essential commodities was an important factor in encouraging urban commercial growth. Finally, the civil aristocrats received income from the *kugonin* (service personnel) attached to them, in itself not a negligible source of support.

An even greater demand for rice and other necessities in Kyoto came from the military aristocracy and their retainers who gathered about the Muromachi bakufu. As Professor Kawai has pointed out, during the Muromachi period Kyoto became both the seat of the bakufu and the residence of a large number of shugo vassals of the shogun. These men provided themselves with great mansions in the capital and also quartered armed guards and even armies in the city.[1] As a consumer group, the military aristocracy was large and exacting. Goods and services had to be provided either directly by the military retainers of the great military houses or indirectly by specially patronized merchant groups.

During the early Muromachi period important new commercial links were forged between the capital and the provinces. Military men of the shugo class employed special merchants called *toiya*, or *ton'ya*, who lived in Kyoto, in nearby cities such as Yamazaki, or in ports such as Sakai, to serve as their agents for forwarding goods and tax revenues from home provinces. In addition, those shugo who were responsible for paying estate rents to civil proprietors sometimes appointed Kyoto moneylenders as their agents for the purpose. In fact, among the moneylenders responsible for collecting rents for civil proprietors, there were many who had the status of rear vassal to one or another of the shugo.

Some shugo operated special ships for sending essential goods from their home areas to Kyoto. This practice became so common that others set up toll barriers in order to profit from the trade. To counter these extortions, shugo resorted to force or negotiation. For example, vessels belonging to the Ōtomo of Bungo and the Kobayakawa of Aki acquired passes for barriers at such places as Hyōgo and were able to travel freely through the Inland Sea. Others tried bluff, pretending to hold legitimate passes of their own. There are records of punishments dealt to ordinary merchants who were caught using this stratagem.

The shugo's control of his lands was not yet as thorough and systematic as that of the later sengoku-daimyo, but he did attempt to take over the old provincial capital and the adjacent ports, which constituted the economic

1. Kawai Masaharu, "Muromachi zenki no shakai to bunka," in *Chūsei buke shakai no kenkyū* (Tokyo, 1973), pp. 203–232.

center of the province over which he held administrative authority. He was constantly on the lookout for ways to expand his local authority and his capacity to extract wealth from the province. Two outstanding examples of this effort by shugo can be found in Obama and Onomichi. Obama was the main port serving the old capital of Wakasa province. The shugo of the province, the Yamana family and later the Isshiki family, established offices in the mansion of a toiya in Obama and from there ruled the entire province. Later the Takeda family, which succeeded to the position of shugo of Wakasa, built a castle near Obama. The Obama market soon became so important to local farmers that according to a contemporary source "hardly a day could pass without their having some business in the town." The shugo then set up a control barrier at Obama. By refusing the passage of goods and persons through the barrier for up to forty or fifty days at a time, the shugo was able to control the economy of the whole province.

Onomichi, a port in Bingo, was used in a similar manner by the Yamana family for nearly a century. For the first fifty years, the Yamana headquarters was at Saionji in Onomichi. Among the rent contracts held by the Yamana was one for the Ōta estate, which belonged to Kōyasan, the great Shingon monastery. The task of shipping rents to the temple proprietor was delegated to a local toiya who also seems to have been an official of the administrative agency for the old provincial capital.[2]

As these cases indicate, the toiya of port towns played an important part in the shugo's control of his province. These same merchants also had close ties with Kyoto merchants and worked with them in the development of commercial routes between the capital and the provinces—routes which in many cases had been in existence from earlier times when the old provincial capitals actually served as centers of imperial administration and tax collection.

In developing its economic foundations, the bakufu also turned to the use of commercial agents, though its reasons for doing so were somewhat different from those of the shugo. The bakufu from the first had trouble in maintaining a strong land base: its directly held estates were small and tended to shrink as time passed. Of necessity therefore, bakufu fiscal policy deemphasized land and actively sought to develop commercial income, either through taxation or through participation in commercial ventures. The first enterprises to attract bakufu attention were the *sakaya* (sake dealers) and *dosō* (storehouse operators), which were already prominent elements in the economy of central Japan when the Muromachi bakufu was established. The power to regulate and tax these commercial houses

2. Toyoda Takeshi, ed., *Ryūtsūshi* (Tokyo, 1969).

was a matter of considerable consequence to the Ashikaga house. When Takauji came to power, approximately 80 percent of the city's sakaya and dosō were controlled by the great monastery of Enryakuji on Mt. Hiei, and the remainder were regulated by the imperial court's police office, the kebiishi-chō. After establishing its headquarters in Kyoto, the Ashikaga house gradually acquired police powers over the city and gained control over its commercial and financial establishments. By 1393, the bakufu had eliminated its political competitors in Kyoto, and an edict of that year denied the authority of the Enryakuji and its agents in Kyoto to regulate or tax brewing and moneylending. In its place the bakufu named its own agents, themselves influential sakaya and dosō, as nōsen-gata (tax collectors) and had them contract for the taxes on the other moneylenders.[3] This system was not uniform, and some lenders paid their taxes directly into the bakufu treasury while others paid through the agency of guilds or corporations attached to patron shrines. Thus in addition to revenues from the go-ryōsho (direct shogunal holdings) a substantial portion of bakufu income, particularly after 1441, came from the fees extracted from the sakaya and dosō.[4]

Another important source of bakufu income was foreign trade and the monopoly of the supply of currency that this made possible (discussed more fully by Professor Tanaka in his essay below). The ability of the bakufu to provide coins enhanced its position in the growing commercial and exchange economy at the same time that it earned vast sums of money for the bakufu.

Two aspects of Muromachi commercial development which only later contributed directly to bakufu coffers but toward which bakufu policy was politically important were guilds (za) and toll barriers (sekisho). For a yet undetermined reason the bakufu did not at first attempt to set itself up as a patron of commercial and craft guilds. During most of its existence the bakufu defended but did not contest the authority of the civil aristocracy or religious institutions over the guilds. At the same time the bakufu encouraged the independent development of the za and used them to control production and distribution. There were some particularly noteworthy cases in which the bakufu permitted the expansion of the rights of certain special za beyond the normal sphere of authority of the original patron. The ability, for example, of the Oyamazaki oil guild to obtain monopoly rights over the purchase and sale of the raw material for lamp oil, even in areas outside the jurisdiction of the Iwashimizu Hachiman shrine, was no

---

3. Kuwayama Kōnen, "Muromachi bakufu keizai kidō no ichi kōsatsu," Shigaku zasshi 73, no. 9 (1964).

4. Toyoda Takeshi, Nihon shōninshi: Chūsei hen (Tokyo, 1949). See sections on sakaya and dosō.

doubt a result of shogunal backing. Thus the bakufu encouraged the spread and stability of the za system, thereby assuring the prosperity of the merchants of the home provinces and the continued flow of income to the civil aristocracy and religious establishments which served as patrons of these organizations.

Only in the post-Ōnin period did the bakufu attempt to become a za proprietor itself and to organize za members directly under its control. In 1547, eighty years after the outbreak of the Ōnin War, the Ōtoneriza, which first produced Nishijin textiles, abandoned its patron, the Madeno-kōji family, and in an effort to maintain its monopoly rights subordinated itself to the shogun and his consort.[5] In the Sengoku period, the sharp decline of the authority of the court even in Kyoto meant that many za members were obliged to seek the protection of the bakufu or the kanrei in the central provinces or of the more powerful daimyo in outlying areas. It is no doubt for this reason that individual merchants and artisans enlisted in the service of the shogun or his consort.

A similar pattern is evident in the bakufu's policy toward the practice of establishing *sekisho* (barriers).[6] During the Kamakura period authority for the erection of barriers lay with the civil aristocracy, and it was customary for the bakufu to recognize and confirm barriers established by the court by issuing its own orders to accompany the formal edicts. After the establishment of the Ashikaga bakufu, the imperial court still possessed nominal authority to establish sekisho and to issue passes for them. When the bakufu wanted to assert its authority over barriers for any reason, it would petition the throne for permission and use the resulting edict as its authority. In 1346 the bakufu issued an order to the shugo forbidding them to erect new barriers and throughout the early Muromachi period continued to issue prohibitions against the establishment of new barriers, each time at the insistence of the civil aristocracy or the religious establishments.

With time, shogunal rights in respect to sekisho grew stronger, until even those barriers directly operated by the court had to display the *kōsatsu* (placards) that signified shogunal approval. As shogunal finances became increasingly straitened, the bakufu began to encroach upon the commercial income of the court aristocracy by setting up its own sekisho and using the income from them for its own purposes. Thus as early as 1434 the bakufu had begun to take from the Saionji family one-third of the dues received from salt food purveyors at the Yodo fish market, and later it took over the principal salt distribution routes as well. The bakufu also brought

5. Toyoda Takeshi, "Za to dosō," in *Iwanami kōza: Nihon rekishi* (Tokyo, 1963), 2: 153–186.
6. Toyoda Takeshi, "Chūsei ni okeru sekisho no tōsei," *Kokushigaku* 82 (1968).

many of the chief sekisho on roads between Kyoto and the provinces directly under its own management. In 1470 it created new barriers at the seven entrances to Kyoto for the ostensible purpose of raising funds for repair of the imperial palace, but Hino Tomiko, Yoshimasa's consort, is known to have squandered the proceeds. Ultimately, the bakufu came to set up its own barriers without pretense of imperial justification and thereby involved itself still more deeply in the circulation of goods.

Clearly, the civil and military aristocracy of the Muromachi period —both by their style of living and by their public policies—did much to encourage the production of goods and the circulation of commodities. As its political power waned and its land income diminished, the bakufu relied increasingly on taxes from the sakaya and dosō and on income from commerce and industry. Therefore it was to the interest of the bakufu to stimulate commercial development. Provincial lords, particularly after their emergence as true regional hegemons, also put great stress on the encouragement of production and on the creation of commercial wealth. The net effect of these trends was that commerce and manufacture began for the first time in Japanese history to have an independent existence. In the process a new urban commercial element was created within Japanese society.

THE EMERGENCE OF URBAN COMMERCE

Although it was not until the Edo period that cities came to occupy a position of greater importance than that of rural villages, towns with clear-cut commercial functions had already appeared in the Muromachi era. What distinguished these communities from large villages was the regular market (teikiichi). In the early part of the Muromachi period, markets met at specified intervals during the month. In contrast to those in the countryside, which met only three times a month, commercial settlements began in the mid-fourteenth century to hold markets as often as six times a month.[7] In Nara the Kōfukuji, having established a north market in the mid-Kamakura period, a south market late in the period, and a central market early in the Muromachi era, operated these markets in such a way that at least one of them would be open on any given day.

Eventually permanent retail shops sprang up in a wide variety of neighborhoods, bringing into being the wholesalers (ton'ya) who supplied them with merchandise. The ton'ya, who occupied a central position in the distribution network of medieval Japan, began as groups called toi or toimaru attached to the shōen estates. Toi were a type of estate officer who

7. Sasaki Gin'ya, Chūsei Nihon shōhin ryūtsūshi no kenkyū (Tokyo, 1972).

operated warehouses in ports near Kyoto and Nara on behalf of the proprietors. They were charged with the storage and shipment of rice received as estate rents and served the proprietors as general transport agents. In time the proprietors began using toi to sell surplus rent rice and other goods in commercial markets. Living as they did at key points in the distribution network, toi often accepted the patronage of several proprietors who shipped through the same port and for this reason tended to become independent merchants who specialized in the entrepot trade.

During the Muromachi period increased exchange between capital and provinces by the proprietary class, the Muromachi bakufu, and the shugo-daimyo led increasingly to the conversion of toi and toimaru into independent businessmen who dealt in the transshipment of goods between the port towns and the great consuming centers of Kyoto and Nara. As this phenomenon became widespread, the term *toimaru*, which designated status as an estate officer, gave way to *ton'ya*, i.e., wholesaler. More importantly, differentiation of function also occurred, the new specialization evidenced in the clustering of tradesmen and merchants by streets and blocks and by the formation of trade organizations. The ton'ya of the central cities, for instance, operated inns *(jōyado)* for provincial merchants which catered to merchants from specific provinces or dealers in specific kinds of merchandise. Such arrangements accentuated the ton'ya's role as a wholesaler with respect to the local producers and retailers: local merchants generally could not sell their goods directly to consumers but had to go through the ton'ya. Similarly, the residents of nearby farming communities, who produced handicraft items as a by-occupation, also began to use the ton'ya as intermediaries in selling their products to consumers.

As an example of how certain commercial houses gained control of commodities on a sale monopoly basis we can cite the case of Sudareya of Nara, who dealt in bamboo blinds. Sudareya bought blinds from the guild that produced them in the Otogi estate of Yamato province and then sold them in Nara, where he held a monopoly. Soon he was selling blinds in Kyoto, where he also received monopoly privileges. In this way Sudareya ultimately came to control the rural za of blind makers. In another example, the za that made and sold sedge hats in the village of Fukae in Settsu province, with operations in markets in Kyoto, Sakai, and Nara, in about 1485 came under the direction of a single ton'ya, probably a resident of Tennōji.[8]

As trade increased, markets gained independence from political interference and became more strictly commercial in their activities. This

8. Wakita Haruko, *Nihon chūsei shōgyō hattatsushi no kenkyū* (Tokyo, 1969).

was particularly true of the bulk commodities markets dealing in rice, fish, fowl, and lumber that grew up in and around Kyoto. Grain markets were established at Sanjō and Shichijō in Kyoto by the late fifteenth century, and the merchants in the markets (*komeba*) were organized into a Kome-baza. Bulk rice, generally brought in by teamsters from Sakamoto and Ōtsu was traded there. The town of Yodo had since the middle of the Ka-makura period served as the locus of a fish market to which special vessels shipped salt and salted marine products from Inland Sea coastal areas.[9]

The spread of the use of *kawase* (drafts for the transfer of funds) was yet another significant economic development which indicates the extent of development of domestic trade. The use of kawase began about the latter half of the thirteenth century when kawashi or kaisen were a common means of transferring funds to Kamakura to pay for the expenses of legal claimants who had to appear before the bakufu court. Eventually such documents were used to send estate rents in monetary form to Kyoto and other destinations. An early example of this is seen in 1311 when the depu-ty shugo of Bingo on the Inland Sea coast sent estate rents to the proprietor in Kyoto. On that occasion he secured from a certain Jirōbyōe no Jō of the fish market at Yodo a kawase, the proceeds of which were to be paid in cash at an inn in Kyoto. The fish market merchant had no doubt gone to Bingo to acquire salt and thus was able to handle the exchange.

During the Nambokuchō period, toimaru of the port towns first began handling kawase on a large scale as estate rents came increasingly to be paid in monetary form and as exchange between Kyoto and the provinces assumed greater importance. There are numerous examples of such doc-uments. Those of the Niimi estate of Bitchū reveal that in the latter half of the fifteenth century there were several merchants who carried kawase from the estate drawn on establishments in Yamazaki, Hirose, Watanabe, Amagasaki, and Sakai in central Japan.[10] The Muromachi period *kaiya* or *kaisenya* who dealt in kawase were usually ton'ya engaged in trade with the provinces rather than specialized exchange houses such as those of later eras, though by the end of the period the kawase they used had already assumed a form similar to that which would be used in the Edo period.

THE CHANGING NATURE OF THE ZA

The term *za* in Japan refers to two quite distinct types of organization, and the early za differed greatly in character from those which began to appear in the Muromachi period. Whereas the early za

9. Toyoda Takeshi, *Chūsei Nihon shōgyōshi no kenkyū*, rev. ed. (Tokyo, 1952).
10. Sugiyama Hiroshi, *Shōen sei kaitai katei no kenkyū* (Tokyo, 1959).

were obliged to perform personal service to the shōen proprietors, the later za simply paid dues *(zayaku)* and enjoyed a relatively free, contractual relationship to the proprietor. Increasingly during the Muromachi period, the original za, which had their bases in the towns of central Japan, were challenged by new groups which emerged outside the jurisdiction of the urban za. The result was that geographical restrictions on commerce became relatively ineffectual so far as za were concerned, and the monopolistic control of the ton'ya in any given area grew correspondingly stronger.

This fundamental change in the nature of the za occurred after the Nambokuchō wars, when a succession of so-called "new za" *(shinza)* appeared, many of them in conflict with the earlier "original za" *(honza)*. For example, the Gion shrine was patron *(honjo)* of the Wataza which controlled the sale of cotton and which operated shops in Sanjō, Shichijō, and Nishikikōji in Kyoto. But the Wataza was undermined by a new za group organized by individuals who were peddlers engaged in sales to villages outside the city. Simply by paying 200 cash each year to the Gion shrine, these persons, who numbered some sixty-four at the time, could participate freely in sales without geographical restriction. In 1343 the original Wataza appealed to the shrine against the activities of the new za, claiming that its members had violated the original za's monopoly rights. But, as was to become typical of such situations, victory went to the shinza. Nara provides a similar example. Among the salt guilds under the protection of the Kōfukuji was the Seizen'in salt za, which dealt principally on a wholesale basis. A second za, a shinza, was organized to include peddlers, and by the time of the Ōnin War it had begun to open shops regardless of previous restrictions on them.

What is especially striking about the za of the later period is the freedom with which they were organized and administered. In the earlier za the control of the patron was strong and there was a pronounced hierarchy of status within the guild itself. The organization was so exclusive and authoritarian that if a member became the leader *(chōrō)* of a za by going over the heads of any above him, those who were passed over had no choice but to resign.[11] In contrast, the members of the later guilds were relieved from personal service to the proprietor and there was freedom both to enter and resign from the group. Individual members had an equal voice in the common activities of the group, and the membership met from time to time in council to discuss such matters as fees owing to the proprietor or sanctions against those who had violated monopoly rights.

The administration of the later za was in the hands of a council of elders called *zatō* or *otona*. The Fusaka oil guild of Nara had eight such elders who

---

11. Tsuji Zennosuke, comp., *Daijōin jisha zōjiki*, 10 vols. (Tokyo, 1931–34), item dated Bummei 5 (1473).

met together and decided the affairs of the group, and at times the members as a whole would convene to express their views. Merchant organizations were also influenced by the practice, increasingly common after the fifteenth century, of holding town or village meetings. Among the za that grew up in rural areas, the kind of geographically based village community described by Professor Nagahara became a model for occupationally differentiated merchant communities (shōnin sō). Just as in the villages, merchants brought legal suit as corporate units and set policy for their groups at common assemblies. Although some codes for the governance of the za were compiled on the authority of the proprietor alone, the membership itself not infrequently set its own internal regulations. One such body of rules was the Kombai zachū hatto, written by the Kombaiza at Nagasaka-guchi in Kyoto in 1517, which contained numerous and detailed provisions. Za laws began to appear in the records after the beginning of the Sengoku period, but discrete rules concerning equality of opportunity in purchase and sales of products were being written by the fifteenth century. As an example, the guild in Nara that dealt in cypress bark provided that whenever cypress trees were delivered to the city their distribution would be carried out in consultation with the guild's membership.[12]

In summary, the Muromachi period saw a steady growth in the quantity of trade and commercial production and in their freedom from proprietary control. Those aspects of the economy which had been limited in production and distribution, but which had been stimulated by the patronage of the aristocratic class, grew in importance and scope. Eventually merchants freed themselves from the control of their patrons and found new markets and new independence of enterprise. Complete freedom of trade was as yet many centuries off. But commerce as a separate component of the economy was coming into its own. This in turn was to have widespread social implications.

FROM SUBORDINATION TO FREEDOM AMONG MERCHANTS AND ARTISANS

One of the most characteristic features of society in the Kamakura and early Muromachi periods was that groups of merchants, artisans, and professional entertainers were subordinate to offices attached to the imperial court, to shōen proprietors, and to religious establishments. Most commercial and service groups were to some extent delimited in their social status as well as economic activities and were known by various terms which reflected inferior position. Kugonin, zōshiki, and kayochō

12. Toyoda, Nihon shōninshi.

served the imperial house and branches of the Fujiwara family; attached to shrines were *jinin* and to temples *yori'udo, hijiri,* and *kunin.* These people received sustenance fields *(kyūden)* or stipends *(hōroku)* and performed special labor services in compliance with the dictates of their powerful patrons.

From the latter half of the fourteenth century, these groups began to lose their subordinate status and to achieve greater autonomy. What had once been a service relationship between servant and patron, for instance, became an economic one in which patron taxed commercial and service groups in return for providing protection. As these service groups broke free of their subordination to the old aristocracy, the guilds (za) came into being. Merchants and artisans congregated in towns or sections of Kyoto and Nara, forming urban communities *(machishū)* which took their place alongside the civil and military aristocracy, the monastic communities, and the villages as integral parts of medieval society. Merchants, like villagers, sought economic and political independence, and we find among them the same patterns of group association for self-protection.[13]

The process by which urban guilds gained independence from estate proprietors can be surmised from the preceding description of the development of urban commerce during the Muromachi period. The first to exhibit such independence were the sakaya and dosō, merchants engaged in sake brewing and moneylending in the Kyoto area.[14] At the outset many such merchants were monks of the Sammon establishment of Mt. Hiei who managed storehouses in Kyoto. Others were wealthy Kyoto townsmen under Sammon control. As Sammon authority declined, the number of laymen involved in moneylending increased. A list of za members dated 1467 indicates how large the proportion of laymen had grown by that time: of 48 names, only 17 were clerics. After the economic recovery of Kyoto following the Ōnin War, lay sakaya and dosō such as Sawamura, Nakamura, and Yasui served as merchant representatives collecting taxes in place of official tax agents. The moneylenders steadily freed themselves from Sammon control and used their affluence to become community leaders in the capital.

Sakaya and dosō occupied central positions in all towns, but in the port towns the operators of *kaisen* (freight vessels) held an equally significant place. In the flourishing foreign trade ports of Hyōgo and Hakata, and in the newly arisen Sakai, these *kaisen-ton'ya* had an influential voice in the running of municipal affairs. Their prominence was, in fact, one indica-

13. The 1419 oath taken by the sake brewers of Kyoto in the name of Kitano shrine is an early example of such action.
14. Toyoda, *Nihon shōninshi.*

tion of the early role that ports played in the development of long-distance trade.

Next to the sakaya and dosō, the most conspicuous occupational groups in the capital were the skilled weavers of Kamigyō. The Ōtoneri weavers who had grown up in the tradition of court handicrafts produced *aya* and other fabrics of superior quality, which they supplied on order throughout the entire country. Rice merchants too held an influential position among the townsmen of their day. At the outset they were subordinate to proprietors such as Iwashimizu shrine, but later, with the emergence of the Kayochōza, rice merchants were organized into a guild under court patronage. By the sixteenth century, this za had attained such a degree of independence that it acted more as an association of rice dealers than as a za subservient to control by a patron. These are but a few examples which illustrate the rise of merchant houses to wealth and influence, with a resultant weakening in their urban communities of the political control which had been exerted by the aristocracy at the beginning of the Muromachi period.

Perhaps the most significant symbols of the newly won status of urban merchants were the councils of elders that appeared in cities throughout the country shortly after the Ōnin War. Such city councils were analogous to the councils of the new za and the new rural village councils. Their members, known by a variety of similar names, including *otona, toshiyori,* and *egō,* came from among the leading citizens (the moneylenders, the ton'ya, and the freight merchants) who had flourished with the expansion of the medieval economy. Undoubtedly the best-known of the councils was the ten-member Egōshū of Sakai, which first appeared in historical records in 1484. But it was hardly unique, for most other towns seem to have had their councils as well. Uji, Yamada, and Ōminato, which lay outside the Ise shrine, for example, all had Egōshū; Kamigyō and Shimogyō in Kyoto each contributed ten representatives called *shukurō* to a joint council.[15]

Under the councils townsmen came to have autonomous responsibility for many of the most important functions of their communities, including the joint collection of taxes owed to the proprietor class. Sakai had a long history of autonomy dating back at least to 1419 when the southern part of the city, Izumi Sakai, paid its dues to the Sōkokuji in the form of a *jigeuke*—a contract between the temple and the residents as a whole. Under this arrangement the temple assigned no official to Sakai but expected the citizens themselves to collect and forward the assessments. Hama-gō, now part of modern Osaka, enjoyed a similar arrangement

15. Toyoda Takeshi, *Nihon no hōken toshi* (Tokyo, 1952), pp. 69–73.

with its proprietor, the Daijōin. The successful operation of markets within the cities led to the creation of urban police forces as well. Regulations originally intended for the governance of markets gradually came to apply to towns as a whole. In addition, proprietors increasingly granted limited authority over the enforcement of such regulations among the local residents. For example, in 1491 the Ōuchi family had the residents of Akamagaseki collect on their own account a fee to pay for the preparations for one of the Ōuchi trade missions to Ming China, and the daimyo permitted them the right to expel those who refused to pay. Finally, town councils were at times obliged to direct the defense of their cities from outside attack. In one instance of this, the residents of Obama provided their town with gates and moats as protection against the depredations of pirates on the Japan Sea coast. A better known case was Sakai's resistance to Oda Nobunaga when he first invaded the Home Provinces in 1568. Notoya and Beniya of the Egōshū directed Sakai's defense on behalf of the Miyoshi family, which was Nobunaga's chief opponent in the area.[16]

While merchants gained increasing freedom from political dominance through their wealth and by group organization, artisans and service personnel followed a somewhat different course in their emancipation from social controls. During the Muromachi period this class of individuals was known as *shokunin*. In modern Japanese this term refers exclusively to artisans and persons engaged in handicraft industry, but at this earlier time *shokunin* had a far more inclusive meaning and was a generic term for persons in a broad spectrum of occupations outside agriculture, including intellectuals, technicians, and entertainers.[17]

One of the characteristic features of Kamakura and early Muromachi society was that groups of shokunin were subordinate to offices of the civil government or to estate proprietors and engaged in profit-making activities under a variety of unfree statuses. The terms by which they were known clearly demonstrate that they were servants of the civil nobility and religious institutions. The relocation of the bakufu in Kyoto provided a new opportunity for the military class to intervene in the relationship between the civil aristocracy and the artisans. By the time of the Ōnin War many of the shokunin were under the direct authority of the shogun. A recent study of carpenters by Ōkawa Naomi has provided a clear case

16. Ibid., pp. 76–77.
17. The best sources available for the study of shokunin are *shokunin utaawase* (poetry games) and *shokunin zukushizu* (drawings), which had shokunin as their subject and were produced by the aristocrats of the Muromachi period. The four extant examples—all to be found in *Gunsho ruijū*, rev. ed. (Tokyo, 1960), 18, nos. 502–503: 43–207—are: "Tōhokuin shokunin utaawase," "Tsurugaoka Hōjōe shokunin utaawase," "Sanjūni ban shokunin utaawase," and "Shichijūichi ban shokunin utaawase."

in point.[18] In the Kamakura period the primary center of large-scale construction projects was the Yamato area, especially the vicinity of the great temples of Nara. With the establishment of the Muromachi bakufu in Kyoto, Nara declined as the scene of building activity and the most important construction projects were those undertaken by successive shoguns. These included the construction of Zen temples, such as Tenryūji and Sōkokuji, and palaces, beginning with the Muromachi Dono, the Kitayama Dono, and the Higashiyama Dono. To build these the bakufu recruited and patronized master builders from Nara, whom contemporary records describe as "the shogun's carpenters, the master builders of Nara" (*kubō on daiku Nara banshō*).[19] The bakufu followed traditional, pre-Muromachi practice to the extent that it left the carpenters subordinate to the great temples and shrines from which they held the privilege of *daiku shiki*. But it was plain nonetheless that they were ultimately responsible to the bakufu itself, since the artisans were also termed *shōgun-ke on daiku* or *kubō on daiku* (i.e., the shogun's carpenters). Clearly they were patronized directly by the shogunal house. Bakufu support of this sort ultimately raised the status of the Nara builders and gave them a degree of independence that enabled them to survive the decline of the Nara temples in the sixteenth century.

Still another kind of shokunin was exemplified by the Iami family of mat makers who became directly subordinate to the Muromachi bakufu soon after its founding. The genealogy of the Iami family records that in the time of Yoshimitsu, a certain Nobukatsu, the son of Tanigawa Shirōzaemon no Jō Munenaga, took the name *Dōbō Iami*, which suggests that he was a member of the shogun's *dōbōshū* entourage. It goes on to say that in the Ōan period (1368–75) the family was appointed official purveyors of mats by the bakufu. Thereafter the descendants of the family served successive generations of the court, the *In*, and the bakufu as makers of *tatami* mats. Although a genealogy written centuries later is not necessarily a reliable source and the Iami family's service in the fourteenth century may be open to question, there is evidence that the Iami, together with Ikegami Gorōzaemon, served as Ontatami Daiku at the coming of age ceremony of the shogun Ashikaga Yoshiteru. Oda Nobunaga and Toyotomi Hideyoshi in their day honored the family with the title of *tenka ichi* ("the foremost mat makers in the empire"). In this fashion, shokunin such as the Iami and the Ikegami benefited from warrior patronage and enjoyed heightened status beyond that of their predecessors. Kyoto itself

18. Ōkawa Naomi, *Banshō* (Tokyo, 1971).
19. "Kammon gyoki," Eikyō 7(1435)/8/12, in *Zoku gunsho ruijū* (Tokyo, 1928).

must have been populated by large numbers of just such individuals as these.

Bakufu patronage meant more than simply the sponsorship of a few individuals or families. It extended as well to organizations such as the za, into which many of the shokunin were organized. Among the most famous of these was the za of the *biwa hōshi*, entertainers who traveled about the countryside chanting *The Tales of the Heike* to the accompaniment of the *biwa*. This za was known as the Tōdōza and was originally under the hereditary patronage of the Koga family of courtiers. In the Muromachi period, it became the custom for the shogun to hold regular performances at his residence in the first and twelfth months of each year by inviting the leaders of the biwa hōshi to chant there the tales.[20] Although the bakufu continued to recognize the proprietary rights of the Koga family through official edicts and appointments, the shogun also gave the performers personal rewards such as house lots.

Even more subservient to the political institutions of early medieval Japan were the *semmin* (base people) who served the aristocracy in a variety of capacities. One category of such people were the *sanjo*, a term which originally designated areas within shōen that were specially exempt from dues owed the proprietor.[21] Later, the term came to apply to the individuals who belonged to such areas and who carried out miscellaneous duties for the proprietor class. Some lived at strategic points of communication, where they engaged in such activities as ferrying; others were craftsmen, such as smiths, metal casters, dyers, or potters; others were fishermen; and, finally, there were entertainers and fortunetellers. Among the latter, the group that won the greatest popularity in the Muromachi period were the puppeteers and other performers at festivals.

By the end of the fourteenth century there was a growing class of people who were not under the control of the estate proprietors, as were the sanjo. Such individuals built shanties on the river flats *(kawara)*—where no taxes were collected—and hired out as sweepers or as gardeners. These were the so-called *kawaramono*. We hear of the kawaramono as a definite group in Kyoto from an incident in 1371 when a dispute arose between the kawaramono and the *inu-jinin* (service personnel) of Gion shrine over who should be entitled to the clothing of corpses. The kawaramono rallied together wearing armor, at which point the *samurai-dokoro* of the Muromachi bakufu interceded to hear the dispute and decided in favor of the kawaramono. Although the civil aristocrats rejected the kawaramono as

20. "Denchū mōshitsugi ki," in *Gunsho ruijū*, 18.
21. Toyoda Takeshi, "Sanjo kara kawaramono e," in *Nihon rekishi*, 300 (1973).

unclean, the warriors accepted them and did not hesitate to use those with specialized abilities. As we shall see in later essays, Ashikaga Yoshimitsu gladly took into his entourage anyone who excelled at his art no matter how low his status, and through his protection several Yamato Sarugaku groups (to one of which the famous Zeami belonged) escaped their menial status as *shōmonji*. Uji Sarugaku performers, by contrast, remained subject to the discipline of the shōmonji and were held accountable to the guild.

One specific means that the warrior aristocracy used to raise the status of the sanjo and kawaramono was to include them in their dōbōshū. The dōbōshū, as will be made more explicit in the essays which follow, were groups of individuals who served in the entourages of the shogun and the daimyo, often as arbiters of taste and as practitioners of the arts. The research of Professor Hayashiya has shown that dōbōshū members acquired respectable status by taking holy orders, and in the court of the Ashikaga shoguns all such members were obliged to take the tonsure as clerics in the Ji sect of Buddhism. Ji sect priests included in their names the characters *a* or *ami* from the name of the Amida Buddha, and the prevalence of names with the suffix *ami* among the artists of the shogunal court attests to the widespread use by the warrior class of Buddhism as a status-elevating institution. Kan'ami and Zeami of the Yamato Sarugaku troupe of nō performers are but two illustrative cases.[22]

This willingness to recognize able men of even the lowest orders of society and to allow them to exercise their talents was common to the newly powerful warriors in general and helps to explain the role played by lower class elements in Kitayama culture. When Yoshimasa became shogun, this tendency became even more pronounced as he actively promoted the *senzui kawaramono*, who were excellent garden designers. Following his example, the daimyo and the temples used these groups. Even the civil nobility, who previously had despised the kawaramono, began to use them as their exclusive gardeners at about this time. As early as 1430, in fact, the retired emperor had employed a member of the kawaramono class as a garden designer. These are small indicators, but they confirm the existence of a general trend toward the gradual improvement of the social status of the shokunin class as a whole.

22. Hayashiya Tatsusaburō and Okada Yuzuru, eds., *Ami to machishū* (Tokyo, 1969).

10

Sakai: From Shōen to Port City

V. DIXON MORRIS

Sakai is the best known of the commercial cities of medieval Japan. Historians have often treated it as a uniquely prosperous community, the most powerful of several "free cities" that presumably withstood the efforts of the great daimyo to impose their control over commerce in the sixteenth century. But in most ways the origin and early development of Sakai was no different from that of dozens of similar cities and towns, both large and small. Like them Sakai first appeared as an entity functionally distinct from the countryside, and with a relatively large and permanent population, in the fourteenth century during the wars of the Nanbokuchō period. Also, like many of these other cities, it grew up as a satellite of the older imperial capitals of Kyoto and Nara, functioning as a point of transshipment of estate rents from the countryside to the aristocratic establishments and religious institutions of the capital area. During the wars between the Northern and Southern Courts Sakai served as a port of military supply for certain of the combatants. What eventually set Sakai apart from the majority of towns, which remained small and did not grow beyond the stage of regional market center, was its involvement in the official tally trade with Ming China late in the fifteenth century. Because the Ming missions were under the control of the bakufu and the shugo-daimyo, they provided a valuable opportunity for the merchants of Sakai to gain the patronage of the military aristocracy. As a result the city's leading merchants were able to shift from dependence on shōen proprietors to an alliance with bakufu and daimyo, thereby extending their operations to a national, even international, market.

This essay will focus upon Sakai's origins as a medieval town, particularly on the economic origins of the city and on the first stages of Sakai's emergence as an independent entity, functionally separate from the shōen out of which it rose. The time span covered is from the fourteenth to the early sixteenth century, that is, just until Sakai developed into the great "free city" described so eloquently by the Jesuit missionaries.

The cities of medieval Japan originated in a fashion quite different from those of either the ancient or early modern periods. Nara and Kyoto, the first capitals, were conscious creations of the imperial government, built as "planned cities" after study of Chinese models. Similarly, the castle towns of the late sixteenth and early seventeenth centuries were the products of political, economic, and social policies of daimyo who sought to strengthen their regimes by stimulating urban growth. They too were in a sense planned cities. As a consequence, the founding of both types of cities was attended by laws, regulations, and plans that have enabled historians to ascertain with relative precision when and why they were established. By contrast, medieval cities, like Sakai, that appeared throughout the Kinai area and at isolated points elsewhere in the fourteenth century grew up for more purely economic, rather than political, reasons. They enjoyed neither official encouragement as towns nor political recognition. Unlike the cities of medieval Europe, no charters marked their rise. Indeed Sakai received no special legal distinction as a city until after it had passed its peak of affluence and urban development. During most of its early life Sakai was treated as part of two shōen, not as a city at all. The lack of records concerning the city's founding makes it necessary, in fact, to infer its origin and the reasons for its early growth from our general knowledge concerning the national economy and only incidentally from references to Sakai itself.

As the previous essay by Professors Toyoda and Sugiyama makes clear, the emergence of cities in medieval Japan was the result of widespread economic changes affecting virtually every phase of life. Improvements in agricultural technology, in exchange facilities, and in the supply of money all contributed to the capability of the economy to support urban populations outside the old capitals. These, in turn, depended on the shift away from the localized self-sufficiency that had characterized Japan prior to the end of the Kamakura period.[1] Commerce was already an important economic factor in the Kamakura era. As the aristocracy, both civil and military, acquired a need for products that were not forthcoming from the rents paid by their estates, trade was the logical outcome. Luxury goods were made available by the China trade, and local specialty products were brought to Kyoto and Nara by the za which were centered there. Artisans organized as za in these urban areas also produced goods to meet the needs of the proprietor class. At first, rice and other goods received as rents

1. Sasaki Gin'ya, "Chūsei shōgyō no hattatsu to zaichi kōzō," *Shigaku zasshi* 61, no. 3 (March 1952): 225–240; idem, "Sengo shōen shōgyō shi kenkyū no shomondai," ibid. 69, no. 7 (July 1960): 864–875. For a contrasting statement, see Wakita Haruko, "Chūsei no toshi to nōson," in *Kōza Nihon shi* (Tokyo, 1970), 3: 189–226.

could be bartered for desired specialty products. Then the coins which flowed in from China provided a more convenient and easily transportable medium of exchange. When the za merchants began to require money in payment, proprietors had to find the means of obtaining currency. They turned to the major source available to them, their estates, from which they demanded rents in money. One of the early bits of evidence we have about Sakai concerns the arrangement whereby Sakai Kita no Shō began paying one *kammon* in cash in lieu of rent in kind in the middle of the thirteenth century.[2] By the end of the century this practice was widespread. Though estate managers could adequately supply their own consumer needs locally, this new imposition of rents in cash meant that they had to acquire coins somehow.[3] The growth of local markets which became so characteristic of the late Kamakura period was obviously an index of the spread of trade and the demand for money.

Another development described in the preceding essay was the activities of the *toimaru*. These men who served as agents for moving rents in kind, largely rice, to Kyoto and Nara, took up residence in the ports around those cities. A reference in the *Teikin ōrai* to "ura-ura no toimaru" (the toimaru of the several ports) suggests how widespread such individuals were in all parts of the country.[4] Unlike the humbler *gyōshōnin* and za members, the toimaru, as members of the estate manager class, did not require the protection of temples, shrines, and nobility.[5] Toimaru were able to maintain extensive warehouses and transport facilities. They were also closely connected with the *kaisen* merchants who moved the goods by ship.

As the toimaru built up their facilities for handling *nengu* rice and rent payments in cash, it was natural that they should move into the business of financial transactions: conversion of goods to cash, moneylending, and the like. Moreover, as in the case of Sakai, these merchants frequently engaged in foreign trade so that they were close to the source of currency. Thus although toimaru began in the service of the estate system, they eventually became merchants free to profit from the patronage of the shugo-daimyo and the other military proprietors. By the end of the Kamakura period we find a whole series of towns growing up on the eastern end of the Inland Sea as ports of transit between the major

2. Toyoda Takeshi, *Sakai* (Tokyo, 1957), p. 1.

3. Inagaki Yasuhiko and Nagahara Keiji, eds., *Chūsei no shakai to keizai* (Tokyo, 1962), pp. 388–402.

4. *Teikin ōrai*, in *Zoku gunsho ruijū* (Tokyo, 1923–30), 13: 1133.

5. Toyoda Takeshi, *Nihon shōnin shi: Chūsei hen* (Tokyo, 1950), p. 97. See also Harada Tomohiko, *Nihon hōken toshi kenkyū* (Tokyo, 1957), pp. 205–255.

political and religious centers of Kyoto and Nara and the estate head-quarters in western and central Japan. Sakai was one such town.

The first documentation that relates directly to Sakai comes from the fourteenth century. Scattered, but concrete, evidence shows that a town was growing up in the area with a relatively large and permanent popula-tion engaged in commercial activities functionally distinct from agricul-ture. In administrative terms, Sakai consisted of two estates, Sakai Kita no Shō, the northern estate, in Settsu province and Sakai Minami no Shō, the southern estate, in Izumi.[6] These shōen passed through several propri-etary hands including Tōji, Sumiyoshi shrine, and Sōkokuji. Since the two shōen were located in different provinces, Sakai came under a variety of shugo jurisdictions, including the Hosokawa, Yamana, and Ōuchi. At a later time, the city of Sakai was brought under direct shogunal control.

Unlike the usual shōen, the documentary evidence shows from the be-ginning that the shōen of Sakai were important for their commercial ac-tivities. Most of the evidence concerns the growth of maritime trade. As early as 1333, Emperor Go-Daigo awarded the proceeds of a tax on ship-ping to the Sumiyoshi shrine, which was near Sakai and held the rights as steward and proprietor (jitō-shiki and ryōke-shiki) of Settsu Sakai.[7] This was one of the earliest indications that Sakai was becoming an important port. Since the tax was on foreign ships (karafune) it is likely that Sakai enjoyed some trade with Yüan China in addition to domestic trade. Again in the 1350s Emperor Go-Murakami issued an order to the shugo, Kusunoki Masanori, forbidding him to interfere with shipping in Sakai Minami no Shō. In 1373 the Hachiman shrine attached to Tōdaiji in Nara received the benefits of taxes from ships calling at Sakai.[8] Upon expiration of that grant in 1376, a second edict extended the tax for another three years, this time placing it on ships at Settsu Sakai. Each of these orders treated the calling of ships at Sakai as a common occurrence, and such taxes on ship-ping implied that there was enough traffic to produce a significant income. When Ōuchi Yoshihiro became shugo of Izumi in 1392, Izumi Sakai became an important terminus for his activities in the capital area.[9]

Since Sakai grew up more as a port than as a market, it did not as yet have al the typical functions of the medieval commercial town. There is some evidence that a market (teiki ichi) existed in Sakai in the fourteenth century, but it was not sufficiently important in the town's economic life to

6. The name Sakai means "border" and refers to the fact that Sakai straddled the Settsu-Izumi boundary; Toyoda, Sakai, pp. 1–2.

7. Toyoda, Sakai, p. 6; Sakai Shiyakusho, ed., Sakai Shi shi (Sakai, 1930), 1: 188 (hereafter cited as SSS).

8. Sumiyoshi Jinja monjo, in SSS, 4: 4–5; Tōdaiji monjo, in SSS, 4: 16–17; SSS, 10: 188.

9. Ōei ki, in Gunsho ruijū, rev. ed. (Tokyo, 1960), 20: 306.

have been mentioned in surviving documents. The activities of za were similarly limited. Representatives of guilds from Kyoto and Nara used Sakai, but the city itself apparently did not become the center of any extensive za activity. During the fourteenth century, for instance, only one za, the Hama Ō-Abura-Za (oil guild), is mentioned in the records of the Sumiyoshi shrine.[10] In all probability this was a small organization that merely supplied lamp oil to the shrine, because the oil market for central Japan as a whole was effectively monopolized by the Ōyamazaki of Kyoto and the Fusaka guild of Nara. The relative lack of evidence concerning za activity does not mean that there was no commerce. In 1377 there was a complaint from the Ōyamazaki guild to the effect that three residents of Sakai Kita no Shō were violating the guild's monopoly in sesame seeds (egoma) from which oil was pressed. As a result of the appeal, the shugo prohibited the three from engaging in the oil business. There were similar protest incidents in later years as well.[11]

Judging by the experience of port cities in general, one would expect to find toimaru in Sakai serving to transmit rent income from estates to proprietors in Kyoto and Nara. An early piece of documentary evidence suggesting such a conclusion is a contract dated 1380 which specified that the steward on a Tōdaiji estate in Suō province in western Japan should send twenty kammon as rent each year. Because of the dangers inherent in sea transport, he was enjoined to send the amount as a bill of exchange (kawase), which could be exchanged for cash at Hyōgo or Sakai.[12] This document implies that exchange services were regularly available at Sakai.

Handicraft producers appear in records relating to Sakai at the end of the fourteenth century. One of the earliest of the special products of the Sakai area was ironwork. In 1385 a certain Yamakawa, a resident of Sakai Kita no Shō, made a gong, which is preserved in a temple in Shikoku.[13] By later centuries Sakai was nationally famous for its metal products, and it became one of the prime producers of guns in the sixteenth century. Tradition helps to supplement the picture presented by extant documents. Textile manufacture is known to have flourished in Sakai during the Ōnin War after artisans fled there for refuge from the fighting in Kyoto. But according to tradition the technique of making brocade had already been introduced to Sakai by Ōuchi Yoshihiro in the 1390s. Originally, brocade

10. Nagashima Fukutarō, "Nara to Sakai," Shirin 35, no. 2 (August 1952): 148.
11. Rikyū Hachiman-Gū, in SSS, 4: 3–4; 1: 306–308.
12. Tōdaiji monjo, in SSS, 1: 314–315. Translated in Delmer M. Brown, Money Economy in Medieval Japan (New Haven, 1951), p. 45.
13. Toyoda, Sakai, p. 16.

makers had been brought from China to Yamaguchi, the Ōuchi head-quarters in western Japan. From there Yoshihiro is believed to have moved them to Sakai. At about the same time *Sakai-nuri,* a kind of lacquer ware, was also being produced in Sakai.[14]

Although we have no clear picture of the nature of the commercial population of Sakai in the late fourteenth century, it is certain that the city already had a number of prosperous residents. A history of Kōyasan, the great monastery in Kii, notes that in 1388 a certain Mozuya, a resident of Izumi Sakai, was the chief contributor responsible for the completion of one of the monastery's main buildings, the Okuin.[15] The wealth of Sakai also supported scholarly pursuits, for Sakai became the site of an early publishing activity. The oldest extant edition of the *Analects* of Confucius printed in Japan is the Sakai Ban (Sakai Edition) made in 1364. A note at the end of the volume states that it was executed by a Sakai resident. Unfortunately, little is known about the circumstances surrounding the printing of the *Analects.*[16] Nevertheless, the fact of its publication provides insight into the growing prosperity of the city and marks the beginning of a printing industry that came to its florescence in the sixteenth century.

Despite the relative obscurity of the origins of Sakai, and the lack of documentation regarding its early development, it is obvious that the town grew up during the fourteenth century as one of several similar ports in the area around the capital. Facilities for the transport of estate rents to Kyoto and Nara provided a nucleus for its development. As the estate system declined during the Muromachi period, these facilities proved capable of being turned toward the service of the bakufu and the shugo-daimyo. Sakai consequently experienced a continuing expansion leading to its dominant position as a port during the sixteenth century. In this transition the year 1399 was an almost disastrous turning point. In that year the shogun Yoshimitsu turned his forces against the Ōuchi house. The final battle between the bakufu forces and Ōuchi Yoshihiro occurred in Sakai. The Ōuchi were defeated and, as the *Ōei ki* recorded, "of the myriad houses in Sakai not one was left, for the town was burned at the same time."[17] The disaster that Ōuchi Yoshihiro shared with the people of Sakai might have spelled doom for the city had the town been simply an armed camp in the service of the Ōuchi house. It did not perish, however, for it had become a distinct entity in its own right, capable of surviving war and the change of political control or patronage.

14. *SSS,* 1: 317–318.
15. "Kōya shunjū hennen shūroku," in *Dai Nihon Bukkyō zensho,* 131 (Tokyo, 1912–13): 221.
16. A photographic reproduction will be found in *SSS,* 1: 326–327.
17. *Ōei ki,* in *Gunsho ruijū,* 20: 317.

Recovery appears to have been slow for Sakai during the first half of the fifteenth century. But the reason for the relative lull in Sakai's growth after 1399 was not that it was so badly damaged that it could not spring back to life. Rather, the explanation seems to lie in the city's close geographical ties to Nara and the Kii Peninsula and its isolation from Kyoto. For while Kyoto prospered and grew in the fifteenth century, and thus added new stimulus to its satellite towns, Nara and its satellites remained relatively untouched by the dynamic commercial development of the age.

During the fifteenth century, while the capital blossomed as the center of a new economy based on the military aristocracy, Nara remained bound to the old economy centering on the great temples. This is not to say that Nara completely stagnated, for religious institutions proved to be more successful as proprietors than the secular nobility. The temples were able to retain and even to expand their holdings in many cases, for they had the manpower to administer their estates directly and effectively. Moreover, many of the monasteries supported bodies of armed monks who were quite capable of defending their rights by force of arms. Finally, court families increasingly allied themselves with religious establishments, using their prestige to protect temple holdings, for in many cases their family members held hereditary posts in the priestly hierarchy. Thus the religious estates were the last to fall under control of the new feudal aristocracy, and rents flowed into Nara and Kōyasan well into the sixteenth century.

Sakai's role as an entrepot for the forwarding of estate rents continued into the fifteenth century. Politically, the city came under the direct control of the Ashikaga bakufu after 1399 but, economically, it remained a satellite of Nara. Sakai had enjoyed a close relationship with Nara through the early medieval period because of the development of communication routes between them: Sakai was essentially Nara's port. Kyoto normally relied on Hyōgo for its communications through the Inland Sea to western Japan. So long as Hyōgo remained available as a port to the authorities in the capital, Sakai had a relatively minor part in their trade. Thus until the Ōnin War severed the connection between Kyoto and Hyōgo, Sakai depended most heavily on the temples and shrines in Nara and the Kii Peninsula, or anti-bakufu shugo such as the Ouchi.

We know little of the recovery of Sakai from the destructive fire of 1399. By 1410, however, there is evidence that the port was back in operation. In that year we learn that the shugo of Satsuma in southern Kyushu, Shimazu Motohisa, changed from sea to land transport at Sakai on his way to Kyoto.[18] Because of Sakai's association with Nara and Kōyasan,

18. *SSS,* 1: 155.

the economic functions of the residents remained largely unchanged for some decades after 1399. There is, for example, ample evidence of the activities of toimaru in the port. In 1415, according to a sixteenth-century document, the Injōji, a Sakai temple of the Ji sect, was granted a tax on toimaru for the purchase of lamp oil.[19] Thereafter, records that reveal the development of the port and the work of merchants of the toimaru type appear frequently.

Toimaru in Sakai depended heavily on forwarding rents to Kōyasan from estates in western Japan. Ōta no Shō, a Kōyasan holding in Bingo near modern Hiroshima, for example, shipped its rents by way of Sakai. The estate's records covering the years from 1439 to 1447 and from 1456 to 1463 show a number of cases in which as many as six shiploads of rent produce were changed into money at Sakai annually. Because almost all commercial transactions in the Muromachi period involved money, it was natural that the toimaru continued to deal in *kawase* and *saifu* (bills of exchange). In 1466 the sum of 90 kammon in rent due the Tōdaiji in Nara was sent as a kawase payable in Sakai, and about that time the Tōji near Kyoto also received its rent from Bitchū (Okayama) in the form of a money order on Bitchūya Hikogorō, a Sakai merchant.[20] By the fifteenth century the toimaru appear to have become independent merchants and not estate officials as they had been at the outset. In 1458 we find a certain toimaru collecting a commission of six kammon for his efforts in handling three hundred *koku* of rice and beans from Ōta. There were also instances in which merchants lent money to Kōyasan with estate rent as security.[21]

Another indication of the extent of the commercial development of Sakai is the increase in the number of names ending with *ya*, a suffix which indicated that the holders were merchants. In addition to Bitchūya, the names Notoya, Naya, Kanedaya, Izumiya, Aburaya, and Shioya appear in contemporary documents.[22] Many of these, as seen in the last two listed above, denoted special products such as oil (*abura*) or salt (*shio*).[23]

19. *Injōji monjo*, in *SSS*, 4: 167.

20. *Tōdaiji monjo*, in *SSS*, 4: 184–185; *Tōji monjo*, in *SSS*, 4: 184; *SSS*, 1: 367–368. Apparently even individuals could take advantage of the kawase system, for in 1453 a resident of Bingo on a pilgrimage found it necessary to borrow ten kan while in Nachi in Kii. On his way home he stopped by Izumi Sakai and arranged to have the money returned to Nachi by money order; Toyoda, *Sakai*, pp. 23–24.

21. One such toimaru was Saburōgorō. In 1442 he exchanged 32 *koku* 9 *to* of rice and beans for 45 *kammon* in money. Two years later when the rent from Ōta no shō was lost, the merchant made it up to the temple. Toyoda, *Sakai*, pp. 20–21.

22. Kobata Atsushi, ed., *Sakai Shi shi zokuhen;* (Sakai, 1971), 1: 433–435 (hereafter cited as *SSSZ*) *SSS*, 1: passim.

23. Toyoda, *Sakai*, p. 26. The names associated with products did not, however, necessarily correspond to the type of goods the bearer sold; *SSSZ*, 1: 433–434.

Evidence of the existence of za based in Sakai remains scanty, and it seems as though the early za activities were the work of guild members from Nara and other areas who had extended their monopolies into Settsu and Izumi.[24] There was a market in Sakai by the beginning of the fifteenth century, and it may have had local za operating from it.[25] It was usual for merchants in such local markets to form their own organizations, and this may well have been true for Sakai.[26]

In the fifteenth century the toimaru continued to dominate the economic life of Sakai. But their superior position resulted at least partly from their transformation from toimaru into ton'ya (wholesale merchants). The emergence of ton'ya, as the essay by Toyoda and Sugiyama explains, was one of the most significant changes in economic organization in the Muromachi period. As toimaru capital was invested in za activities, it made possible a new style of control over the special rights to markets and sources of supply that the za had once gained from the patronage of their proprietors.[27] In Sakai, for example, the right to control both the purchase and sale of sedge hats had been in the hands of two sedge hat za which paid dues to religious institutions in Nara and to court families in Kyoto. Late in the fifteenth century a ton'ya secured these rights for himself by paying the dues to the proprietors on behalf of the za members. In this fashion, the ton'ya came to control all aspects of that market not only in Sakai but in Tennōji, Nara, and Kyoto as well, where the guilds' monopoly extended.[28] Though this man was probably not a resident of Sakai, it is highly likely that Sakai's toimaru followed this same route to control of products in the Kinai market.

On balance, the evidence for Sakai during the period from 1399 to the outbreak of the Ōnin War in 1467 shows that the city grew as a result of the activities of the old toimaru. The basic direction of the city's economy, therefore, was not substantially different from what it had been in the previous century. Sakai remained tied to the estate system and the forwarding of estate rents. Yet there was at least one essential difference. The toimaru were no longer tied to single proprietors as they had been when

---

24. See, for example, "Rikyū Hachiman-Gū," in *SSS*, 1: 306–308; 4: 3–4.
25. *SSSZ*, 1: 350. There were also place names in Sakai containing the term *ichi* (market) in the fifteenth and sixteenth centuries; Kikō Daishuku, "Shoken nichiroku," in Tokyo Daigaku Shiryō Hensanjo, ed., *Dai Nihon kokiroku* (Tokyo, 1964–), 4: 66; *Akuchi Jinja monjo*, in *SSS*, 4: 165.
26. Toyoda Takeshi, *Hōken toshi*, p. 15; idem, "Toshi oyobi za no hattatsu," in Nishioka Toranosuke, ed., *Shin-Nihonshi kōza* (Tokyo, 1947–49), 4: 34–36.
27. See also Wakita Haruko, *Nihon chūsei shōgyō hattatsu shi no kenkyū* (Tokyo, 1969), pp. 325–343, 395–417.
28. Ibid.

they were estate officials. Now they were independent merchants who could devote their commercial facilities to the service of new patrons.

The Ōnin War marked the beginning of a new age for Sakai and put the city on the path toward becoming the leading port in Japan. The war disrupted the power balance in the home provinces, necessitating different configurations of patronage. The most direct event that affected Sakai was that when access to the port of Hyōgo was lost to the Hosokawa, they turned to Sakai as an alternative. This in itself would not have been so significant had it not been for the fact that the Hosokawa house was one of the prime sponsors of Japan's official trade with Ming China. Sakai was consequently drawn into the vortex of the expanding overseas trade of this period.

In 1467, the first year of the Ōnin era, the bakufu dispatched a regular embassy to China from Hyōgo. Of the three ships which comprised the fleet, one was sponsored by the shogunate (*Izumi Maru*, 3000 koku), another by the Hosokawa (*Miya Maru*, 1200 koku), and the third by the Ōuchi (*Tera Maru*, 1800 koku). The envoys left Japan just as the Hosokawa and the Yamana were drawing up their troops for their confrontation in the Ōnin War, and they were alert to possible trouble on the return journey. As the returning ships approached Japan they learned that war had in fact begun and that the Ōuchi had joined the Yamana army against the bakufu and its Hosokawa supporters. Since the Ōuchi controlled the eastern end of the Inland Sea including the port of Hyōgo, the bakufu and Hosokawa ambassadors, fearing capture of their valuable cargoes, decided to avoid the customary Inland Sea route and Hyōgo. Instead, they sailed south past southern Kyushu and Shikoku and landed at Sakai.[29] This event of the year 1469 marked a new epoch in the history of Sakai, for it proved to be the beginning of the city's profitable association with the official Ming trade, and with the military rulers based in Kyoto.

Over the course of the next four decades the bakufu used Sakai as a base for its Ming embassies, even during times when the political rivalries between the Ōuchi, the bakufu, and the Hosokawa had been eased and the Inland Sea route became available again. Altogether three embassies of three ships each sailed from Sakai in 1476, 1483, and 1493. A fourth left in 1506 from Sumiyoshi no Ura immediately to the north of Sakai, and Sakai merchants seem to have been responsible for the outfitting of the Hosokawa ship on that mission.[30] Although this does not on the surface

---

29. Tsuji Zennosuke, comp., *Daijōin jisha zōjiki*, 10 vols. (Tokyo, 1931-34), 4: 321 (hereafter cited as *DJZ*).

30. Kobata Atsushi, *Chūsei Nisshi kōtsū bōeki shi no kenkyū* (Tokyo, 1969), p. 106.

seem like a trade sufficient to transform a city into a major entrepot, it was enough, given Sakai's existing domestic trade, to make the critical difference.

Professor Tanaka describes in the following essay the main characteristics of Japan's official trade with China. Such trade was, in the first instance, "official" in that it was carried out in the guise of official tribute missions to the Chinese court. Missions were headed by an ambassador who bore tribute from the Japanese head of state to the Ming emperor. The sponsoring agency needed legitimacy, and in this context the qualified body was normally the bakufu, its daimyo officers, or their designated deputies, including religious institutions. To ensure legitimacy the Chinese obliged the ambassadors to present books of tallies (*kangō*) that would identify them as official representatives. For this reason and because of the profits involved, each mission was preceded by keen competition for the right to outfit the ships. In the case of the third embassy to sail from Sakai, for example, the principal applicants were the Kenninji and the Sōkokuji among the temples and the Ise, Hosokawa, and Ōuchi families among the daimyo. As with most of the missions of the time, the Hosokawa and the Ōuchi were in the forefront of the competitors, and the Hosokawa secured the rights to operate all three ships.

A second fact that characterized the Ming missions was that their important commercial business was delegated to private individuals. Sponsoring groups, whether bakufu, shugo-daimyo, or temples, relied on their favored merchants to outfit their ships. Thus the Ōuchi tended to use merchants from Hakata while, after the fall of Hyōgo, the Hosokawa used Sakai merchants.[31] Merchants bid for the privilege of outfitting the fleets. In the second Sakai embassy the city's merchants offered the bakufu four thousand kan for the rights to outfit each of the vessels and outbid Hakata, which offered only three thousand.[32] This same mission also provides a detailed illustration of how the merchants shared the huge costs involved. These were distributed among large numbers of merchants who were anxious to go along. Each of them paid a fare of twenty kan plus another twenty kan for each *da* (literally one horse load) of freight. Those with ten da of goods were exempted from paying passage and could take one other person along free of charge. Twenty da of goods entitled one to free passage for himself and two other persons. Though the minimum of forty kan was still a high price, it was low enough to enable many private

31. Ibid., pp. 90–101.
32. Ibid., p. 251. Four thousand kan was an extraordinarily large sum at the time. By comparison, the normal annual rent of Izumi Sakai in this period was 730 kan; "Onryōken nichiroku," in *Dai Nihon Bukkyō zensho*, 131: 1381–1382.

merchants to take part, and therefore capital could be widely mobilized throughout the city and surrounding areas.[33]

In return for their investment private traders could expect sizable rewards. Though lack of documentation prevents a clear accounting of profits, impressionistic evidence suggests that.they were great. On the embassy of 1476, for example, the Chinese at one point offered 38,000 kan for the nontribute articles alone.[34] This amounted to many times the value of the average annual rent shipment that passed through the city.

The Ming trade also provided Sakai with an important new subsidiary role as an international entrepot. The missions took years to outfit and often involved gathering goods from distant areas. The cargo of the first mission, for example, included horses, sulphur, folding fans, screens, agates, swords, and other arms.[35] Such goods were naturally not produced in Sakai but came from Kyoto and elsewhere in Japan. Moreover, many of the goods that were presented to the Chinese were not native to Japan and had to be acquired from other parts of Asia or even Africa. Pepper was a common tribute item that was not produced in Japan, and on at least one occasion the Chinese noted gifts of rhinoceroses and elephants from Japan.[36] Such items were normally acquired from Ryukyu, because it had commercial relations with a number of countries that could supply them. Sakai had to develop significant dealings with other Japanese commercial centers and with the southern islands in its capacity as a staging port for the Ming missions.[37]

Sakai ultimately lost its role as the point of departure of official missions to China, but individual merchants from the port continued their participation in foreign trade into the sixteenth century. After 1510 there were three official embassies from the bakufu to the Ming Court, and all of these were controlled by the Ōuchi family. Therefore, merchants from Hakata, Moji, and other cities in the Ōuchi territories at the western outlet of the Inland Sea took over most of the important places in the tribute ships. But men from Sakai were not completely excluded. The Ikenaga

33. Kobata, pp. 246–247. See also Toyoda, *Sakai*, p. 35.

34. Yi-t'ung Wang, *Official Relations between China and Japan, 1368–1599* (Cambridge, Mass., 1953), p. 69. The total value would amount to several tens of thousands of kan. Kobata, pp. 243–257, gives the best accounting; see also *DJZ*, 9: 38.

35. Tōkyō Daigaku Shiryō Hensanjo, ed., *Dai Nihon shiryō*, series 8, pt. 8 (Tokyo, 1922): 302–305.

36. Wang, p. 94.

37. In 1471, just as Sakai was gathering tribute and merchandise for its first embassy, the bakufu sent an order to the Shimazu of southern Kyushu that noted the increasing frequency of Sakai vessels traveling to Ryukyu and authorized them to turn back any ships without proper credentials and to confiscate any coins on board; *Satsuma kyūki*, in *SSS*, 4: 61–62; Toyoda, *Sakai*, p. 40.

family, in particular, had a close relationship with the Ōuchi as trade agents. As early as 1506 a certain Ikenaga Shuri of Izumi Sakai sailed from Sumiyoshi no Ura on an Ōuchi vessel, and a man of the same name was on the following voyage in the 1520s. Moreover, the number of participants from the city in the last two embassies rose sharply, and among those who have been identified as Sakai merchants were Ikenaga Munetomo, Ikenaga Shinzaemon, and Ikenaga Jirōzaemon.[38] One cannot state with certainty what their part in the missions was, but they seem to have been influential members of the merchant groups that accompanied the Ōuchi embassies. The Ikenaga were particularly mentioned in connection with a council of four that controlled the interests of the Sakai traders on the voyages. In this way the enterprise of its citizens meant that Sakai was able to enjoy the profits of at least a portion of the tally trade until it ended at mid-century.

The importance of these officially sponsored Ming missions can be understood partly in terms of alternatives available to the city, one of which was the traditional role of handling estate rents. As late as the 1540s Sakai still forwarded rent payments for temples in the home provinces. In 1542 an estate in Nagato sent 20 kammon to Daitokuji by way of Sakai, and five years later there was another transfer of 51 kan from Suō to Tōfukuji.[39] But clearly estate rents were dwindling in importance. After the Ōnin War they declined both in number and in the value of individual shipments. Before the outbreak of the war Sakai handled rents as high as 551 kan 500 mon per transaction.[40] None of the rents after the war approached such a figure. Clearly, Sakai no longer could rely on rent shipments for more than a small part of its economic existence.[41]

The most viable alternative to the Ming trade as an economic basis for Sakai was the Kinai (capital region) market itself. By the early decades of the sixteenth century the Kinai region, where daimyo development was relatively retarded, had grown into a unified market in which farmers produced handicraft goods for sale in urban shops. This brought into being a whole series of new towns which served the farmer-craftsman.[42] Sakai benefited from this development. With capital accumulated in trade, its merchants could control production and sale of specialized com-

38. Kobata, pp. 130–131, 261–264.

39. Tōfukuji monjo, in Tōkyō Daigaku Shiryō Hensanjo, ed., Dai Nihon komonjo, Iewake monjo series 20, pt. 2 (Tokyo, 1956): 459–460.

40. Toyoda, Sakai, p. 20.

41. Tōdaiji monjo, in SSS, 4: 186; Temmon nikki, in SSS, 4: 186; Kobayakawa-ke monjo, in Dai Nihon komonjo, Iewake monjo series 11, pt. 2 (Tokyo, 1927): 115–116.

42. For example, Tomita, Ikeda, Itami, Nishinomiya, and Kaizuka. See Wakita, "Chūsei no toshi," p. 223.

modities. Sakai was on the way toward becoming a completely urban city based on a commercial economy. Indeed, as early as 1438 the proprietor of Sakai Minami no Shō had commented that it collected its taxes on the basis of houses, since no farm land remained.[43] Moreover, its population of thirty thousand in the 1530s made it one of the largest urban areas in the entire country. Already the beginnings of urban self-government had been laid with the appearance of the ten-man council of elders, the *egōshū*. Soon the merchant community was to arm itself to the point that it could successfully hold off for considerable time such powerful generals as Oda Nobunaga.

43. "Onryōken nichiroku," pp. 1381–1382.

11

Japan's Relations with Overseas Countries

TANAKA TAKEO
with Robert Sakai

THE EAST ASIAN TRADING COMMUNITY

Japan's foreign relations in the premodern period were greatly influenced by the system of tributary relationships established between China and the lesser members of the East Asian community. According to Chinese theory, the concept of *t'ien hsia* (all under heaven) defined a world in which the many races of mankind were united under the virtuous rule of the *t'ien tzu* (son of heaven, i.e., emperor). The Son of Heaven, legitimized by the Mandate of Heaven, extended his virtue and brought the four corners of the earth under his sway. The rulers of the "four barbarian regions" were expected to request formal relations with the Son of Heaven by presenting their local products, either personally or through representatives, after which the Son of Heaven granted them an audience. These political rites constituted the essence of the ceremony surrounding imperial tribute.

The relationship of dependency concluded between the ruler who presented tribute and the Son of Heaven usually was expressed in terms of familial or personal relationships, although in some instances such relationships were not specified and only the imperial tribute was presented. Tribute-bearing foreign rulers were invested with appropriate titles such as "king" by the Chinese emperor. In return for the tribute goods the Son of Heaven also customarily made a gift of a large quantity of articles, and thus this exchange of tribute for gifts contained the essential characteristics of trade.

Japan's great distance from China, and particularly the difficulty of the sea voyage, strongly influenced Japan's relations with the continent. Although Japanese rulers frequently sent missions to China, the element of tribute did not play an important role. Only in two instances does it

---

This essay is based on the following works by the author: *Chūsei kaigai kōshōshi no kenkyū* (Tokyo, 1959); *Wakō to kangō bōeki* (Tokyo, 1961); "Chūsei kaigai bōeki no seikaku," in *Nihon keizaishi taikei*, ed. Nagahara Keiji (Tokyo, 1965); and "Higashi Ajia tsūkō kikō no seiritsu to tenkai," in *Iwanami kōza: sekai rekishi*, no. 16 (Tokyo, 1970).

appear that Japanese rulers accepted investiture by the emperor of China as "king of Japan." The first occurred in the sixth century during that period of Japanese history known as the era of the "five kings of Wa" (Yamato). The second occurred when the Ashikaga shogun was invested by the Ming emperor. In this second instance it was the shogun, not the emperor, who was so invested. During the Sui and T'ang dynasties, tribute was presented by Japanese envoys to China but no investiture took place. In the tenth and eleventh centuries, it is generally assumed, private trade was carried on without a tribute relationship, although the Sung government looked upon the voyages of Japanese priests to China as a kind of tribute mission. During the Yüan dynasty and in the Ch'ing period prior to the nineteenth century, no official relations between Japan and China existed, and trips were made by private commercial vessels. Thus even during these intervals, thanks to the traffic of persons and commodities, a lively cultural exchange did take place.

The Sino-centric international order also governed the relations among non-Chinese countries. Korea's traditional policy in foreign affairs was to assume an attitude of "barbarian toward the great [i.e., China], interaction with neighbors." In other words, Korea would submit to China, which was a great country, and treat Japan, which was a neighboring country, on a basis of equality. Japan, on the other hand, always considered its neighbor to be one rank beneath itself and tried to deal with Korea as a tributary state. This attitude was a legacy of the ancient period when Japanese had inhabited the state of Mimana at the southern tip of the Korean peninsula and extremely close cultural and political ties had been maintained between Japan and the three kingdoms of Koryŏ, Paekche, and Silla. When the embassy to Silla was discontinued in 799 A.D., Japan's relations with its peninsular neighbor became sporadic, ceasing altogether in the Koguryo period which began in 918. Korea and Japan were once more brought into close, though hostile, contact with each other as a result of the Mongol expeditions of 1274 and 1281 against Japan and the activities of the Wakō. In the Muromachi period, under the supervision of the Sō family of Tsushima, Japan's relations with Korea were reestablished and formalized. The diplomatic institutions thus established survived periods of strain caused by Japanese piracy and even invasion to remain in effect until the middle of the nineteenth century.

The only other country with which Japan maintained overseas relations during the early Muromachi period was Ryukyu, present-day Okinawa. Because so few of the islands were identified in the early historical records, it is impossible to describe the exact nature of Japan's relations with the southwestern archipelago until after the fourteenth century, when Ryukyu became an important participant in East Asian international relations. Following unification of the islands into a kingdom, its king received investiture by the emperor of China, and its ships played an active role in overseas activities, making frequent voyages to the various lands of Southeast Asia, to the China mainland, and to Japan.

THE WAKŌ OF THE FOURTEENTH AND FIFTEENTH CENTURIES

Although at the beginning of the Muromachi period Japan's overseas relations were not extensive, the Mongol invasions had stimulated shipbuilding, and Japanese sailors and traders were increasingly venturing out of the coastal waters of western Japan to conduct a trade that was not regularized and frequently required the use of force. Under these circumstances, trade and piracy became indistinguishable. Thus for many generations the most common form of contact between Japan and the Asian continent was carried out by the Wakō. This was the term applied by the people of Korea and China to piratical groups which presumably originated in Japan and operated along the coasts of the Korean peninsula and the China mainland.

Wakō groups appeared with increasing frequency along the coast of the Korean peninsula from the beginning of the fourteenth century, but only after 1350, when attacks became more regular and violent, did "Wakō" become a fixed concept. In the year 1350 six large raids took place, and thereafter for twenty-five years the records show an average of five a year. Then suddenly between 1376 and 1384 the average rose to over forty a year. Wakō presented the Koryŏ dynasty with one of its most difficult problems. And in the end they were credited with helping to bring the dynasty to its demise.

At first limited to the southern part of the Korean peninsula, the area of Wakō activity broadened in successive years to the neighborhood of Kaegyong, the Koryŏ capital city, and to the coasts of the Yellow Sea and the Japan Sea. What had once been sporadic occurrences in which a few ships sought to trade or forcibly seize goods was transformed into organized raids by well-armed fleets and landing forces. Whereas Wakō fleets initially numbered from several ships to at most several tens of ships, gradually the scale grew so that some raids are recorded to have been made up of as many as 400 ships carrying 3,000 men. Eventually, even the interior areas distant from the coast became subject to Wakō attacks involving cavalry units.

The Wakō active during the fourteenth and fifteenth centuries appear to have been made up mainly of Japanese, although the composition of Wakō bands is by no means certain. In Korea there is a phrase, "Wakō of the three islands." One may surmise that this referred to the Japanese islands of Tsushima and Iki and the region of Matsuura in Hizen. A rugged terrain made a self-sufficient agrarian economy difficult to achieve in these areas, and the inhabitants there may have been forced to seek a livelihood from the sea. Of course, in addition to the "Wakō of the three islands," Japanese pirates of the Inland Sea to the east of Shimonoseki may have joined the attacks on Korea. Furthermore, it is likely that Korean outcasts and other non-Japanese participated in the raids and helped guide the Japanese. There were probably instances also in which Korean people carried out plunder disguised as Japanese, thus expanding the area of so-called Wakō penetration and increasing the attendant destruction.

In pursuit of their primary objective, rice and other cereal grains, the Wakō would first attack the warehouses in which government tax grain was stored and the ships which transported the grain. Easy to find and seize, rice also served as the medium of exchange in the Koryŏ economy. The second objective of Wakō plunder was slaves. Some contemporary records state that over a thousand coastal people were taken at one time. What was done with these people is not at all clear, but there is some evidence that the captives provided cheap labor for agricultural production within Japan.

The Koryo government, weakened both politically and economically, its military forces reduced to impotence by the Mongol occupation from 1231 to 1356, proved unable to keep the Wakō from running rampant. In a resort to diplomacy, envoys were sent to Japan to seek the prohibition of the Wakō. But diplomacy was hardly the answer: at that time it would have been hard to find any power in Japan capable of enforcing such a prohibition.

The Yi government which followed the collapse of the Koryŏ dynasty in 1392 continued the policy initiated in the Koryŏ period of carrying on diplomatic negotiations for the suppression of the Wakō. But it also increased its military forces, strengthened its coastal defenses, and attempted a new policy of conciliating the Wakō. This vigorous new policy produced different reactions among Wakō leaders: some surrendered to Korea, accepted government positions, and received grants of food, clothing, and shelter; some tried to gain legitimacy by becoming the trade representatives of leading daimyo of western Japan or by becoming licensed foreign trade merchants; and some chose to continue their piratical activities with a fresh start in the direction of the China mainland.

Legitimate trade was formalized from time to time with such daimyo as the Ōuchi and Ōtomo, but in the long run it was the Sō of Tsushima who received the favor of the Korean government. Responsibility for supervision of all ships crossing from Japan to China was eventually given to the Sō, who served as the prime intermediaries between Japan and Korea.

ASHIKAGA YOSHIMITSU AND THE MING COURT

An envoy to Japan from the Koryo court approached the Muromachi bakufu in 1366 to request the suppression of the Wakō. The bakufu, although it did not respond to the request, sent the envoy back with horses, mirrors, long swords, and other gifts. Still in its early phase of development, the bakufu possessed neither sufficient power nor authority to suppress the Wakō or to carry on diplomacy with the continent. But its expressions of goodwill extended in a semipublic capacity attested to its strong desire to establish diplomatic relations overseas.

The opportunity to pursue an active foreign policy presented itself in 1368 with the founding of the Ming dynasty. As part of his program to eradicate the influence of the Mongol conquest over China, the Ming emperor T'ai-tsu sought to revive the Sino-centric international order as a basis for foreign relations in East Asia. Accordingly, in 1369 T'ai-tsu dispatched an envoy to Japan (and thence to Champa, Java, and the other countries of Southeast Asia) with a diplomatic message addressed to the "King of Japan" containing two main points: that Japan should enter into the international order in which China occupied the central position and that Japan should suppress the Wakō who were creating disturbances along the China coast. Japan was at the time divided between the Northern and Southern Courts, and it so happened that the Ming envoy, arriving in northern Kyushu at the city of Hakata, found the area under the control of the *Sei-sei shōgun-fu* (Headquarters of the Generalissimo for the Subjugation of Western Japan), an office established by the Southern Court and headed by Imperial Prince Kanenaga. Given the circumstances, Prince Kanenaga could neither accept nor comply with T'ai-tsu's demands. Instead he detained the Ming envoy, executed some of his staff, and refused to conclude diplomatic ties.

Notwithstanding this drastic action, the Ming government sent another envoy to the Sei-sei shōgun-fu in 1370. This time Prince Kanenaga was more conciliatory, and the envoy returned to China with gifts such as horses and with over seventy Chinese men and women who had been captured by the Wakō. After this the Ming government and the Sei-sei shōgun-fu entered into negotiations, though official relations between

Japan and China remained stalled. Prince Kanenaga's letters to the emperor of China were frequently defiantly worded, and Wakō continued to pillage the China coast.

Formal relations between Ming China and Japan were established eventually by Ashikaga Yoshimitsu, who had harbored hopes for diplomatic ties with the Ming for some time. Yoshimitsu had sent envoys to China in 1374 and 1380, but the emperor T'ai-tsu did not recognize Yoshimitsu, refusing to allow diplomatic relations or commerce on the pretext that the form of the diplomatic correspondence was improper. Following the capitulation of the Southern Court in 1392, the Ashikaga shogun emerged clearly as the prime political figure in Japan, the one with whom China would have to deal. Anxious to reopen negotiations with the Ming, Yoshimitsu appointed a mission to China in 1401 headed by the priest Soa as chief envoy and Koetomi, a Hakata merchant, as deputy envoy. The delegation took with them such gifts as gold, horses, paper, folding fans, screens, armor, swords, and inkstone cases along with some Chinese captured by the Wakō. The conciliatory tone of the memorial carried by Soa made a favorable impression on the Chinese, and the delegation returned to Japan the following year accompanied by an envoy from the Ming emperor. The diplomatic document from the Ming emperor referred to Yoshimitsu as "King of Japan," and at the same time Yoshimitsu was presented with the Chinese imperial calendar.

According to diplomatic usage then, acceptance of the Chinese imperial calendar implied that the Chinese year names and dates would be utilized in official documents as an indication that the ruler had come under the sway of the Middle Kingdom. Earlier, when the issue of dependency based on the concept of the imperial calendar had been raised during the negotiations between Prince Kanenaga and the emperor T'ai-tsu, Prince Kanenaga had refused to accept the calendar. Yoshimitsu received the Chinese envoys with great courtesy, however, and accepted designation as "King of Japan." Yoshimitsu's nominal subservience to China aroused opposition within the capital, especially from the court nobility, but his interest in trade profits apparently overrode any misgivings which he himself might have had.

In 1403 another Japanese delegation, led by the Zen priest Kenchū Keimi, headed for China. Kenchū was accompanied by the returning Ming envoy, who bore with him a state letter drafted on behalf of Yoshimitsu by the priest Zekkai Chūshin. The document which Kenchū Keimi presented to the Ming emperor Ch'eng-tsu (Yung-lo), a document congratulating the emperor upon his enthronement and indicating that tribute would be presented, opened with the words, "Your subject, Minamoto, King of Japan." The expressions "King of Japan" and "Your subject" had never before been used in Japan's foreign documents, and their use in this case deviated from Japan's customary diplomatic practice. The emperor Ch'eng-tsu was greatly pleased with the arrival of the Japanese delegation and provided them a warm welcome. He immediately drafted a reply to Yoshimitsu's letter and sent an envoy to Japan in the company of Kenchū.

Ch'eng-tsu's diplomatic document referred to Yoshimitsu as "King of Japan" and stated that a gold seal would be presented. (Such a seal was customarily presented by the Chinese emperor as a token of investiture.) The gold seal, which was said to have been so heavy that it could barely be lifted using both hands, had a tortoise-shaped knob for attaching a cord and bore the inscription, "Seal of the King of Japan." Matching sheets of paper called *kangō,* or tallies, were sent to Japan at this time also.

Following the establishment of this new relationship, the Ming government sent three successive delegations to Japan—in 1405, 1406, and 1407. The first of these missions brought a message of praise from the emperor for the Japanese suppression of Wakō activity, and the letter presented in 1407 commended Yoshimitsu for returning Chinese captives. There were, in addition, gifts of silver and copper coins.

A description of the tally system may be helpful here. *Kangō,* or tallies, provided evidence by which the official tribute ships from Japan were distinguished from the ships of smugglers and pirates. Issued by the Li Pu (Board of Rites and Ceremonies, one of the Six Boards of the Ming government), tallies were produced in series, a new one for each succession of a Ming emperor. Tallies valid between China and Japan were issued six times, namely, in the reigns of Ch'eng-tsu, Hsuan-te, Ching-t'ai, Ch'eng-hua, Hung-chih, and Cheng-te. The two characters for "Nihon" were divided on the matching tallies, one tally being called the "sun" character tally and the other the "origin" character tally. A hundred tallies of each were made, both numbered in sequence. For purposes of comparison two registers for the "sun" character tallies and two registers for the "origin" character tallies were prepared.

When ships left Japan for China, they carried the sequentially numbered "origin" character tallies beginning with number one. At Chekiang and Peking these tallies were checked against the register and notations made on the reverse side of the tally sheet of the quantity of tribute goods brought for the Ming emperor, the articles brought by the chief envoy and his subordinates, the cargo of the merchants aboard the ships, the number of ships, and the number of crew members on the ships. When Ming ships left for Japan, presumably the situation was reversed, but there is no known case in which a Chinese ship carrying "sun" character tallies actually arrived in Japan.

From the time the first tally ship was sent to China in 1404 until the last ship was dispatched in 1547—a period of approximately 150 years—seventeen trips were made with a total of 84 ships making the voyages. There is evidence that, although the Japanese were anxious to send as many ships as possible, the Chinese government was intent on limiting the amount of goods exchanged between the two countries. In the latter half of the fifteenth century the Ming government set maximums of three ships per voyage, three hundred official passengers and crew per ship, and one trip every ten years. As a result the total number of officially recognized ships which made the trip was not large, although profits were immense.

The number of merchants permitted aboard a tally ship depended on its size and the nature of its cargo. Generally speaking, there were 150 to 200, and it seems merchants usually comprised more than half the total number of people on board any given ship, evidence of the fact that the tally ships were very commercial in character.

In the early period most ships sent to China departed from Hyōgo. Although large ships were necessary for the overseas voyage, they were not newly constructed for the purpose. Instead the usual practice was to charter ships according to need. The captains of the ships, the helmsmen, and the sailors for the voyages were hired from various ports along the Inland Sea. The mission which departed for China in 1465 is illustrative. On that occasion three ships were readied. But since their cargoes could not be completely supplied at Hyōgo, they sailed along the Inland Sea taking on copper at Onomichi and sulphur at another coastal port. The ships were not fully outfitted as an official fleet until they arrived at Hakata.

Once preparations were completed at Hakata, ships bound for China went to the Hirado or Goto area (in present-day Nagasaki prefecture) where they awaited seasonal winds. The voyage across the China Seas was made with no other calls along the way, generally in the spring, although occasionally autumn winds had to be used. Since navigational techniques were still in their infancy, it was not a rare occurrence for the ships to wait for over a year for appropriate winds. In one case, a ship that had set out for China became becalmed and had to be towed back.

Landfall was somewhere near Ningpo, and after the fleet entered Ningpo harbor the crewmen were lodged at the Chekiang municipal shipping office. Here the cargo was landed, inspected, and stored in the warehouse. The officials at the municipal shipping office began comparing the tallies and looked after all matters pertaining to the treatment of the delegation of the tribute mission. The tribute goods from Japan as well as the products to be purchased by the Ming government were sent to Peking together with the envoy, except in the case of commodities of large bulk to be purchased by the Ming government, such as sapanwood, red dyestuff, pepper, and copper. Only samples of these commodities were sent ahead to Peking with the embassy, the total shipment being sent later. As time went on these goods were not always sent to Peking but instead disposed of at Nanking.

The delegation had to wait at Ningpo for permission to enter Peking before setting forth for the capital. The number of people permitted to proceed to Peking varied. The mission to China in 1453, for example, consisted of nine ships carrying 1,200 persons of whom only 350 were allowed to continue to Peking. Fearing that delegation members might create disturbances along the way, the Ming government generally limited their number to about 300 during the fifteenth century, and after 1511 the limit was reduced to 50.

Rivers and canals dictated the route of the journey to Peking, and the Ming government assumed complete responsibility for providing the necessary food, coolies, carts, boats, donkeys, and other necessities. At the capital, upon completion of the presentation of the diplomatic document in the name of the "King of Japan" and the offering of the tribute goods, the Japanese envoy was granted an audience by the emperor.

Once the collation of the tallies and other formalities had been completed, attention was turned to trade. For goods relating to the official trade carried on with the Ming government, the price was set at Peking and payment for these goods and the copper coins for the chief envoy and his subordinates were transferred at Nanking. The private trade carried on by the chief envoy and by the merchants took place in Peking too. But private trade could also be carried on along the return route from Peking to Nanking. Upon arrival at Nanking, payment in copper coins was made for the goods sold to the government at Peking. In addition, the Ming government allowed private trade at Ningpo with especially privileged merchants known as *ya hung* (licensed brokers for the sale of goods on commission) of the goods brought by the ship's crew (as distinct from tribute goods).

After completion of the commercial transactions at Ningpo, the official delegation departed from China for the homeward journey, generally retracing the route to Hyōgo. When in the sixteenth century tension between the Hosokawa and Ōuchi houses in Japan turned to violence and made the Inland Sea route too dangerous, the ships used the roundabout course going south of Kyushu and northward around Shikoku to the city of Sakai. As a result, Sakai for a time became the main arrival and departure point for the official fleets to China.

THE LATER TALLY TRADE

Diplomatic relations with the Ming were discontinued by Ashikaga Yoshimochi after his father Yoshimitsu's death. This action apparently dealt a heavy blow to Ming hopes for establishing and maintaining a Sino-centric international order, and for a time the Ming emperor Ch'eng-tsu even contemplated sending troops to attack Japan. But this plan was never carried out. Ch'eng-tsu sent emissaries to Japan in 1417 and again in 1419, hoping to restore friendly relations and to secure Japanese suppression of piracy. Yoshimochi, however, was adamant in rejecting these overtures.

Yoshimochi was succeeded as shogun by his younger brother Yoshinori, who soon resumed amicable relations with China. From the Japanese point of view Yoshinori's diplomacy was something of an improvement over the subservient attitude adopted by Yoshimitsu. But Yoshinori's interest in the political and economic prospects of a renewal of relations with Ming China overcame any repugnance to acceptance of investiture by the Ming emperor. The first envoy sent by Yoshinori to China arrived in 1433. The document carried by this envoy referred to Yoshinori as "Your Japanese subject, Minamoto Yoshinori" and, although the term "King of Japan" was not used, the year period designated on the document was that of the emperor Hsuan-te. The Ming emperor, satisfied with this diplomatic gesture, sent the Japanese delegation back with an envoy carrying an imperial rescript that invested the shogun with the title of "King of Japan." The Ming envoy also brought 100 tally sheets.

During the periods when Yoshimitsu and Yoshimochi were shogun the ships from Japan to China sailed entirely in the name of the bakufu, which was the principal sponsor of the trips. After contact with China had been established by Yoshinori, the bakufu was joined in its sponsorship by various powerful temples and shrines and by some of the shugo daimyo of Japan, as detailed in table 1.

Beginning in the middle of the fifteenth century this traffic dropped off sharply, one reason being restrictions imposed by the Ming government. The nine ships of the tribute mission of 1451 had carried such a large amount of goods that the Chinese were alarmed and, as mentioned earlier, Japanese tribute missions were thereafter limited to one every ten years,

TABLE 1
Summary of Tally Ships

Order of Trip	Year of Departure	Year of Arrival in China	Number of Ships	Sponsorship of Ships
1	1404	1404		Bakufu
2	1405	1405		Bakufu
3	1406	1407	38	Bakufu
4	1408	1408		Bakufu
5	—	1408		Bakufu
6	—	1410		Bakufu
7	1432	1433	5	Bakufu; Sōkokuji; Yamana; ships of thirteen daimyo, temples, and shrines; Sanjūsangendo
8	1434	1435	6	Bakufu; Sōkokuji; Daijōin; Yamana; Sanjūsangendo
9	1451	1453	9	Tenryūji; Ise Hōrakusha; Kyushu Tandai; Ōtomo; Ōuchi; Yamato Tōnomine
10	1465	1468	3	Bakufu; Hosokawa; Ōuchi
11	1476	1477	3	Bakufu; Sōkokuji; Shoman'in
12	1483	1484	3	Bakufu; Dairi
13	1493	1495	3	Hosokawa; Bakufu
14	1506	1511	3	Ōuchi; Hosokawa
15	—	1523	3	Ōuchi
	1520	1523	1	Hosokawa
16	1538	1540	3	Ōuchi
17	1547	1549	4	Ōuchi

with a maximum of three ships per mission and three hundred persons aboard each ship.

Another important reason for the decline in the Japanese-China trade was the political instability in the Japanese islands. The struggle between the Hosokawa and Ōuchi houses, which was to result in the Ōnin War, led to competition between these two houses for trade advantage with China. Thus in 1465 the Hosokawa and Ōuchi had participated jointly with the bakufu to dispatch the tenth tally fleet, but when the fleet returned the Ōnin War had already broken out, and the ships of the opposing Hosokawa and Ōuchi daimyo sailed back separately. By the time of the fourteenth and fifteenth missions in the first quarter of the sixteenth century, the Ōuchi and Hosokawa were engaged in a fierce struggle for possession of tallies and as a consequence sent their fleets independently. The arrival at Ningpo in 1523 of separate Hosokawa and Ōuchi delegations triggered a clash between them, following which members of the Ōuchi mission went on a rampage in Ningpo. The Ming government thereupon closed the Ningpo office. Before relations between Japan and China were completely terminated, two other missions were dispatched as monopolies of the Ōuchi family, who by that time had full control of the Inland Sea. But the Chinese were reluctant to deal with the Japanese, and when the Ōuchi family lost its political influence after 1550 the tally trade came to an end.

We have noted that in the trade between Japan and Ming China there were three types of transaction: tribute exchange, official trade, and private trade. Among the items brought back to Japan from China were first of all the gifts made by the Ming emperor to the shogun in return for the latter's tribute goods. These gifts included silver ingots and, to a lesser extent, high quality silken fabrics, which were given to the shogun and his consort in certain set quantities. In addition the shogun received a large amount of copper coins and a rich variety of special artifacts such as procelain, bronze objects, brocade, and the like.

The copper coins imported from China were of particular importance to the bakufu for, although currency was circulated and exchanged over a wide area of Japan, there was as yet no unified currency, and Chinese coins came to be accepted as the standard currency. The fact that the shogun was the importer of Chinese currency had the same effect as if he were the issuer of the standard currency.

Japanese goods sold in both official and private transactions were paid for by the Chinese with copper coins, silk goods, or hemp. In a later period, the Japanese merchants no longer took all the copper coins back to Japan but rather exchanged some for Chinese commercial products. At times copper coins were even taken out of Japan for the purpose of purchasing Chinese commodities. Private traders began importing, in addition to silk thread and silk fabrics, such goods as cotton, hemp, pharmacopoeia, sugar, ceramic wares, books, calligraphic scrolls, various kinds of copper ware, and lacquer products.

The commodities exported to China included the tribute goods sent by the shogun and the articles taken for official and private trade. Among the tribute goods were horses, sulphur, arms (particularly long swords, armor, and spears), and artistic craft works (inkstones, folding fans, and screens). For the official and private trade the export items were swords, sulphur, copper, sapanwood, and artistic craft goods such as fans, lacquer ware, screens, and inkstones. Sulphur and copper were the major bulk commodities. The mission of 1453 carried a recorded 150,000 catties of copper and 364,000 catties of sulphur as "supplementary articles," that is, for official and private trade.

The export of sulphur and copper was a continuation of an earlier feature of trade between Japan and China, but the dramatic increase in the quantity of swords exported is a special characteristic of this period. At one point, in fact, the Japanese brought 30,000 swords for sale, to the consternation of the Ming authorities. Disagreement over the price which Japanese swords fetched in China became a major source of friction in the latter days of the trade.

Sapanwood, which was grown in the East Indies, was highly valued in China for its qualities as red dyestuff and for medicinal purposes. It became a major item of Japanese export to China, and the 1453 mission carried 106,000 catties of it. In this case, Japan served as a middleman of a rather unusual sort. China had previously engaged in direct trade with countries of the South Seas. The Ming government, however, adopted an isolationist policy which aimed at curbing the activities of piratical groups, such as the Wakō, and at consolidating the government monopoly over foreign trade. The result was that sapanwood, which had once been imported to Japan through China, now entered Japan through Ryukyu and was reexported to China by the Japanese. Thus goods which had formerly flowed from Southeast Asia to China to Japan were routed through a new course which went from Southeast Asia to Ryukyu to Japan and finally to China. This development raises the question of the role of Ryukyu within the East Asian trading community, a subject to which we now turn.

THE RYUKYU KINGDOM AND
ITS OVERSEAS ACTIVITIES

The latter half of the fourteenth century witnessed a burst of maritime activity in East Asian waters, and peoples from the various regions of the southern seas began making visits even to Japan. The trend continued into the fifteenth century as trading opportunities greatly expanded in East Asia due to the Ming prohibition on overseas travel by Chinese merchants. This act opened the waters of the North and South China Seas to other nationalities. The Ryukyu Islands were well placed geographically to take advantage of this situation, and Ryukyu ships began operating overseas on a broad scale in the fifteenth century. After Shō Hashi completed the unification of Ryukyu in 1423, trade between the Ryukyu kingdom and the lands to the south became quite lively. Ryukyu ships navigated to China, Korea, and Japan and southward to

Annam, Siam, Malacca, Sumatra, and Sunda (the northwestern part of Java).

Ryukyu had been involved extensively in the Chinese tribute system from 1350 when King Satto of Chūzan concluded ties of dependency with China. Having no natural resources or indigenous industries, Ryukyu was heavily dependent upon the tribute trade for income. When the Ming government imposed limits on the number and size of tribute missions from Ryukyu in 1472, this was a heavy blow for the island kingdom. Even though the Ryukyu government won an agreement from the Ming in 1507 restoring the original mission per year schedule, Ryukyu authorities decided to abandon the policy of sole reliance for trade on China and instead expanded their overseas activities, which included trade with Japan.

At the beginning of the Muromachi period, envoys from Ryukyu were sent regularly to the bakufu, generally about once every three or four years. In addition to presents for the shogun, their vessels carried scented and medicinal products (such as aloes), sapanwood, *namban* silk, and wines. The latter, originally brought from Southeast Asia, were later obtained from Portuguese and Spanish traders. Another, and very important, item was copper coins from China.

When after the Ōnin War the number of Ryukyu ships sailing to Japan slowly dwindled to zero, the merchants of Hyōgo and Sakai lost their suppliers of pharmacopoeia, spices, and dyestuffs. To deal with this situation the Sakai merchants, who had by now gained the upper hand over the merchants of Hakata, began to finance their own voyages to Ryukyu. Such a step was a serious threat to the financial life of the bakufu, and a bakufu order to the Shimazu in 1471 indicates that the government intended to keep this trade under its own control. The bakufu order warned that, though in recent years many traders had been in the habit of sailing from Sakai to Ryukyu, henceforth such voyages would be prohibited except for ships which carried bakufu permits. In particular, ships which had copper coins on board would be apprehended and returned to the capital area.

In issuing this order the bakufu was obviously relying on the Shimazu daimyo to perform a service on behalf of the bakufu for control of the Ryukyu trade. Shimazu, being the shugo with closest proximity to Ryukyu, had from an early time maintained a special relationship to the islands and attempted to monopolize Ryukyu trade much as the Sō of Tsushima endeavored to monopolize the Korea trade. The Shimazu family claimed that the Ryukyu Islands had been granted to them by the Muromachi bakufu in 1441, even though Ryukyu was never made aware of this. The Ryukyu king had continued to maintain an independent position, though he did send ships on diplomatic missions to the Shimazu bearing congratulations on the occasion of accessions to the headship of the domain or for military victories over neighboring provinces.

In 1508 Shimazu sent a letter to the king of Ryukyu requesting that, henceforth, if any merchant should voyage to the latter's kingdom without a certificate of authorization by the Satsuma government, an investigation should be made and the ship and cargo confiscated. This was clearly an effort to gain recognition for a Shimazu monopoly over the Ryukyu trade. In 1559 a letter from an official of Naha to a Shimazu vassal stated that ships which did not have Shimazu permits would not be allowed to trade, an indication that the monopoly system was in actual operation.

By the start of the sixteenth century, the importance of Ryukyu in the trade of East Asia began to diminish, and by mid-century it had collapsed completely. Failure of the Ming government's policy of curbing overseas travel by Chinese merchants opened the China Seas again to Chinese traders, who by now began to sail directly to the ports of Southeast Asia and Japan. Yet another major change was brought about by the Portuguese occupation of Malacca in 1511. Portuguese ships soon proceeded northward along the China coast and by the 1550s had established direct trade ties with Japan. With these changes controlled trade through government monopoly was no longer possible. A new period of piracy, freebooting, and open trade—a new period of Wakō activity—was in the making. Thus the entrepôt trade so long enjoyed by Ryukyu was taken away by Chinese, European, and Japanese merchants who now sailed at will to China or to the south, leaving the role of Ryukyu merchants in East Asian waters drastically reduced.

JAPAN, KOREA, AND THE SŌ FAMILY

If Japan and China were bound by a tributary relationship in which the Ming emperor appointed the Ashikaga shogun "King of Japan," a much more complicated relationship existed between Japan and Korea. Multiple relationships had been established: between the Korean king and the "King of Japan" (the Ashikaga shogun) and also between the Korean king and certain daimyo and even merchants of Japan. The common denominator in these relationships was that they were all regulated by the Sō family of Tsushima.

Kings T'aejo and T'aejong of the Yi dynasty, whose reigns extended from 1392 to 1418, through their dual policy of conciliation and military defense had succeeded in suppressing the Wakō. Once peaceful relations between Japan and Korea were reestablished, Japanese sailed to Korea in increasing numbers in search of trade, to such an extent that officials along the Korean coast began to complain of the burden which these visits placed upon them. Moreover, the quantity of cotton goods taken out of Korea as a result of the Japanese trade was having an adverse effect upon the economy. Consequently the Korean government decided to limit the number of Japanese admitted to Korea. To enforce this limitation, the Koreans turned to the Sō family of Tsushima, who were ideally placed to do this since all ships from Japan bound for Korea had to pass by Tsushima.

Formal ties between Sō Yorishige, the ruler of Tsushima, and the Korean king were concluded in 1397. Yorishige's successor, Sō Sadashige, continued friendly relations with Korea and exerted himself in suppressing the Wakō. His activities were highly appreciated by the Koreans, who grew anxious after his death over a revival of Wakō activity. Thus in 1419 the Korean government, believing that Tsushima had again become a breeding ground for Wakō, sent a large expeditionary force against the island. The expedition aborted because the landing party retreated in fear of an approaching storm.

Sejong, T'aejong's successor, returned to the policy of diplomacy and conciliation, implementing new institutions for diplomatic and trade relations between Korea and Japan. One was the system whereby the representatives of various Japanese daimyo came under controlled and favored treatment, receiving copper seals from Sejong as proof of diplomatic status. Sejong also reinforced the limited authority that had been delegated to the Sō family by ordering Korean officials to deny port facilities to Japanese ships which did not have a certificate of authorization from the Sō. Also as part of the regularization of Japanese trade, Sejong specified certain ports for trade and as places of residence for foreigners. Elaborate regulations were established for the route to be taken by the emissaries to the capital and for the manner of reception of the diplomats at the court. There were regulations on the size of ships, the number of ships per trip, and the number of trips permitted to each recognized authority in Japan. The Sō received such special privileges as the right to send fifty ships to Korea each year, the right to receive annual supplies of rice and pulse, and the right to send a ship under special conditions. In return, the Sō were expected to give positive support to the policies of Sejong.

Meanwhile the Muromachi bakufu had begun formal relations with Korea in 1397. In 1404, following the shogun's investiture by the Ming emperor, Yoshimitsu sent an envoy to Korea for the first time as representative of the "King of Japan." Some sixty more such envoys were dispatched between then and the mid-sixteenth century. Their missions were to convey messages of good wishes, congratulations, and condolences to the Korean king; to request Buddhist sutras and altar objects; to raise funds for the construction of temples and shrines; to seek Korean mediation in behalf of Japan's efforts to reopen relations with China; and in general to seek profits. Korea reciprocated by sending diplomats and messengers to Japan to return the compliments. Although official relations of this sort were maintained between the Korean king and the Ashikaga shogun, Korean officials perceived that the actual authority of the bakufu did not extend over all of Japan. Thus in actual practice the Koreans relied more directly on the Sō to enforce their trade control measures.

In 1510 Japanese-Korean trade relations were again disrupted. By this time Korea was finding it difficult to meet the Japanese demands for trade. The three ports of Pusan (Fusan), Naeip'o (Naiji), and Yomp'o (Empo) having been opened for Japanese ships and Japanese residents, the Japanese population in these places had increased greatly since the fifteenth century. As pressure for more exchange of goods mounted, these ports became centers for a smuggling traffic which embarrassed the Korean officials responsible for maintaining control. When King Chunjong, ascending the throne at the beginning of the sixteenth century, ordered strict enforcement of the restrictions on Japanese activity, the Japanese residents in Korea joined in a revolt against Korean authorities. Following the incident, all Japanese residents at the three ports were rounded up and sent back to Tsushima, and trade was broken off between the two countries.

After repeated overtures to Chunjong to reconsider his policy, the Sō managed in 1512 to reopen relations with Korea. But the previous terms of trade were reduced by half, resulting in an even tighter Tsushima monopoly over Japan's trade with Korea. Whereas, before, certain daimyo of Kyushu and western Japan had been permitted their own direct relations with the Korean court under Sō superintendence, now only the Sō were permitted to represent the Japanese. The Japan-Korea trade as it developed under these new regulations had certain peculiar features. The Korean economy differed considerably from that of China. Consequently the trade commodities exchanged between Korea and Japan were quite different from those traded between China and Japan. While in the early period of Wakō activity the principal objects of plunder had been government rice and the people residing on the coast, once peaceful relations were established, textiles and Buddhist sutras were the main objects sought by the Japanese, and only Tsushima imported rice and pulse as foodstuff.

The large export of textiles to Japan was closely related to the fact that the fabrics woven in Korea were used as a form of currency. In the Koryo period, hemp had been used as the medium of exchange, but during the Yi dynasty paper currency and copper coins were also manufactured. Because such a specie was not widely accepted, cotton cloth and hemp cloth became the chief media of exchange. This naturally stimulated textile production in Korea. Since cotton cloth was still in short supply in Japan, it was only natural that textiles would become an important commodity in the Japan-Korea trade.

A year by year survey of the goods imported from Korea by Japan shows that at first the major items were tiger skins, leopard skins, fancy matting, hemp, and silk pongee, followed by ginseng, pinon nuts, and honey. After 1423 hemp sloth and silk pongee predominated, and by 1443 cotton cloth, along with hemp and silk pongee, was being imported in large quantities. It is reported that in 1475 Japan imported 27,208 *hiki* of cotton cloth. (The *hiki*, a bolt of cloth about 68 cm. wide and 10.6 m. long, was equivalent to two *tan*, and it was assumed that one *tan* was sufficient to make the apparel for an adult.) By 1476 the import figure had reached 37,421 hiki, rising to an estimated 500,000 hiki in 1486 and a startling 100,000 hiki during the three summer months of 1488 alone. As a result, the Korean government warehouses were so depleted that at one point the country as a whole had a bare 800,000 hiki in storage.

The greater part of this vast quantity of imported textiles was cotton cloth. The Tsushima envoy who was sent to Korea in 1490 stated, when requesting cotton cloth, that silk and hemp cloth were available in Japan but the country had no cotton cloth. Eventually, of course, cotton came to be produced widely in Japan, and the Japanese demand for Korean cotton diminished. With this development the Korean trade lost its critical significance.

Another important import item from Korea was the *Daizōkyō,* the great compendium of Buddhist sutras and commentaries. In the Koryŏ period Buddhism had flourished in the Korean peninsula and the work of printing the *Daizōkyō* was carried on with great vigor. During the Yi dynasty, however, Confucianism was encouraged, and Buddhism, which had previously occupied the position of a state religion, came under attack. Thus it became possible for Japanese to acquire copies of the *Daizōkyō.* The production of the *Daizōkyō* was an immense undertaking. The work was in some 6,000 fasicules and required 80,000 blocks for its printing. When the value of these collections dropped in Korea as a result of anti-Buddhist persecution, they became an appropriate item for export. In the hundred and fifty years from 1389 to 1539 Japan made eighty-three requests for the

Daizōkyō and received forty-three sets. At one time the Japanese even tried to acquire the wood blocks used for printing the work but, predictably, the request was turned down.

Of the Japanese articles exported to Korea, some were produced within Japan and others were merely transshipped. Among the former were copper, sulphur, and other minerals; after the middle of the sixteenth century silver came to be a major item for export. Long swords and folding fans are also recorded as important exports, though not in as large quantities as were shipped to China. Among the items transshipped from Japan were products from Southeast Asia and China—dyestuffs, spices, medicinal materials, ceramic wares—many of which came by way of Ryukyu.

SOME CONCLUDING OBSERVATIONS

The preceding pages have dealt with the diplomatic, cultural, and economic aspects of Japan's relations with the countries of East Asia during the Muromachi period. It seems appropriate to conclude with a discussion of the special nature of what we look upon as the "foreign relations" of this period.

Heretofore the mainstream of research into the history of Japan's foreign relations has been concerned with the growth of trade. This emphasis probably reflects the fact that scholars were influenced by the importance of trade in the establishment of the modern Japanese state. But trade, or to put it more broadly, economics, does not alone suffice to explain the foreign relations of the Muromachi period, for diplomacy and national political conceptions were closely involved. Moreover, although some scholars have discussed the cultural exchange of the period, their interest has been limited largely to one aspect: the travels of Buddhist priests, especially those of the Zen sect. Unless we examine Japan's international relations within the full context of the evolving East Asian order and consider the political, economic, and cultural aspects of this as a single whole, a true understanding will elude us. Viewed in this way, the investiture of Ashikaga Yoshimitsu by the Ming emperor becomes not simply a whimsical or willful act by an upstart military dictator, but rather an important step in the establishment of Japan's position in East Asia. In the history of Japan's foreign relations this was an epoch-making event, not only for what it meant to the other countries of East Asia but for the implications it had for the place of the shogunate within Japan itself.

Secondly, from the origin of the Japanese imperial state in the seventh century, control of diplomacy and foreign relations traditionally had resided with the emperor. Moreover, though Japanese emperors may have conformed to the formalities of presenting tribute, none had acknowledged China as suzerain nor demonstrated dependency by using Chinese year names. The diplomacy of the Muromachi period broke with both of these traditional practices. When Yoshimitsu accepted the title "King of Japan" and began using Ming year names in his diplomatic correspondence, he made his control over diplomatic affairs explicit. This action bespeaks the acquisition of a new increment of political power by the shogun and established the precedent for later military hegemons who assumed control over diplomacy. The Ashikaga exerted a tremendous influence in this respect upon the subsequent governments of Nobunaga, Hideyoshi, and Ieyasu, for each in his way acted the complete monarch in determining Japan's foreign policy.

Yet having made this observation we must make clear that a concept of "national authority" was not yet fully developed. It is still a special characteristic of this period that the various rights associated with diplomacy and trade were held in a private manner, just as political rights were associated with feudal states. With regard to Ming China, diplomatic and trade privileges were shared by the bakufu, the various daimyo such as the Hosokawa and Ōuchi, certain powerful temples and shrines, and even to some extent the merchants of Sakai and Hakata. With respect to Korea, besides the interests of the bakufu and of the various daimyo of western Japan, the Sō family acquired a large monopoly interest. These interests could in turn be divided up into smaller parts among the lord's vassals, just as land was granted in fief by the feudal lords of the time. The same held true with respect to the rights held by the Shimazu in the Ryukyu trade. The concept of absolute national control over foreign relations and foreign trade had yet to be established.

Finally, with respect to trade itself, it is clear that foreign trade had not yet been accepted as a normal and desirable economic activity. Neither China nor Korea looked upon it as a national asset but rather tolerated trade for political reasons. Thus Japanese traders faced unusual difficulties in establishing secure commercial opportunities, and for various lengths of time trade could only be accomplished forcibly or illegally. Trade in the guise of tribute was still the accepted pattern for much of East Asia.

PART FIVE

Cultural Life

While the previous parts of this book have dealt with the political, economic, and social aspects of the Muromachi period, the parts that follow are concerned with the aesthetic and religious life of the Japanese of the fourteenth and fifteenth centuries. By and large, the cultural aspects have received the most attention outside Japan, for these include the much admired artistic achievements of *nō*, *kyōgen*, landscape gardening, tea ceremony, *shoin* architecture, and monochrome painting. It has long been recognized that "Muromachi culture" is one of Japan's most distinguished historical legacies. Yet, as we have already noted, there has been a tendency to treat this legacy as something disembodied from its historical context, as an almost "pure art" phenomenon which happened as if in spite of the main historic currents of the Muromachi age.

There are two primary messages in the essays that follow. The first is that the cultural life of the Japanese of the Muromachi age cannot be looked upon simply as an aristocratic achievement. The Muromachi cultural phenomenon, as we now see it, was much more complex and variegated than ever imagined. Alongside, or underlying, the activities of the aristocracy and high priesthood was an equally important popular culture which reflected the interests and capacities of the common people. Moreover the "great" and "little" traditions were often closely interlocked, as when aristocratic themes were "vulgarized" in popular literature or when members of "base" social strata were picked up as decorators or performers by aristocratic patrons. It has become increasingly apparent that the popular dimension of Muromachi culture is worthy of attention, not only for what it tells us about the lives and thoughts of the common people but for what it reveals about the indigenous roots of many of the elite aesthetic genre.

The second point which these essays make is that Muromachi culture needs to be looked at in the context of the profound changes in political organization and social composition which occurred during the fifteenth and sixteenth centuries. The breakup of the shōen economy and the consequent weakening of the court aristocracy, the adoption of aristocratic ways by the military elite, the acquisition of new freedoms by village communities, the emergence of an independent merchant and tradesman society—all of these changes which have been described in the previous essays had their share of influence on the look of Kyoto and on the composition of the society which gave rise to Muromachi culture in its fullest sense.

In the arts, new centers of wealth and political influence brought into existence new sensibilities, new interests, and new styles. No better illustration of the impact of changing life style on culture can be found than in the essay by Professor Itō which describes how something as concrete as architectural form changed to accommodate the ways of the new military aristocracy. New patterns of patronage led to the involvement of new groups, whether this meant the use of *dōbōshū* by Yoshimitsu or the tremendous popularity of *etoki* and *biwa hōshi* among villagers and townspeople. There were new regional activities as well. As the essays of the first part of this book have demonstrated, decentralization of political power and the growth of trade made for the emergence of regional centers of government and commerce outside the home provinces. Conspicuous cultural achievements were no longer confined to Kyoto or Nara. Artists, poets, and religious leaders traveled widely throughout the country as did the jongleurs who appealed to both townsmen and country villagers. The priest Rennyo was ever on the move between the capital area and Echizen. The poet Sōchō traveled between the capital and the eastern province of Suruga. And daimyo sought to fashion their provincial capitals into "little Kyotos."

Two further observations follow from these major themes. First, much of what was new and creative in the culture of the Muromachi period served as prelude to the art forms which we most closely associate with the Edo period. As Professor Keene suggests, the popular renga style of versification led directly to the perfection of Edo haikai poetry. Professor Rosenfield's description of the more intellectually motivated painting of the fifteenth century shows that it preceded the development of the literati (*bunjin*) style of Edo painting. And as Professor Ruch suggests, Saikaku was prefigured by the *etoki* and Kumano bikuni. Much of what has been considered peculiarly Edo turns out to have been foreshadowed in the Muromachi age. Or to put it another way, it becomes clear that the flowering of a vigorous urban culture in the late seventeenth century can now be explained in terms of a lengthy preparation which started in the Muromachi age.

The second point stems from the first, namely, that one is struck by the essential modernity of many aspects of Muromachi art and thought. This is so not only because many of the art forms perfected during the period have continued as living elements of contemporary Japanese culture, but because the Muromachi expression itself had begun to break away from the highly aristocratic values of the old court society. In *kyōgen* the military aristocracy looked at itself with an objective humor which transcended social class and historic generation. *Shoin* architectural style, which emerged to suit the freer social life of the military aristocracy, possessed the capacity to serve all classes and subsequent generations of Japanese as the basic modular form of house interior. It was during the fifteenth century, as Professor Rosenfield suggests, that the mainstream of Japanese painting moved out of the temple and acquired a purely secular imagery. Or finally, as Professor Ruch believes, the popular jongleurs of the age had begun the creation of a national literature in the modern sense.

The vitality and richness of Muromachi cultural life is such that a comprehensive coverage of its many aspects would require many more studies than can be presented in this book. The following essays have been selected for the new light they can shed on the above mentioned themes. Some familiar subjects such as nō-kyōgen, landscape gardening, and tea, and some unfamiliar ones such as the music of the nō or of the ballad singers have been omitted, either because they are familiar enough or because of lack of space. The main effort in the following essays, as brought out in the description of the "world of Kitayama" by Professor Varley, is to link together our understanding of social change, patronage, and cultural life.

12

Ashikaga Yoshimitsu and the World of Kitayama: Social Change and Shogunal Patronage in Early Muromachi Japan

H. PAUL VARLEY

The Kitayama epoch of the late fourteenth and early fifteenth centuries was one of the great watersheds in Japanese cultural history. For it was around this time that all of the major new artistic and intellectual pursuits that were to flourish in the Muromachi period, becoming in the process key elements of the Japanese cultural tradition, had their origins. It is the aim of this essay to trace the origins and evolution of Kitayama culture within the context of social change in early Muromachi Japan. I will also seek to emphasize the critically important part played by the shogun, Ashikaga Yoshimitsu (1358–1408), not only in creating the "world of Kitayama" but also in setting standards of shogunal patronage of the arts and learning that were to be followed by the Ashikaga shoguns for the remainder of the Muromachi period. Yoshimitsu's historical significance as the most powerful of the Ashikaga shoguns and as the architect of the balance of power between the shogun and the shugo that provided nearly a century of relative stability in this otherwise politically and militarily restless age has been duly noted in Western scholarship. Far less attention has been given to Yoshimitsu as the first great shogunal patron of the arts. In attempting to assess Yoshimitsu in the latter role, we must first seek to analyze the motivations of this complex man.

Yoshimitsu was clearly driven by a exceptionally strong desire to become the complete ruler. The decentralized, feudal conditions of fourteenth century Japan precluded the likelihood or in fact the possibility that anyone, even Yoshimitsu, might assert himself as a truly national autocrat. But within the limitations which political conditions imposed upon shogunal authority, Yoshimitsu became a very powerful man. He utterly dominated the elite society concentrated in Kyoto, which included the imperial family, courtiers, shugo, and prominent ecclesiastics. And, most significantly, he exerted his dominance not only in the political and military spheres but also in the cultural.

There is no reason to question the sincerity of Yoshimitsu's attraction to art for its own sake. At the same time, it is hard to imagine that he was devoted to art simply for its aesthetic reward. Yoshimitsu was first and foremost a political man, and the records show clearly that he sought to enhance or complete his rulership by assuming the mantle of supreme patron of the arts as well as that of warrior hegemon of the country. In Confucian terms, he attempted to merge the *bun* (the cultural) and the *bu* (the military).

Yoshimitsu's assumption of the role of leading patron of the arts was of special importance because he, more than anyone else, was responsible for broadening the formally accepted scope of higher culture in Japan to permit the inclusion within it of the various new art forms, some of them distinctly plebeian in origin, that were evolving at the time. The *kuge,* of course, continued to act as custodians of the Heian court tradition. Although some courtiers came to participate in the new arts of Muromachi, it is quite unlikely that the kuge as a class, conservative and protective of traditional ways as they were, would have been either able or willing to sponsor the kind of cultural diversity that so distinctively marked the Kitayama epoch.

The other feature of Kitayama culture to which Yoshimitsu contributed was its social variety. Participation in the various new trends in art and scholarship of the Kitayama epoch tended to come from two particular groups: first, the courtiers of low rank and people from the lesser social orders who, on the basis of personal talent alone, assumed professional or quasi-professional status as poets, actors, playwrights, arbiters of taste, and the like; and second, priests, particularly those of the Rinzai sect of Zen Buddhism, who lived in the monasteries which clustered on the northern and eastern outskirts of Kyoto. In terms of their respective cultural interests, the first group was devoted largely to advancement of the new indigenous arts of early Muromachi, including *renga, nō,* and *kyōgen,* while the priests, who came to serve as transmitters of a fresh wave of art and learning from China, concerned themselves primarily with such "foreign" pursuits as Chinese poetry, Sung Neo-Confucianism, and monochrome painting. The study of Kitayama culture lends itself logically to an analysis of these two groups, of their activities, and of the patronage they received.

In 1334, a year after Emperor Go-Daigo (1288–1336) began his ill-fated Kemmu Restoration, a list of anonymously composed lampoons was publicly displayed at the intersection of Nijō Avenue and the Kamo riverbed in Kyoto. These celebrated Nijō-Kawara lampoons began: "Among the things commonplace in the capital these days are nighttime attacks, robbers, counterfeit edicts, prisoners, fleet horses [to carry urgent messages], groundless quarrels, severed heads, the shedding of holy robes [on the one hand] and the unauthorized taking of vows [on the other], upstart daimyos . . . wanton battling . . . sychophantic and slanderous priests, and *gekokujō* parvenus."[1] The author or authors of the lampoons went on to comment acidly about such things as the spectacle of boorish eastern warriors aping the ways of courtiers and, conversely, courtiers ineptly pursuing the popular martial games of the bushi. Among the passions of people of all classes were *dengaku* (although it was said that, along with dog fighting, it had caused the downfall of the Kamakura shogunate),[2] tea and incense judging parties, and linked verse. In the composition of linked verse, the lampoons inform us, the vulgar Kamakura and elegant Kyoto styles were freely intermixed, distinctions between hereditary and newly formed renga schools were ignored, and everyone deemed himself qualified to serve as a judge at versing competitions.[3]

The tradition of political and social satire in the form of publicly displayed lampoons dates far back in Japanese history. But it was not until the fourteenth century that lampoonery began to appear conspicuously in the chronicles. Although those posted at Nijō-Kawara in 1334 are the best known, many other lampoons are recorded in the pages of works like the *Taiheiki* and the later wartales of the Muromachi period. This sharp increase in satirical comment represents, among other things, an important index to social change. Societies with rigidly drawn class lines are not apt to give rise to the expression of grievances by means of satire. Rather, it is the advent of social flux and rising expectations among less privileged classes and groups that is most likely to produce derisive witticizing of this sort.[4]

Among the social groups with rising expectations in Kyoto during the restoration period of the 1330s were not only bushi and certain new commercial elements but also middle and lower ranking members of the courtier class. There had always existed a great gap between courtiers of the

---

1. *Kemmu nenkan-ki,* in *Gunsho ruijū,* rev. ed. (Tokyo, 1960), 25: 503 (hereafter cited as *GR*).

2. This attribution has traditionally been made on the basis of the account in the *Taiheiki* of the great passion for dengaku and dog-fighting of the last ruler of the Kamakura shogunate, Hōjō Takatoki. See Gotō Tanji and Kamada Kisaburō, eds., *Taiheiki* (Tokyo, 1960), 1: 161–164.

3. *Kemmu nenkan-ki,* in *GR,* 25: 504.

4. Sakurai Yoshirō has analysed the *Taiheiki* as a product of the spirit of the emergent commercial (*machishū*) class of Kyoto. He believes that the lampoons contained in the *Taiheiki* reveal in particular an antiauthoritarian attitude on the part of townsmen toward both courtier and warrior elites of the country. See "Machishū bunka no senkuteki keitai," in *Chūsei Nihonjin no shii to hyōgen* (Tokyo, 1970).

first three ranks and those below, and no amount of ability on the part of
the latter could truly serve to overcome their birth into families not
hereditarily entitled to ascend above the fourth rank. In earlier times, these
middle and lower ranking courtiers had presumably accepted their fates
with resignation, serving as clients of the higher nobility. But from the
restoration period on some found an important new avenue of advancement opened to them through the offering of their literary and other artistic skills to the new warrior chieftains who flowed into the capital.

To free themselves from the restraints imposed by their inherited social
statuses and thereby to render themselves, so far as possible, classless,
these courtiers often became Buddhist priests by means of the relatively
simple act of *jiyū shukke* (the "unauthorized taking of vows" criticized in the
Nijō-Kawara lampoons). In the literature of the age such priests were
known as *tonseisha* (or *inja*)—those who had retired from the routine activities of everyday life—and they were carefully distinguished from members of the regular Buddhist priesthood. These tonseisha, whose ranks also
included people from the lower classes, usually established no formal ties
with particular temples or sects and in many cases continued to live quite
as they had before taking the tonsure.

The best known tonseisha around the time of the Kemmu Restoration
was Yoshida Kenkō (1283-1350), author of the miscellany, *Tsurezuregusa*.
Kenkō, who took Buddhist vows about 1313, probably wrote *Tsurezuregusa*
from approximately 1319 until 1331.[5] Thus the work gives no specific information about Kenkō's reactions to the radical social changes that occurred in Kyoto after 1333. Nevertheless, *Tsurezuregusa* contains much
lamentation for the passing of the leisured and elegant courtier ways of old
as well as criticism of the *nariagari* (parvenu) or *haikin* (money mad) spirit
of the age. Kenkō was an outspoken antiquarian who acknowledged, "In
all things I yearn for the past. Modern fashions seem to keep on growing
more and more debased."[6] And *Tsurezuregusa* has long been admired as a
kind of textbook dealing with those aspects of etiquette and aesthetic sen-
sibility that were central to the Heïan cultural condition.

It may be perplexing to find Kenkō, who so deplored social upheaval
and cultural debasement, hobnobbing with the new military leaders
following the Ashikaga rise to power in the late 1330s. But the fact is that
Kenkō was a frequent guest at the social affairs of such men as Ashikaga
Takauji, his brother Tadayoshi, Sasaki Dōyo (1306-73), and "upstart
daimyos" like Kō no Moronao.[7] Perhaps Kenkō simply could not resist

5. Kadokawa Genji and Sugiyama Hiroshi, eds., *Nihon bungaku no rekishi* (Tokyo, 1967), 5: 446.
6. Donald Keene, trans., *Essays in Idleness: The Tsurezuregusa of Kenkō* (New York, 1967), p. 23.
7. Kadokawa and Sugiyama, 5: 442.

the lure of the material benefits that association with these warrior chieftains could bring. At the same time, there is the strong likelihood that he was happily surprised to find the new masters of Kyoto to be men who sincerely esteemed the arts, even though their temperaments might incline them toward the ostentatious and flamboyant.

The leaders of the newly founded Ashikaga shogunate were themselves alarmed over what they regarded as a shocking decline in the moral values and behavior of the times. Echoing the sentiments of the Nijō-Kawara lampoons, they piously sermonized in the Kemmu formulary of 1336: "These days people give themselves over entirely to that form of extravagance known as *basara*. One's eyes are dazzled by fashionable attire . . . and by such adornments as finely wrought silver swords. It is indeed madness itself! The wealthy are ever more vain, while the shame of the less fortunate knows no bounds."[8] Moreover, men "are addicted to the pleasures of loose women and engage in gambling. . . . Under the pretext of holding tea parties and poetry competitions, they make great wagers, and their expenses are beyond calculation."[9]

The hyperbolic and outraged tone of these admonitions suggests that the shogunate officials were less concerned with extravagant and dissolute conduct as such than they were with the fact that the wrong kind of people were engaging in it. The Ashikaga shoguns and their higher officials regarded themselves as warrior aristocrats sharing a commonality of class interest with the kuge. Had such "extravagant" conduct been confined, as in the past, to the elite sectors of society, the authors of the Kemmu formulary might not have felt the need officially to speak out so forcefully against it. Their use of the term basara—which bears connotations not only of extravagance but also of blatant vulgarity and even rowdyism—was probably intended primarily to castigate the upsurge of exuberant activity during this age on the part of such people as lower-class bushi retainers, guildsmen, and merchants.

But in other records of the age, including the Nijō-Kawara lampoons and the *Taiheiki*, we find basara applied specifically to the doings of military figures like Sasaki Dōyo. Formerly an official of the Kamakura shogunate, Dōyo had joined forces with Ashikaga Takauji at the time of the overthrow of the Hōjō regime in 1331; he emerged after the middle of the fourteenth century as one of the more prominent shugo. Dōyo, as revealed in the pages of the *Taiheiki*, seems to have been archetypical of many independent-minded bushi chieftains of Muromachi Japan who recognized no authority superior to naked power and the relations generated by it. At the same time, he also appears to have been a man of strong

8. *GR*, 22: 33.   9. Ibid., 22: 34.

artistic proclivities and, indeed, a key figure in the evolution of Kitayama culture.

The *Taiheiki* account of the state of affairs in Kyoto about mid-fourteenth century notes that, whereas kuge were steadily descending into impecunity, buke were "increasing their wealth a hundredfold day by day." The provincially based shugo, now obliged to live in Kyoto, "beginning with Sasaki Dōyo," were especially conspicuous for their frequent and munificent parties. At such gatherings, we are told, seating places were adorned with leopard skins, tiger skins, and precious cloths, while exotic sweets and delicacies, as well as sake, were provided in lavish quantities. *Tōcha* or "tea competitions," then the rage, aroused much excitement among the assembled merrymakers, who made ever higher wagers on successive rounds of competition.[10]

Included among the people at these parties, according to the *Taiheiki*, were not only shugo and their personal guests but also such types as *sarugaku* and *dengaku* performers, courtesans, *shirabyōshi* dancers, and tonseisha.[11] Inasmuch as the last named are lumped together with humble entertainers and are referred to specifically as being "in the company of" or "among the entourage of" the shugo, we may deduce that they were not courtier tonseisha like Yoshida Kenkō. Rather, the tonseisha mentioned in this passage of the *Taiheiki* were the forerunners of the *dōbōshū* or "companions" who were to play an increasingly important role in the cultural activities of the Muromachi period.

There has been much debate among scholars over the origins and character of the class of tonseisha who evolved during the late fourteenth and fifteenth centuries into the dōbōshū and came to serve the Ashikaga shogunate as official "men of culture."[12] On at least two points, however, there is general agreement: virtually all of these tonseisha came from lowly, if not base, social backgrounds and all assumed names that ended with the characters for *ami*. *Ami*—an abbreviation of Amida Butsu—implies that such men were believers in Pure Land Buddhism and particularly in the Jishū or Time sect of Pure Land, since it was the Jishū people who most commonly engaged in the practice of adding *ami* to their religious names. The earliest Muromachi tonseisha of this sort (i.e., incipient dōbōshū) appear indeed to have been followers of Jishū. But it is doubtless incorrect to conclude, therefore, that all subsequent dōbōshū must have been believers in this sect. The use of *ami* in assumed, professional names

10. Gotō and Kamada, *Taiheiki*, 3: 252–253. For a description of the way in which *tōcha* were conducted, see Murai Yasuhiko, *Nihon bunka shōshi* (Tokyo, 1969), pp. 210–213.

11. Gotō and Kamada, 3: 253.

12. Murai Yasuhiko provides an excellent discussion of the origins of the dōbōshū and the major points of dispute concerning them in "Buke bunka to dōbōshū," *Bungaku* 31, no. 1 (1963).

was practiced universally by the dōbōshū from at least the Kitayama epoch. But such usage had by that time become largely formalistic and probably had little to do with the actual religious beliefs or commitments of individual members of the dōbōshū fraternity.[13]

The chronicles record that, from the fourteenth century on, it was the practice of Jishū priests to follow armies into battle in order to tend the dying and the dead. An account of Kusunoki Masashige's tenacious defense of the Chihaya fortification in 1333, for example, states that some two hundred such priests were with the forces of the Kamakura shogunate as they converged on Masashige's position.[14] In addition to offering *nembutsu* salvation to the mortally wounded, these priests gathered and buried the dead and, in some cases, returned their personal effects to widows and families and even gave verbal reports about how they had fought and died. The Jishū priests who thus served with the armies of the fourteenth century were undoubtedly of quite humble social origins. Nevertheless, their status as priests or tonseisha made them, as it did courtiers like Yoshida Kenkō, to some degree classless and certainly more mobile socially than they would otherwise have been.

By the Kitayama epoch, many tonseisha from the lower orders bearing names ending in *ami* had achieved a special position in Muromachi society. They were men, employed by warrior houses, who were expected to perform miscellaneous services that included participation in *renga* parties and tea competitions, the decoration of banquet chambers (*kaisho*), the handling of imported works of art and craftsmanship (*karamono* or "Chinese pieces"), and the running of errands. The conversion of these tonseisha into dōbōshū or bodies of cultural attendants to the shogun, however, had just begun by Kitayama times; not until the Higashiyama epoch did the dōbōshū become a distinct group. Historically the most influential of this type were the celebrated "three ami"—Nōami (1397–1471), Geiami (1431–1485), and Sōami (d. 1525)—who served Yoshimasa as experts in painting, poetry, and Chinese art.

Characteristic of the dōbōshū was the diversity of the services and skills demanded of them. They were not given the luxury of concentrating on only one or two artistic pursuits.[15] Thus it appears that the evolving dōbōshū-type tonseisha of the Kitayama epoch should be clearly distinguished from artists like Kan'ami and Zeami, who earned renown in one field, in this case the nō theater. The latter also assumed ami designations, and very likely they were viewed by the shogun as similar in

13. Ibid., p. 73.
14. Okami Masao and Hayashiya Tatsusaburō, eds., *Nihon bungaku no rekishi* (Tokyo, 1968), 6: 233.
15. Kōsai Tsutomu, "Dōbōshū zakkō," in *Zeami shinkō* (Tokyo, 1962), p. 86.

many respects to dōbōshū. Yet, unlike the latter, they did not become
official functionaries of the Ashikaga shogunate. Kan'ami, Zeami, and
other practitioners of the performing arts were products of special guilds or
za by means of which they retained a significant degree of professional and
artistic independence.

There is a famous passage in the *Taiheiki* dated 1361—the eve of the
Kitayama epoch—that reveals much about how the buke came to use
their tonseisha retainers. The occasion was the fourth (and final) recap-
ture of Kyoto by the forces of the Southern Court from the Ashikaga, who
found themselves temporarily weakened by the defection of one of their
leading commanders. Among those forced to leave the capital with
Ashikaga Takauji was Sasaki Dōyo who, anticipating that a general of the
Southern Court would soon take occupancy of his mansion, decided to
leave it suitably ordered and well provisioned. According to the *Taiheiki*
account, Dōyo

> spread rush matting with boldly emblazoned crests on the floor of the six-bay
> banquet chamber *[kaisho]* and arranged everything in its proper place, from the
> triptych of hanging scrolls to the flower vase, incense burner, tea kettle, and
> server. In the study *[shoin]* he placed a Buddhist verse in grass-writing by Wang
> Hsi-chih and an anthology by Han Yü, while in the sleeping chamber he laid
> silken night-garments beside a pillow of scented aloe wood. He provisioned the
> twelve-bay guardhouse with three poles bearing chickens, rabbits, pheasants,
> and swans and with a three-*koku* cask brimming with sake. Finally, he directed
> two tonseisha to remain behind, giving them precise instructions that "if some-
> one should come to this dwelling, greet him with a cup of wine."[16]

In fact, it was Kusunoki Masanori of the Southern forces who shortly
thereafter took possession of Dōyo's mansion. And so impressed was Masanori with his reception in absentia that, when he himself was forced to
retreat from Kyoto in the face of an Ashikaga counterattack a few weeks
later, he left the guardhouse even more abundantly supplied than he had
found it. In addition, he placed a treasured suit of armor and a silver-
worked sword in the sleeping chamber as personal gifts for Dōyo.[17]

This anecdote of elegant and chivalrous conduct in the midst of a bitter-
ly fought war is especially illuminating. First, it is the earliest account
of the use and studied decoration of a special room or chamber (*kaisho*) in
a private buke mansion that prefigured development of the *shoin*-style of
domestic architecture and interior decoration of Higashiyama times. And
second, it adumbrates what was to become the basic role of the dōbōshū-
type tonseisha in the mid-Muromachi period. Although some of the more

16. Gotō and Kamada, *Taiheiki*, 3: 373–374.   17. Ibid., 3: 374.

famous Higashiyama dōbōshū such as Geiami and Sōami are well remembered for their paintings in ink, their work in landscape gardening, and their putative role in the evolution of the tea ceremony, tonseisha of this kind, whether the retainers of daimyo or the shogun, seem primarily to have been utilized as connoisseurs or men of taste and artistic discrimination. In particular, they were entrusted with the preparations for and supervision of formal receptions and entertainments.

In this passage from the *Taiheiki* we observe the tonseisha of one military lord functioning as servant-hosts for another. Later on dōbōshū and other tonseisha appear conspicuously in the chronicles as attendants during the ceremonial processions (*onari*) of the shoguns to the Kyoto mansions of the leading shugo.[18] The increasing frequency of these processions and the ever greater attention devoted to them were clear indications that, with the decline of Ashikaga governing power, there was a strong tendency toward the ritualization of shogunal rule and buke society. It was precisely in this area that the dōbōshū came to function so prominently.

The early evolution of tonseisha as connoisseurs during the Kitayama epoch was centered mainly on their handling of works of art and articles of craftsmanship imported from the continent. Such Chinese pieces or *karamono*—including paintings, lacquerware, porcelains, tea utensils, and incense burners—had been steadily transported to Japan by merchants following the renewal of semiformal contacts with Sung China in the late Heian period. But it was chiefly under the auspices of Zen priests that karamono were brought over in significant quantity from the mid-Kamakura period on. A century later we find karamono (Sung and Yüan pieces) in great demand in the buke-kuge society of Kyoto. Prominently displayed, they created a highly exotic atmosphere at the social affairs of men like Sasaki Dōyo.

Among the works of art imported to Japan around this time were ink paintings by Mu Ch'i, Liang K'ai, Yu Chien, and others. And so avidly did the Kyoto aristocracy covet these works that they were prepared to pay exorbitant prices for them, a fact which no doubt encouraged both Chinese and Japanese merchants to supply the Kyoto market with paintings of questionable authenticity and even with forgeries. Not until the Higashiyama epoch did the Japanese—particularly the dōbōshū—cultivate a degree of connoisseurship sufficient to discriminate among and to catalog the main corpus of Sung, Yüan, and Ming art that had been brought to their shores during the preceding centuries.[19] This does not

18. Okami and Hayashiya, 6: 166–169.
19. The main catalog of such art is contained in the *Kundaikan sōchō-ki*, a work generally believed

mean, of course, that the Japanese of the Kitayama epoch were totally lacking in discrimination of this sort. Sound judgments were, for example, passed on certain of the more prominent paintings in Yoshimitsu's personal art collection.[20]

One new challenge presented by karamono was how to display them to best advantage for the appreciation of viewers. Although the Japanese had of course long been knowledgeable in the studied placement of Buddhist statuary and other icons for purposes of religious celebration, they had heretofore done their main forms of secular art either on dwelling fixtures or articles of household utility, such as sliding doors and folding screens, or on horizontal hand-scrolls that were kept in storage when not being viewed. The new impulse to display such karamono as vertical hanging scrolls and porcelain pieces was a crucial factor in the eventual creation by the Higashiyama epoch of the *shoin*-style room with its characteristic alcove (*tokonoma*) and *chigaidana* shelves. This phenomenon is the subject of Professor Itō's essay below.

As noted at the outset of this study, the other groups of special participants in Kitayama culture were priests of the monasteries which flourished in the environs of Kyoto. Among them the activities of the Zen priesthood were particularly important. One aspect of Zen that made it especially appealing to the buke rulers of Japan was the capacity of its priesthood to serve as bearers of a new wave of cultural influence from China. Buddhism had declined precipitously in China after the persecutions to which it was subjected in late T'ang times. Zen was the only organized sect that managed to survive as an influential force in Chinese life, and during the Sung dynasty Zen even came to enjoy considerable patronage at the imperial court and among the literati class in general. Hence, when the Japanese of the late Heian period began once again to look admiringly to China and Chinese culture, they were inevitably attracted to Zen.

Among the founders of the "new sects" of Kamakura Buddhism and their followers, only those who embraced Zen were motivated to journey to China for inspiration and study. It was largely for this reason that members of the Zen priesthood came to play a prominent role not only in the importation of Chinese culture to Japan but also in trade and general

---

to have been undertaken by Nōami and completed by his grandson, Sōami. Text will be found in *GR*, section 361.19.

20. Yoshimitsu used two seals bearing his Buddhist names Tensan and Dōyū respectively to place the imprint of ownership on his paintings. Selection of the Tensan seal was apparently intended to indicate that a picture was judged to be of more superior quality than those imprinted with the Dōyū seal. See Okada Yuzuru, "Karamono e no keitō," in *Ami to machishū*, ed. Hayashiya Tatsusaburō and Okada Yuzuru (Tokyo, 1969), p. 124.

intercourse with China during the medieval age. At the same time that Japanese traveled to China in quest of religious training, Chinese Zen priests came to Japan. Two of the more distinguished of these foreign clerics were Rankei Dōryū (1213–1278) and Mugaku Sogen (1226–1286), founders of Kenchōji and Engakuji of Kamakura. Through the extension of patronage to such men, the buke rulers of Kamakura sought both to increase their knowledge of Zen and to enhance the cultural atmosphere of their new military capital in the eastern provinces.

Still another Chinese Zen master to come to Japan in the closing years of the Kamakura period was Issan Ichinei (1247–1317). After a period of residence in Kamakura, Issan moved to Kyoto, where he became head abbot of Nanzenji and converted the former emperor Go-Uda (1267–1324), among others, to Zen. Issan thus contributed to the shift in the center of Zen influence from Kamakura to Kyoto that occurred about this time.

But the person who played the most important role in promoting Zen among both kuge and buke leaders in Kyoto during the first half of the fourteenth century was the Rinzai priest Musō Soseki (1275–1351). Musō, who was from the eastern province of Kai, had studied both Kegon and Shingon Buddhism before entering the Zen priesthood, and he became one of a growing number of Japanese devotees whose Zen was liberally infused with esoteric thinking and practice. As Professor Akamatsu's essay in this volume suggests, this intermingling of Zen with esotericism (mikkyō) was in part a natural result of the syncretic inclinations of the Japanese in the religious realm.[21] In addition it also served to make Zen more readily acceptable to the Kyoto courtiers. Beyond this, the mixing of Zen and esotericism may be viewed as a manifestation of the cultural and social symbiosis that evolved between buke and kuge in the early fourteenth century.

It is within the context of the crucial role of the Zen priesthood in bringing together—and to a considerable extent helping to meld—the buke and kuge elites of Kyoto that we must view the importance of Musō Soseki, for Musō was highly instrumental in shaping the course of Zen in Muromachi Japan. Quite apart from his manifest persuasiveness as a religious leader, Musō was an exceptionally astute politician. For example, after an earlier, almost peripatetic life of journeying about the country, he was several times recalled to Kamakura in the waning years of the shogunate. But Musō saw clearly that the trend of history was running

---

21. There are in fact certain particularly striking similarities, observable even to the non-specialist, between mikkyō and Zen. Both, for instance, assert that Buddhahood or enlightenment is attainable in this life, and both stress the practice of direct, secretive transmission of their doctrines. For further remarks concerning these similarities, see Ōsumi Kazuo, "Nairan-ki no bunka," in Iwanami kōza: Nihon rekishi (Tokyo, 1963), 6: 200. See also the essay by Professors Akamatsu and Yampolsky below.

against the Hōjō regime. He therefore willingly accepted the invitation of
Emperor Go-Daigo in 1325 to become head abbot of the prestigious
Nanzenji in Kyoto, a temple closely associated with the imperial family.
Musō was obliged to return to Kamakura the following year, but upon the
overthrow of the Hōjō in 1333 he resumed his duties at Nanzenji, once
again at the personal request of Go-Daigo, who was now the architect of a
triumphant Imperial Restoration.

When the Ashikaga abruptly terminated Go-Daigo's restoration in
1336, Musō retired quietly to a temple in the outskirts of Kyoto. But
before long he was summoned from his self-imposed "retirement" to the
presence of the Ashikaga brothers, Takauji and Tadayoshi, where he
received their patronage. Thus he secured the backing to make his school
of Zen the dominant one under the Ashikaga shogunate. Musō's particular style of Zen practice and his influence over the establishment of the
gozan system of Zen monastic organization is described more fully in the
essay below by Professors Akamatsu and Yampolsky and need not be
elaborated here, since our concern is primarily with the cultural role of the
Zen priesthood.

The two prime cultural and intellectual achievements of *gozan* priests of
the Kitayama epoch outside the religious realm were in the field of Neo-
Confucianism and what has been labeled "gozan literature." The first
subject is made difficult of study in part by a scarcity of primary evidence.
It is also complicated by the fact that Japanese Zen priests often obscured
the character of Confucianism by seeking either to demonstrate its in-
feriority to Buddhism or to utilize it as merely an introductory discipline
to the higher study of Buddhism. Actually, this handling of Neo-
Confucianism by the Zen priests of medieval Japan was a direct outgrowth
of the philosophical and religious attitudes that came to surround both
Zen and Confucianism in China during the course of the evolution of Neo-
Confucianism in the late T'ang and Sung periods. Neo-Confucianism
became a highly syncretic product which contained much that was Buddhist, and particularly Zen. But, despite their extensive incorporation
of Buddhist thought, the Neo-Confucianists of China attacked Buddhism
itself as an alien and harmful creed. The Buddhists, in turn, counter-
attacked by asserting the superiority of their religious beliefs to the newly
developed tenets of Neo-Confucianism. It was the spirit of this desire on
the part of Buddhists to meet or overcome the competition, so to speak, of
Neo-Confucianism that was transferred by Zen priests to the Japanese setting during the medieval period.

The first books on Sung Neo-Confucianism to reach Japan appear to
have been brought from China in 1241 by the returning Japanese Zen

priest Enni (1202–1280).[22] From at least the mid-thirteenth century on, therefore, Neo-Confucian writings were directly accessible to the Japanese. But, apart from the fulminations of certain priestly successors to Enni over its anti-Buddhistic bias, Neo-Confucianism seems to have attracted little serious interest or independent study in late Kamakura Japan.

There are references in the diary of the ex-emperor Hanazono (1297–1348) to the fashion for Sung Confucian ideas among certain ministers at court in the years leading to Go-Daigo's Kemmu Restoration, but again we have almost no way of knowing how sophisticated these ministers really were in their understanding of Neo-Confucianism.[23] If Hanazono's experience is any criterion, Confucian studies at the Kyoto court in the early decades of the fourteenth century were still predominantly of a traditional kind, and it is unlikely that Go-Daigo's ministers could have had much opportunity to receive serious training in Neo-Confucianism from others. Hanazono himself was of a very studious bent and was wide-ranging in his scholarly interests. Yet his readings in Confucianism were mostly confined to the classics as they were recognized in pre-Sung times. Hanazono, moreover, was clearly skeptical in his personal feelings about the possible merits of the Sung Confucian synthesis. Increasingly drawn toward Zen, he was concerned about the potentially detrimental effects of mixing Buddhism and Confucianism.[24]

The first major figure of the Muromachi period to acquire an unquestionably high level of knowledge about Neo-Confucianism was the priest Gidō (1334–1388). A native of Tosa and a disciple of Musō Soseki, Gidō spent more than twenty years among the gozan temples of Kamakura before being personally summoned in 1380 by Yoshimitsu to Kyoto. Appointed to serve as the head abbot of Kenninji, Gidō was expected also to be available to instruct the young shogun in both Confucianism and Zen.

Yoshimitsu had already begun reading such primary Confucian texts as the *Analects* and the *Mencius* under the direction of scholars from the imperial court, including Sugawara Yoshikata and Higashibōnojō Hidenaga.[25] Working with Gidō from 1380 on, Yoshimitsu also undertook study of the remaining two works—the *Doctrine of the Mean* and the *Great Learning*—of the Neo-Confucian classical canon of "four books." One day, dur-

---

22. Wajima Yoshio, *Chūsei no Jugaku* (Tokyo, 1965), pp. 67–68.

23. Hanazono's journal is virtually the only source for information about this subject; ibid., pp. 100–111.

24. *Hanazono Tennō shinki*, in *Shiryō taisei* (Kyoto, 1965), 2: 299–300.

25. Usui Nobuyoshi, *Ashikaga Yoshimitsu* (Tokyo, 1960), p. 202. The two families traditionally most noted at court for their Confucian scholarship were the Sugawara and the Kiyowara.

ing a discussion of the *Mencius,* Yoshimitsu queried Gidō about apparent discrepancies in comments on this work contained in the lectures of the courtier scholars. It was at this point that Gidō explained to Yoshimitsu the distinction between the "old" and the "new" forms of Confucianism and between their variant interpretations of ancient texts.[26] Yet even while thus enlightening his student about such a critical Confucian distinction, Gidō was preparing to shift Yoshimitsu's attention more fully to Zen as the ultimate source of truth. And indeed, in 1382, he stopped discussing Confucianism altogether and urged Yoshimitsu to intensify his practice of Zen meditation.[27] To Gidō, Confucianism was of value as a means for learning the art of practical rulership; otherwise he considered it useful merely as an introductory discipline in opening the way to Zen.

The extent to which Yoshimitsu became devoted to Zen during this period of his life is perhaps best illustrated by the events surrounding an excursion he led in the tenth month of 1382 to view the maple leaves at Saihōji in southwestern Kyoto.[28] Among the priests, courtiers, and military chieftains who accompanied him were Gidō, the imperial regent Nijō Yoshimoto, and the shogunal deputy Shiba Yoshimasa. After a light repast, the group entered into a party of versification in both Japanese and Chinese. But before long Yoshimitsu withdrew from the party and, changing into holy robes, retired by himself to meditate. Sometime after nightfall he summoned Gidō and had him talk about his former master and the founder of Saihōji, Musō Soseki, about Musō's death, and about the priestly line he had founded. And even after all the other guests had returned to their homes or private apartments, Yoshimitsu remained into the small hours of the following morning at Saihōji to practice alone his Zen austerities.

In addition to his high standing as a Zen cleric and scholar of Confucianism, Gidō also came to be regarded, along with Zekkai Chūshin (1336–1405), as a dominant figure in the field of gozan literature. It is somewhat ironic that this should be so, since he, perhaps more than any other member of the gozan priesthood, forcefully admonished his colleagues to resist the tendency to secularize Zen and to become excessively immersed in the pleasures of pure literature.

Dedicated to the quest for enlightenment through direct perception of the truth of human existence, Zen by its very nature eschewed use of the written word—that is, scriptural exegesis—and stressed instead transmis-

26. Gidō Shūshin, *Kūge nichiyō kufū ryakushū,* ed. Tsuji Zennosuke (Tokyo, 1939), p. 147. An account of the relationship between Gidō and Yoshimitsu may be found in George Sansom, *A History of Japan, 1334–1615* (Stanford, 1961), pp. 161–166.
27. "Gidō ni tsuite," in *Kūge nichiyō kufū ryakushū,* p. 20.
28. This excursion is recounted in Usui, *Ashikaga Yoshimitsu,* pp. 207–210.

sion of its beliefs from person to person or from master to disciple. In actual practice, of course, it was virtually impossible for the adherents of Zen, even with their strongly "antitextual" bias, to resist the use of writing to pass on the essentials of their creed, and even before the Sung period in China it had become accepted practice among Zen priests to compile the sayings and experiences of their masters in the form of "analects" (in Japanese, *goroku*) and also to assemble anthologies of admired parables and allegories.[29]

To this was added an interest in poetry. During the Sung period certain branches or subsects of Zen began to flourish among the literati at the Chinese imperial court. One important result of this was an extensive Zen secular literature, much of it in the form of poetry. This literature, in turn, was conveyed to Japan. The person usually credited with initiating these forms of Zen literary activity in Japan was the Chinese Zen priest Issan Ichinei. But there were many Japanese monks as well who perfected their capacity to write Chinese either in China or Japan. Stimulated and enriched by the writings of such luminaries as Kokan Shiren (1278–1346),[30] Gidō, and Zekkai, gozan literature reached its zenith of excellence in the Kitayama epoch. The most popular form of this literature was Chinese poetry, although the gozan priests of Japan also compiled goroku and geju, kept personal diaries, and even ventured to compose prose miscellanies in Chinese. There is little doubt that the erudition and cosmopolitan cultural elegance of the gozan litterateurs were much admired by the other participants in the world of Kitayama. At the same time, it is hard to escape the feeling that gozan literature remained something of an incongruity in Muromachi Japan, an alien pastime that stood apart and could never truly be ingested by the Japanese. After the age of Yoshimitsu, gozan literature declined steadily in both quality and range of appeal.

Although Yoshimitsu did not assume full control of the political powers of the Ashikaga shogunate until the end of the 1370s, he had already amply demonstrated certain personal preferences in the realm of art and a penchant for the pomp and glamor of courtier life. In 1374, for example, he attended his first performance of *sarugaku* (partly at the urging of Sasaki Dōyo).[31] He had promptly extended the patronage to Kan'ami and Zeami

29. A good, concise discussion of these and other documentary and literary forms used by Chinese Zen priests may be found in Tamamura Takeji, *Gozan bungaku* (Tokyo, 1966), pp. 107–147.

30. Kokan Shiren is best remembered as the author of *Genkō shakusho*, a history of Buddhism (with the main emphasis on its introduction to and development in Japan) completed in 1322.

31. Sasaki Dōyo and the tonseisha Ebina Nan'ami appear to have been the ones chiefly responsible for arousing Yoshimitsu's interest in sarugaku. Before 1374, Ashikaga chieftains had

that enabled them to transform sarugaku into nō. Earlier buke leaders, from the Hōjō on, had enjoyed sarugaku's companion form of theatre, *dengaku*. But there is no evidence that any of these buke leaders envisioned the possibility of dengaku's being shaped into something more than an essentially diversionary (and probably not quite proper) kind of entertainment. Thus Yoshimitsu's extension of patronage to sarugaku and the opportunity this presented for the development of nō must be regarded as epochal in the cultural history of Japan.[32]

Yoshimitsu's aspirations to live the life of the courtier were manifested at an early age. Following his designation as shogun in 1368, he became the recipient of appointments from the imperial court to ever higher ranks and offices. As a result, he had by 1380 reached (at age twenty-two) the highest rung in the ladder of the court ranking system, junior first rank (*jū-ichii*).[33] He had also advanced rapidly in the hierarchy of courtier offices. In 1381 he was appointed Great Minister of the Center (*naidaijin*), in 1382 Great Minister of the Left (*sadaijin*), and finally in 1394 Chancellor (*daijō daijin*). He thus became only the second buke leader (Taira Kiyomori was the first) to hold the exalted position of Chancellor at court.

But Yoshimitsu's penetration of the world of the kuge was not limited to the acquisition of court ranks and offices. Having taken as his wife Hino Nariko, member of a prominent courtier family, he gained special entry at court.[34] In visits to the court from 1378 on he was invariably accompanied by entourages that included ministers from such preeminent kuge families as the Kujō, Nijō, and Konoe.[35] Before long Yoshimitsu also began to use a kuge-style cipher or signature (*kaō*). At first he reserved this for written communications to courtier and religious institutions, but eventually he abandoned his buke *kaō* entirely and affixed the kuge cipher to all of his official documents.

To provide an appropriate physical setting for the role he was fashioning for himself as the grand overlord of both kuge and buke, Yoshimitsu in 1378 had a munificent shogunal palace constructed in the Muromachi section of northwestern Kyoto. Called the *hana no gosho* or "Palace of

attended only the theatrical performances of dengaku. See Okami and Hayashiya, *Nihon bungaku no rekishi*, 6: 179.

32. The best study of nō in English is Donald Keene, *Nō: The Classical Theatre of Japan* (Tokyo, 1966).

33. The rank of senior first grade (*jō-ichii*) was only bestowed posthumously.

34. The Hino were descended from the northern branch of the Fujiwara and had for generations served as Confucian scholars and waka poets at court. The first and second Ashikaga shoguns, Takauji and Yoshiakira, had married into buke families, the Akabashi and the Shibukawa.

35. Usui, *Ashikaga Yoshimitsu*, p. 37.

Flowers" because of its profusion of blossoming plants and trees (a number of the finest specimens of which were "donated" by kuge from the gardens of their own mansions), it was by all accounts a fitting monument to Yoshimitsu's burgeoning political and social aspirations.

Yoshimitsu had for several years been receiving instruction from Nijō Yoshimoto in the manners, ceremonies, and other traditional courtier accomplishments. With this background in kuge training he had Yoshimoto in 1381 arrange a formal visit or procession to the Palace of Flowers by Emperor Go-En'yū (1358–1393) and a party of courtier attendants. Over the course of some six days, Yoshimitsu and his illustrious guests enjoyed a carefully planned round of entertainment, including music, dancing, *waka* poetizing, football, and boating. And on the day of his departure the Emperor issued a special decree bestowing promotions in courtier rank upon Yoshimitsu's mother and wife and upon other ladies and ministers closely associated with the shogun. The entire occasion could hardly have proceeded more auspiciously for Yoshimitsu, fulfilling his ostensible aims of having the Palace of Flowers imperially sanctified as a new center for the meeting of kuge and buke and, beyond that, of confirming his own courtier status in intimately social as well as strictly formal terms.

Although thus obliged to be a party to Yoshimitsu's quest for ever greater influence and prestige in Kyoto society, Go-En'yū was by no means pleased with the relationship that had evolved between him and the shogun. In 1382, the year after his visit to the Palace of Flowers, Go-En'yū (who was exactly the same age as Yoshimitsu) abdicated in favor of his five-year-old son Go-Komatsu (1377-1433) and opened an office of the ex-emperor (In-no-chō). Yoshimitsu thereupon had Nijō Yoshimoto, his frequent companion and mentor in the kuge arts, appointed regent for Go-Komatsu. He himself assumed the position of chief administrator in Go-En'yū's office of the ex-emperor. The northern branch of the imperial family and the Kyoto kuge class as a whole were now completely under Yoshimitsu's control, and henceforth no one at court could dare oppose him. Even the assignment of kuge ranks and offices—most of them by this time were ornaments of social status—could not be made without Yoshimitsu's approval.

The personal frustration experienced by Go-En'yū over this course of events that had brought the court aristocracy to a state of utter subservience to the shogun was manifested in 1383 in an outburst of passionate anger against one of his favorite concubines, Azechi no Tsubone, whom he suspected of having had intimate relations with Yoshimitsu. So distraught and fearful was the ex-emperor in the aftermath of this outburst that he is even believed to have contemplated suicide; and for a while thereafter rumors persisted that the shogun was planning to send Go-En'yū into exile.[36]

At the same time that he was forcing the members of the Northern Court to accept his will in all matters, Yoshimitsu was also laying plans to strengthen the hegemony, geographically limited though it was, of the Ashikaga shogunate. From about 1385 on he undertook a series of journeys into the provinces, most of them for the ostensible purpose of visiting religious institutions and famous sites but also quite clearly to observe the power alignments among his shugo subordinates and any remaining backers of the Southern Court. Owing in part to the strategic assessments and arrangements he made while on these journeys, Yoshimitsu was able to deal successfully with the uprisings of the Toki and Yamana families in 1390 and 1391, and in 1392 to bring about a reunion of the Northern and Southern Courts. With these triumphs to his credit, Yoshimitsu in 1394 transferred the office of shogun to his young son Yoshimochi (1386-1428) and took for himself the civil title of Chancellor.

Yet Yoshimitsu seems not to have been satisfied with the unique eminence he had achieved by this time. It appears that he desired to transcend all remaining limits imposed by birth and to assume a social and ritual status second to none in the land. Accordingly, in 1395, he took Buddhist vows—tacitly obliging many leading kuge and buke to do likewise—and began openly to follow the life style and ways of an ex-emperor. His construction two years later in the Kitayama suburbs of northern Kyoto of the elegant kinkaku or Golden Pavilion and a private mansion in obvious imitation of the palace of the ex-emperor was simply one of the more conspicuous of Yoshimitsu's gestures to impress upon one and all the extraordinary degree of influence he had actually achieved within the courtier-warrior aristocracy of his age.

Since the Golden Pavilion remains today the most striking physical reminder of the age of Yoshimitsu, it seems fitting to enquire further into its attributes—both architectural and aesthetic—in the hope of making clearer some of the more dominant aspects of the spirit and tastes of the Kitayama epoch of Japanese culture. Yoshimitsu acquired the property for his Kitayama estate from the Saionji, a branch family of the Fujiwara that had exercised great influence at court during the Kamakura period. In 1224 Saionji Kintsune (1171-1244) constructed on these grounds the Saionji temple (from which his family took its surname) and a complex of residential buildings for himself and his descendants.[37] But, owing to a

36. Ibid., pp. 50–52.
37. The construction and layout of the Saionji temple and estate by Kintsune is described in Part Five ("Uchino no Yuki") of the *Masukagami*.

decline in family fortunes after the overthrow of the Kamakura shogunate,[38] the Kitayama estate fell into disrepair in the late fourteenth
century. Yoshimitsu refurbished and converted to his use many of the
older Saionji family buildings on the Kitayama grounds during the course
of construction of his own estate over a period of some ten years, from 1397
until 1407. After Yoshimitsu's death, the newly refurbished Kitayama estate was designated the Rokuonji temple of the Zen sect. As a result of
warefare, looting, and natural calamity over the years, none of the
buildings survived into modern times except the famous Golden Pavilion,
which was itself put to the flame by a demented acolyte in 1950.

A lack of primary documents makes it impossible to reconstruct or even
to envision with any real clarity the layout of the Kitayama estate in
Yoshimitsu's day. We know that the first important structure Yoshimitsu
built at Kitayama was the *minami gosho* or "Southern Palace" to which he
moved in 1398 and which later became the formal dwelling place of his
wife, Hino Yasuko.[39] Yoshimitsu's own personal residence, the *kita gosho* or
"Northern Palace," was finally completed in 1407.

Among the many other structures that came to comprise Yoshimitsu's
sprawling Kitayama estate was still a third palace built for Lady Suken-
mon'in, the mother of Go-En'yū and the grandmother of Go-Komatsu.
All of these palaces were built in the traditional *shinden* style of courtier
architecture, with the most important of the three, the Northern Palace,
situated in appropriate relationship to the Kyōkochi, a large pond with ar-
tificial islands, jutting rocks, and a lovely background of mountains and
slender, towering pines. Kyōkochi Pond was the central element in the formal garden originally constructed by the Saionji during the Kamakura
period and has probably retained its shape and appearance without
significant alteration through the ages. The only structure adorning it today is the rebuilt Golden Pavilion, which stands alone on the northern
bank of Kyōkochi Pond. Formally designated as a *shariden*, or reliquary, of
the Rokuonji temple, the Golden Pavilion is an extremely light, almost
fragile looking edifice. And so exquisite does it appear in its "natural" setting, it is difficult to imagine that in a former age the Golden Pavilion was
simply one of a cluster of buildings that constituted the seat of the most
powerful military ruler of the country.

Despite its modest size, the Golden Pavilion is both a masterpiece of

---

38. Saionji Kimmune (1310–1335) was executed as a result of his participation in a plot to
reestablish the military power of the Hōjō.
39. Yoshimitsu's principal consort was Hino Nariko. But Nariko had by this time lost the favor
of the former shogun and it was her niece, Yasuko, whom Yoshimitsu installed as his "wife" in
the Southern Palace at Kitayama.

architectural design and an invaluable historical record of the evolving aesthetic tastes and cultural values of the Kitayama epoch. Whereas the *shinden*-style palaces that Yoshimitsu erected at Kitayama attested to the continuing use by buke of the traditional form of courtier architecture, the Golden Pavilion is striking evidence of the incorporation or adoption of newer styles to a building that was also originally intended for residential use.

The Golden Pavilion is a three-story structure with a short, covered passageway extending outward from its western side into the Kyōkochi Pond. Its first two floors are rectangular in shape and are done essentially in the shinden manner. But the third floor, which is square and much smaller in size, has features such as bell-shaped windows and "Chinese" doors *(karado)* that clearly link it to new architectural features most closely associated with Zen Buddhist temples.[40] Apart from its interest to architectural historians, the Golden Pavilion suggests much about the changing patterns of socializing and cultural activity in Yoshimitsu's age. Its slender wooden pillars, low ceilings, and gently sloping roofs endow it with a feeling of intimacy unlike the earlier homes or informal meeting places of Japan's kuge and buke elites.[41]

Kitayama culture in general has often been said to possess the qualities of "elegance and sensuous beauty" *(yūga enrei)*. In the vocabulary of the Kitayama age, the two terms that together probably best connoted these qualities were *basara* and *yūgen*. We have seen that *basara* was loosely used in the early years of the Muromachi period to describe a wide spectrum of exuberant, extravagant, and even vulgar social behavior on the part of people ranging from newly affluent merchants to prominent military leaders. By the Kitayama epoch, however, the term *basara* seems to have been tempered to mean essentially a love of things exotic (particularly foreign objects of art) and a kind of showy elegance such as Yoshimitsu presumably sought to capture in his Kitayama estate.

Yūgen, on the other hand, is an aesthetic term (written with the characters for "indistinct" and "unfathomable") that conveys an aura of mysteriousness. The highest expression of yūgen was achieved in the *nō* theater. Although fashioned by commoners under buke patronage,

---

40. Before its destruction in 1950, the first floor of the kinkaku, called the *hosuiin,* contained a statue of Amida with his attendant bodhisattvas (Amida *sanzon*), a wooden likeness of Yoshimitsu in priestly robes, and a portrait of Musō Soseki. The second floor or *chōonkaku* contained a statue of Kannon and was apparently used on occasion for socializing purposes, especially for viewing the Kyōkochi Pond. The third floor *(kukyōchō)* was a Zen sanctuary in which there was installed a plaque with an inscription in the hand of Emperor Go-Komatsu.

41. Takeda Goichi, "Rokuonji Kinkaku no kenchiku," in Shigaku Chirigaku Dōkōkai, *Muromachi jidai no kenkyū* (Kyoto, 1937), pp. 151–184.

nō—based as it was on a sense of high refinement and on a "visuality" of resplendent color harmonies—represented, in content and style as well as aesthetic values, an extension or advancement of primarily kuge culture. Little imagination is required to see in the Golden Pavilion both the basara spirit and the yūgen aesthetic of Kitayama times. Moreover, as a structural amalgam of courtier shinden and Zen temple architecture, the Golden Pavilion is a reminder of the transitional characteristics of Kitayama culture.

Emperor Go-Komatsu visited Yoshimitsu at his Kitayama estate in 1408 for twenty days of gala entertainment.[42] Still a young man in his twenties, Go-Komatsu had for many years been treated by Yoshimitsu as virtually an adopted son, and his procession to Kitayama on this occasion was surrounded by much the same aura as that of the ceremonial visits traditionally made by emperors to the residences of former sovereigns. It was also on this occasion that Yoshimitsu formally introduced to Kyoto society his fourteen-year-old son Yoshitsugu, whom he doted upon and whom he seems openly to have envisioned elevating to a position comparable to that of imperial prince and perhaps even successor to the throne itself.

Within little more than a month, however, Yoshimitsu died suddenly of illness at the still vigorous age of fifty. He may well have been on the verge of claiming the imperial succession for his own progeny. And so compelling had his presence and aspirations been that the imperial court, in its first reaction to the shock of his death, was even moved to bestow posthumously upon him the title of *daijō hōō* or "priestly retired emperor." This unprecedented act was prevented by Yoshimochi, who strongly resented his father for the greater love he gave Yoshitsugu and who, with the backing of the former shogunal regent Shiba Yoshimasa, moved swiftly now to secure real power in the shogunate.

Yoshimitsu was a unique personality, and no one could have hoped to succeed truly to the position he had attained. The political and military balance over which he presided between shogun and shugo ultimately deteriorated after his death and finally collapsed in the Ōnin War. While Yoshimitsu reached a pinnacle of power and prestige that most of the later Ashikaga shoguns could not realistically aspire to, he bequeathed to his successors a new and vital heritage of what might be called the cultural (as distinct from the strictly "legal") right to rule. This does not mean that all the shoguns who followed Yoshimitsu attempted to emulate precisely his

---

42. A quite detailed account of Go-Komatsu's visit to the Kitayama estate may be found in the *Kitayama Gyōkō-ki*, written by the imperial regent Fujiwara Tsunetsugu, who was in attendance upon Go-Komatsu.

role as the high lord of kuge-buke society, much less his apparent pretensions to imperial status. But they were the leaders now of a true warrior aristocracy and not merely military hegemons obliged to pay respectful obeisance to the cultural (and possibly ethical) superiority of the kuge. Regardless of how effectively they were able to exercise the purely administrative authority of their office of "barbarian subduing generalissimo," the Ashikaga shoguns—like leading members of the kuge ruling class before them—possessed the patrician right to patronize and even to set the standards for the arts and learning. For this reason, it may properly be said that Yoshimitsu's age of Kitayama brought about the final transition from courtier to warrior rule in premodern Japan.

13

The Unity of the Three Creeds: A Theme in Japanese Ink Painting of the Fifteenth Century

JOHN M. ROSENFIELD

During the lifetime of Yoshimasa, the eighth Ashikaga shogun, Japanese ink painting (*suibokuga*) became a coherent, fully mature pictorial language in both artistic and social terms.[1] Despite its foreign origins, this art form had reached the point where it could express the basic cultural values of the leaders of Japanese society. Members of the Ashikaga family were enthusiastic collectors and patrons of painting; Yoshimochi, the fourth shogun, was himself an accomplished artist. Ink painting was seriously practiced in several ranking Zen monasteries of Kyoto and Kamakura, and the taste for ink painting was adopted by provincial samurai and monks. By the 1450s paintings of eloquence, subtlety, and high technical proficiency were being executed by men under the tutelage of the Sōkokuji monk Tenshō Shūbun, who is thought to have served Yoshimasa as *goyō eshi*, or official court painter.

Ink painting was also closely related to other forms of expression in a broad but unified cultural movement that had appealed to the Japanese intelligentsia from the thirteenth century onward. The unity of this movement has been widely recognized by scholars and its parts well defined, but to my knowledge the only overall name it has been given is *gozan bunka* (*gozan* culture), or *gozan bungei* (*gozan* art), which is not entirely satisfactory. It deserves a name as broad and meaningful as the term "Renaissance" in Western history, for it was equally inclusive and equally consistent intellectually. It was also equally enduring, for it flourished despite the civil wars of the sixteenth century as one of the most central features of Japanese civilization. The scope of this movement ranged from

---

1. Two introductory books have appeared recently in English: Tanaka Ichimatsu, *Japanese Ink Painting: Shūbun to Sesshū*, The Heibonsha Survey of Japanese Art (Tokyo, 1972); and Matsushita Takaaki, *Ink Painting*, The Arts of Japan (Tokyo, 1974), vol. 7. See also Jon Carter Covell, *Under the Seal of Sesshū* (New York, 1941).

philosophic speculation to the shape of the implements of daily life; it included state symbolism, architecture, garden design, painting, calligraphy, essays and poetry, the establishment and spread of the Zen Buddhist community, the nō drama, the tea ceremony and flower arrangement, and the collection and manufacture of ceramic ware.

Although ink painting was only one part of this larger complex, it reflected almost all the other parts, and its symbolic content was extremely varied. Its iconic motifs came from traditional Mahayana Buddhist art, Zen Buddhist traditions, Confucian and Taoist legends, Chinese nature poetry, and Japanese poetic traditions. Despite this diversity in subject matter, the vast majority of ink paintings and their inscriptions prior to the 1470s were made by Zen Buddhist monks. Whether true to the severe monastic discipline, as most were, or monks in name only, these painters expressed in their works values that were not exclusively those of Zen Buddhism but were part of the broader gozan cultural matrix of which Zen itself was a part.

The meanings of Japanese ink painting, as in any other pictorial language, were conveyed in two different ways: symbolically through the verbal content of the subjects depicted (often reinforced by poems and comments written on the paintings themselves) and nonverbally through the nuances of expression imparted by the artist's choice and handling of his materials. I should like in this essay to focus on the former, the symbolic or verbal content, without denying the importance of the purely visual dimension.

It is not yet possible to make a complete iconological review of all themes of Japanese *suibokuga;* this would demand the labor of several lifetimes. As a test case, however, I will explore here fifteenth-century examples of one major theme that appears steadily throughout the history of Sino-Japanese ink painting well into the modern era, that of the Unity of the Three Creeds—Buddhism, Confucianism, and Taoism.[2] This test case will suggest some of the nuances of meaning possessed by paintings of the Higashiyama era, some of the historical perspectives of the Kyoto artists, their awareness of Chinese painting and poetry, and something of the matrix of consciousness from which their perception of art emerged.

As is true for other didactic motifs in suibokuga, we begin to grasp the conceptual meaning of the Three Creeds theme only after analyzing many examples and after considering its historic origins. Even then, the student

---

2. The importance of the theme is noted by Matsushita, pp. 47–53. See also Haga Kōshirō, *Chūsei Zenrin no gakumon oyobi bungaku ni kansuru kenkyū* (Tokyo, 1956). My essay has also made extensive use of Uemura Kankō, "On Viscount Suematsu's Study in the Thought of the Three Religions," *Kokka,* nos. 338, 340, 341 (July, September, October 1918).

must inevitably contend with a certain amount of uncertainty. Inscriptions on paintings are often difficult to decipher accurately and then to translate and interpret in English. They often contain puns, with double and triple meanings, or references to obscure Chinese poems. Inscriptions recorded in gozan literary texts were sometimes inaccurately copied; whole stanzas have been lost or a single character altered enough to distort the meaning of an entire poem. In addition, the verbal content of paintings of the Unity of the Three Creeds was often intentionally obscure. Such themes were heavily tinged with irony, contradiction, and paradox. They depended on the use of metaphor and, above all, incompleteness, obliging the observer to form his own conclusions to an unfinished chain of thought or to complete in his imagination a picture that is undetailed and indefinite. One does not find in suibokuga the hieratic and strictly logical symbolic system of a Buddhist mandala or a French Gothic cathedral façade; the symbols in suibokuga are often indirect, understated, or purposely concealed. Nonetheless, the symbolism was meant to be understood.

Despite such interpretive difficulties, the theme of the Unity of the Three Creeds is particularly important because it expresses a point of view that pervades the entire gozan aesthetic system. The paintings on this theme express the principle of the fundamental unity of man, nature, and society and of political-ethical, religious, and artistic concerns. It is a principle that dissolves the boundaries between the sacred and the profane, the self and the nonself, the animate and the inanimate, the beautiful and the ugly, between social classes and between nations. The principle of the transcendental oneness or identity of all things has ancient roots in the metaphysics of both Mahayana Buddhism and Taoism; but, as in many other elements of the Muromachi cultural movement, this old notion is given new and effective application.

The paintings on the theme of unity illustrate yet another important feature of Muromachi art, and that is its secularism. During the fifteenth century, the mainstream of Japanese painting was finally and conclusively freed from its subservience to traditional Buddhist art. The appearance of a truly secular imagery in suibokuga—birds, animals, flowers, topographic landscapes, Confucian and Taoist figures—marked the final fading away as a major creative art form of the international tradition of hieratic painting that had flourished since the introduction of Buddhism to Japan. This is a great watershed, a point of demarcation in Japanese cultural history remarkably similar to that in the West between the arts of the Renaissance and those of Medieval Christianity from which they emerged.

Finally, the paintings on the theme of unity give evidence of the appearance in the Higashiyama period of the ideology of the Chinese *wen-jen* or *literati* tradition. The ideal of the wen-jen, an ancient one in Chinese civilization, was that of the amateur of the arts whose pursuit of personal cultivation must be free from all external compulsion. The model wen-jen would be a man with a private income or a political sinecure, who was poet and painter, antiquarian and collector, living simply and informally in a rural setting, treasuring above all the circle of his friends—their warm comradeship in walking trips, drinking parties, and poetic gatherings —avoiding involvement in political and social affairs. Despite the long prevalence of the wen-jen ideal, it did not produce a distinct school of painting in China until the fifteenth century and the emergence of such men as Shen Chou (1427–1509) and Wen Cheng-ming (1470–1559). Not only did these painters consciously pursue the life style of the literati, they also developed a pictorial style that was a scholarly review of modes of the past done often with a simplicity and artlessness that sustained their pose as amateurs. In Japan the wen-jen movement became an organized, articulate force devoted to the literati style of painting only in the mid- and late-Edo period, when it nurtured such giant talents as Yosa Buson, Ike no Taiga, or Uragami Gyokudō. Nonetheless the ideal gained currency and had a palpable influence in the fifteenth century, as an analysis of the emblems of the Unity of the Three Creeds will show.

THE THREE LAUGHERS OF THE TIGER RAVINE

The concept of the Unity of the Three Creeds was symbolized in painting by three motifs so closely related that, on occasion, they cannot be distinguished one from the other: the Three Laughers of the Tiger Ravine, the Men of the Three Creeds Tasting Vinegar, and the Patriarchs of the Three Creeds. The most familiar of the emblems is that of the Three Laughers, illustrated in this essay by an inscribed painting of the second half of the fifteenth century (see figure 2 below). As an allegory set in circumstances remote from fifteenth-century Kyoto, its main figures were famous in ancient Chinese cultural history: the Buddhist monk Hui-yüan (334–416), the poet T'ao Yüan-ming (ca. 365–427), and the Taoist scholar and wonder-worker Lu Hsiu-ching (ca 406–477). Their biographies were well known to the Japanese monks of the Muromachi period, and we must familiarize ourselves with certain details in order to understand their symbolic value.

Hui-yüan was born in northern Shansi and given a sound education in both Confucian and Taoist classics.[3] At the age of twenty-one, he heard

3. Tsukamoto Zenryū, in *Eion kenkyū*, ed. Kimura Eiichi (Kyoto, 1962), 2: 3–87; *Kao seng-chüan: Taishō shinshū daizōkyō*, 6: 357.3–361.2 (or pp. 240 ff. in the English translation by E. Zurcher, *The Buddhist Conquest of China* [Leiden, 1959]).

the celebrated Buddhist theologian Tao-an expound the doctrine of Perfection of Wisdom. He was so deeply impressed that he declared Confucianism, Taoism, and other schools of philosophy to be no more than chaff and became Tao-an's disciple. In 373, Hui-yuan established himself south of the Yangtze on Mount Lu. Remaining in his Hermitage of the Eastern Grove, he exerted a strong personal influence on the spread of Mahayana Buddhism in South China. Once established at Mount Lu, Hui-yüan lived strictly by the monastic regulations. His official biography states that during the more than thirty years in which he lived there his shadow never left the mountain; his steps never reentered the profane world. When seeing off guests or taking a walk, he would make the Tiger Ravine the limit beyond which he would not go.

T'ao Yüan-ming (T'ao Chien) was born into a gentry family of Kiukiang south of the Yangtze.[4] Although his family had fallen onto hard times, he was educated in the Six Classics and entered official service. But he soon retired to live as a farmer, refusing to have further dealings with officialdom. He proclaimed that his instinct was all for freedom; he would tolerate no discipline or restraint. He would rather endure hardship, hunger, and cold than do things against his will. "Whenever I have been involved in official life," he once wrote, "I was mortgaging myself to my mouth and belly." As a poet-recluse, he lived a simple life near the southern slopes of Mount Lu, cultivating his fields and his favorite flower, the yellow chrysanthemum. He was a contemporary of Hui-yüan; however there is no record of the two men having met.

T'ao Yüan-ming's poetry, in its simplicity and straightforward style, was a source of inspiration to later Chinese literati. It was also long known and studied in Japan. Of the three men depicted in the Three Laughers paintings, T'ao was probably the most familiar to Japanese, assuming something of the role of prototype for the literati ideal. An example of his prominence in Japanese gozan circles is a handsome painting of the poet standing in profile before his chrysanthemums; it was inscribed in 1425 by a distinguished monk Ishō Tokugan (1365–1434) who extols T'ao's detachment from the political world (figure 1).[5]

The third of the Three Laughers was a pioneer in compiling the canon of Taoist religious texts and in organizing its doctrines.[6] Lu Hsiu-ching, a native of Wu-hsing in Chekiang province, learned Taoist fortunetelling and prognostication at an early age. Becoming a mountain-dwelling ascetic, he visited famous mountain retreats in search of Taoist texts and in

---

4. James Hightower, *The Poetry of T'ao Chien* (Oxford, 1970).
5. Matsushita Takaaki, *Muromachi suibokuga* (Tokyo, 1960), pls. 22–23. Ishō Tokugan, a prolific writer, was a member of the Rinzai sect who lived in Nanzenji and Tenryūji in Kyoto. The shogun Yoshimochi invited him to lecture at Sōkokuji.
6. Kimura, *Eion kenkyū*, 2: 384–433.

210

FIGURE 1.
T'ao Yuan-ming.
Inscribed in 1425
by Ishō Tokugan.

424–425 sold medicines from village to village. Finally, in 453, he set up a simple, solitary retreat at Mount Lu near a waterfall. Lu was noted as an eloquent opponent of Buddhism.

In its simplest form, the allegory of the Three Laughers tells that one evening, after T'ao and Lu had visited Hui-yüan in his hermitage on Mount Lu, the monk walked with them as they were returning home.[7] Lost in conversation, Hui-yüan inadvertently crossed the bridge over the Tiger Ravine and at that moment a tiger roared. Suddenly realizing that Hui-yüan's vow had been broken, the three burst into laughter. In paintings of the theme, Hui-yüan is often shown wearing the patchwork robe of

7. The historical basis of the legend is explored carefully by Nawa Ritei, *Geibun* 15, no. 5 (1922).

a Buddhist monk, T'ao Yüan-ming a leopard-skin cape, and Lu Hsiu-ching a tiny cap. On occasions, a servant boy is shown watching the event.

The legend of the Three Laughers seems to have been accepted as a truthful account in 1072 by a court official, Ch'en Shun-yu, in his *Record of Mount Lu (Lu-shan-chi)* and thereafter passed quickly into general currency. The oldest record of a painting of the theme dates from approximately the same time. The Sung poet Su Tung-p'o (1036–1101) wrote an inscription on a painting of the theme found on the walls of a villa of his patron Ou-yang Hsiu (1007–1072). The painting, long since lost, was attributed to the eccentric master Shih-k'o, active at the end of the tenth century.[8] Su Tung-p'o's inscription may be translated:

> They three
>   are sages;
> In gaining the concept
>   words are forgotten.
> Instead they utter
>   a stifled laugh
> In their pleasure
>   and innocence.
> Ah! this small boy
>   watches them
> As the deer
>   watches the monkey.
>
> You! What do
>   any of you know?
> Your very laughter
>   fills the world.
> What is despicable?
>   What is admirable?
> Each laugh
>   is that laugh.
> One cannot know
>   which of you is superior.

Su Tung-p'o and his circle of eminent friends around the beginning of the twelfth century were the most specific point of origin for the subsequent Japanese imagery of the Three Laughers. This may be seen in another

8. Shih K'o was a satirical painter originally from Ch'eng-tu and active around 965 in K'ai-feng. A master of the *i-p'in* (untrammeled) style, he loved to shock and disturb his audience through his paintings. See Oswald Siren, *Chinese Painting* (New York, 1965), 1: 160–165; and Shimada Shūjirō, *Bijutsu kenkyū*, no. 161 (1950). The latter was translated by James Cahill and appeared in *Oriental Art* 7, no. 2 (1961): 66–74; 8, no. 3 (1962): 130–137; 10, no. 1 (1964): 19–26.

early example of the theme, a poem from Su Tung-p'o's close friend
Huang Ting-chien (1045–1105). Composed in 1102, this poem was based
on an earlier one by the famous Ch'an monk and painter Ch'an-yüeh of
the late T'ang–early Five Dynasties period, who lived for many years in
the Hermitage of the Eastern Grove on Mount Lu. Huang began with an
explanatory preface in prose, then quoted Ch'an-yueh's verse:

> The monk Hui-yüan, dwelling on the slopes of Mount Lu, observed the rules of
> pure asceticism and fanatically refused the honeyed water which might have
> saved his life. However, when composing poems, he would turn to wine and
> drink with T'ao Yüan-ming. When he bade farewell to his guests, whether they
> were high or low in rank, he would not cross the Tiger Ravine. However, when
> accompanying Lu Hsiu-ching, the Taoist sage, he went a hundred steps beyond
> and, giving a great laugh, then parted from him. Ch'an-yüeh's poem went as
> follows:

> > Being fond of T'ao the Senior Official,
> >   he drunkenly plodded onward;
> > Bidding farewell to Lu the Taoist
> >   he tottered at a snail's pace,
> > And crossed the Ravine to buy wine,
> >   breaking all his solemn precepts.
> > What kind of person is the monk
> >   who would do such a thing?

> Whereupon I [Huang Ting-chien] have written the following imitation:

> > When greeting T'ao Yüan-ming
> >   he would take a cup of wine;
> > When bidding farewell to Lu Hsiu-ching
> >   he crossed the Tiger Ravine;
> > His heart, which held all learning,
> >   was pure like a mirror.
> > That of the ordinary man, drunk
> >   on the things of this world, is like dirt.[9]

Antecedent to this theme of unity, of course, had been centuries of competition between the three creeds in China, a vast topic outside the scope
of this essay. The Confucians, for example, had long complained that
Buddhism was a foreign creed based on legends that were irrational, extravagant, and unverifiable; that its monasteries took men out of service to
society; that it was hostile to orderly government and the system of family-
state loyalty. Attempts to minimize or reconcile points of difference were

9. *Kō Sankoku*, in Kurata Junnosuke, ed., *Kanshi taikei* (Tokyo, 1967), 24: 217–219.

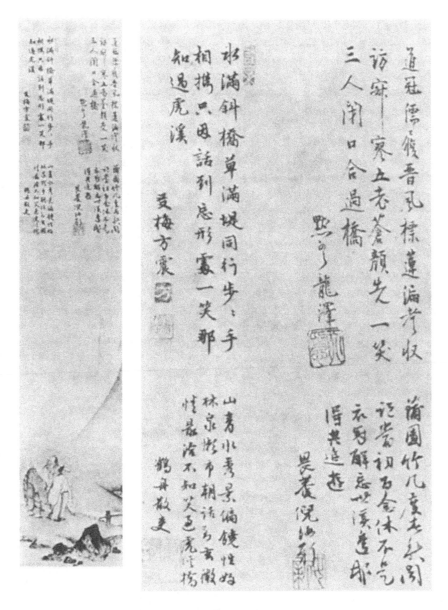

FIGURE 2. The Three Laughers of the Tiger Ravine, ca. 1500, and detail of inscription. Courtesy of Asano Collection, Tokyo.

made again and again. In the mid-T'ang period, especially in Ch'an Buddhist circles, doctrines of the equivalence of the three creeds became fashionable and thus served as a background for the enthusiasm shown for the idea by the Northern Sung literati. But always in the background of this theme was the harsh historical fact that Buddhism had been persecuted repeatedly in China; especially damaging was the suppression of 845 by the Emperor Wu-tsung, who was inspired in this by Taoists.

Japanese Buddhists were well aware of this conflict, but neither Confucianism nor Taoism had the authenticity and status in Japan that they possessed in China. Arguments about the relative merits of the creeds were secondhand reflections of an issue that was much more serious on the mainland. Moreover, by the fifteenth century the argument had subtly changed in character. While traces of the earlier religious disputes may be seen in the later poems and paintings, the three creeds had come to be subordinated to a higher principle, namely, the ideology of the Chinese literati. It is this principle which is particularly evident in the Japanese examples of the Muromachi era.

Dating no later than 1492 is the painting of the Three Laughers reproduced in figure 2.[10] Although the painter's name is unknown, his style is close to the Oguri school which had emerged from the circle of Tensho Shūbun. Above the painting are four poems that were added at presumably the same time in a formal gathering or ceremony. Each poem comments on the theme of the painting and adds a twist to its meaning. The upper right corner, normally the place of most prominence, is here occupied by an inscription by Moku'un Ryūtaku,[11] a well-known figure in gozan literary circles:

> A man in a Taoist hat,
>   a man in Confucian shoes
>   in the style of Chin;[a]
> As the lotus clock marks
>   the passing hours,[b]
>   the old ones gather to visit
>   at the lonely hermitage.
> Near Wu-lao Peak[c]
>   the monk's wizened face
>   is the first to break out
>   in laughter.
> The three men together,
>   saying nothing of it,
>   together cross the bridge.

[a] The Eastern Chin dynasty, 317–420.
[b] A water clock made of lotus leaves, devised on Mount Lu by Hui-yao, a disciple of Hui-yüan.
[c] One of the southern peaks of Mount Lu.

10. *Kokka,* no. 385 (1922).
11. Moku'un Ryūtaku was a native of Harima who came to Kyoto at the age of ten, became an active scholar, and lived for a long period at Kenninji. He was a prolific poet, and his inscriptions are found on many paintings of the last two decades of the fifteenth century.

The second poem is by Yubai Hōshin, a monk not recorded among major gozan figures:

> Water rushing under
>   the makeshift bridge;
>   the embankment choked
>   with weeds;
> Walking together
>   step by step,
>   leading each other
>   by the hand.
> Discussing things
>   of deepest profundity,
>   and forgetting
>   all formalities, [a]
> Then they laugh,
>   realizing that
>   they have crossed
>   the Tiger Ravine.

The third inscription (lower right), the most difficult to translate, was written by a monk with the unusual name Ian Geijoshin:

> Seated meditating
>   on a mat of rush,[b]
>   leaning against
>   an arm-rest of bamboo,
>   they have passed the seasons
>   in self-cultivation.
> But from the moment
>   they hear
>   each other speak
>   all anxieties cease.
> When wearing
>   their formal garb
>   they had not understood
>   unworldliness.[c]
> Past the boundary
>   marked by the Ravine
>   they are able
>   to continue their ramble.

---

[a] A Taoist phrase indicating the point where one no longer recognizes distinctions in experience.
[b] A circular mat used in Buddhist monasteries when sitting in meditation.
[c] Literally "forget the world," that is, of daily affairs and formalities, routine and obligation.

The last poem is by an unidentified man, perhaps a Chinese, who
signed his name Kakushū Sanri:

> On the verdant mountain
>   with sparkling streams,
>   the vista opening
>   richly to one side;
> By natural inclination
>   they prefer secluded woods and springs,
>   and cannot abide the vexations
>   of official life.
> Their conversation reaches
>   profound subtlety;
>   their sentiments attain
>   the utmost harmony.
> Without knowing it,
>   and in laughter,
>   they cross the bridge
>   at the Tiger Ravine.

It will be noted that these inscriptions contain a willful contradiction. The
poem of Moku'un states that Hui-yüan intentionally violated his vow and
laughed before he crossed the bridge. The second and fourth poems
describe the men crossing the bridge unwittingly. But on a more fundamental issue all poems are in agreement: the three men represent
Buddhism, Confucianism, and Taoism. The third poem, however, states
that if the men retain their formal identities as Buddhist, Confucian, or
Taoist they will not "understand unworldliness." "Unworldliness" is
thereby offered as a condition of thought and life that is higher than any of
the three creeds. Thus a major overtone of the Three Laughers motif here
is not simply that representatives of three creeds are united, but that they
are united by awareness of a higher reality that transcends the original
beliefs. Hui-yüan violates his most solemn and historically prominent vow
as a monk. T'ao Yüan-ming is a poor representative of the Confucian
social ethic, since he gave up official life to become an eccentric recluse
devoted to gardening, drinking, and poetry. All of this is permitted in the
name of a transcendental higher reality.

If the three creeds are unified by recognizing a higher principle, I have
not found a name given to that principle. None of the four poems
translated above names it. In fact a specific, concrete answer would not be
in keeping with the spirit of this tradition of thought. The higher reality or
principle can be understood, however, in a negative and partial way. By

crossing the Tiger Ravine, the men gain freedom from narrow orthodoxy. The Three Laughers symbolize spiritual and intellectual freedom guided by the principles of nonduality and nondiscrimination.

THE MEN OF THE THREE CREEDS TASTING VINEGAR

Another variation of the theme of unity, usually labeled the Men of the Three Creeds Tasting Vinegar, presents the same three sages in a different context. A handsome painting of the theme (figure 3) comes from the brush of the monk Reisai, who was active in Kyoto from around 1435 to the late 1460s.[12] He seems to have worked at Tōfukuji in the painting tradition established there by Kitsuzan Minchō (died 1431) two generations earlier. Reisai must have specialized in Buddhist themes. His surviving works and those mentioned in old records include such subjects as the white-robed Kannon, the Nirvāna of Śākyamuni, Manjusrī seated on a lion, and the Totō Tenjin. His painting of the vinegar-tasting theme, however, is among his most original surviving works. Its prose inscription is written by Yaun Eitsu, a monk for whom no biographical data have been found. It may be rendered in translation as follows:

> The man of Han [T'ao Yüan-ming], the old Taoist from Chin [Lu Hsiu-ching], and the monk of Tai [Hui-yüan]! A marvelous thing, marvelous indeed! In one place, intimate together. Ah, each one a sage! But inadvertently, suddenly (. . . owing to the stuff that makes up the wine . . .) the vat holds a great treasure. The three creeds become a single doctrine. Oh, oh, good gracious! You there! Tiny beetles! Can it be true? The men endure the sour taste and knit their brows, standing face to face in silence. A dominant religion is an affliction to man.
>
> Playfully written by Yaun

The three sages are surprised; the wine has turned to vinegar. The sourness has silenced them; they are united before this strong, astringent reality. But they also discover tiny insects in their cup, wine beetles that dwell in the vat. The beetles are not apparent in the painting, which is an object lesson on the degree to which the conceptual meaning of this imagery depends on the inscriptions, for the beetles add an important dimension to that meaning.

The theme of vat beetles is an old one in the Chinese Taoist tradition. It appears, for example, in Chuang Tzu where Confucius is described as saying to a disciple after a discussion with Lao Tzu, "As far as the Way is concerned, I was a mere gnat in the vinegar jar! If the Master had not

12. Watanabe Hajime, *Bijutsu kenkyū*, no. 87 (1939).

FIGURE 3. The Men of the Three Creeds Tasting Vinegar, ca. 1450, by Reisai, with inscription by Yaun Eitsu.

taken off the lid for me, I would never have understood the Great Integrity of heaven and earth."[13] Thus the three sages see in the vat beetles a reflection of their own limited vision. The beetles swimming in the cup shock them into recognizing a higher reality.

Reisai's painting is the only example of this theme surviving from the Higashiyama period, but the motif must have been quite popular at the time. Preserved in the gozan texts are inscriptions written on several paintings of the period that have been lost. One monk, also from Tōfukuji,

13. Burton Watson, *The Complete Works of Chuang Tzu* (New York, 1968), pp. 225–227; Kurata, 24: 43–47.

Gen'un Gesshū, seems to have been particularly fond of the theme.
Translated below are two of his poems:

> Wearing Confucian shoes, a Taoist cap,
>   and a Buddhist robe,
> Three men taste vinegar
>   standing in the setting sun.
> Later it will be changed
>   into a cup of wine.
> They are T'ao, Lu, and Yüan;
>   T'ao will support the drunken one
>   when they return home.

> It is true that between China and India
>   is the vast interval between east and west;
> Although different mouths taste the sourness,
>   the faces are wrinkled alike.
> Within the vat, moreover,
>   is enclosed the vastness of heaven.
> The three men together
>   are like a single vat beetle.[14]

THE PATRIARCHS OF THE THREE CREEDS

The simplest and most direct expression of the concept of the
Unity of the Three Creeds is the painting theme usually labeled *Sankyō-zu*
showing the founders of the three doctrines standing together, visually
unified in a single compositional unit. In this version the three Chinese
personages—Hui-yüan, Lu Hsiu-ching, and T'ao Yüan-ming—are not
used to carry the symbolism. This is done by the patriarchs themselves.
The most prominent remaining version of the theme in Japan is attributed
to the monk Josetsu, active at Sōkokuji in the first two decades of the
fifteenth century. Josetsu painted the celebrated Catfish and Gourd picture ordered by Ashikaga Yoshimochi and was considered by Sesshū and
later generations to be the father of Japanese suibokuga. His painting
of the Three Creeds (figure 4), done in the highly economical, rapidly
brushed style of Liang K'ai, shows Confucius in the foreground, Lao Tzu
behind him, and the bearded Sākyamuni farthest to the rear.[15]
The inscription directly above the picture dates from 1493, as much as a

14. Uemura, *Kokka*, no. 338.
15. *Kokka*, no. 348 (1919); Jan Fontein and Money Hickman, *Zen Painting and Calligraphy*
(Boston, 1970), pl. 39; Watanabe Hajime, *Higashiyama suibokuga no kenkyū* (Tokyo, 1949), pp.
45–78.

FIGURE 4. The Patriarchs of the Three Creeds, ca. 1400, attributed to Josetsu. Inscribed in 1493 by Seishū Ryūtō. Courtesy of Kenninji, Ryōsoku-in Collection, Kyoto.

century after the presumed date of the original painting. It was written by a well-known monk, Seishū Ryūtō, and reads in part:

> Gautama, Confucius, and Lao. The three are like one. One is like three. Together the three produce all virtues. They may be compared to three boatmen in the same great vessel containing heaven and earth and laden with the sacred and profane. They sailed for 108,000 leagues with the rudder twisting; they sailed for 108,000 leagues to the east while the compass needle pointed to the south. For 350 years they drifted with the wind, then for 350 years they used the sail. Strange, is it not?[16]

16. *Gozan bungaku shinshū* (Tokyo, 1970), 4: 124. The writer Ryūtō, a native of Yamashiro, spent most of his life in Nanzenji and died in 1498.

FIGURE 5. Three Sages, ca. 1475, by Sessō Tōyō. Courtesy of the Museum of Fine
Arts, Boston.

The content of this inscription is ironic. The Three Patriarchs are first
praised and then made fun of; the sages are likened to boatmen lost and
aimlessly wandering. The inscription may be nearly a century later than
the painting, so we cannot be certain that the artist had precisely the same
point of view, but it is clear that he did not conceive of the patriarchs as
heroic, ideal figures. They were painted in a humble guise, almost like
caricatures.

Similar in composition is a picture in the Museum of Fine Arts, Boston,
bearing the seal of Sessō Tōyō, active in the third quarter of the fifteenth
century (figure 5).[17] The painting is not inscribed, and the identity of the
three men is uncertain. There is no doubt that they symbolize the Unity of
the Three Creeds and that they are shown as humble men—not as all-
knowing sages or deities. Thus, as with other versions of the unity theme,
the three creeds are united as each realizes its limitations in the face of a
higher reality, which is never named or defined.

While historical records indicate that the Three Patriarchs theme had
been painted by Chinese masters such as Ma Yüan, Ch'en Ch'ing-po, and
Hsu Tao-ning, all Sung-period examples apparently have been lost. An

17. Tanaka Ichimatsu and Nakamura Tanio, *Sesshū: Sesson*, in *Suiboku bijutsu taikei* (Tokyo,
1973), 7: pl. 54.

FIGURE 6.
The Patriarchs of the Three Creeds,
ca. 1300. Painting bears the seals of
Yin-t'o-lo and an inscription by
Ch'ing-cho Cheng-ch'eng but may be
an early Japanese replica of lost original.
Reprinted by permission
from *Sadō bijutsu zenshū* 12
(Tokyo, 1971), pl. 20.

exception may be a picture bearing the seals of Yin-t'o-lo, a monk-painter
of the late thirteenth to early fourteenth century who was much admired
in Japan but almost completely ignored in Chinese records. The painting (figure 6) has an inscription signed by Ch'ing-cho Cheng-ch'eng
(1274–1339), a monk from Fukien who came to Japan in 1327. He resided
at Kenchōji and Engakuji in Kamakura and later at Kenninji in Kyoto.
The painting is not widely accepted as a genuine work of Yin-t'o-lo; it and
the inscription may be an early Japanese replica of a lost original.[18] The
inscription reads:

> The Magistrate of Lu [Confucius]
> The Pillar of Chou [Lao Tzu]
> And who is the person in front of them?
> The princely son of Suddhodana [Śākyamuni]

18. Reproduced in *Sadō bijutsu zenshū* (Tokyo, 1971), 12: pl. 20.

> The three are all masters.
> Choose among them a good one,
> And follow him!

1335, early spring. Respectfully written by the *śramana* of Kenninji.

Ch'ing-cho Cheng-ch'eng

The poem makes no mention of incompetence or inadequacy. Indeed, most early poems and inscriptions on the subject have a positive air and stress that the result of the unity of the three creeds is greater than the sum of the parts. An important example is the prose-poem written on a lost painting of the theme by Wu-chun Shih-fan (1177–1249). As the abbot of the Wan-shou-ssu near Hangchou, Wu-chun was perhaps the most important single figure in the flowering of the Southern Sung Ch'an community; a painter and calligrapher, he was a strong supporter of the concept of the Unity of the Three Creeds as seen in this translation:

> The one is three.
> The three are one.
> The three are one.
> The one is three.
> Apart, they cannot be separated.
> Together, they cannot form a group.
> Now, as in the past,
> They join together
> In silence,
> For the simple reason
> That within the creeds
> Are many vessels.

Two disciples of Wu-chun undoubtedly helped to implant the doctrine of the Unity of the Three Creeds in Japan. The Japanese priest En'i Ben'en (1202–1280), later known as Shōitsu Kokushi, studied with Wu-chun and after returning to Japan founded Tōfukuji. Records show that in 1275 he lectured to the Retired Emperor Kameyama on the subject. The other disciple was Wu-hsüeh Tsu-yüan (1226–1286), a Chinese monk who traveled to Japan and founded the great Kamakura monastery of Engakuji.

Another Chinese monk who had a hand in disseminating this theme in Japan was Ming-chi Ch'u-chun (1262–1336). He arrived in Japan in 1329 and served for a period as spiritual adviser to the Emperor Go-Daigo; later he became abbot of Kenchōji in Kamakura and of Nanzenji and Kenninji in Kyoto. In his *Zaitōroku* is this text inscribed on a lost painting of the Three Creeds:

The saintly ones of the three creeds.
Each established his own doctrine:
Confucius' law of great integrity
That administers firmness without injustice;
Śākyamuni's law of the great enlightenment
Whose inherent universal harmony transcends all obstacles;
The law of the great vision of the Tao
Whose magnanimous wisdom flows without cease.
Like a tripod standing on three legs,
It is not possible to break one off.
Be that as it may,
Which among the three saintly ones
Should receive the devotions of men and gods?
There can be no agreement.[19]

The above citations do not by any means exhaust the many examples of the theme of unity, either pictorial or poetic, to be found in the works of the Muromachi period. They give evidence, however, of the prevalence of this theme in China and Japan and to certain other aesthetic and historical insights.

Clearly in Japan the complex system of religious and artistic activities which takes the name of *gozan bungei* rested heavily on a lineage of ideas that can be traced directly back to late eleventh-century China, to the circle of Su Tung-p'o, Huang Ting-chien, Fo-yin Ch'an-shih, and the painters Mi Fu, Li Kung-lin, and Wang Shen. This group included Ch'an monks and was considerably influenced by the so-called Southern tradition of the sect. The group gave impetus to a cultural movement—informal and humanistic—that imparted a new meaning to the ancient ideal of the man of letters, the wen-jen. In this view, the amateur artist (poet-calligrapher-painter-scholar-musician) embodied the highest of all human attainments. Through his superior character and intellect, he rises to the· rank of artist-philosopher. The professional artist who works mechanically from old copybooks and is content to satisfy the demands of his patrons is a poor thing by comparison. The true artist seeks spontaneity and directness, not technical perfection, and will defend his freedom—personal, intellectual, and spiritual—against encroachment from any source. His spirit is exalted by his experiences in nature, by his love of the arts of the past, by the comradeship of his friends, and by the good, clear wine that helps him break the bonds of anxiety and worldly care.

With the fall of the Northern Sung government in 1126, the wen-jen ideals were sustained in the Southern Sung state and its capital at

19. Uemura, *Kokka*, no. 338.

Hangchou. There, in the last half of the twelfth and the early thirteenth centuries, the movement attained a brilliant flowering, more so in painting than in poetry. The artists were of diverse vocation: laymen, members of the court painting academy *(hua-yüan)*, and monks of the nearby Ch'an and T'ien-t'ai monasteries. (The term *wu-shan*, meaning gozan, comes from the fact that the Ch'an monasteries were administered under a system of that name.) A central figure in the artistic circle was Wu-chun Shih-fan, abbot of the Ch'an monastery atop Ching-shan. Meanwhile, in Japan, the Zen sect had come into its own as a separate and favored order. Along with the establishment of Zen temples in Kamakura and Kyoto, the wen-jen tradition was communicated to Japan as part of the gozan monastic and cultural tradition.

In Japan, with the support of the Kamakura and Ashikaga shogunal regimes and the powerful Zen monasteries, the gozan system achieved a stronger impact than it had attained in China, and its heritage in later centuries was more enduring. Ink painting developed on the model of Southern Sung masters such as Mu Ch'i and Ma Yüan, whose imagery became a classic ideal for later generations in Japan, and the Southern Sung style persisted there at the time when, in China, the more in-dividualistic wen-jen style was chosen by the most original and creative painters.

Historically the gozan (wu-shan) cultural system in both Southern Sung China and Muromachi Japan was buttressed by the doctrine of the Unity of the Three Creeds. Under this doctrine, there was no contradiction between the ruler's concern for civic welfare, the monk's preoccupation with spiritual salvation, and the poet's search for private insight. All shared common goals, and the ruler who supported the monastic establishment as well as a circle of poets and painters had promoted the principles of right conduct.

In China, however, the gozan cultural system declined rapidly after the Mongol conquest, the impoverishment of the Ch'an community, and the rise in the Ming period of the wen-jen as the dominant ideal for cultivated men. In Japan, the very success and long life of the gozan cultural system, and the continued vitality of the great Zen monasteries of Kyoto, post-poned by two centuries the day when the literati school would emerge as a separate, well-defined artistic movement.

14

The Development of
Shoin-Style Architecture

ITŌ TEIJI
with Paul Novograd

As life styles change, so does architecture. In few other ways can we see so directly and concretely the changes in the social and cultural life of the Muromachi elite as in the development of *shoin*-style architecture and the invention of the new form of domestic structure known as the *kaisho*.

Traditionally the Muromachi age has been characterized as a time when the new military aristocracy sought to emulate the life style of the court nobility. The presence of many elements of the older palace-style (*shinden*) architecture in the early shoin architecture associated with the military aristocracy bears this out. The crumbling of the old rigidly stratified society, the spread of freer, more casual relations between members of the military aristocracy or between upper and lower levels of society, as well as the emergence of new cultural pursuits such as the tea ceremony, *renga* composing parties, and the rage for displaying Chinese art and artifacts led to new forms of architecture to accommodate these changing patterns in social behavior and cultural life.

Although today the predominant building style of the ruling classes in the Tokugawa period is commonly referred to as "shoin-style architecture," the term *shoin* actually is of quite late origin. There is no record of its use before 1842 in Ise Teijo's *Teijo zakki*.[1] Moreover, because Ise offered no clear definition of the term, the earliest example of its use to designate a specific type of architectural style is to be found in Sawada Natari's *Kaoku zakkō* of about the same date.[2] Sawada singled out as identifying characteristics of shoin style:

1. Entrance vestibule, writing alcove, guest room, room with a raised floor, and private chamber in the ground plan of the building

---

1. Ise Teijo, *Teijo Zakki*, in *Kojitsu sōsho*, ed. Imaizumi Sadoyoshi (Tokyo, 1899–1906).
2. Sawada Natori, *Kaoku Zakkō*, in *Kojitsu sōsho*.

2. Decorative alcove, split-level shelves, writing alcove, or other distinctive innovations
3. Sliding door and wall panels (versus the hinged wooden doors of palace style)

From the Meiji period on, architectural historians like Itō Chūta, Sekino Tei, Tanabe Tai, Ōkuma Yoshikuni, Sekino Masaharu, Horiguchi Sutemi, and Ōta Hirotarō, while agreeing with Sawada on the above basic elements, have proposed various and increasingly detailed definitions.[3] Fundamental departures from palace style in shoin architecture as noted by these scholars include:

4. No distinction between central chamber and outer veranda (as there had been in palace style)
5. Tatami mats covering the floors (versus the plain wood boards of palace style)
6. Square posts (versus the round posts of palace style)
7. Ceilings (a rarity in palace style)
8. Structures of any one complex built contiguously without the covered walkways necessitated by the spatial arrangement of buildings in palace style
9. Roofs of more complex design than in palace style

The fact that shoin architecture is generally defined by comparing it with the palace-style architecture of the Heian and Kamakura periods reflects its evolutionary relationship to the earlier style. Shoin architecture did not totally replace palace architecture but, in a lengthy process which did not reach completion until the Momoyama period in the latter half of the sixteenth century, modified it in adaptation to new social and cultural practices. What we see in the Muromachi age is a phase of transition from one to another form of architectural design. Thus while most of the elements which distinguished true shoin architecture were incorporated in the aristocratic residences of the late Muromachi period, there was not yet at that time an awareness that these comprised a distinct style. Moreover, all Muromachi structures contained a number of elements of the former palace style which were eventually to be dropped in the final evolution of the shoin style.

3. Itō Chūta, *Kōhon teikoku bijutsu ryakushi* (Tokyo, 1901); Sekino Tei, *Kōgyō daijiten* (Tokyo, 1913); Tanabe Tai, *Nihon jūtakushi* (Tokyo, 1934); Ōkuma Yoshikuni, *Kinsei buke jidai no kenchiku* (Tokyo, 1935); Sekino Masaharu, *Nihon jūtaku shōshi* (Tokyo, 1941); Horiguchi Sutemi, *Shoin-zukuri ni tsuite* (Tokyo, 1943); and Ōta Hirotarō, *Shoin zukuri* (Tokyo, 1966).

FIGURE 1. Traditional use of round posts and hinged wall panels *(shitomi)*. Photograph courtesy of Shokokusha, Tokyo.

THE VESTIGIAL ELEMENTS

We begin our analysis of Muromachi residential architecture therefore with a study of the vestigial elements which, despite lack of functional utility, were retained from the older palace style. There were in all five: the covered entrance arcade, horizontally hinged wall panels, swinging doors, slatted windows, and round posts. An inquiry into the reasons for their retention reveals a great deal about the efforts of the military aristocracy to emulate the life style of the court nobility.

Covered Entrance Arcade (chūmonrō)
This is a long, narrow structure (6′ wide and anywhere from 12′ to 45′ long) built out from a corner of one of the main palace buildings, generally with one of the long sides open and the other formed by a wood board wall (see figure 2). Functionally it served as a passageway for the entrance or exit of the host and his guests when grand occasions necessitated the presence of numerous attendants.

FIGURE 2. Detail of painting showing covered entrance arcade (*chūmonrō*), slatted
windows (*renjimado*), and swinging doors (*itakarato*).

One of the last palace-style elements to be abandoned, such arcades
were found in many formal, upper class buildings of the Tokugawa period.
During the Muromachi period the covered arcade still had a practical purpose in the main buildings of the shogunal and temple complexes but in
early modern shoin structures, its function having been taken over first by
the entranceway called the *kuruma-yose* and later by the vestibule (*genkan*,
had become a merely symbolic appendage. The arcade was a necessary
element so long as the priesthood and the military houses of the Muromachi period continued the ceremonies that the Heian nobility had once conducted. This is revealed by the fact that it was almost never attached to the
private living quarters of Muromachi residences. Such rooms, being unrelated to any public ceremonies, had no need for the entrance arcade.

Hinged Wall Panels (shitomi)
Wall panels of the *shitomi* variety first appeared in the Heian period as partitions between interior and exterior spaces in palace-style residences (see
figure 1). Affixed in pairs, one above the other, at each 6' bay, they made
excellent fixtures from the point of view of temperature control during the
summer because they could be opened to allow cool air to enter. During

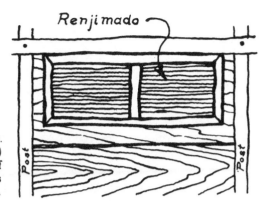

FIGURE 3.
Slatted windows (*renjimado*)
of the guest house of
the Kangakuin abbot's
residence.

the winter, however, they had to be completely closed to keep out the cold, plunging the interiors into darkness. This disadvantage is what probably stimulated the invention of sliding wall panels, which saw steadily increasing use during the Kamakura and Muromachi periods.

The trend is evident in the main ceremonial buildings of the successive shogunal residences during the Muromachi period, although at least the front of the houses continued to be fitted with shitomi. For the shoguns, the shitomi were not only devices for controlling room temperatures but also a symbol of noble status. A typical example of this was the shinden of Yoshinori's Muromachi palace. The whole of the southern (i.e., main) side and a portion of the east side had shitomi, with sliding panels employed throughout the rest of the structure. It should be borne in mind that the shogun's shinden was intended primarily as a place for public ceremonial purposes. Thus the drawbacks of the shitomi in daily living quarters were not a great problem. What it indicates is that, just like the entrance arcade, the shitomi were viewed by the warrior class of the Muromachi period as a symbol of the culture of the old nobility. There are any number of examples to show that this awareness of their symbolic meaning persisted into the architecture of the Momoyama period—the audience chamber of the Jūraku-dai and the front shoin of Daigoji Sambō-in, among others—as well as construction plans in manuals on carpentry produced in the early Tokugawa period. But the shitomi did not last as long as the entrance arcades.

Swinging Doors (itakarato)
It is generally supposed that originally these were a necessary accompaniment to the shitomi, for once the shitomi were closed it was impossible to leave or enter a building save through a doorway of this kind. With the in-

troduction of sliding partitions, itakarato were no longer an absolute
necessity, but like the shitomi they did remain as a symbol of the old
aristocratic culture, showing up in such early modern shoin-style structures as the guest quarters in Kōjō-in and Kangaku-in at Onjōji and the
central audience chamber of Edo Castle (see figure 2).

Slatted Windows (renjimado)
These small windows, covered by horizontal strips of wood and placed in
the wall of the entrance arcade facing the main entrance, permitted a person on the inside to have a view of the exterior without being seen. An
entry in a court diary for 1175 states that slatted windows were only permitted in the residences of those with high noble rank. Thus they were
status symbols even in Heian times. Slatted windows served to screen the
lord of the house when he spoke to a person of lower rank. The *Heike
monogatari* describes, for instance, an audience that the Cloistered Emperor
Goshirakawa granted to Minamoto Yoshitsune while sheltered behind his
slatted window. Due to a lack of source materials, it is not clear exactly
how extensively these windows were used by the Muromachi military
aristocracy, but their incorporation in such later structures as the central
audience chamber of the Jūraku-dai and the guest quarters of Onjōji's
Kangaku-in, together with their inclusion in a plan for an audience
chamber contained in an early Tokugawa carpenter manual, seems to
prove that Muromachi residences also had slatted windows.

Round Posts
The fact that shoin-style construction used square rather than round posts
had deep significance. In palace-style buildings, except for the posts on the
extreme exterior which supported the outmost eaves, all posts were round.
In shoin-style construction, square posts were used exclusively. There was
a structural reason: as sliding door and room divider panels came into use,
round posts had to be replaced by square ones in order to form a tight
joint with the sliding panels. The Ashikaga shogunal residences provide an
illuminating illustration of how the process of change from round to
square posts took place. The main building of Yoshimitsu's Kitayama
palace (1398) had square posts on the exterior supporting the eaves,
whereas in the interior the posts were round. The same arrangement was
followed in the Seiryō-den of the imperial palace and is, in fact, typical of
all Heian palace-style structures (see figure 1 above). By the time
Yoshinori's Muromachi residence was built, however, only the southern
half of the interior of the main building had round posts, the northern half
being fitted with square ones. In other words, the square posts were in the

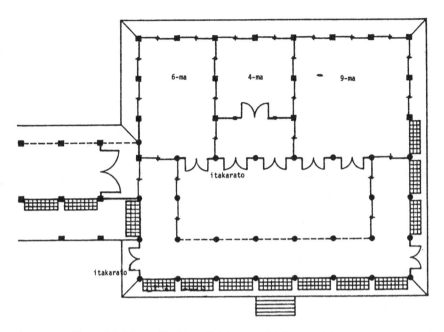

FIGURE 4. Plan of Ashikaga Yoshinori's Muromachi-dono residence showing use of both round and square posts.

process of completely replacing the round. That round posts—together with the shitomi—were used in the southern half was because public ceremonies were still held in that portion of the residence (figure 4).

THE NEW ELEMENTS

If the retention of the five elements described above long past their usefulness in the emerging society represented an extreme consciousness of continuity with the old Heian culture, early shoin architecture was also distinguished by a number of new elements clearly adopted to serve a new life style. Such were the carriage shelter, entrance vestibule (*genkan*), sliding door (*shōji, yarido*), and sliding wall panels (*fusuma*). In addition, three elements in particular—the raised-floor alcove (*toko*), split-level shelves (*chigai-dana*), and the writing alcove (*shoin*)—were fundamentally associated with the maturation of shoin style. It is these architectural innovations that derived most directly from the changing life style of the dominant military aristocracy. In modern shoin architecture the three elements have come to be installed as an integrated unit, forming a distinct mode of interior design. In the Muromachi period, however, they were used independently of one another and were combined only later.

Raised-Floor Alcove (toko)

The term *toko* changed in meaning from the Kamakura-Muromachi period to modern times, so we must first clarify this difference. Today *toko* denotes the *tokonoma*, an alcove for the display of hanging scrolls and other decorative articles, whereas in the Muromachi period the term had a different and less precise meaning. In his *Shoin-zukuri*, Ōta Hirotarō defines this earlier usage as "a general name referring to a raised-floor, built-in-seating area, or any platform-like portion of a house, such as the *tsuke-shoin*." Reference to raised seating areas as toko are found in numerous Muromachi-period writings. A description of the *kaisho* at Yoshimasa's Higashiyama palace states, "To the south of the Kari-no-ma is a raised seat 3 *chō* square." In effect, this "raised seat" was simply a room with a raised floor. Several of the rooms in the new Imperial Palace and Lesser Palace (built in 1456) were described in one record as having raised floors, while in another these same rooms are referred to as toko. Clearly at this time a toko was simply a room with a raised floor. Moreover, when tatami were spread over a portion of wooden flooring, the raised portion so formed was referred to as a toko in distinction to the lower floor. Thus it is evident that the toko of later times derived its primary form and purpose from an architectural element different from the toko of the Kamakura-Muromachi period. Rather than the raised seat, it was a simple decorative board known as *oshi-ita* that became the primary ingredient of the later tokonoma.

Decorative Platform (oshi-ita)

Originally the oshi-ita was no more than a portable wooden table or plank placed under the hanging scrolls that decorated the walls of the palace-style rooms as a platform for decorative or religious objects. Eventually it came to be a built-in structure. To judge from extant examples and source materials of the Muromachi period it appears to have measured 1½' to 2' wide and from 6' to 18' long and was set about 6" to 12" above floor level. In the portion of the illustrated *Boki-e* generally believed to have been painted in 1351 a portable oshi-ita is depicted being used as a desk, while in the portion thought to have been painted in 1482 there is a built-in oshi-ita. This would seem to indicate that sometime between the late fourteenth and early fifteenth centuries the oshi-ita began to be a built-in element. How this came about is not absolutely certain, but it most likely has to do with the continuing interest in the acquisition and display of imported

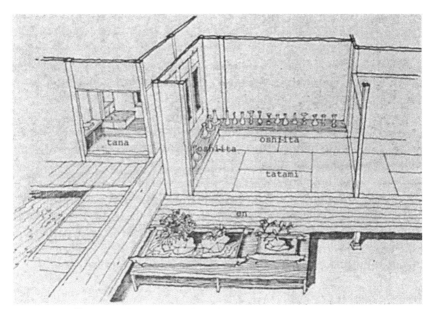

FIGURE 5. Decorative platform (*oshi-ita*) in a typical kaisho.

Chinese vertically mounted scroll paintings. With the establishment of an accepted mode for arranging these objects of art, permanent facilities for their display became necessary.

Having emphasized the oshi-ita as the main element in the formation of the tokonoma, it should be pointed out that tokonoma in early modern and even contemporary Japan show a dual derivation. On the one hand there is the reliance on the tradition of the Muromachi oshi-ita, a thick board placed on the floor, long and narrow, with no frame delineating a clearly defined alcove. On the other hand there developed out of the tradition of the Muromachi toko the tatami-covered raised platform within a clearly delineated framework deeper but not so wide as the oshi-ita. This type may be seen in the shoin of Katsura Rikyū as well as most contemporary residences and tea rooms (see figure 5). Functionally both were used as places for religious objects and hanging scrolls, but the latter was occasionally used—just as in the Muromachi period—as a place where an honored guest might sit.

Split-Level Shelves (chigai-dana)
A third element found in the shoin tokonoma consisted of split-level shelves, generally accompanied by cabinets above and below, though sometimes the cabinets were omitted. The oldest extant shelves of this type

are those at the Tōgu-dō (1485) at Jishō-ji. It is believed that these developed from older portable types of shelves, for it is known from historical sources that even in the Muromachi period portable shelves saw considerable use as interior fixtures. It was in Yoshimasa's time that built-in shelves first appeared. Contemporary evidence shows that these were installed in Yoshimasa's Kokawa palace and Higashiyama residence.

Most often these shelves held books—a direct outcome of the tremendous scholarly interest which Zen monks at this time displayed in Chinese literary and philosophical studies and of the immense numbers of books then being imported as a result of trade with China and Korea. The second most important class of articles placed on these shelves was tea utensils, usually including tea cup, tea caddy, tea whisk, food cannister, tea ladle, portable fireplace, feather broom, ember poker, and water bowl. From these examples it should be clear that the shelves of Yoshimasa's time were not without their functional uses, but their main purpose was to provide a place for the artistic arrangement of books and tea utensils.

Writing Alcove (tsuke-shoin)

It is this element that gave to shoin-style architecture its distinguishing name. In the Muromachi period the tsuke-shoin was generally referred to simply as shoin, by which was meant the framed alcove with four shōji placed on the side of the tokonoma in the manner of modern shoin architecture. The alcove was built around a wooden desk or bench-like structure. Built-in desk alcoves may be seen in picture scrolls of the late thirteenth and early fourteenth century, and it is safe to assume that they first appeared at the end of the Kamakura period. Originally they were probably functional fixtures where one read or wrote, but by the time of Yoshimasa they were built in such a way that it was clearly impossible to sit and read or write comfortably in them. Thus they had become completely decorative in function.

In keeping with its origin as a writing alcove, the shoin was used for the display of writing implements. The oldest recorded description of the contents of such a shoin is in a reference to the kaisho of one of the subtemples at Daigoji in 1430 which listed a water jar, pitcher, inkstone, brush, brush tray, short knife, seal case, and scrolls. In the *Kundaikan sōchō-ki*, a manual on the tea ceremony dated 1511, there is only one picture illustrating shoin decoration, suggesting that at the time it was written shoin decoration had become completely standardized.[4]

Today the oshi-ita (tokonoma), split-level shelves, and shoin form a unit of decoration in the main rooms of every shoin-style structure. This type of

4. See *Gunsho ruijū*, rev. ed. (Tokyo, 1960).

standardization did not exist in Muromachi times, although there were a few instances even then where these newly developed elements were consciously grouped together. Why and how did these three particular elements, whose original functions are so disparate, come to be grouped together? A study of the available examples of fifteenth-century structures in which two or more of these architectural elements are included reveals that these combinations most frequently occurred in what was known at the time as the kaisho, a room or building primarily used for social gatherings. Thus the kaisho was of undeniable importance in the development of the interior design scheme of shoin-style architecture. Moreover, since kaisho architecture both developed and fell into desuetude within the Muromachi period, it consequently represents the most distinctive feature of Muromachi architecture.

The word *kaisho* (lit. gathering hall) appeared first in the Kamakura period, the oldest mention being found in Kamo no Chōmei's *Mumyōshō* (1211-12).[5] This does not mean, however, that the unique form of architecture denoted by that term had developed yet. Rather the word was used to indicate the various rooms or buildings in palace-style architecture that were used for informal gatherings.

The appearance of the kaisho as a completely independent structure did not come until at earliest the end of the Kamakura period. Yoshimitsu's Muromachi palace, built in 1378, marks the first instance in which a kaisho structure was included in a shogunal residence. This, of course, was not the first use of the kaisho in residences of the military aristocracy. As cited in Professor Varley's essay above, the *Taiheiki* states that Sasaki Dōyo had a large kaisho at his residence at the time of his flight from Kyoto in 1361.

Not having been designed to accommodate any traditional formalities of social or ceremonial conduct, the kaisho did not have the symbols or the traditions of the Heian nobility, for example the shitomi. All that was necessary was to have fixtures that suited the functions of the kaisho and adequately controlled room temperatures. As a result, the new sliding door and wall panels came into very early use here. This in turn meant that the kaisho was built with square not round posts. The kaisho was consequently a force in the evolution of the external features of residential architecture in the direction of the mature shoin style (see figure 6).

The internal arrangement of the kaisho resulted primarily from the social activities which took place in them. Kaisho were regularly used for such special occasions as *tanabata* festivities, flower-arranging and vase competitions, *sarugaku* and nō performances, tea-guessing, the monthly

5. Ibid.

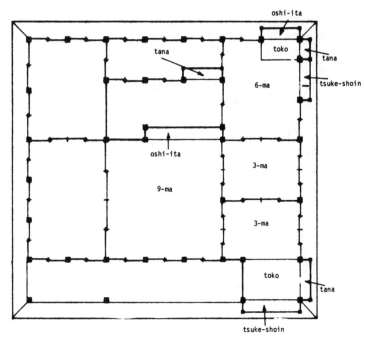

FIGURE 6. Kaisho of Higashiyama residence.

Chinese and Japanese linked-verse meetings, moon-, flower-, and snow-viewing parties, and even on occasion for Buddhist ceremonies. Since these activities required no unusual interior fixtures, they probably had little direct influence on the development of the combined toko, split-level shelves, and shoin unit as part of the interior decorative design.

But the banquets held by the military aristocracy, frequently for purely social purposes after formal interviews or state ceremonies, undoubtedly were a factor in kaisho design. In the shogunal residences particularly, kaisho were used for regular audiences and meetings as well as for receptions and banquets for especially honored members of the nobility and clergy after their formal audiences in the audience chambers. It was on such occasions that the kaisho was used to the fullest extent of its capabilities, with emphasis on a display of objects of art. A kaisho so decorated was described by Prince Sadafusa in his *Kammon gyoki:* "The splendor of the articles and treasures on display astonished the eye. The magnificence of the garden was something beyond description. Surely the splendor of Paradise must be something like this."[6]

Against the background of the new and more gregarious culture and the types of banquets and entertainments that went along with it, one can see

6. Prince Sadafusa, *Kammon gyoki,* 2/7/1431, in *Zoku gunsho ruijū.*

how important the combination of shoin, split-level shelves, and oshi-ita became as places where decorations could be placed to add to the sumptuousness of the room. Thus it was in the kaisho that the change toward the shoin style was earliest and most profoundly felt, and it was the kaisho which acted as a force in drawing the whole of residential architecture toward the shoin style as it eventually was formalized in the late sixteenth century (see figure 7).

FIGURE 7. Idealized rendition of the mature shoin style.

15

The Comic Tradition in Renga

DONALD KEENE

Renga (linked verse) was the most typical literary art of the Muromachi period. The many court poets of the traditional *waka* undoubtedly believed that their chosen form of poetry possessed greater dignity, and even the renga masters would probably have concurred in this opinion, not only because of the great antiquity of the waka but because of the miraculous powers with which it was credited, even to moving the gods and demons. However, it is surely significant that the twenty-first and last imperial anthology, the *Shin zoku kokin shū* (1439), now totally forgotten, appeared between two important collections of renga that were accorded the unprecedented privilege of being ranked "immediately after" (*jun*) the imperial anthologies. A few waka poets of the Muromachi period still command our attention, notably Shōtetsu (1381–1459), who excelled also as a critic of poetry. Some poets like Nijō Yoshimoto (1320–1388) or Shinkei (1406–1475), though accomplished in both waka and renga, are remembered today only for their renga, another indication of the decrepit state of the waka at the time. It is clear that, even at the court, renga composition had come to occupy the place of importance formerly reserved for the waka. Elsewhere in the country, as the result of the dispersion of the bearers of the court culture during the Ōnin War, major and minor magnates eagerly sought to attract renga poets to their castles.

The prose writings of the period are of more interest than the waka, whether they are cast in the pseudoclassical manner adopted at the court in imitation of Heian models or in the more vigorous (if often inartistic) popular and religious tales, but we know nothing about their authors, and the works themselves attracted little attention from the literary men of the day. The only form comparable in literary importance to renga during the Muromachi period was nō. The texts, especially those by Zeami, include masterpieces, and the painstaking care with which they were composed is revealed in Zeami's critical writings. In translation, moreover, they are certainly more appealing than any renga sequence. But even though these plays are by our standards the supreme literary works of the age, in their own day they were considered hardly more than the libretti for sung and danced performances and belonged only indirectly to the established literary traditions. In this sense, if not necessarily in terms of absolute worth, renga was the representative literary art of the period. Innumerable manuscripts of renga have been preserved, too many ever to be printed, and the number of "links" composed at sessions for which the records have been lost must be staggering.

Long neglected even by scholars of Japanese literature, renga has attracted wider attention in recent years.[1] In the West too there has been a surprising awakening of interest in renga composition, especially in the basic principle of a group of poets submerging their own identities for the sake of a larger composition produced by the confluence of different poetic insights.[2] What for long had been the chief stumbling block in the path of appreciating renga even in Japan—its lack of a unifying theme or even of any overall structure—has come to appeal to poets seeking to transcend the limitations of isolated experience by engaging in a formally organized but free conversation with other poets at the highest level of receptivity. Although modern examples of renga (certainly those composed in the West) do not observe the traditional codes of composition, in spirit at least they resemble the works of the Japanese poets of the Muromachi period who, living in an age of conflict and uncertainty, sought comfort in the creating of works of art that revealed complex textures of mutual stimulation and response. Octavio Paz, who has himself composed renga, wrote, "We are witnessing the end of the idea of art as aesthetic contemplation and returning to something that the West has long forgotten: the rebirth of art as collective action and representation, and the rebirth of their complementary opposite, solitary meditation."[3]

Renga, almost from its inception, was composed in two distinct moods: as a lighthearted, often indecorous, literary game and as an artistic expression of what might be called a multiple stream of consciousness. In terms of the quantity of verses composed, those of the *mushin* (inelegant) style must have far outnumbered those of the *ushin* (elegant) style, but the triumphs of ushin poetry are usually recorded as if they constituted the entire history of renga. Certainly, judged in terms of literary worth, the ushin

---

1. Masaoka Shiki's curt dismissal of renga as not being "literature" was certainly one important factor in the demise of renga during the Meiji period, but it had been in a state of marked decline for years.
2. The volume *Renga* published in 1971 contains poetry by four poets—Octavio Paz (Mexican), Jacques Roubaud (French), Edoardo Sanguineti (Italian), and Charles Tomlinson (English) —each composing in his own language according to a special code of renga.
3. Octavio Paz, *Alternating Current,* trans. Helen R. Lane (New York, 1973), p. 21.

style is incomparably superior, but the mushin style led directly to the formation of what would prove to be the most popular of all varieties of Japanese poetry, the *haiku*, known originally as *haikai no renga*. Sōchō (1448–1532) was a central figure in the development of this comic form of renga. Though neither so celebrated nor so accomplished as some of his predecessors—notably Sōgi (1421–1502), the supreme master of the art—Sōchō is an exceptionally interesting poet, both because of what he revealed of himself in his writings and because of his immediate connection with the creation of *haikai* poetry.

By way of introduction to my account of Sōchō I have briefly described the early history of linked verse, then devoted attention to two commanding figures, Nijō Yoshimoto and Sōgi. Much of this material will be familiar to those who have read the studies in renga by contemporary Japanese scholars, but I felt it was desirable to make some such presentation in view of the almost total lack of any descriptions of renga in English. I have not, however, gone into the technicalities of composing renga, intriguing though they are, since my interest here lies in tracing the comic tradition of renga through history into Sōchō's work and beyond.[4]

EARLY HISTORY

It was long traditional to trace the origins of renga to an exchange of poems recorded in the *Kojiki*. The hero Yamato-takeru-no-mikoto asked an old man by the road a question in the form of a poem:

Niibari	How many nights
Tsukuba wo sugite	Have I slept since passing
iku yo ka netsuru	Niibari and Tsukuba?

The old man demonstrated he was equal to the test by replying in verse:

kaganabete	The days put together
yo ni wa kokonoyo	Make of nights nine
hi ni wa tōka wo	And of daytimes ten.[5]

Mention of the place-name Tsukuba later gave rise to the term "the way of Tsukuba" as an elegant manner of referring to the art of renga, but this pair of verses bears no resemblance, even of the most rudimentary kind, to mature renga. It consists of two *kata-uta*, the first somewhat irregular, in lines of five, seven, and five syllables. Together they make a *sedōka*, an archaic poetic form, but the question and answer do not really make a

4. The mechanics of renga composition are illuminatingly discussed by Konishi Jin'ichi in his *Sōgi* (Tokyo, 1973), pp. 178–242.
5. See also Donald Philippi, trans., *Kojiki* (Tokyo, 1968), p. 242.

single poem except in the sense that they have a certain number of syllables and lines. Singly or together, the utterances of the prince and the old man are devoid of literary value, but the renga poets of later times revered these compositions not for their beauty but for their antiquity, which enabled the court poets to compose renga with confidence in its pedigree.

A more suitable candidate for the oldest extant example of renga is poem 1635 in the *Manyōshū*. A note before the poem states, "A nun wrote the 'head' Yakamochi, responding to the nun's challenge, completed a waka by adding a 'tail' verse."

Saogawa no	The one who dammed up
mizu wo sekiagete	The waters of the Saho River
ueshi ta wo	And planted the fields.
karu wasaii wa	Should be the only one
hitori narubeshi	To eat the harvested rice.

Many explanations have been offered for this cryptic poem, including the allegorical interpretation that the nun's daughter, whom she had carefully reared, was taken possession of by Yakamochi as his "harvest."[6] Whatever the true meaning of these verses, they marked a first stage in the creation of a short renga—a single waka composed by two people. This is the only example of a renga in the *Manyōshū*, but the absence of others does not necessarily mean that the renga was a rare form of poetic expression; there is evidence to suggest the contrary, including the use of the word *hokku* to designate the first three lines of a waka.[7]

During the Heian period the short renga developed into a kind of social pastime. Often a riddle was presented in the *maeku* (first verse) and the poem was completed by another person with a *tsukeku* (added verse) of wit and ingenuity. The more complicated or absurd the situation described in the maeku ("a deer is standing in the middle of the sea"), the greater the achievement of the person who could make sense of the whole by adding a cleverly explicative two lines ("the reflection of the mountain is cast on the waves"). The short renga tended to be a demonstration of wit rather than poetic depth, though the tone is occasionally moving, as in the episode in *Ise monogatari* which describes how a maeku written by a woman was completed by a man, apparently with romantic intentions:

6. Shimazu Tadao, *Renga shi no kenkyū* (Tokyo, 1969), p. 8. Omodaka Hisataka, *Manyōshū chūshaku* (Tokyo, 1957–68), 8: 289–293, gives many ingenious explanations of this poem. Nose Asaji, *Renku to renga* (Tokyo, 1950), pp. 70–71, interpreted *hitori* as *hi* (water pipe) and *tori* (take), as well as *hitori* (one man).

7. *Manyōshū*, no. 1657; Omodaka, 8: 320.

> kachibito no   Since ours was a relationship no deeper
> wataredo nurenu   Than a creek too shallow
> e ni shi areba   To wet a foot-traveler's garb . . .

The last two lines were missing, and with a bit of charcoal from a pine torch he supplied these:

> mata Ausaka no   I shall surely again cross
> seki wa koenan   Ōsaka Barrier.[8]

Such examples of renga did not go beyond the composition of a single waka by two people. No attempt was made to impart to the maeku (in seventeen syllables) an independence of content, and the tsukeku (in fourteen syllables) merely completed the thought, without any special overtones of association.

The first imperial anthology to contain a section of renga poetry was *Kinyōshū* (1127), compiled by Minamoto Toshiyori (d. 1125), who has been styled the "perfecter" of the short renga.[9] Toshiyori insisted on the integrity of each "link" of renga. A short renga could be started either with the "main verse" (in three lines) or the "subsidiary verse" (in two lines), but "within each verse one must express completely the sense of whatever is to be said. It is bad to leave it to the next man to complete a thought."[10] The insistence on the integrity of each link disassociated his short renga from the previous ideal of two people creating what appeared to be a waka composed by a single person. The renga, especially after it broke the confines of the thirty-one syllables of the waka and was prolonged to one hundred or even more links, was compelled by "codes" to preserve the completeness of each link, and even to change the season and subject repeatedly so as to avoid giving the impression of a single, unified poem. In this respect the Japanese renga differed most conspicuously from its closest Chinese equivalent, *lien-chü*, which sought unity rather than diversity.[11]

8. Translation by Helen Craig McCullough in *Tales of Ise* (Stanford, 1968), p. 117. The main point of the response was the pun *mata au* (we shall meet again) imbedded in Ausaka.
9. Kidō Saizō, *Rengashi ronkō* (Tokyo, 1971–73), 1: 83–103.
10. Minamoto Toshiyori, *Toshiyori zuinō*, in *Nihon kagaku taikei* (Tokyo, 1956), 1: 124.
11. The *lien-chü* (renku) dates back as far as the Han dynasty. In the early examples, poets each contributed one "link" on a set topic, but there was no suggestion of response to the "link" of the preceding poet. Later examples, such as the dialogue between one Chia Ch'ung and his wife, a work of the fourth century A.D. (translated in Donald Keene, *Japanese Literature* [New York, 1955], p. 34), reveal the distinct voices of the participants, but there are few poetic overtones. The height of the *lien-chü* was reached in the mid-T'ang, when poets joined efforts to produce a poem that might have been the work of one man; an example is given in Cyril Birch, *Anthology of Chinese Literature* (New York, 1965), p. 265. The Japanese renga, as will be clear from the above, was not inspired by Chinese example.

In another important respect Toshiyori's renga differed from the waka, even when the two links seemed to form a single short poem: unlike the normal waka, the expression tended to be cerebral rather than emotional. Toshiyori's short renga usually had for their central point a pun, related word (*engo*), or some other variety of verbal play, often comic in effect. It is true that there was a *haikai* (comic) section of waka in the *Kokinshū*, but in Toshiyori's short renga verbal play was not merely a rare possibility but the *raison d'être* of the composition. One example of his ingenuity will suffice:

tsuki wa hiru	The moon can be seen
hi o wa yoru to mo	In daytime, and the sun
miyuru kana[12]	Even at night.

The surface meaning of these lines is a paradox, if not an absurdity, but when read together with the prefatory note ("Composed by the weir at Uji when the moon was bright") we become aware of puns that yield a quite different meaning: at the weir the whitebait *(hio)* can be seen swarming *(yoru)* because tonight the moon is as bright as day.

Toshiyori devoted similar ingenuity to his tsukeku, which often echo the puns or wordplays in the maeku. When read together, the two lines often suggest less a waka than parallel couplets of an epigram. The short renga having reached this point, it was a small step to break down the original limitations of the thirty-one syllables of a waka and create a poem comprising a series of indeterminate numbers of links.

Fukuro zōshi (1159), a work of poetic criticism by Fujiwara Kiyosuke (1104–1177), includes a section on the principles of the renga. At one point the author states that the *hokku* (opening verse) of "chain" *(kusari)* renga must be in seventeen syllables and not in fourteen,[13] a clear indication that chain renga (that is, renga in more than two links) was being composed commonly enough to require rules. Only two examples of twelfth-century chain renga have been preserved, in *Ima kagami* and *Kokon chomonjū*. The example found in *Ima kagami*, apparently written before 1130,[14] concludes with a remark indicating that this kind of renga was already popular with the aristocracy.

| Nara no miyako wo | My thoughts go out |
| omoi koso yare | To the capital at Nara. |

12. Kidō, 1: 86. I have departed from my usual romanization in order to make the puns between *hi wo ba* and *hio wa* more evident.
13. Quoted in Shimazu, p. 31. Fujiwara Kiyosuke's *Fukuro zōshi* (text in *Nihon kagaku taikei*, 2) is hard to date; the particular section quoted (p. 10) may have been added toward the end of his life. See Kidō, 1: 118.
14. Kidō, 1: 115–116.

To this the general added the lines:

yaezakura	The double-petaled cherry
aki no momiji ya	And the red leaves of autumn—
ika naran	How are they now?

Echigo no Menoto added:

shigururu tabi	Every time the rain sweeps down
iro ya kasanaru	The colors grow the brighter.

This was praised for years afterward. Such things often happened.

The links in this sequence in no way recall the cleverness of Toshiyori's renga, but the prevailing tone is nevertheless intellectual rather than emotional, and it is clear that the aptness of the response was more highly prized than the depth or intrinsic beauty. The way had been opened for the development of renga as a distinct poetic art, but as yet it had not achieved its characteristic tone.

The example from *Kokon chomonjū* describes a renga sequence of 1165 which required the participants not only to respond appropriately to the link composed by the previous poet but to begin each successive link with the next in order of the *i-ro-ha* syllabary. This clearly implies that by this time renga sequences in forty-seven links (the number of *kana* in the *i-ro-ha* syllabary) were being composed.[15]

By the early thirteenth century, when the Retired Emperor Go-Toba gathered the best poets at his court, renga chains in fifty or one hundred links, apparently modeled on waka sequences of those lengths, were frequently composed. In *Yakumo mishō*, the work of poetics by Emperor Juntoku written mainly before 1219, it is stated, "In the past there was no such thing as composing fifty or one hundred links . . . The creation of chains in the present manner originated in middle antiquity. I imagine that the *fushimono* also originated about that time."[16]

Presumably "middle antiquity" (*chūko*) referred to the period of a hundred years earlier, though no extant evidence indicates that either the chain renga or the fushimono existed at that time. The fushimono (prescribed themes) were an important, even indispensable feature of the early renga and were retained in vestigial form well into the Muromachi period. The use of fushimono represented a first stage in the creation of rules of renga composition; without rules, renga could never have become more than a game. Originally the fushimono were topics that had to be mentioned in the two links of a short renga. Fujiwara Teika in *Meigetsuki*

---

15. See Nagazumi Yasuaki and Shimada Isao, eds., *Kokon chomonjū*, in *Nihon koten bungaku taikei* (Tokyo, 1966), 84: 151–152.

16. Quoted in Shimazu, p. 41.

248   DONALD KEENE

listed about forty varieties of fushimono such as "fish and birds," "things that float and things that sink," etc. In almost every instance the fushimono consisted of two associated objects or concepts. The person who composed the maeku had to mention the first of these two topics, and the writer of the tsukeku the second. The skill with which the participants responded to the challenge of composing verses on prescribed themes was evaluated by the judges, who declared the winners. Before long it had become customary to award prizes at renga sessions, and bets on the lucky verses were placed by participants. Indeed, renga sessions resembled gambling parties and were accompanied by wine, women, and song.[17] Renga and gambling continued to go together for centuries, and at times renga gatherings were prohibited because of the undesirable riffraff they attracted.

The importance of the fushimono is apparent from the earliest surviving rules of renga composition, listed in *Yakumo mishō*. Most of the fifteen articles are concerned with the fushimono; the remainder elucidated the principle of *sarikirai*, the restrictions on the repetition of words or themes in a chain renga.[18] As time went on, more and more complex regulations developed and the fushimono lost their importance. The masterpiece of renga, *Minase sangin*, bears the fushimono of *nanibito* (what kind of man?), and the presence in the hokku of the word *yama* (mountain) satisfied the technical requirement of the fushimono because it could be combined with the word *hito* to form *yamahito* (mountain man). But by the time of *Minase sangin*, 1488, there were so many other rules that the fushimono were the least of the poets' problems. Indeed, the rules had proliferated so much that not even the poets could be expected to know them all. Instead, it was left to a referee (*shuhitsu*) to determine if a link observed exactly all the regulations; if not, it was sent back for correction.[19]

The evolution of codes of composition may have been intended mainly to make the game more challenging to experts, but the result was to raise the level of renga, if only because participation became restricted to poets capable of complying with the complex rules and of catching the allusions to classical literature and ancient customs, the basic materials of composition. Entertainment, however, was still the main reason for holding renga sessions. At Go-Toba's palace there were two distinct groups of poets, the ushin and the mushin, and competitions between the two were held frequently between 1206 and 1217. Almost all the surviving examples are in

17. Ishida Yoshisada, "Chūsei shoki renga no fushimono," *Kokugo to kokubungaku*, March 1959, p. 34.
18. Kyūsōjin Hitaku, *Kōhon yakumo mishō to sono kenkyū* (Tokyo, 1960), pp. 17–20.
19. Konishi, *Sōgi*, pp. 72–73.

the ushin manner associated with Teika's lofty conception of poetry, but the mushin renga continued to be composed by way of diversion, even though generally not recorded. The collection of edifying anecdotes, *Shaseki shū*, compiled between 1279 and 1283 by the priest Mujū (1226–1312), contains various examples of short renga which the compiler himself characterizes as being clever or witty.[20] After Sōgi has spent several painful hours composing serious renga with a not especially gifted baron and his entourage, probably all the participants were delighted to turn to informal composition promoted by generous libations of sake. Professor Konishi Jin'ichi has written concerning one renga session held at the Imperial Palace in 1480 and attended by Emperor Go-Tsuchimikado, the former Chancellor Ichijō Kanera, the then Chancellor Konoe Masaie, and other notables that it is difficult to tell whether the main object of the gathering was the renga or the sake.[21] No doubt the renga composed on that occasion verged on the mushin style.

The main stream of renga composition, however, was directed toward evolving a poetic form marked by the kind of elegance and seriousness that characterized the waka. The composition of formal codes (*shikimoku*) made of renga a demanding and ultimately satisfying art. Some sort of code apparently existed even in Go-Toba's day, but the earliest surviving one dates from 1278. It in turn served as the prototype for the later, more complicated codes. From the fourteenth century on the ushin renga dominated, not only at the court but among the commoners, whose activities in renga became steadily more pronounced. The combination of the poetic skill of a commoner poet and the authority of a nobleman poet created the mature art of renga.

NIJŌ YOSHIMOTO (1320–1398)

Yoshimoto, the son of a chancellor (*kampaku*), belonged to the highest rank of the nobility. Extraordinary honors were accorded him, even as a child, thanks to his birth. At seven he became a captain of the Left Palace Guard (*sakon shōshō*) and two years later was appointed an Acting Middle Counselor. His rise in rank and position, though the honors were usually hollow, continued without break through the crises of the day—Go-Daigo's unsuccessful revolt and exile, his restoration to power, and his flight to Yoshino. Yoshimoto, an adherent of the Northern Court, became Minister of the Right in 1343, and in 1346 became Chancellor of the Northern Court, retaining this position until 1358. His

---

20. Watanabe Tsunaya, ed., *Shaseki shū*, in *Nihon koten bungaku taikei* (Tokyo, 1960), 85: 242–246.
21. Konishi, p. 76.

brilliant career probably owed less to his political ability than to his birth
and his decision not to follow Go-Daigo into the mountains of Yoshino. At
a time when the Imperial Court was virtually without power, the duties
even of a chancellor or regent were more a matter of appearance than of
reality, but to people of the time appearances were of the highest importance. Yoshimoto was learned in court ceremonials and precedents and
seems to have spent his days in such studies rather than in practical
politics. Late in life he became the adviser of the youthful shogun
Yoshimitsu and wrote at his request a manual of court ceremonial.

Yoshimoto's absorption with precedents and rules is apparent also in
his writings on renga. He was esteemed as a waka poet too, but his poems,
derived from the conservative traditions of the Nijō school, are lifeless and
conventional; by contrast, his renga poetry and criticism are still of interest, though he never freed himself from the traditions. His mentor in
renga, the priest Kyūsei (1284–1372),[22] belonged to the commoner poets
known as *hana no moto* ("under the blossoms"), who may have been the
source of such originality as Yoshimoto's renga possesses. Yoshimoto
bestowed the highest praise on Kyūsei's poetry, describing it as "beautiful
and skillful, evocative and bewitching."[23] Although he himself was a *dōjō*,
or aristocrat poet, in his writings on renga he did not consider it necessary
even to mention the names of other *dōjō* poets.

Yoshimoto's willingness to associate with persons of a distinctly inferior
social class was not confined to renga. Recently discovered documents
show that the boy Zeami, twelve years old at the time, first visited
Yoshimoto's mansion in 1375. Enchanted by the boy's precocious talents
and good looks, Yoshimoto bestowed on Zeami the name Fujiwaka, apparently taking the *fuji* from the name of his own clan, the Fujiwara.[24] The
boy subsequently participated in renga sessions with Yoshimoto and other
masters, holding his own so successfully that at one gathering in 1378 his
tsukeku to a maeku by Yoshimoto was pronounced "truly outstanding."[25]

The close relationship between the arts of renga and nō, discussed at
length by Professor Konishi,[26] is confirmed by the striking similarity in the
vocabulary of criticism of the two arts. Moreover, although both were
dominated by aristocratic preferences in literature—the imperial anthologies of waka, *Genji monogatari*, *Ise monogatari*, and the most familiar Chinese

22. The name is pronounced *Gusai* by some authorities, including Ijichi Tetsuo in *Renga shū*, in
Nihon koten bungaku taikei (Tokyo, 1960), p. 29.

23. Kidō Saizō and Imoto Nōichi, *Rengaron shū: Hairon shū* (Tokyo, 1961), p. 242.

24. Fukuda Hideichi, "Zeami to Yoshimoto," in *Geinōshi kenkyū*, no. 10, p. 51.

25. Ijichi Tetsuo, "Higashiyama Gyobunko-bon 'Fuchiki' . . . ," *Kokubungaku kenkyū* 35
(1967): 39.

26. Konishi, pp. 105–107.

poems—the chief practitioners were commoners, some of extremely humble origins. Sōgi, whose position in renga is analogous to that of Teika in waka, is said by some to have been the son of a *gigaku* performer, though there is virtually no information on his antecedents. Nevertheless, he associated on familiar terms with such members of the high nobility as Sanjōnishi Sanetaka and with daimyós all over the country, even on occasion serving as the judge of renga written by the Emperor himself. His disciple Sōchō, though acutely aware of his base birth (as he conceived it), did not hesitate to mingle with the great political and military figures of the day. Of course, the fact that Kyūsei, Sōgi, and Sōchō were (in appearance at least) Buddhist priests made it easier for them to move in aristocratic circles, but priestly garments would not have easily won them a place in the court society of a previous age.

Although Yoshimoto stated his conviction that "renga is one of the many forms of waka,"[27] he clearly recognized that its potential was different. His discussion of the language appropriate to renga suggests this awareness: "The poet should seek in his language to find the flower among flowers, the jewel among jewels. But among beginners there are always those who try to make their language as elegant as possible, even when the thought is absolutely trivial, supposing that the use of such phrases as 'a spring dawning' or 'an autumn evening' is proper in renga even today . . . It is true that in general the language of renga should be confined to the vocabulary of the successive imperial anthologies of waka, but there is no objection in renga to the use of neologisms or even of vulgar words . . . It is the closeness in correspondence between one verse and the next that determines excellence in renga, and it therefore does not necessarily seem a fault even if the language is somewhat ugly."[28]

Yoshimoto's reluctant tolerance in renga of words not found in the standard poetic diction opened to renga areas of experience impossible to describe in the waka. He also recognized the importance of the present, as opposed to the waka poets' belief that perfection had been achieved in the past. He wrote, "As the times change, so styles also change, and there is no need to defend the old ways. One should accept the common preferences and, without insisting on narrow prejudices, respect the leading poets of our time and current usages."[29] Many years later (in 1491) Sōgi, in most respects a highly conservative poet, also stated, "In general it is true that a work is unlikely to succeed, no matter how respectful it is toward the past, unless the present is also included."[30] The elegant phraseology with which Yoshimoto and Sōgi clothed their compositions

27. Kidō and Imoto, p. 35.   28. Ibid., pp. 40–41.
29. Ibid., p. 36.   30. Quoted in Konishi, p. 40.

makes it difficult for us today to detect the contemporary touches, but close examination reveals them. Yoshimoto's contact with poets of the commoner class enriched his renga, though not his waka. Even at its most exalted the renga would not lose a touch of this-worldliness.

Yoshimoto distinguished fifteen different ways of linking renga verses, including the straightforward continuation of the thought of the preceding verse, the link established by plays on words and other verbal elements, and the link that catches the faint associations thrown off by the preceding verse.[31] The more remote the link the more highly it was esteemed by such poets as Shinkei (1406–1475), but a judicious combination of closely and remotely associated links was necessary for balance in a long sequence.[32]

Yoshimoto's most complete statement of his theories of renga was presented in *Tsukuba mondō* (1372), a set of seventeen questions with responses ostensibly given by an old man well versed in renga lore. Most questions were specific, e.g., on the nature of the hokku or the *wakiku* (second verse) or on the ideal number of participants in a session, but one question asked if renga is of help in governing a country, and another if renga leads to enlightenment. The old man answered both these questions affirmatively, explaining that every syllable in a renga sequence must conform to morality and citing the numbers of holy men who had devoted their lives to renga. Not only men, but the buddhas of past and present had all composed poetry, and, of the different varieties of poetry, renga with its perpetual shifts of subject and mood corresponded most closely to the mortal world itself.[33]

The religious aspect of renga composition, irrespective of content, is apparent from the frequency with which sequences were offered to temples and shrines. Renga sequences were composed by way of prayer for recovery from illness or for victory in war. In 1471 a hokku offered by Sōgi to the Mishima Shrine in Izu was credited with having effected the miraculous cure of a child; and in 1504 Sōchō offered at the same shrine a renga sequence in a thousand links in order to assure the victory of the daimyo he served.[34] The elevation of the "dignity" of renga from the level of an after-dinner entertainment to an art credited with miraculous powers was largely the work of Buddhist monks who readily found parallels between renga and the teachings of the Buddha. Yoshimoto himself was not a priest, but such men as Shinkei compared the Three Bodies of the Buddha, assumed to save men of different capabilities, to the different

31. Kidō and Imoto, pp. 50–52. See Konishi, pp. 124–133, for an analysis of the different varieties of links, together with examples by Kyūsei illustrating each.
32. See Konishi, p. 124.
33. Kidō and Imoto, pp. 81–83.   34. Konishi, pp. 18, 21.

levels of renga composition practiced by poets ranging from beginners to masters of the art.[35] Such writings contributed to the enormous prestige enjoyed by renga, making it a medium suitable for expressing the loftiest sentiments.

The daimyos in different parts of the country, eager to learn about the kind of poetry most in vogue in the capital, often asked the guidance of the masters. In 1376 Yoshimoto wrote *Kyūshū mondō* for Imagawa Ryōshun (1325-1420), the *tandai* of Kyushu and himself a distinguished poet. In 1379 he wrote *Renga jūyō* at the request of Ashikaga Yoshimitsu. Yoshimoto declared in this work that he had held back no secrets or oral traditions but, as if to contradict this statement, his last work of renga poetics, presented in 1383 to Ōuchi Yoshihiro (1356-1399), bore the title *Jūmon saihi shō* (Ten questions: A most secret selection). These critical works reveal Yoshimoto's increasing independence of views on renga. He seems to have left behind his master Kyūsei, perhaps as the result of his study of Sung poetics.[36] The following brief passage suggests this influence:

> Question. What should the style of renga be?
> Answer. It is stated in *Yü-hsieh*, a work dealing with Chinese poetry, "Avoid all vulgarity of meaning, language, or tone." The same holds true of renga.[37]

Yoshimoto contributed to renga not only his own compositions and criticism but his compilation (with the collaboration of Kyūsei) of the renga anthology 2Tsukuba shū (1356). The compilers clearly intended to make a classic anthology of renga that would proclaim its importance, much as the *Kokinshū* had done for the waka. In this effort they largely succeeded: thanks apparently to pressure exerted on the court by Yoshimoto and Sasaki Takauji (Dōyo, 1306-1373, high-ranking military adviser of the Ashikaga shogunate, and an enthusiastic amateur poet), *Tsukuba shū* was in 1357 officially ranked as "immediately after" the imperial anthologies of waka.[38]

Tsukuba shū consisted of 2,170 verses, arranged for the most part in pairs of maeku and tsukeku, though some single hokku were also given. This arrangement indicates that even though renga sequences in a hundred or

---

35. Kidō and Imoto, p. 201.
36. Shimazu, pp. 83-84. See also Konishi Jin'ichi, "Yoshimoto to Sōdai shiron," *Gobun*, no. 14 (1968), for a study of the influence of Sung poetics on Nijō Yoshimoto.
37. Kidō and Imoto, p. 111. The Chinese work mentioned was the collection of *shih-hua*, or talks on poetry, *Shih-jen yü-hsieh* (Jade chips from the poets), edited in 1244 by Wei Ching-chih. See Yoshikawa Kōjirō, *An Introduction to Sung Poetry*, trans. Burton Watson (Cambridge, Mass., 1967), p. 183.
38. Ijichi, *Renga shū*, p. 20.

more links were appreciated as integral works with a form of their own, the heart of renga composition still remained the skillful catching of the overtones of a maeku with an effective tsukeku. In this collection the writers of the maeku are normally not identified, no doubt because the emphasis was so heavy on the skill of the response. Kyūsei is represented by the largest number of tsukeku, followed by Yoshimoto. The following may suggest Yoshimoto's characteristic renga techniques:

| yama wa shika no ne | In the hills the cries of deer, |
| no ni wa naku mushi | In the fields the chirping insects. |

mono goto ni	In everything
kanashiki kana ya	What sadness is apparent
aki no kure[39]	This autumn evening

The maeku tells of the mournful cries of deer yearning for their mates in the late autumn (a familiar waka subject) and the last feeble chirps of the insects before winter comes. In the tsukeku Yoshimoto stated the significance of these sounds: it is in the nature of an autumn day for everything to seem heartrendingly sad.

Yoshimoto was entirely confident about the future reputation of *Tsukuba shū*. He wrote, "I imagine that men of future times will look up to our day because *Tsukuba shū* was chosen as an imperial collection and preserved many different forms of poetry."[40] It was much more common for Japanese writers to look back to some distant golden age than to congratulate themselves on being alive in their own time, but Yoshimoto evidently felt quite sure that *Tsukuba shū* would arouse the envy of yet unborn poets.

Yoshimoto's mention of the different forms of poetry in the collection may be a reference to the haikai poems in the nineteenth book of *Tsukuba shū*, a reminder that the mushin tradition was not dead. The humor in these poems is often strained and is unlikely to provoke laughter, but after eighteen books of overwhelmingly ushin poetry the haikai poems provided a welcome change of style. Most often the humor revolved around puns or even double puns, as in this tsukeku by the former Major Counsellor Tameie (1179–1275) composed in response to a maeku associating a horse and some carp:

uma no se ni	I wonder what kind
ika naru fuchi no	Of spots there might be
aru yaran[41]	On the horse's back.

39. Fukui Kyūzō, *Tsukuba shū*, in *Nihon koten zensho* (Tokyo, 1951), 1: 116.
40. Kidō and Imoto, p. 79.
41. Fukui, 2: 273.

The point of this lame poem is the puns on *se* ("back" but also "shallows of a river") and on *fuchi* ("spots" but also "pools"), giving an underlying river imagery that matches that of the maeku. A somewhat more interesting example bears the title, "When I called somebody's aunt who was in the public bath."

furo no uchi ni te	I called his aunt
oba wo yobikeri	Inside the public bath.
wa ga oya no	She was in the water
Ane ga kōji no	At the bathhouse his father runs
yu ni irite[42]	On Elder Sister Lane

The humor here involves the play on *ane* (elder sister) of the man's father and the street-name Ane-no-kōji in Kyoto; it is appropriate for the person's aunt (his father's elder sister) to be in the bathhouse on that street. Beyond the rather childish humor of the play on words, there is some interest in the subject itself: no one ever mentioned a public bath in ushin poetry.

A better example, anticipating the haikai style of the sixteenth century, had a tsukeku by Kyūsei:

warai wa suredo	They laugh, it is true,
anazuri wa sezu	But they never mock.
taka no oru	The flock of crows
mori no kozue no	In the treetops of the wood
muragarasu[43]	Where a hawk lurks.

The maeku along leads the reader to suppose that the unexpressed subject must be human beings, but Kyūsei interpreted it instead as a nonhuman creature which laughs. He wrote therefore about a flock of crows noisily cawing ("laughing") at a hawk but too afraid of being seized to make fun of him. This was precisely the kind of haikai response found in the collection of *Inu tsukuba*, compiled about 1542.[44]

SŌGI (1421–1502)

There is no haikai section in the next important collection of renga, *Shinsen tsukuba shū*, compiled in 1495 by Sōgi and his associate Ken-

---

42. Ibid., p. 280. This *tsukeku* was written by the priest Jūbutsu, who was otherwise known as the author of *Daijingū sankeiki* (1341).

43. Ibid., p. 265.

44. I am thinking of such riddles as *kiritaku mo ari kiritaku mo nashi*. See Suzuki Tōzō, *Inu tsukuba shū* (Tokyo, 1965), p. 76, where three different *tsukeku* are given for this *maeku*.

zai (1452?–1510) at the request of Ōuchi Masahiro, the powerful daimyo of Yamaguchi.[45] Members of both the court and the military nobility participated in the planning of the collection, and the variety of authorship attests to the widespread popularity of renga at the time. Compared with *Tsukuba shū* there are far fewer poems by emperors and other high-ranking nobles and many more by soldiers and professional renga poets. In view of the increased participation by members of the commoner class it would be natural to expect that haikai poetry, which was especially identified with that class, would be generously represented. Certainly the lack of a haikai section in *Shinsen tsukuba shū* cannot be taken as evidence that comic renga had become unpopular. Shinkei, whose book of criticism *Sasamegoto* (1463) is the loftiest enunciation of the ideals of renga, decried the prevailing situation in the countryside: "The renga verses I have heard recently in country districts have none of the earmarks of a disciplined, conscious art. The poets seem to be in a state of complete confusion. Indeed, ever since such amateurs have grown so numerous the art of composing noble, deeply felt poetry seems to have come to an end. Renga has become nothing more than a glib chattering, and all mental discipline has vanished without a trace. That is why when one passes along the roads or the marketplaces one's ears are assaulted by the sounds of thousand-verse or ten-thousand-verse compositions, and even the rare persons who have real familiarity with the art employ it solely as a means of earning a living. Day after day, night after night, they engage in indiscriminate composition together. Our times would seem to correspond to the age of stultification and final decline of the art."[46]

Sōgi no doubt shared the prejudices of his teacher Shinkei against the countrified renga, and by excluding haikai verses from *Shinsen tsukuba shū* he was probably doing his best to impart dignity to an art imperiled by indiscriminate poets. He nevertheless threw open his collection to all poets regardless of their social position. When the forthcoming compilation was announced he and the other editors were so deluged with contributions that they were forced to establish a deadline for submissions.[47] The nationwide mania for renga, about which Shinkei complained in 1463, grew more intense after the outbreak of the Ōnin War in 1467. The professional poets, finding it impossible to live in the capital under such dangerous conditions, dispersed all over the country, wherever they could find

45. But see Konishi, *Sōgi*, p. 49, where he suggests that Sōgi probably put the idea into Masahiro's head.

46. Kidō and Imoto, pp. 162–163. Shinkei used the Buddhist terms *zōhō* and *mappō*, the last two stages of the world after the death of the Buddha. I have rendered the words freely as "stultification" and "final decline."

47. Ijichi, *Renga shū*, p. 24.

patrons to support them. A hokku by Shinkei bears the headnote: "Composed after going down to the East when the world was in turmoil during the Ōnin era."

kumo wa nao	The clouds still possess
sadame aru yo no	Some semblance of order:
shigure kana[48]	They bring the world rain.

A hokku by Sōgi has the headnote: "On the same theme, written at a gathering when thoughts weighed on my mind."

yo ni furu mo	To live in the world
sara ni shigure no	Is sad enough without this rain
yadori kana[49]	Pounding on my shelter.

Sōgi was known as a traveler-poet, but this reputation did not stem from mere wanderlust. On occasion, it is true, he journeyed to see with his own eyes the "famous places" which had inspired the poetry of the past, and in his critical writings he devoted much attention to these *utamakura*. But his travels were also spurred by the uncertainty of the times and the passionate desire of the military men to acquire culture. Sōgi was celebrated in his own day not only for his renga but for his profound knowledge of the Japanese classical literature, and this knowledge gave him access to the most exalted quarters. During his lifetime Sōgi made many lengthy journeys—seven times to the province of Echigo (as the guest of the daimyo Uesugi Fusasada), twice to Yamaguchi, and even as far as Kyushu in 1480, a journey commemorated in his diary *Tsukushi no michi no ki*. Although the days spent on the road must have been painful and even dangerous, life in the Ōuchi mansion in Yamaguchi was undoubtedly more agreeable than life in the war-torn capital, and Sōgi was royally welcomed. But although travel had its compensations, and Sōgi seems to have enjoyed hobnobbing with the great, his poetry is rooted in the traditions of the wandering priests for whom travel was part of their vocation.

Sōgi's reputation in his day was unparalleled, but modern scholars generally agree that Shinkei's poetry was more deeply moving and evocative.[50] Sōgi's respect for Shinkei is evidenced by his inclusion of more examples of renga by Shinkei than by any other poet represented in *Shinsen tsukuba shū*. Indeed, Shinkei's work shows to best advantage in the form of the two-verse extracts given in this anthology: his aristocratic tempera-

---

48. Ibid., p. 263. The meaning is ironic: the clouds, generally used as a symbol of inconstancy, are actually more dependable than men, for at least one knows the clouds will bring rain, whereas nothing can be predicted about men.
49. Ibid., p. 312. See also Konishi, *Sōgi*, p. 10.
50. Konishi, *Sōgi*, p. 52.

ment may have inhibited him when it came to composing extended renga sequences. Shinkei was sure that the comprehension of renga was inevitably limited to a minute group of initiates. He once remarked sardonically, "These days there doesn't seem to be anyone who hasn't embarked on a career as a poet. I wonder if we are living in a golden age?" Elsewhere he expressed his doubts concerning the frequently voiced conviction (in China and Europe as well as Japan) that the greatest poetry should be intelligible even to an ignorant peasant. He declared, "No art worthy of the name is intelligible to persons of shallow understanding who have not mastered it. No doubt even the most untalented and ignorant poets may be pleased by pedestrian verses and a banal style, but it is inconceivable that anyone only vaguely familiar with the art could understand poetry of an elevated and profoundly beautiful nature."[51]

Despite his haughty attitude, Shinkei spent much time, especially during the years of warfare, forming and improving literary taste in the eastern region where he had taken refuge. In 1474 he served as judge of the waka competition (uta-awase) held in Edo by command of Ōta Dōkan, the traditional founder of the city; this is the oldest surviving example of such a competition being held under the sponsorship of a military leader.[52] The participants in the poetry competitions over which Shinkei presided were all other soldiers or priests, an indication of how far removed he was from the traditional milieu of poetry, the court. He seems rarely to have had the good fortune to associate with poets of equal stature who could have joined with him in extended renga sequences of the first importance.

Sōgi's reputation, on the other hand, stems not so much from his criticism or his individual links as from his extended sequences. Two are particularly important: *Minase sangin* (Three poets at Minase), composed in the first month of 1488,[53] and *Yunoyama sangin*, composed in the tenth month of 1491. On both occasions his partners were his disciples Shōhaku (1443–1527) and Sōchō (1448–1532). A solo renga sequence by Sōgi composed in 1499 and called *Nanibito hyakuin* has been acclaimed as supremely beautiful renga by Professor Konishi.

Although the three poets who joined efforts at Minase and Yunoyama were not equally gifted, Sōgi being superior to the other two, their abilities were nearly enough matched for a magnificent series of verses to unroll, each man catching the overtones and associations of the words uttered by the man before him. There is no unity of thought behind these poems; in-

51. Kidō and Imoto, p. 143.
52. Inoue Muneo, *Chūsei kadanshi no kenkyū: Muromachi zenki* (Tokyo, 1961), p. 229.
53. He was soon afterward appointed to the exalted post of *renga kaisho bugyō* (the supreme master of renga) by the shogun Yoshihisa.

deed, the rules the poets observed made it quite impossible to achieve unity. The interest lay in the variety and change, the closeness or remoteness of the links, the alternation of verses that produced a strong impression *(mon)* with others that were relatively bland *(ji)*, and in those verses that developed a half-spoken theme as opposed to those which resolutely changed the direction of the flow of thought.[54] Sōgi's links maintained a difficult balance in these sets of possibilities in a manner superior even to Shinkei's, let alone of any other renga poet. Yet it is not easy to detect his particular voice when reading a sequence. The expert will recognize the superiority of Sōgi's contributions to those of his collaborators, but the reader is less aware of his individuality than of his skill in using familiar materials. Neither in his renga nor in his diaries does a distinct personality emerge. His commentaries on the classics were more satisfying than the explanations of obscure words that were the traditional stock in trade of scholars of Japanese literature, and we can only assume that his understanding was based on a genuine love of these works. But it is significant that we know hardly a single fact about Sōgi before he was forty and little else of a personal nature even for his later years, except that he seems to have enjoyed robust good health.

Sōgi's manner was precisely the opposite of that of the romantic artist. To paraphrase the opening of Rousseau's *Confessions*, Sōgi was not any different from other renga poets of his day, only much superior. The closest parallel to his art in the West may be in music rather than in poetry. We can detect the unmistakable voice of Schubert or Chopin even in a piece we hear for the first time, and we not only prize this quality but would feel disdain for any composer who so successfully imitated the style of Schubert or Chopin as to defy detection: mimicry is not a revered art. With respect to baroque music, however, we tend to have different standards. We do not try to recognize, say, the distinctive voice of Albinoni or contrast his voice with that of Vivaldi or Corelli, and it really makes little difference even if we know that Bach took over whole sections of Vivaldi. We can enjoy a work of baroque music without caring who the composer was, appreciating the fertility of invention, the contrasts in moods and rhythms, the general elegance of the age of baroque. Shinkei wrote, "The supreme renga is like a drink of plain boiled water. It has no particular flavor, but one never wearies of it, no matter when one tastes it."[55]

With Sōgi the renga reached the apex of its development, although many men wrote renga during the century after his death. Shōhaku, the senior of his collaborators at Minase and Yunoyama, was undoubtedly an accomplished poet, but so self-effacing that it is hard to attribute to him

54. See Konishi, *Sōgi*, pp. 53, 117.   55. Quoted in Shimazu, p. 146.

any new development in renga. He ranks as a worthy follower, a smaller-sized edition of Sōgi. Sōchō, however, emerged in his prose writings and haikai verse especially as a distinctive personality. His place in Japanese literary history has been relatively obscure because he was overshadowed by Sōgi, but he deserves recognition as a practitioner not only of the *ga* (elegant) but of the *zoku* (familiar) style.

Even in Sōgi's day, when the ushin renga had become established as the only acceptable style, mushin renga was still being composed as a diversion both at the palace and in the villages. Sōgi himself on occasion composed haikai links, as the following example shows. It is prefaced by the note: "Written when Sōgi attended a renga gathering wearing a short-sleeved robe *(kosode)* of twilled silk *(aya)*."

ayashi ya tare ni	Very suspicious! From whom
kariginu no sode	Did you borrow that silk robe?
Sōchō	

kono kosode	A certain person
hito no kata yori	Presented me with this robe
kurehatori[56]	Of figured silk.
Sōgi	

The surface meaning of this exchange is only the pretext for the elaborate puns. Sōchō's exclamation *ayashi ya* (how suspicious!) contains the word *aya* (twilled silk); and *kariginu* (a silk cloak) contains the word *kari*, meaning "to borrow." In Sōgi's reply *kata* (direction) is the homophone of the word for "shoulder," suggesting that the robe was formerly on someone else's shoulders; and *kurehatori*, the name of a figured silk originally woven in China, contains the verb *kure*, "to bestow." A similar kind of humor was displayed by other poets of the day. Such play on words are unlikely to provoke much laughter (even when not subjected to the cruel process of translation). This pedantic humor would be developed by Matsunaga Teitoku and his school in the seventeenth century and was present even in some poems by Bashō. Various anecdotes that recount examples of the wit of Sōgi and his disciples are found in later collections, but it is hard to be sure which are authentic.[57]

It is clear, however, that one collection of haikai poetry already existed during Sōgi's lifetime, the recently discovered *Chikuba kyōgin shū* (1499). The compiler's name is not known, but he seems to have been an elderly priest who lived in the vicinity of Kyoto. Some haikai poems given in *Chikuba kyōgin shū* were taken word for word from the haikai section of

56. From *Shinkyū Kyōka Haikai Kikigaki,* courtesy of Professor Konishi.
57. Suzuki, pp. 266–267.

Tsukuba shū, others were slightly modified,[58] but the compiler claimed to have included only verses he had actually heard people recite; this would explain the many variations, characteristic of oral transmission. At any rate, the publication of *Chikuba kyōgin shū* in 1969 changed the history of haikai poetry, upsetting the long-held assumption that the oldest collection was *Inu tsukuba shū*, compiled by Yamazaki Sōkan. Many verses from *Chikuba kyōgin shū* appeared unaltered in Sōkan's collection, though it is not clear whether they were borrowed directly or were part of a "floating population" of comic poetry circulated from generation to generation.[59] Certainly the prevailing tone of the two collections is quite dissimilar: *Chikuba kyōgin shū* depends on refined plays on words to achieve its humorous effects, while *Inu tsukuba shū* brims with an earthiness that belongs to the *zoku* tradition. This tradition, present in the mushin renga in former times, was embodied in the comic work of Sōgi's disciple Sōchō.

SŌCHŌ (1448-1532)

Sōchō gave a brief autobiographical account of himself in the journal *Utsuyama no ki*, written in 1517:

> I was born the son of an unskilled artisan, but in my eighteenth year I became a priest and underwent the rituals of ordination (*jukai*), preparatory discipline (*kegyō*), and baptism (*kanjō*). The country broke out in disorder while I was in my twenties, and this lasted for six or seven years. There was fighting also in the province of Tōtōmi for three years running. I mingled with the dust of the encampments, but in my diet (if in no other respect) I remained a priest, eating thistles and suchlike vegetarian food. Afterward, forgetful of the powerful virtue (*toku*) of my own province, I was drawn to the holy shrines of the capital, to the Seven Great Temples of Nara, and to Kōya, and visited them all. For more than forty years I enjoyed a close relationship with that cultivated gentleman Sōgi and learned from him the rudiments of composing renga. He died when he was over eighty, having become a celebrity among both the nobles and the military men. That is how it happened that even a base-born person like myself was able to attend formal gatherings of the nobility. How strong the bond must have been between us from a former existence! On my recent visit to the capital I was often reminded of him.
> While in this province I became acquainted with a woman who washed and sewed my clothes, and eventually two children were born. One is a boy. I left him at birth with Angen[60] to rear, and decided he would become a priest. This boy, to whom I at first gave a worldly name, has become an acolyte and is

---

58. Kimura Miyogo, "Chikuba kyōgin shū," *Biburia*, no. 43 (1969), pp. 57–58.
59. Ibid., p. 60.
60. Saitō Angen, a high-ranking officer of the province. See below.

called Shōha. He is now eleven. My daughter is thirteen. I had planned also
that she become a nun, but a certain man was fond of her, and at the close of
the year I learned that they were engaged. It is a relief for a man in his seventies
to have both children disposed of. Even if I were to confront my last hour now, I
would probably feel that nothing had been left unfulfilled. But all the same I
somehow feel sorry for them.

kore kare ni	Though we have parted
kakehanaruredo	Going this way and that,
aware nari	How deep is my grief!
ko wo omou yami wa	There is no way to describe
iu kai mo nashi[61]	The anguish of a parent's love.

This is by no means the only biographical information available about
Sōchō, but it alone tells us more about the man than we know about other
renga masters. Sōchō mentioned first his humble ancestry. There is reason
to believe that he was the third son of a hereditary family of swordsmiths.
His father was the fourth to bear the name Gisuke, and descendants who
took the same name continued to make swords until the 1740s.[62] The
family lived in the province of Suruga, near the modern city of Shizuoka,
and Sōchō felt so strong an attachment to his birthplace that he seems
rather embarrassed to have traveled to Kyoto and Nara, as if admitting
thereby that their holy sites were more remarkable than those in Suruga.

Sōchō described his ordination in terms that suggest that his sect of
Buddhism was Shingon.[63] However, apart from his mention of visiting
Mount Kōya, Shingon Buddhism seems to have meant much less to him
than Zen. His journals are dotted with references to the Daitokuji, the Zen
temple at Murasakino, and to the Shūon-an, the hermitage outside Kyoto
where Ikkyū lived and died. Sōchō does not mention when he first became
acquainted with Ikkyū; possibly it was while in service under the daimyo
Imagawa Yoshitada (1442–1476). When he went to Kyoto soon after
Yoshitada's death it was largely because he wished to see Ikkyū, and their
relationship continued until Ikkyū's death five years later. The importance
of Ikkyū in Sōchō's life will be discussed below.

The "disorder" Sōchō mentioned in his account was undoubtedly the
Ōnin War. When the war broke out, Imagawa Yoshitada went to Kyoto
with 1,000 men and for over 200 days stood guard outside Ashikaga

61. *Gunsho ruijū*, kan 480, p. 404. An "official" biography of Sōchō by Kurokawa Dōyū (d. 1691)
entitled *Sōchō koji den* is little more than a translation into classical Chinese of this and similar
materials; see *Zoku zoku gunsho ruijū* (Tokyo, 1902–12), 3: 392–394.
62. Ijichi Tetsuo, "Sōchō-den kōsetsu," *Renga to haikai* 1, no. 4: 15.
63. Kidō, *Rengashi ronkō*, 2: 597, quotes a document which states that a priest from the Daigoji, a
Shingon temple near Kyoto, officiated.

Yoshimasa's palace, the Hana no Gosho. Yoshitada returned to Suruga with his forces at Hosokawa Katsumoto's command and maintained order there in face of spreading disturbances.[64] Sōchō was on unusually intimate terms with Yoshitada; indeed, mention in the journal *Sōchō shuki* of having served at Yoshitada's side "day and night for many years" has suggested to some modern commentators that their relationship went beyond the normal ties between master and vassal.[65]

The three years of fighting in Tōtōmi described by Sōchō probably refer to disturbances that broke out in 1475. Yoshitada, in the course of putting down a revolt by some *rōnin*, was struck by a stray arrow and killed, apparently in the spring of 1476.[66] Sōchō's precise duties while he "mingled with the dust of the encampments" are not clear, though we know that he composed renga to pray for victory or to thank the gods for success in battle.

We know more about Sōchō's efforts on behalf of Yoshitada's son Imagawa Ujichika (1473–1526). In 1517 Sōchō successfully served as the negotiator for peace when a fortress belonging to Ujichika was besieged. Sōchō's journals also reveal a most unusual interest in fortifications, moats, sources of water supply, and the like; it may well be that he profited by the relative ease with which renga masters could move around the country, even in time of war, to spy for the Imagawa family.[67]

After Yoshitada's untimely death in 1476 a succession dispute arose between the adherents of the infant Ujichika and of Yoshitada's brother. For a time Ujichika and his mother had to go into hiding. This may have been the direct cause of Sōchō's decision to leave for Kyoto. An undated entry in his journal *Sōchō shuki* states, "When Ujichika was a small child I took leave of him and made my way to Murasakino."[68] His other reason for going to the capital (apart from his admiration for Ikkyū) was to study with Sōgi. Some accounts state that Sōgi had been impressed to read renga composed by Sōchō when the latter was a boy of twelve, but their first meeting probably occurred in 1466, when Sōchō was in his nineteenth year. Sōchō invited Sōgi, who was passing through the town of Okitsu on his way to the East, to a renga party at the famous temple Seiken-ji.[69] Their next meeting probably took place soon after Sōchō's arrival in Kyoto at the end of 1476. Sōgi was then at the height of his fame both as a

64. Ibid., 2: 577, quoting *Imagawa ki*.
65. See Ijichi, "Sōchō-den," p. 17; Kidō, 2: 576. The source is *Sōchō shuki*, in *Shinkō gunsho ruijū*, kan 326, p. 698.
66. For theories as to the date of Yoshitada's death, see Kidō, 2: 577.
67. *Sōchō shuki*, pp. 579, 645.
68. Ibid., p. 698.
69. So stated in *Sōchō shuki*, p. 662, about fifty-eight years after the event.

poet and as an expert in the classics. In the following year his lectures at his "hermitage" on *Genji monogatari* were attended by Sanjōnishi Sanetaka, and he traveled to Nara to participate in a renga party held by Chancellor Ichijō Kanera (1402–1481). We do not know how close Sōchō had become to Sōgi during this first year as his disciple, but in 1478, when Sōgi journeyed to Echigo, he took Sōchō along. During the journey he instructed Sōchō on *Hyakunin isshu*. In the following year Sōchō attended Sōgi's lectures delivered in Echigo on *Ise monogatari* (his lecture notes are still preserved). The two men returned to Kyoto from Echigo only to set out again in 1480, this time traveling to Yamaguchi and from there to northern Kyushu, composing renga together at various places on the way.

Sōchō was to spend much of the next thirty years in travel. He returned from time to time to Suruga and continued to receive financial support from Imagawa Ujichika, but his main source of income was probably the gifts received from various daimyos with whom he composed renga. The renga masters were well-off, probably enjoying larger incomes than most members of the nobility.[70] Undoubtedly Sōchō derived more pleasure and satisfaction from his sessions with Sōgi and Shōhaku than from his "professional engagements," but renga masters often had no choice in their partners.

His serious activities as a poet begin when he was about thirty, after his arrival in Kyoto. Ten years later he had established himself as a first-rate renga master. Although he was to develop into a writer of marked individuality, his vocabulary and themes were for the most part almost indistinguishable not only from those of other renga poets of his day but even from the standard waka collections. Suggestion and elegant simplicity had become the twin ideals of renga, and an atmosphere of lonely beauty pervaded the verses. Oda Takuji in his brilliant analysis of Sōchō's renga described how exactly he conformed both to the general divisions in a standard waka collection and to the specific topics under each heading. For example, under "summer" Sōchō composed poetry in the approved manner about summer clothes, lingering blossoms, green leaves, hollyhocks, irises, moonflowers, short nights, fans, evening showers, the *hototogisu*, etc., but flies, mosquitoes, sweat, heat rash, and similar summer topics were naturally excluded. Although Sōchō's haikai-style renga were overt to the point of being scabrous when they treated love, his ushin renga on love kept to such stereotyped themes as "hidden love," "waiting love," etc. with no suggestion of personal experience.[71] His manner of linking

70. Nakamura Yukihiko, "Bunjin to Sōchō," *Bungaku* 31, no. 5: 509–510, traces the beginning of "writing for a living" to the commoners who taught waka and renga during the middle ages.
71. Oda Takuji, *Renga bungei ron* (Kyoto, 1947), p. 58.

verses was also quite conventional. The renga by Sōchō included in *Shinsen tsukuba shū* were probably among his works most admired at the time, but they hardly go beyond bland competence, as two examples will indicate:

yukiki mo kage ni	They come and go in the shade
shigeki aoyagi	Of thickly growing green willows.
tsubame tobu	The swallows fly
haru no kawazura	Over the springtime river;
mizu sumite[72]	The water is clear.

The maeku (by an unknown poet) suggests people coming and going under the willows along a riverbank, but Sōchō's tsukeku interprets the unspecified subject as being swallows, rather than people. We can imagine them flickering through the willows, their reflections streaking the clear springtide water. The images are all familiar and the link is made between such obviously related words as "willow" and "river." The following example depends for its effect on a poetic allusion:

natsu no yo wa	Was the summer night,
tada toki no ma no	I wonder, only the space
hodo nare ya	Of a moment of time?
nakeba kumo hiku	When it sang, the clouds trailed forth:
yama hototogisu[73]	The mountain *hototogisu*.

The full meaning of Sōchō's tsukeku can be apprehended only in terms of the poem by Ki no Tsurayuki in the *Kokinshū*:

natsu no yo no	On a summer night,
fusu ka to sureba	About to crawl into bed,
hototogisu	At the single cry
naku hitokoe ni	Of a *hototogisu*
akuru shinonome	The daybreak clouds grow bright.

The shortness of summer nights was a hackneyed theme of poetry, but Tsurayuki, in a display of hyperbole, declared that the dawn came so swiftly that he hardly had time to go to bed; it took only the cry of one *hototogisu* (a kind of cuckoo) to induce the clouds to the east to grow bright. Sōchō repeated much of this imagery.

Such tsukeku, if lacking in originality or individuality, show elegance and unobtrusive skill, exactly the qualities most desired of a partner in a renga sequence. Conspicuous virtuosity would disrupt the mood of three voices blending, and Sōchō in particular disapproved of contrived or un-

72. Ijichi, *Renga shū*, p. 333.   73. Ibid.

usual effects.[74] He was so anxious not to stand out that he restricted himself to mentioning places known from the lists of *utamakura*, even though he must have seen in the course of his travels many other sites worthy of being described in poetry.[75] His renga criticism is also orthodox to such a degree that he contributed nothing new beyond the refinement of a few details. Yet even in his most conventional statements the expression sometimes betrays his unconventional mind. Sōchō compares, for example, a renga poet's store of knowledge to a beggar's wallet; like a beggar who gladly accepts whatever alms people may bestow on him, the renga poet treasures not only the poetry of his great predecessors but every other kind of utterance, from the proverbs of farmers to the loftiest Buddhist doctrine.[76] The following passage from his work of criticism *Renga hikyō shū* is typical of his combination of orthodox views and unorthodox expression:

> Question. Is it true that the skillful poet achieves golden expression by linking things that would never strike an inept poet as being related, and that the inept poet, because he writes only commonplaces, turns out verses that are in no way unusual but even grating on the ears?
>
> Answer. That is not the case. Some faces are handsome and others ugly, some aristocratic and some mean, but all are alike in having seven apertures and two eyebrows. The beauty or ugliness of a face depends on its shape, size, and coloring, on the opening of the eyes and mouth, and on the way ears and nose are attached. The same is true of renga. There is no difference from poet to poet in the seventeen or fourteen syllables of a link, and the use of associations and related words is the same, regardless of the poet; it is the manner in which the poet composes his verses that determines whether he is a master or a poetaster. If you decide that something is not unusual because people have been saying similar things since ancient times and you reject allusions in favor of expressions that have no textual authority (*honkyo*), it is as ugly as if you drew a person's eyes so that they rose up vertically instead of horizontal, or made a nose spread out horizontally instead of being vertical.[77]

Sōchō's preference for ordinary, familiar expression, like Shinkei's praise of plain boiled water, was normal in the renga masters of the day, but his manner of stating it was characteristically plebeian. Although he opposed conscious originality or individuality in renga composition, subconsciously his personality revealed itself. In a sense this was true of all the great renga poets. As Professor Konishi has pointed out, the individuality of Sōgi, Shōhaku, or Sōchō revealed itself despite the prescribed forms of expression: "Individuality is not erased by the forms (*kata*); what is

74. Oda, p. 70.   75. Oda, p. 60.
76. Ijichi Tetsuo, *Rengaron shū* (Tokyo, 1956), 2: 166.   77. Ibid., 2: 171–172.

destroyed is actually no more than the closed shell of the individual."[78] The use of kata, whether in renga or nō, imposed order on a performance, and the kata themselves were the products of many artists' experience, far transcending what any individual could discover for himself. In the end, moreover, the individuality of the poet or actor will shine through the kata more convincingly than if each word or movement was totally original because the connoisseur will detect the slight differences from man to man in performing essentially the same act. When Sōchō composed renga with other men he gladly submerged the differences between his personality and theirs in a mutual effort to create a work of art. His ideal was a harmony of effects. He compared renga to a sword and its ornamental knot (sageo): a common leather cord attached to a golden sword would be unsuitable, but it would be equally unsuitable to attach a magnificent sword knot to a utilitarian sword.[79] He compared renga also to a series of pictures hung on one wall: each picture is complete and independent, but unless it blends with adjacent pictures there will be an impression of disharmony that destroys the initial worth of each picture.[80] He desired nothing more than to have the links he contributed fit smoothly into a sequence, with no suggestion of ostentation.[81]

The first product of the collaboration of Sōgi, Shōhaku, and Sōchō was the celebrated Minase sangin (1488). Although he was the youngest of the three poets, Sōchō's reputation was already secure; ever since 1485 he had been frequenting Sanjōnishi Sanetaka's salon, the ultimate mark of recognition. He was perhaps slightly inferior to the other two poets, but they were nearly equals; otherwise, the sequence would surely not have achieved its reputation. By the time of their next collaboration, when they composed Yunoyama sangin in 1491, Sōchō's progress as a renga poet was unmistakable and there is little to choose among the three participants. Perhaps it was a new sense of self-assurance that enabled him, composing within a prescribed framework, to introduce occasionally a characteristic touch of wit, as in the following:

michikuru shio ya	The tide rushing to the shore
hito shitauran	Seems to yearn for someone there.
Shōhaku	
suteraruru	Abandoned though it is,

78. Konishi, Sōgi, p. 146.
79. Ijichi, Rengaron shū, 2: 174.
80. Ibid., 2: 180.
81. Kidō, 2: 587, states that Sōchō's tsukeku rarely plumb the emotional associations of the maeku but tend to develop their associations in a matter-of-fact manner.

kataware obune   The battered little boat
kuchi yarade[82]   Does not rot away.
        Sōchō

There is certainly nothing comic about Sōchō's tsukeku, but its ingenious use of personification, shifting the subject from the tide mentioned in the maeku to the little boat that longs for its master, impressed the commentators by its wit.

Sōchō's close relations with Sōgi lasted until the latter's death in 1502.[83] He accompanied Sōgi on his final journey and was at his side when Sōgi died near Hakone. His account of Sōgi's death, *Sōgi shūen ki*, is not as coherently organized as we might desire, but it contains some moving passages, especially the description of Sōgi's death:

> At some time past midnight he seemed to be in great pain, so I shook him out of his troubled sleep. He said, "I have just been dreaming I met Lord Teika," and he recited the poem, "Jeweled thread of my life, if you must break, do break." Those who heard him thought, "That poem is by Princess Shikishi." Then he whispered a verse which, I believe, was a maeku in his recent thousand-link sequence:

nagamuru tsuki ni   I step out and am borne up
tachi zo ukaruru   To the moon at which I gaze.

> "I found it very difficult to add a verse to this," he said. "All of you try to add something." So speaking in jesting tones, like a flame that flickers out, he breathed his last.[84]

After Sōgi's death Sōchō was indisputably the best renga poet, but he refused the honors that came his way, preferring to withdraw to a hermitage.[85] His reluctance to remain in the capital may have been occasioned by the new life he began about this time in Suruga. Having been accorded in 1504 the protection of Saitō Angen, an important official of the province, Sōchō was enabled to build a retreat at the foot of Utsuyama called Saiokken. In the following year, as he mentioned in his autobiographical account, he became intimate with the woman who washed his clothes. They had a daughter and, two years later, a son. Although such indulgence was prohibited to Buddhist priests, Sōchō had never led a monastic life and his formal religious ties were apparently minimal.

82. Kaneko Kinjirō, *Sōgi sakuhin shū* (Tokyo, 1963), p. 84.
83. See Ōshima Toshiko, "Sōchō nempu," *Joshidai kokubun* 24 (February 1962): 38–43, for a list of poetry Sōgi and Sōchō composed together.
84. Kaneko Kinjirō, *Sōgi tabi no ki shichū* (Tokyo, 1970), pp. 114–115. Sōchō's text was completed in the year of Sōgi's death; see Ōshima, p. 43.
85. Oda, pp. 105–106.

Perhaps here too the example of the wayward Ikkyū had inspired him.[86]

Sōchō's new domesticity by no means confined him to his hermitage, as is evident from repeated mentions in his diaries of activities in many parts of the country. We know, for example, that he took to the capital 100 pairs of two-link renga, composed in 1508, and asked Shōhaku to judge and make comments on these pairs—which Sōchō had matched in the manner of the old *uta-awase*. Three months later he made the same request of Sanjōnishi Sanetaka. The exceptional combination of poet and commentators should have made this a most interesting document, but *Sōchō hyakuban renga-awase* rarely satisfies a modern reader, either as poetry or as criticism. Here are the verses of the twenty-seventh pair:

Left	
futari tomo	If we were together
araba semete no	At least we could share
kari makura	A temporary pillow.
tsuki wa mono ii	But is this the kind of sky
kawasu sora ka wa	That makes us praise the moon?
Right	
yuku hito mo naki	Autumn alongside a road
michinobe no aki	Where no one ever travels.
wa ga kage ni	I gaze at the moon
tomonaitsutsu mo	Even as it accompanies
tsuki wo mite	My shadow.

Sanetaka: The Left poem, though shallow in conception, does seem to convey a feeling of intimacy over the years. The Right poem is in the manner of the line in Su Tung-po's second prose-poem on the Red Cliff: "Our shadows appeared on the ground, and looking up we saw that the moon had risen." Even on the way to the Lin-kao Pavilion one might well have feelings similar to those communicated by these verses; because they are incomparably richer in overtones, I consider the Right pair to be superior.

Shōhaku: Each pair has something to recommend it. It is hard to choose between them.[87]

86. Sōchō's irregular amorous activities are further indicated by the writings of Satomura Jōha, who visisted the Saiokken and vicinity in the spring of 1567. He met a man named Okitsu Bokuin who, by his own testimony, had been Sōchō's lover many years before. He claimed that he still possessed love letters he had received from Sōchō. When Jōha visited Sōchō's hut on Utsuyama a plaque inscribed "Saiokken" in Ikkyū's hand still hung over the door. See Satomura Jōha, *Jōha Fujimi no michi no ki*, in *Gunsho ruijū*, kan 339, pp. 791-793.

87. Ijichi Tetsuo, ed., *Katsuranomiya-bon sōsho* (Tokyo, 1955), 18: 21. The Lin-kao Pavilion is mentioned, along with the quoted line, near the beginning of the second Red Cliff prose-poem. See Burton Watson, *Su Tung-po* (New York, 1965), p. 91, for the translation I have used.

In the Left pair the speaker wishes he could have the temporary con-
solation of being with some intimate friend, even though they would not
have the pleasure during this bad weather of talking to each other about
the moon. The Right pair is more conventional, but it appealed to
Sanetaka because he sensed an association with Su Tung-po, in an age
when Sung poetry was idolized.

A better example of Sōchō's skill as a renga poet is the second set in the
forty-fifth pair:

yūgure fukaku	As the evening darkness falls
hito kaeru nari	Someone is returning home.
miyako ni ya	In the capital
tabi no yatsure wo	She must be wondering,
shinoburan[88]	"Is he worn with travel?"

Sanetaka commented that the second two lines of the tsukeku were
"witty" (*okashi*), and Shōhaku praised the skill of the tsukeku as a whole.
Their admiration was aroused by Sōchō's unconventional linking of the
two verses. Instead of choosing one element in the maeku as the *yoriai*
(association) for the tsukeku, he linked the entire meaning of the maeku, at
the same time shifting it from the mere description of a traveler returning
in the dark to the apprehensions of a woman who, seeing this traveler,
wonders about the safety of her own lover. This kind of linking anticipates
the manner of the Danrin school of the seventeenth century; Professor
Konishi called Sōchō the pioneer of *kokorozuke*, linking by meaning, as opposed to linking by purely verbal elements.

Two selections of Sōchō's renga with notes by himself have been
preserved. He apparently made these selections about 1528, when he was
eighty, and sent them to two men, Okitsu Masanobu and Mibu Tsunao.[89]
In his commentaries Sōchō patiently explained the allusions (generally
from such well-known collections as the *Kokinshū!*) and occasionally made
general comments on the art of renga; but only rarely did he indicate the
poetic value of the lines he was elucidating. The first example in the selection he sent to Okitsu Masanobu is given one of the most interesting of
Sōchō's commentaries:

kasumeru hodo zo	There is no way to define
waku kata mo naki	Just how far the mists extend.

88. Ijichi *Katsuranomiya-bon*, 18: 54.
89. Ibid., 18: 11. Okitsu Masanobu was probably the same man mentioned in footnote 86
above.

kesa wa mata	This morning again
kozo ka kotoshi no	The sky is clear; is it last year's
sora saete	Or this year's weather?

As described above, it is not certain whether the mist in the morning sky at the beginning of the day belongs to last year or this year.

toshi no uchi ni	The spring has come
haru wa kinikeri	Before the old year was out;
hito tose wo	Should we say of the spring
kozo to ya iwan	It belongs to last year,
kotoshi to ya iwan	Or that this year's has come?

haru tatsu to	Is it merely because
iu bakari ni ya	This is the day spring begins?
mi Yoshino no	At holy Yoshino
yama mo kasumite	The mountains this morning
kesa wa miyuran[90]	Appear swathed in mist.

What is called *yoriai* [association] in renga involves borrowing the theme of a source poem *[honka]*, or taking its words, or else mentioning associations that exist in original texts, whether in Japanese or Chinese poetry. If the maeku is only slightly related to the source poem or original text, it is proper in the tsukeku to emphasize the association somewhat in order to bring out the relation. But if in the maeku many words have been borrowed from the source poem or original text, the tsukeku should merely suggest the association. In either case, this is determined by the maeku. The echo should seem to be in love with the voice. One should devote one's attention to the faint glimmerings of depth in the maeku and consider how to achieve beauty of form and overtones in the tsukeku. If both upper and lower verses are crude and vulgar, this no doubt reflects the character of a contemptible man. When one speaks of suggestion *[yosei]*, it means that a poem sounds somehow impressive *[yū]*, quite beyond its themes and words, and that deeply moving *[ushin]* images are evoked. Even when one is not at a renga gathering, if one seeks out in one's daily life, even at wakeful moments in the night, the thoughts and words of the men of the past, this will surely reveal itself when one comes to responding to a maeku. Of course, even if a poet does not show such devotion, he may all the same produce a fluent verse, but it will not come from his heart. Quite apart from the occasions when a man is composing renga or waka, who will dislike or abuse him if he observes this precaution? And if the man is by himself, it will enable him to be calm, to enjoy life naturally, and not feel lonely.[91]

90. The first waka is the opening one of *Kokinshū* by Ariwara no Motokata. The second, by Mibu no Tadamine, is from *Shūishū*.
91. Ijichi, *Katsuranomiya-bon*, 18: 95–96.

Although these views on renga are confusingly presented, they at least suggest Sōchō's attitudes when he set about responding to a maeku. He took for granted the importance of associations with poetry and other texts of the past but emphasized the necessity of achieving a balance between extremely close and extremely remote references to the sources. His statement on suggestion seems to reflect a famous passage in the *Mumyōshō* of Kamo no Chōmei,[92] and his pious generalizations on poetry being the product of the whole man, not just his brains, have many antecedents. Only in one line—where he likens the tsukeku's relation to the maeku to that of an echo in love with a voice—do we seem to catch a note of Sōchō's individuality.

To the end Sōchō remained a faithful and orthodox follower of Sōgi in his renga, but there was another, more eccentric aspect to his work. It will be recalled that when Sōchō first went to Kyoto in 1476 he headed directly for Murasakino, the Daitokuji, where he could find Ikkyū. *Sōchō shuki*, written in Sōchō's old age, contains many references to temples associated with Ikkyū, evidence of the persistence of his admiration over many years. Ikkyū was already eighty-two years old when Sōchō visited him in 1476 and he had only five more years to live. During this period Sōchō was away from the capital, traveling with Sōgi, for at least half the time, so the two men could not have been together very long. Yet Ikkyū's great influence on Sōchō can hardly be doubted. Kidō Saizō wrote, "The influence of Ikkyū was absolute, and it dominated Sōchō for the rest of his life."[93]

An extreme example of Sōchō's devotion to the memory of Ikkyū is given in an entry in his journal for the sixth month of 1526. A messenger arrived at the Shūon-an (where Sōchō had been staying) with word that Imagawa Ujichika had suddenly died. It was Sōchō's urgent duty to return to Suruga, as his relationship to the daimyo commanded, but he decided not to go. He had long since made up his mind that he would die either at the Daitokuji or (like Ikkyū himself) at the Shūon-an. When he left Suruga earlier that year for the capital it was in the belief that he had little time left to live, and he could not risk the possibility of dying elsewhere, no matter what his duty as a faithful vassal might be.[94]

Sōchō's devotion to Ikkyū revealed itself in many ways. He repeatedly contributed money for the rebuilding of temples associated with Ikkyū, on one occasion (in 1525) selling his prize possession, the set of *Genji monogatari* he had devotedly read for many years, in order to raise funds for this purpose.[95] He also commissioned an artist to paint a portrait of Ikkyū

92. Robert H. Brower and Earl Miner, *Japanese Court Poetry* (Stanford, 1968), p. 269.
93. Kidō, 2: 582.   94. See *Sōchō shuki*, p. 697.   95. Ibid., p. 667.

with a long sword in a vermilion scabbard and asked a well-known calligrapher to add an inscription originally composed by Ikkyū.[96] The completed portrait was apparently hung in the Shūon-an. Sōchō mentions, for example, worshiping the portrait and offering incense before it in the fifth month of 1526. He was exhausted after his long journey from Suruga, but when he saw the portrait he "felt the weight of old age fall" from his shoulders.[97] It is not absolutely clear that this is the portrait he commissioned in 1488, but a later entry in his diary states that he was "moved and enlightened" when he gazed at the portrait of Ikkyū with a sword, suggesting that it probably was the same picture.[98] On this occasion he composed two waka, of which the first was:

uchiharau	The great sword in its scabbard
yuka no atari ni	Resting on the clean-swept floor
oku tachi no	Is brilliantly clear;
sayaka ni izuko	Nowhere is it clouded
kumoru chiri naki[99]	By a particle of dust.

It is obvious that the sword stands for Ikkyū's mind, brilliantly clear and unclouded; in the second waka the phrase *togishi kokoro* (honed mind) has the same effect. This portrait of Ikkyū probably resembled the painting now preserved in the Shinju-an at the Daitokuji.[100]

It should be evident from the above how deeply Sōchō venerated Ikkyū; the question is what form this influence took on Sōchō's work. It might be noted first that his avocations were strikingly similar to Ikkyū's. The two men shared a fondness for the music of the *shakuhachi*, for the tea ceremony, and for nō.[101] Sōchō's preferences outside his chosen field of renga undoubtedly stemmed from his personal tastes, but the knowledge that Ikkyū shared the same preferences probably confirmed his own bent.

96. The traditional date for the picture in 1526, but Nakamoto Tamaki in "Ikkyū Sōjun to Saiokken Sōchō," in Hiroshima Chūsei Bungei Kenkyū Kai, ed., *Renga to sono shūhen* (Hiroshima, 1967), p. 258, argues convincingly that 1488 is correct. It is interesting that Sōchō himself refused to have his portrait painted while he was alive. Jōha saw a portrait of Sōchō in the Saiokken in 1567. It had two poems inscribed on it by Sanjōnishi Sanetaka, who died in 1537, just five years after Sōchō. The portrait, no doubt painted shortly after Sōchō's death, showed him dressed in pale green robes, as he had requested; Satomura Jōha, pp. 791–792.
97. *Sōchō shuki*, p. 679.
98. Ibid., p. 685.
99. Ibid., p. 686. There is a *kakekotoba* on *saya* and *sayaka*.
100. Reproduced in color in Haga Kōshirō, *Daitokuji to Sadō* (Tokyo, 1958), p. 11.
101. For example, he mentioned in *Azumaji no Tsuto*, in *Gunsho ruijū*, kan 339, spending the night drinking with the nō dramatist Miyamasu Genzō (p. 773), seeing *ennen no sarugaku* and drinking with the troupe of twenty actors (p. 780); in *Utsuyama no ki* he quotes a dengaku song (p. 403); in *Sōchō shuki* he describes drinking with the nō actor Komparu Shichirō; and in *Sōchō nikki* he mentions having heard a musician sing jōruri (p. 1265).

But it was especially his defiance of convention, so striking in a renga poet of Sōgi's school, that reflected the influence of the intransigent Ikkyū, who delighted in shocking his fellow priests with overt references to his amorous exploits and who loathed above all the mealy-mouthed hypocrisy of venal priests. Sōchō's open admission that he had had two children by a washerwoman was in the vein of Ikkyū, and there was also an overtly sexual, sometimes salacious side to his writings. In his last journal, *Sōchō nikki* (1530–31), written when in his eighties, he confessed that he was turning increasingly to "crazy writings" (*kyōhitsu*), citing the following waka as an example:

negawaku wa	I only hope and pray
naki na wa tataji	I won't get a false reputation:
ware shinaba	If I should die
yaso amari wo	I'm sure the gods won't realize
kami mo shiraji yo[102]	I was over eighty years old!

The poem suggests that Sōchō's conduct, even in his eighties, was such that rumors were likely to spread about his involvements. A more earthy example of his comic waka bears the headnote, "At the beginning of the ninth month [of 1524] I went a distance some four or five *chō* from my house. On the way back I fell off my horse. My body was half racked with pain and I could not use my right hand.

ika ni sen	What am I to do?
mono kakisusabu	Without the hand I use to write
te wa okite	For my amusement,
hashi toru koto to	How can I hold my chopsticks
shiri noguu koto[103]	Or wipe my behind?

There are many mentions in the journals of the pleasure Sōchō derived from composing haikai poetry. The examples he gives range from the kind of genteel wit of which Sōgi might have approved to out-and-out bawdiness. He spent the last days of 1523 at the Shūon-an where, under the benign auspices of Ikkyū, he and six or seven cronies (including Yamazaki Sōkan) sat around the hearth composing haikai. Here are a few examples:

chigo ka onna ka	Is it a boy or a girl
nete no akatsuki	Sleeping there? The morning after.

mae ushiro	On my hand that gropes
saguru te ni tsuki no	Before and behind, the light
ariake ni	Of the moon at dawn.

102. *Sōchō nikki*, p. 1252.   103. *Sōchō shuki*, p. 663.

hito no nasake ya	People's emotions
ana ni aruran	Are concentrated on a hole.
onna fumi	A woman's letter:
kashiko kashiko ni	"That's the place, that's it!"
kakisutete	Carelessly dashed off.
tanomu wakazō	The young man I counted on
amari tsurenaya	Was oh so very chilly.
hikkunde	Grappling with him
sashi mo ireba ya	I would like to thrust in my sword
chigaeba ya[104]	And die from his thrust!

In the above examples I have chosen throughout the most indecent meanings, but each link is full of wordplays that make possible quite respectable utterances; if this were not the case, half the fun of such composition would surely have been lost. For example, the second pair of renga could also be interpreted in this way:

hito no nasake ya	People's emotions
ana ni aruran	Reach their peak in wonder.
onna fumi	A woman's letter
kashiko kashiko ni	Carelessly signed,
kakisutete	"Very respectfully."

The link between the two verses is verbal, the familiar expression *ana kashiko*, an exclamation of awe and wonder. *Ana* alone has much the same meaning, but it is also the homonym of the word for "hole." Women's letters were commonly signed *kashiko*, meaning "with awe," but it is the homonym of a word meaning "that place."

Such examples of double entendre had undoubtedly formed an important part of the mushin tradition for many years. The emphasis on homosexual relations in these verses seems to reflect life in Buddhist temples were acolytes *(chigo)* often served as the outlet for the sexual desires of priests forbidden to have intercourse with women. However, but for the accident that Sōchō chose to record these comic verses in his journal, we would be as badly informed on the mushin verses of this time as on those of the period a hundred years earlier. The haikai selection in *Sōchō shuki* also includes examples of maeku with different tsukeku supplied by Sōchō and Yamazaki Sōkan, the traditional founder of haikai no renga:

oitsukan	He must be running
oitsukan to ya	So hard because he wants

104. Ibid., pp. 655–656.

hashiruran	To catch up at all costs.
Kōya hijiri no	A man with a spear behind
ato no yarimochi	The Holy Man of Kōya.
Sōkan	

Kōya hijiri no	A lovely girl ahead of
saki no hime goze	The Holy Man of Kōya.
Sōchō	

Sōchō immodestly commented that he thought his own verse, linked by the meaning (*kokorozuke*), was superior to Sōkan's tsukeku. Certainly the surface meaning is funnier if one imagines the Holy Man running after a woman, despite the prohibition, but Sōkan's tsukeku, based on the pun on *oitsuku*, "to catch up," and *oi tsuku*, "to stab through an *oi* (a kind of portable altar carried by priests on their backs)," displayed even greater ingenuity.[105]

This and other examples of haikai poetry composed jointly by Sōchō and Sōkan firmly establish the connection between Sōchō and the early haikai poetry, but if Sōchō tended to prefer his own tsukeku to Sōkan's, the reverse was equally true. The famous opening verse of the collection *Inu tsukuba shū* (The mongrel Tsukuba collection), compiled by Sōkan, is this maeku:

| kasumi no koromo | The hems of the garment |
| suso wa nurekeri | Of mist have been wetted. |

This verse appears in *Sōchō shuki* with the following tsukeku by Sōchō:

nawashiro wo	The wild geese depart
oitaterarete	Having been chased away from
kaeru kari[106]	The rice-seedling bed.

But Sōkan evidently preferred his own tsukeku, given in *Inu tsukuba shū*:

Sao hime no	Now that spring has come
haru tachinagara	Sao, the goddess,
shito wo shite[107]	Makes water standing.

Sōchō's tsukeku was in his characteristic kokorozuke style, taking the entire meaning of the maeku, which fancifully describes the spring mist as looking darker, as if wet, at its lower edges close to the ground. The tsukeku, reinforcing the early spring imagery, describes the wet field where rice seedlings have been planted. The only touch of humor is the play on

105. Ibid., p. 656. See also Suzuki, pp. 62, 239.
106. *Sōchō shuki*, p. 655.   107. Suzuki, p. 11.

the verb *kaeru*—"to return" when used of wild geese returning in the spring but "to depart" when these geese are chased away by an inhospitable farmer. Sōkan, in a much bolder flight of the imagination, supposes that the garment of mist is wet because Sao-hime, the goddess of spring, has been urinating while standing up. In both tsukeku the verb *tatsu* appears, the word used for early spring "rising," but it has special meanings in context.

It is difficult to say, comparing the half-dozen poems with tsukeku by both Sōchō and Sōkan, who is the more daring, more representative of the old mushin renga. Sōkan seems so in his tsukeku on the spring goddess, but his tsukeku to the maeku beginning *hito no nasake ya* (People's emotions) is decidedly more restrained than Sōchō's. Sōkan almost always links through some verbal association, no doubt the reason why he was so esteemed by Matsunaga Teitoku and his school, but Sōchō's kokoruzuke is more closely related to the Danrin poets.

Sōchō's fondness for unconventional poetry apparently had another aspect. He has been credited with the compilation of the anthology of popular songs (many quite earthy) called *Kangin shū*, completed in 1518.[108]

The mushin traditions in renga would be carried on by men who knew Sōchō well. The legendary founder of haikai no renga, Yamazaki Sōkan, closely associated with Sōchō, as we have seen. Arakida Moritake (1473–1549), another pioneer of this style, also received guidance from Sōchō. His special respect for Sōchō is demonstrated by *Sōchō tsuizen senku*, the solo renga in one thousand links he composed in the third month of 1532, exactly three weeks after Sōchō's death, in mourning for his teacher.[109] From Sōkan and Moritake the line of descent to haikai poetry of the seventeenth century is unquestionable.

The comic renga of the Muromachi period has never been systematically studied. Most of the verses composed by way of relaxation were never intended to be preserved and one must search for them in diaries, books of anecdotes, kyōgen plays,[110] and similar scattered sources, as well as in the rare collections beginning with *Chikuba kyōgin shū*. The literary value of these poems by no means approaches that of the serious renga, but these lightly composed verses provide us with tantalizing glimpses of the personal lives of the poets—and suggest in embryonic form the course that future poetry would take.

108. Shimma Shin'ichi, ed., *Chūsei kinsei kayō shū*, in *Nihon koten bungaku taikei*, 44 (Tokyo, 1959).
109. Jingū Shichō, ed., *Arakida Moritake shū* (Tokyo, 1951), p. 82.
110. See Sasano Ken, ed., *Nō kyōgen* (Tokyo, 1945), 2: 190 ff.

16

Medieval Jongleurs and the Making of a National Literature

BARBARA RUCH

TOWARD THE RECONSTRUCTION OF A THEORETICAL FRAMEWORK

The Barriers of Tradition

During the last half century, since Muromachi fiction first attracted some small stirring of interest in the academic world, a number of barriers have inadvertently been erected that greatly hinder our understanding of literary developments from the fourteenth to sixteenth centuries. In general these barriers have easily withstood subsequent attack because they are composed of elements well known to resist the force of logic and evidence: tradition and predilection. Perhaps the most pernicious barriers are, first, an elitism with regard to what is worthy of literary study; second, the inordinate dependence of literary scholars on concepts borrowed from political history; and, third, a traditional scholarly vocabulary consisting of terminology that only inadequately applies to the literary phenomena observable during the Muromachi period. Specifically this means there is, first, a tendency to make light of, or even to ignore, medieval literature produced outside the purview of the imperial or the shogunal courts and thus a reluctance to see literary value during the Muromachi period anywhere but in *nō* drama or classical poetry. There is, second, a surprising willingness to partition literature into political periods, or rather a disinclination to concede that literary history may flow at a pace and in conformations unrelated to the occurrence of wars or the rise and fall of governments. As a result, literary history books are littered with such all-but-meaningless terms as "Muromachi period literature" or "*gekokujō* literature" (the literary products of sociopolitical upheaval) which we are

The author wishes to thank Professor Akiyama Terukazu of the University of Tokyo and Professor Gunji Masakatsu of Waseda University for their kind assistance in obtaining photographs of several of the items included here as illustrations as well as permission to reproduce them.

279

forced for the time being to employ for want of well thought out and agreed upon alternatives. It is clear that the time has come to give Japan's many rich and varied periods of literary output names that reflect the unique characteristics of the genre, the literary movements, or the writers, and not the politics of the age. Third, there is almost no mutually agreed upon scholarly vocabulary (outside of the fields of nō and classical poetry) whereby we can discuss the development of new forms of medieval literature except for such widely and inadvisably used terms as *otogi zōshi* (companion stories) and *Nara e hon* (Nara picture books), anachronistic appellations whose origins remain unclear and whose use is disconcertingly inconsistent among scholars. Clearly neither is a suitable vehicle for the advancement of theoretical studies of medieval fiction.

The barriers of inappropriate period and genre terminology are outside the main concerns of the present essay, but the problem of elitism must be disposed of before we can start to build our theoretical framework. Elitism is difficult to counter because it is apparent that Japanese literature itself began with the patronage and participation of the elite and by the tenth to twelfth centuries had been honed to an aesthetic perfection inconceivable outside leisured wealthy circles. As a result, the standards and preoccupations of the classical court tales or *monogatari* and various forms of classical poetry have exerted, among connoisseurs, an influence so overpowering that these standards have become for many scholars, even today, a measure for all other periods and genre. The problem is exacerbated by the fact that the Ashikaga shogunal court continued to patronize aristocratic literary arts, and it encouraged the application of courtly aesthetics to new arts, such as nō performances, which under other circumstances might not have felt the reach of formal aesthetics.

Interpretations of Japanese literary history based on such elitist standards have nurtured several common predispositions, observable among both Japanese and Western scholars, that must be laid to rest before we can make progress in understanding the unique nature of medieval literature. The first of these views is that the Muromachi period is a dark age for nonpoetic literature. Although the classical Heian monogatari definitely met its end during this period, there is no evidence whatever to support a "dark age" thesis, irrespective of the gloom one may be tempted to find from time to time in the political, economic, or military history of the age. In the past two or three decades a sufficient number of medieval texts has been uncovered to prove the fertility of these centuries.

The second notion is that the medieval period is really essentially a transitional period for fiction that in some enigmatic fashion links the Heian monogatari and the Edo period *ukiyo zōshi* of Ihara Saikaku (1642–1693).

It should be obvious that four hundred years is far too long a period to be accurately described as transitional. Even the two hundred and fifty years or so of the Muromachi period represent too long a stretch of time and too wide a variety of unique literary developments to belong to a "transitional" category. To use such a term because the before and after of the so-called transition is well understood (i.e., Heian and Edo literature), while the product of the intervening Kamakura and Muromachi periods is still insufficiently studied, is to do an injustice to scholarship and to discourage research.

A third view, and the one most frequently repeated, is the contention that medieval fiction is the degenerative end of the Heian monogatari tradition, or worse, a vulgarized imitation by the masses of what used to be a high art. Coupled with this view is the related notion that during the Muromachi period there first emerged a "*shomin*-ization," i.e., a popularization (vulgarization) of Japanese literature. Whether this is considered a degeneration of aristocratic literature or the bursting through of a common people's literary energy, almost all writers customarily associate popularization with a lowering of quality. That there were no new rivals to the *Genji monogatari* is indisputable, and as far as aristocratic monogatari are concerned there was a rapid drop in both quantity and quality. But this was due less to the "popularization" of this genre than to the altered state of the aristocracy itself and to a decline in its interest in the monogatari genre. If by popularization we mean the rendering of literature intelligible to everyone from top to bottom of the population, then that phenomenon did occur. Nevertheless, as we shall see, such popular literature was not an outgrowth of the fading Heian monogatari tradition; it was a new type of literary art fashioned by medieval religio-secular jongleurs.

The "quality" of this literature must be measured differently from that of the Heian monogatari. One cannot speak of the first literary products of a newly emerging corporate culture as degenerated anything. That the writers or tellers of new forms of literature chose the picture-scroll format or a medieval version of the classical language does not mean they were laboring to imitate Heian traditions; such choices were natural as the only readily available options. But surface similarities to earlier models should not lead us to expect to find the old aesthetics as well. Nor should it blind us to those things which were truly revolutionary about the new literature. Clearly the three persistent views outlined above are actually different expressions for one and the same elitist view of Muromachi literature. Once we remove the aristocratic monogatari from the fulcrum of the argument, therefore, all three hypotheses of a dark, vulgarized, transitional age of literature collapse. Of course it is always possible to find a few Heian monogatari and imitative Kamakura *giko* monogatari still being read in elite circles during the Muromachi period. But such works belong to a world completely outside the main stream of Muromachi fiction. The literature produced during the Muromachi period has little if any direct relation to the Heian monogatari; as we will demonstrate below, it represents the birth of a new national literature.

The Concept of Shomin-ization and the Machishū

The reverse of elitism can also be found in studies about medieval literature; it manifests itself in a propensity to see literary developments in the light of upwardly mobile common people. The literature of the period, therefore, if not referred to as *gekokujō* literature, is sometimes described as literature of the common people (*shominteki bungaku*). The concept of the *shomin*-ization of Japanese literature, however, also has its drawbacks. Such terminology does more, perhaps, to obscure than to clarify the actual observable processes of literary change. *Shomin*-ization implies a shift in class. In the context of literature this means a shift either in the class of the creators of literature, in that of the audience, or in both. Changes did indeed occur: there was a widening of the circle of people involved in one way or another in literary arts, and the most energetic contribution to the new forms of literature came largely, but by no means exclusively, from people outside the court or the houses of the military elite. But we emphasize shifts in social class at our peril. There is nothing unusual in a swelling of the numbers and types of participants in a nation's literary production as the written language slowly penetrates to all levels of society. Every nation has experienced the identical phenomenon. It is not the simple and natural widening of the circle of literates alone that changes literary history. The newly literate learn from the previously elite and model their skills on the examples provided by their mentors. New learners are not the iconoclasts of literary tradition; they are, by and large, its fascinated and devoted followers. In some societies where written literature is looked upon mainly as a practical means to political or economic advancement, literacy takes on special and sometimes fearful dimensions. In Japan, nonpoetic writing in the native language, however, was never viewed primarily or even secondarily in this light. The growing literacy of the people at large, therefore, is not the major factor in the revolutionary changes that occurred in Japanese literature. In the case of *renga*, for example, where practitioners could be found from court to street corner, it was not the newly literate stableboy nor the prostitute who shook the poetic

world with verbal experiments in poetic scurrility or lewdness, but priests
with sound literary educations.

Related to the question of social class is the widely discussed hypothesis
of Hayashiya Tatsusaburō, according to which Muromachi culture as a
whole is the product of a newly formed group, the *machishū*.[1] Consisting of
the politically enfeebled aristocrats, the newly powerful bushi, and the
craftsmen, manufacturers, merchants, and others in commercial activities
in Kyoto, the machishū were the city dwellers at whose hands an essentially urbanized set of cultural values and way of life were created. Although
this stimulating thesis has created important breakthroughs in our view of
medieval history, in the context of medieval fiction it is somewhat less
satisfactory. The problem is that it is difficult to find any hard evidence to
support the existence of machishū as major literary producers of fiction.
The only known author of medieval fiction is one samurai-turned-priest,
who may or may not have been a machishū. In other cases where we can
make fairly sound guesses as to authorship we find, for example, an
overwhelming number of instances of noncity origin: priests of Nikkō
(*Gemmu monogatari*), Koya *hijiri* (*Sannin hōshi*), *sekkyōshi* of Kashima (*Bunshō
no sōshi*), etc. Other medieval works such as the *Heike monogatari* and the
Soga monogatari, as we shall discuss below, were the products of wandering
religio-secular performers, who by their very nature are the antithesis of
city dwellers. There are certain works set in Kyoto which depict the
successful rise in life of plebian heroes. Fictional works of this kind are
frequently alleged to be the product of the energetic and upwardly aspiring townsmen because they are considered to reflect the resourcefulness of
this social group (*Monogusa Tarō, Fukutomi zōshi, Issun bōshi*). Yet even these
works do not, on close examination, support the thesis of machishū
authorship. These heroes do not succeed because of their resourcefulness
as machishū: Issun bōshi was a *mōshigo* (child born as a result of prayer) of
Sumiyoshi shrine and Monogusa Tarō was a mōshigo of Zenkōji as well
as the abandoned child of an aristocrat. For such as these, success was inevitable, predetermined by fate. The intent of the Fukutomi story is not to
urge people to exploit their humble talents to gain success, but rather to
warn against envying the talents of others and to recommend that one be
satisfied with his own place in life. Even in that curious genre *irui
monogatari* that centers on animals, birds, or other *irui* (nonhumans),
almost all the upwardly mobile irui marriages (i.e., an animal marries into

1. See Professor Hayashiya's essay in this volume as well as his basic studies on the subject,
Chūsei bunka no kichō (Tokyo, 1955) and *Machishū* (Tokyo, 1964). For discussion of his theory by
other scholars, see Hayashiya Tatsusaburō, ed., *Kyōto no rekishi* (Tokyo, 1967–), 3 (1968): 545 ff.,
569 ff.; 4 (1969): 95 ff.

a human family) end in failure, in the taking of the tonsure, and in salvation. In short, the main agent in medieval fiction is fate, not ambition; the essential core of Muromachi literature is restoration of the proper world order, not gekokujō. There is much evidence that the machishū made intent audiences and supported the theater and book commerce that converged on Kyoto; as recipients of the literary arts, the machishū were certainly active as viewers, patrons, and buyers. It is still questionable, however, whether the evidence will support the machishū as the major creators of medieval fiction; the present essay will suggest different candidates for this role.

Characteristics of Medieval Literary Arts

Before discussing the specific originators of Muromachi literature, it is of great importance that we be aware of the fundamental difference between Japanese literary arts whose quality depends upon the development of an aesthetic theory and those literary arts whose basic strength lies not in conforming to theoretical aesthetic codes but upon capturing an audience and delivering an emotional impact. The first type (waka, renga, and in its later development nō), whose history was built upon a growing body of theoretical and critical works (karon, rengaron, nōgakuron, for example), was reinforced by collections of practitioners' works (wakashū, rengashū, yōkyoku) that were felt to conform well to stated aesthetic principles. The quality of such literary arts is judged less by the intensity of emotional response elicited in an audience than by how fully the product represents a mastery by the practitioner of the aesthetic principles involved. Typical in the practice of such literary arts is the importance of a judge who is also a practitioner of the highest skill.

The second type of literature (Heikyoku, etoki, sekkyō bushi, Kowaka bukyoku, kojōruri, kayō, and later bunraku and kabuki) is represented by arts that have no history of aesthetic codes, no body of criticism upon which practitioners based their activities. Their primary aim was to draw the listener deeply into an orally delivered narrative and to cause, above all, an emotional response (nostalgia, tears, laughter, pride, joy, astonishment, gratitude, religious conversion) in an audience. Such literary arts were transmitted from practitioner to practitioner mainly through repertory texts and were taught by oral mimesis alone. Perfection was sought in the verbal, aural, and in some cases visual techniques which elicit emotion, not in recondite wording employed to demonstrate erudition nor in the mastery of poetics that ensure the creation of an aesthetic atmosphere. In poetry and nō, only the best practitioners were expected to appreciate fully the best products. In Heikyoku, etoki, sekkyō, and jōruri, it was crucial that the majority of one's audience, no matter how disparate, be reached and moved, despite ignorance of the artistic principles or techniques employed by the performers. For simplicity's sake, although the terms are not fully adequate, I will call these two types of literature practitioner-oriented canonical literature and audience-oriented repertory literature.

Several literary art forms lie someplace between these two major and distinct types of Japanese literature. Although I mentioned nō as an example of practitioner-oriented canonical literature, such a definition is somewhat anachronistic. Save for the intervening hand of Ashikaga Yoshimitsu (1358–1408) it is highly likely that nō would have remained an audience-oriented repertory literature where it originated and where its companion kyōgen remained until the seventeenth century, despite a certain aesthetic self-consciousness stimulated by its close association with nō. Probably it was due to the influence of *rengaron*, to which he was exposed after his association with Yoshimitsu, that Zeami (1363–1443) wrote his *nōgakuron*, and this act thrust nō into a kind of *hashigakari* (bridge) position linking the world of pure oral mimesis with that of canonical aesthetics. In contrast to waka and renga, nō had always been performed by one group for another group. No matter what the original intent of *dengaku* and *sarugaku* nō performances might have been, however, the objectives shifted considerably after the fourteenth century. An intent to move the majority of a disparate audience of nonpractitioners gave way to an intent to meet the aesthetic standards of a highly informed audience which included many amateur practitioners of the vocal, instrumental, or choreographic aspects of the art. Such changes isolated nō even more from its point of origin and propelled it further into the literary world of the practitioner-oriented canonical arts.

The classic monogatari, too, lies between these two basic types of literature, but for different reasons. Like poetry and poetic diaries with which it had a close association, the monogatari had always been written with little consciousness of an audience apart from the small numbers that constituted the literary salons of the court. In short, the readers and writers were for all practical purposes the same people; they wrote for each other and not for a general audience. In subsequent periods the enthusiasm generated by the *Genji monogatari* sprang largely from the poetic and aesthetic interests of poets and antiquarians—not, as far as our evidence goes, from the interest of aspiring fiction writers or from any audience demand.

Most of the literary arts that emerged during the middle ages belong clearly to the category of audience-oriented repertory literature. These arts were not canonical but repertory arts, and they were not based on aesthetic theory but on emotional need. Aimed not at a practitioner-elite but at wide and disparate audiences of whom little or no demands were made, they had a great impact on Japanese society as a whole. It was this category that altered the course of Japan's literary history, and out of which was born Japan's first national literature.

Vocal Literature
There was one other characteristic that was fundamental to medieval Japanese literature: all of the many new forms of literature that blossomed during the thirteenth through sixteenth centuries involved the art of voice projection or the intoning of a prose/poetry text—a literature I shall call "vocal literature" (*onsei bungaku*). Some practitioners added to their cantillations various sounds, rhythms, or musical settings produced by means of vocal cries, the beat of a fan on the palm, or by drum, bell, *biwa*, or *sasara*. To certain types of vocal literature body movement or even choreography were added, while others used such props as picture scrolls and books, clay dolls or puppets, religious artifacts such as *gohei*, or costumes and masks. But no matter what the literary art form was, be it *dengaku* or *sarugaku nō, kyōgen, etoki, Heikyoku, enkyoku, Kowaka bukyoku, kojōruri, sekkyō*, or any of the many other vocal literary arts that sprang out of medieval soil—all were arts of intoned and embellished literature, and all such literature was a unique product of the age. Of equal significance is the fact that none could have existed without texts, whether read from, declaimed from memory, or improvised upon according to predetermined techniques.

I would like here to clarify the singular role played in Japan by literature involving voice projection and to define more precisely the term *onsei bungaku*. Japanese "vocal literature" is quite a different thing from what we normally speak of as "oral literature" (*kōshō bungaku* or sometimes *denshō bungaku*). I choose the word "vocal" as opposed to "oral" in order to eliminate the inapplicable and misleading nuances that the term "oral literature" carries. Oral literature is a product of and flourishes in a world of illiteracy. It is most often employed in reference to word arts in societies that have no written language or it is applied to stages in a society's literary history prior to the introduction of script. If used in the context of a modern nation, it is associated with folklore, with the fireside storyteller whose fairy tales flourish in some remote corner of society where few have as yet learned to read or write fluently or where such skills play a minimal role. Thus oral literature usually implies illiteracy on the part of the producer of a story, on the part of the audience, or both. Oral literature did and does exist in Japan.

Japan's vocal literature, however, shares few characteristics with the illiterate world of oral literature. From the beginning of its history, vocal literature has had firm ties to the written language; indeed it was usually based upon written texts: sutras, chronicles, sermons, and many other types of writing. Further, it was more often than not recorded into *daihon* or libretto texts.[2] Illiteracy, among either practitioners of vocal literature or audiences, is a peripheral factor. Some practitioners were highly literate, as were preachers such as the *shōdōshi* of the Agui school, or actor-playwrights such as Zeami. Some, blind from birth, obviously had no knowledge of or use for writing, but we know in the case of the blind lute-playing priests—the *biwa hōshi*, for instance—that many worked in an environment where the colleagues on whom they depended were both sighted and literate. Others, such as the great master of *Heikyoku*, Akashi no Kakuichi (d. 1371), became blind in adulthood after having achieved a high level of literacy as a priest. There were of course other performers of vocal literature who are depicted in contemporary picture scrolls as little more than blind beggars, and that in itself would seem to assure their illiteracy. But records support our assumption that at least some performances by such men and women were based on the same general repertory as that of others in their calling who were more literate and prosperous. Thus, even illiterates had close ties to written texts.

The audience of vocal literature should not be thought of in terms of illiterates either. The records make it clear that audiences represented the full range of literary accomplishment, or lack of it, from scholar-aristocrat to illiterate beggar. At any of the command performances in the mansions of the wealthy elite we assume a literate audience. A street-corner performance of the same repertory would be more likely to attract an audience in which literacy was rare. At way stations on pilgrimages, at temples, and on numerous other occasions the audience for a performance of vocal literature, as we can see depicted in contemporary *emaki*, might include representatives from several such social levels. It cannot be denied that wandering priests and nuns, whose aim was the conversion of as broad a base of the Japanese people as possible, created or adapted vocal literature on a level easily understood by everyone. But literacy or illiteracy was not a concern. If their narratives avoided demonstrations of erudition, it was

2. It is a particular feature of Japanese literature that a highly developed written tradition and a highly developed vocal literary tradition existed simultaneously until the seventeenth century; furthermore, many types of vocal literature from this period remain alive today. Kenneth Butler, "The *Heike monogatari* and Theories of Oral Epic Literature," *Seikei Daigaku Bulletin of the Faculty of Letters* 2 (1966): 37–54, provides an excellent analysis of the relation between written and oral traditions in the *Heike monogatari;* Butler uses the term oral literature but is actually describing what is defined here as vocal literature.

where it could not be appreciated by the ear. If they placed a minimal emphasis on aesthetic subtleties, it was because their touchstone was not a literary canon but the human heart; the appeal was direct and emotional and transcended social class.

The Literary Revolutions of Media and Content

A profusion of diverse performers, both religious and secular, were active between the fourteenth and sixteenth centuries and contributed to these developments. Two specific types, however, played major roles in the formation of Japan's first national literature and in determining both the format and content of the vocal, reading, and dramatic literature of subsequent centuries. Both of these two types were performers of vocal literature and yet they were fundamentally different from each other. The first were the *etoki* or "picture explainers," men and women who used paintings and illustrated texts as visual props and whose narrative performances played a crucial role in introducing the emaki and ehon to all levels of society (see figures 1–5). The second general type were the *biwa hōshi* and *goze* groups, blind men and women whose vocal arts created a universally loved repertory of stories inspired by the Gempei wars that holds a prominent position in Japan's literary history (see figures 6–7). Together, these two types of medieval jongleurs did more than probably any other groups to build what can be called Japan's first body of truly national literature and to spread it throughout the country. We will examine in some detail what is known of the first, the "picture explainer" group—men and women known respectively as *etoki hōshi* (picture-explaining priests) and *Kumano bikuni* (nuns of Kumano).

In order to understand the roles played by these medieval jongleurs it is important to keep in mind the basic literary revolutions of which they were both product and participant. In broad terms there were two. The first, which I have discussed elsewhere in more detail, is the twelfth-century revolution.[3] Here we witness a radical and massive shift of focus from salon literature for reading aloud and for private reading to a new "media" literature where narratives become so closely allied to the emaki through the practice of etoki that the visual illustration of literature and its oral delivery came to equal if not surpass in importance the text itself. Painting, story, chanter, and even the sounding of musical instruments (often pure sound rather than music) combined to create a total audio-visual experience rare, if not unique, in the premodern history of world literature. The process can quite supportably be termed the cinemization of Japanese literature, and the product, "media literature." (I use the word media

---

3. Barbara Ruch, "The Religious Picture Scroll in the Development of Medieval Japanese Fiction," *Journal of Asian Studies*, forthcoming.

絵解

FIGURE 1.
A secular etoki.
From a fifteenth-century scroll,
Sanjūniban shokunin uta awase,
in the collection of
Mr. U. Sakai, Tokyo.

much as we use it today for the television and cinema arts.) Inherent in this shift was a clear separation between author-performer and audience. Literacy or the lack of it was not an issue. This was not a class revolution but a conceptual revolution, one that affected attitudes toward narrative literature from the top to the bottom of society. This distinct and dramatic shift to literature as media can clearly be attributed to the activities of talented, enterprising, and often devout religio-secular jongleurs, etoki of various sorts who, with no intent whatsoever to revolutionize literature, brought about a major change in the course of Japanese literary history. Without a recognition of what was started by the twelfth-century revolution we will fail to see, for example, that the art of Chikamatsu Monzaemon (1653–1724) was a natural and inevitable culmination of this medieval media literature. His art was based on the ingenious combination of puppet, samisen, and *jōruri* chanter, and in this regard he achieved what no man had successfully done before. But this combination of the visual aid, the audio accompaniment, and the chanter/narrator was already by his day deeply rooted in Japanese society and represented the mainstream of nonpoetic, non-Chinese literature in Japanese literary history. Chikamatsu's puppet, samisen, and jōruri chanter are predated by four or five hundred years; their predecessors were the Kamakura-period picture scroll, the biwa, and the pre-jōruri chanting style of the twelfth-century *shōdō* priests of the Agui school, battle singers, etoki, and other practitioners of media literature who have yet to be fully researched.

FIGURE 2. A secular etoki playing his biwa in the marketplace. Detail from "Fukuoka no ichi" section of *Ippen shōnin eden* (1299), owned by Kankikōji, Kyoto.

Whereas the twelfth-century literary revolution was a conceptual one affecting medium, the second major revolution of the thirteenth and fourteenth centuries radically altered content and produced Japan's first "national literature." Although this second revolution took place in at least two stages, the agents involved were again medieval jongleurs. No longer court-oriented, the new narratives were conceived on battlefields and sacred mountains, in shrines and temples, and reflected, as had the media revolution, the energy born out of the wedding of newly risen Amidist sects and native Shinto cults. During the first stage the subject of love that had dominated court literature was replaced by the suffering and salvation of military heroes and deities as well as themes that reveal the anxieties and concerns of the new and turbulent age. The highly developed aesthetic vocabulary of the court gave way to modes of expression that reflected the techniques of religio-secular chanters and responded to the requirements of viewer-listeners. By the fourteenth century the creative surge of new military and religious narratives had come to an end. A new stage of secularization was in motion, however, that was to produce a body of literature known and loved by people in all walks of life: Japan's first national literature.

FIGURE 3. A Kumano bikuni and her young assistant performing etoki at the roadside. Detail from a pair of twofold screens, "A Festival at the Sumiyoshi Shrine," seventeenth or eighteenth century, courtesy of the Smithsonian Institution, Freer Gallery of Art, Washington, D.C.

A National Literature

By "national literature" I do not, of course, mean the whole body of literature produced by a nation nor even the certain unique and highly developed literary arts by which a nation wishes to be known abroad (for Japan, nō, for example, or haiku). On the contrary, I refer to a combination of themes, heroes and heroines, predicaments, ethical dilemmas, resolutions, and emotional attitudes which are, as a composite, unique to a given nation but which at the same time are not the product or property of a particular literary coterie at any one level of society. A national literature is a certain core of literary works the content of which is well known and held dear by the majority of people across all class and professional lines, a literature that is a reflection of a national outlook. Such literature never

292

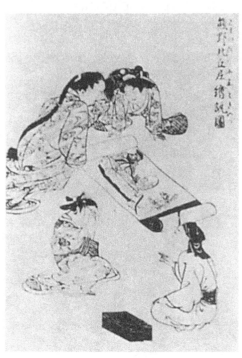

FIGURE 4.
A Kumano bikuni performing etoki
for ladies either at court or
in a wealthy townsman's home.
Illustration from second volume
of a woodblock-printed book,
Kinsei kiseki kō by Santō Kyōden,
published in Edo in 1804.

shocks or revolutionizes; it is constituted of favorite themes that recur again and again and of which the people never tire. It gives comfort because, as a composite, it fits the national character. For this very reason it may be the least exportable of literary products, the least appreciated or understood beyond national borders. This national literature may, indeed must, cross genre lines. It is substance rather than form. *Heike monogatari*, *Gikeiki*, and *Soga monogatari*, for example, and the medieval *engi-honji* narratives that circulated with or interacted with them, are products of this fourteenth-century revolution. They are "national literature" because they contain all the treasured themes and sentiments that Japanese on all levels of society wanted to hear recounted again and again. Their subject matter permeated major literary genre from nō and medieval fiction to *kowaka* and *jōruri*, to *kabuki*, *ukiyo zōshi*, *yomihon*, and even to Meiji novels and modern cinema and television. How forcefully they have spoken, even to the late twentieth century, we can observe, for example, in some of the masterpieces of Mishima Yukio.

A national literature cannot develop if a society is isolated into geographical pockets or fragmented by stringent class lines. Neither of these was the case, however, in fourteenth- and fifteenth-century Japan. But it is not enough to say, as many have, that Muromachi literature was created when the aristocratic *kuge-bushi* culture of Kyoto was transported to pro-

FIGURE 5.
A Kumano bikuni.
From a mid-seventeenth-century
hanging scroll, courtesy of
the Church of World Messianity,
Atami Art Museum, Atami.

vincial centers and when local cultures were carried to the city to be refined and polished and to vie for attention. The creation of a national
literature involves more than just a stirring of the pot. The ingredients of
Japan's national literature were a cataclysmic event, a religious response,
and the artistic utilization of both by medieval jongleurs. The themes, the
heroes, the predicaments that gripped the imagination of everyone during
this period, that permeated every literary genre, that created new ones,
and that proved to have a retentive power that has lasted centuries sprang
specifically and primarily from the cataclysmic events of the Gempei wars
and from the magico-religious world of the deities with whom the warring factions were associated. The Gempei catastrophe struck home on all
levels of society and for centuries subsequent wars and disasters were
measured by it and subsumed under it; religious proselytizers established
links between these events and the healing powers of local deities; religio-
secular narrators then bore the product from one corner of Japan to
another. No body of literature had, until then, been so universally embraced. For the first time Japan in the Muromachi period came to share
one body of heroes and heroines, one sense of pathos, a consciousness as
to what constitutes tragedy, a more or less unified attitude toward such
problems as suffering, resignation, self-sacrifice, the transience of the individual yet the immutability of the social order. Even a national ethic, a
national sentiment, was formed that was without question the product of

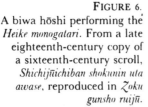

FIGURE 6.
A biwa hōshi performing the
Heike monogatari. From a late
eighteenth-century copy of
a sixteenth-century scroll,
*Shichijūichiban shokunin uta
awase*, reproduced in *Zoku
gunsho ruijū*.

the religio-secular missionary-jongleur of the fourteenth and fifteenth centuries.[4] During these two centuries they had built a body of myth that loomed larger than the central mythology of the *Kojiki* and *Nihongi* ever had or would, and whose heroes and heroines replaced at center stage most of the almost legendary celebrities of the Heian period as well. Japan's medieval jongleurs created a new literature, a panorama of life attitudes in repertory, that not only determined the nature of much of Edo period literature but which remains alive today as national lore.

THE MAKERS OF A NATIONAL LITERATURE

Etoki

It has been suggested that a revolution took place in the twelfth century when the mainstream of narrative literature shifted to an audio-visual media. It may well be asked what is all this about a "revolution," since the Japanese have always had a great deal of illustrated literature from at least the mid-Heian period. We must be careful, however, in discussing the audio-visual revolution to distinguish between the reading aloud of il-

---

4. As just one example, Atsumi Kaoru, in her *Heike monogatari no kisoteki kenkyū* (Tokyo, 1962), has demonstrated clearly the evolution of ethical attitudes through an analysis of various texts of the *Heike monogatari*. Kenneth Butler has also endorsed this view in "The *Heike monogatari* and the Japanese Warrior Ethic," *Harvard Journal of Asiatic Studies* 29 (1969): 93–108.

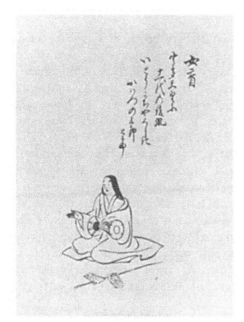

FIGURE 7.
A goze performing the
Soga monogatari. From a late eighteenth-centu
copy of a sixteenth-century scroll,
Shichijūichiban shokunin uta awase,
reproduced in *Zoku gunsho ruijū*.

luminated texts and a performing of the emaki.[5] In the former, illustrations
are only supplements to the literature; the paintings and the literature
they illustrate, though related, may be appreciated independently. In the
latter, literature and pictures were integral parts of a total experience,
and they cannot be considered separately without the danger of mis-
understanding their value and function. Their relationship is analogous to
picture and text in the context of film or television: neither can exist alone
meaningfully.

The performance of emaki emerged during the twelfth century in major
shrines and temples through an activity known as *etoki*, or "picture explanations," performed by *etoki hōshi* or "picture explaining priests," who
were sometimes also called simply *etoki*, "picture explainers." *Engi emaki*
(illustrated histories of shrines and temples and of the origins of the deities
worshiped there) and *kōsōden emaki* (illustrated biographical works depicting events in the lives of important priests and founders of sects) were displayed in temples on certain occasions and an etoki hōshi would give an
etoki performance by providing a narrative for the viewers.[6] The practice
of etoki must have had a long history in Japan. Since the etoki of wall

5. Ruch, "Religious Picture Scroll."
6. For a survey in English of the history of emaki, with color plates, see Hideo Okudaira, *Emaki: Japanese Picture Scrolls* (Rutland, Vt. and Tokyo, 1962); and for a survey in English of Kamakura religious emaki, Akiyama Terukazu, "New Buddhist Sects and *Emakimono* in the Kamakura Period," *Acta Asiatica* 20 (1971): 51–76.

paintings and scrolls was a Buddhist activity known in China, it seems
probable that priests imported the practice to Japan along with many
other religious customs sometime after the introduction of Buddhism.[7]
The illustrations used in China were of three types: murals, horizontal
scrolls, and hanging scrolls (usually several to one set). In Japan, the
earliest known examples were murals: the so-called *Shōtoku Taishi eden*,
which portrayed events in the life of Shōtoku Taishi (573–631) and which
decorated the inner walls of the Hōryūji in Nara and the Shitennōji in
present-day Osaka, temples of which Shōtoku Taishi was the founder-
patron.[8] The earliest documentation of an actual etoki performance of the
Shōtoku Taishi eden, however, is not until the twelfth century when Fujiwara
Yorinaga (1120–1156) mentions several such occasions in his diary, *Taiki*.
Yorinaga appears to have requested etoki every time he went to worship at
Shitennōji, so perhaps this was the customary practice for aristocrats at
the time. He mentions that after offering prayers before a portrait of
Shōtoku Taishi he went to the picture hall and had etoki of *Shōtoku Taishi
eden* performed for him.[9]

It is difficult to determine what the men were like who first performed
etoki in the temples. There is no documentary evidence from Yorinaga's
day to establish the social status or rank of these priests. In later years this
category of temple personnel came to be referred to as *etoki hōshi*, the term
hōshi (priest) normally being an appellation for people on a very low level
in society who performed religious and semireligious ceremonies for
shrines and temples. People in such a category were also known as *sanjomin*
(residents of the *sanjo*) because the institution with which they were
associated permitted them to live in a part of its tax-free property known
as sanjo in exchange for their services, which included the performance not
only of ceremonial tasks but of such menial ones as cleaning and gardening. The performance of the etoki of treasured engi and eden murals or

7. As early as the T'ang period in China, priests served as popular lecturers and storytellers in
Chinese temples, and the texts for these lectures or stories are called *pien wen* (Japanese, *hen bun*).
To date there is no evidence that Japanese texts are translations of *pien wen*, but the practice of
using illustrated texts for oral performances had been observed by Japanese priests in China
(Ennin saw such a performance in Ch'ang-an, for instance) and the possibility of direct in-
fluence is great. The most important research on *pien wen* in English is in Eugene Eoyang,
"Word of Mouth: Oral Storytelling in the Pien Wen" (Ph.D. diss., Indiana University, 1971).
See also the following studies: Umezu Jirō, "Hen to henbun," *Kokka*, no. 760 (1955): 191 ff.;
Okami Masao, "Etoki to emaki-ezōshi," in *Nihon emakimono zenshū* (Tokyo, 1960), 6: 39–49;
Akiyama Terukazu, *Heian jidai sezokuga no kenkyū* (Tokyo, 1964); Konishi Jin'ichi, "Shōdō
bungaku," in *Minzoku bungaku kōza* (Tokyo, 1960), 5, *Chūsei bungei to minzoku*, ed. Wakamori
Tarō, pp. 103–108; and Kawaguchi Hisao, "Tonkō henbun no seikaku to Nihon bungaku:
Etoki no sekai," *Nihon Bungaku* 12, no. 10 (1963): 27–41.
8. Akiyama, *Heian jidai*, pp. 169–172, 197–200.
9. *Taiki*, items under Kyūan 2 (1146)/9/24, 1147/9/14, 1148/9/14, 1148/9/17, and 1148/9/21.
For the original text, see *Taiki*, ed. Takatō Chūzō (Tokyo, 1898), pp. 158 ff.

scrolls for aristocratic patrons who came to worship at temples was certainly not a menial task. It is reasonable to postulate that aristocratic patrons who requested special performances received them from priests of appropriately elevated rank. In general, however, such highly specialized performing arts seemed to be the province of people from the bottom level of society who were associated with temples but not fully involved in religious pursuits. This phenomenon, found in many medieval performing arts, has not as yet been adequately explained.

Research concerning etoki has been hampered by the fact that there were at least two distinct types of performers who bore the appellation etoki, but no attempt has been made to treat them separately. One is the temple etoki hōshi. We actually know almost nothing about him personally except that he performed engi and eden emaki in the temples and received a fee. There are no pictures of him, and so we do not know what he looked like, but many examples of the visual props he used remain. The other etoki, however, is an entirely different type of man. Medieval paintings are extant that show him at work as a secular artist by the roadside and in the marketplace. We know precisely what he looked like, but we have no known examples of the pictures he used. The secular etoki is depicted in *Sanjūniban shokunin uta awase*, a Muromachi emaki dating from sometime in the Bummei period (1469–1487). This etoki (figure 1) is clearly not a priest but is dressed as a low-ranking samurai. On the lid of the open traveling case in front of him rests a large folded painting with loops by which it can be hung in front of an audience by the roadside or wherever he is called to perform. In action, he would accompany himself on the biwa while delivering his narration; stopping now and then, he would point with a pheasant feather on a stick to the pertinent scenes hanging before him.[10] Unfortunately, in the several extant versions of this crucial picture of the secular etoki his paintings remain folded and we do not know their subject matter.

The poet-priest Ikkyū (1394–1481) inadvertently helps us to know at least one item in the lay etoki's repertory. In his *Jikaishū*, Ikkyū tells us that one day a fellow disciple, Yōsō, brought in a portrait of their master and, unrolling it, urged him to look at the words he had prevailed upon the master himself to inscribe. In a biting comment Ikkyū writes that Yōsō at that moment looked just like an etoki who interrupts his playing on the biwa to point with his feather and say: "That is Hatakeyama Rokurō. These are Jūrō and Gorō of the Soga clan."[11] Ikkyū had obviously seen an

---

10. The pheasant feather pointer was no doubt used to protect the delicate pigments of the painting.

11. Okami Masao, "Machishū no bungaku: Otogi zōshi," in *Nihon bungaku no rekishi: Bungaku no gekokujō* (Tokyo, 1967), 6: 366–367.

etoki performance of episodes from the Gempei wars. Further, the nature of his remarks makes it clear he assumes everyone had seen such a performance and would therefore immediately recognize the etoki's mannerism he has mockingly pointed out.

Figure 2 shows a lay etoki playing his biwa in the marketplace in *Ippen shōnin eden* (1299). This etoki looks just like his colleague in the *Sanjūniban shokunin uta awase*, though he dates from two hundred years earlier. We are struck by the fact, however, that he is not performing etoki (no paintings are hung or spread, no traveling box is nearby), but clearly he is in the act of playing his biwa. We are left to speculate: is this an etoki caught at a moment of relaxation strumming randomly on his biwa, or does he represent the lay etoki profession before it had adopted visual props and before it came to use the name etoki?

It has been maintained that some temple etoki hōshi were blind and that their "picture explanations" were actually a vocalization of memorized material. This is a highly controversial point, and there is confusion as to whether etoki were blind or not.[12] One source of confusion may be that sometime between 1318 and 1330 a resident of the Tōji sanjo, referred to as the lay priest Fujitsugu, made a successful application to become an etoki hōshi, prompting a flurry of protest from blind groups.[13] This incident has been interpreted to mean that etoki hōshi had always been blind and therefore resented the threat a sighted man posed to their exclusive right to the etoki profession. But it is not at all certain who the protesting blind groups were, nor is it precisely clear why they were protesting. It seems just as logical to assume that the controversy centered not on a sighted person becoming an etoki but on a sighted person applying to be an etoki with the intent of accompanying his performances on a biwa, the instrument used as a means of livelihood by blind people for many centuries. There is no evidence that etoki of eden or engi had ever been accompanied by a biwa. Yorinaga's frequent notations about etoki performances in the twelfth century never mention the biwa or other musical accompaniment. Neither does he mention blindness. Further, an analysis of engi emaki such as *Kegon engi*, later used as visual props for etoki performances in temples, does not support a thesis of blind etoki hōshi. Indeed, all the evidence points to etoki who memorized or extemporized on their narrations but who read the snatches of conversation written on the pictures of the scrolls as they reached out to point to scenes.

At some point in history, then, either a temple etoki hōshi had to take

12. See Okami, "Etoki to emaki-ezōshi," p. 41; Hayashiya, *Chūsei bunka no kichū*, pp. 34–38; and Hayashiya, *Kyōto no rekishi*, 2: 358.
13. Hayashiya Tatsusaburō, "Kankyaku: Chōshū no hensen," in *Minzoku bungaku kōza* (Tokyo, 1960), 3, *Geinō to bungaku*, ed. Wakamori Tarō, p. 95.

up the biwa or a secular sighted person competent on the biwa had to conceive of the notion of adding the visual dimension of emaki to his art. The latter alternative seems more likely, since there developed no subsequent tradition of engi etoki to the accompaniment of the biwa, although there did emerge a tradition of secular, sighted, biwa-playing etoki. Possibly it was the lay priest Fujitsugu himself who took that first creative step. In any case it was shortly thereafter, during the late fourteenth and fifteenth centuries, that etoki as lay professionals were seen and heard everywhere. They were frequently hired for an afternoon or evening's enjoyment of vocal literature together with artists of *Heikyoku* or nō and puppet performers.[14]

In addition to the temple etoki performer of religious murals and scrolls and the secular etoki performer by the roadside or at the mansions of the wealthy, there was a third type, the "salesman of the faith." In the face of financial crises in the temples and as a result of a rising pitch of evangelical fervor, particularly among the Amidist sects, these etoki hōshi traveled the countryside with their *kakejiku* (illustrative hanging scrolls) and emaki to proselytize and to raise funds for their home institutions. We do not have evidence to call the missionary etoki hōshi a transition between the other two types of etoki; probably by the thirteenth and fourteenth centuries all three types of etoki were at work simultaneously. Without question, however, it was the missionary type and the lay performer who played a crucial role in popularizing the emaki and in helping to establish on all levels of society a body of narratives known and loved by all.

Kumano Bikuni

Kumano bikuni, or the nuns of Kumano, were the female counterpart of etoki hōshi. Very little is known of their origins, but it may be assumed that these nuns, like most professionals with religious names, started their activities at a religious center. As their name suggests, they were probably associated with the three sacred mountains of Kumano, one of the most important centers of popular religion during the middle ages. In spite of the geographical isolation and the difficulty of the roads, Kumano attracted pilgrims in all walks of life, from the emperor on down; a popular saying at the time likened the swarms to "ants on pilgrimage to Kumano" (*ari no Kumano mairi*). Lyrics of popular songs (*enkyoku*) recounted travels

14. "Kammon gyoki," Eikyō 5 (1433)/9/3, in *Zoku gunsho ruijū*, supplement 2 (Tokyo, 1958); "Oyudono no ue nikki," Bummei 12 (1480)/8/2, in *Zoku gunsho ruijū*, supplement 3 (Tokyo, 1957). See also Tsuji Zennosuke, ed., *Daijōin jisha zōjiki* (Tokyo, 1931), item for Eikyō 12 (1440)/3.

15. Matsumoto Takanobu, "*Kumano no honji* dan seiritsu ko: Minzoku bungaku to shite mita Muromachi jidai monogatari," in *Chūsei bungaku: Kenkyū to shiryō, Kokubungaku ronsō* (Tokyo, 1958), 2: 89.

along the roads to the sacred site,[16] and *Tendai shōdō* priests from the Agui center in Kyoto included in their proselytizing texts their version of the origins of the divinities at Kumano.[17] Much of this popularity was unquestionably due to the active missionary campaigns which the three shrines of Kumano had conducted at least as far back as the middle Heian period. Agents from these shrines toured the whole country seeking donations, and Kumano bikuni were no doubt among them.

Few records exist concerning these bikuni until after they began their decline, first as entertainers and later as prostitutes. The nuns were apparently known by several names: Kumano bikuni was the most common, but they were also referred to as *uta bikuni* (singing nuns), *etoki bikuni* (picture explaining nuns), and *kanjin bikuni* (money raising nuns), reflecting various aspects of their art or function. From the few pictorial representations of these nuns that exist, although probably none dates earlier than the seventeenth century, we gain a fairly good notion not only of the early religious etoki they performed but also of their later secular activities (figures 3, 4, and 5). Possibly the different Kumano bikuni portrayed are indicative of stages through which the profession passed, from religious to secular; nevertheless at least from the fifteenth century on, all three types of nun depicted were apparently carrying out their respective activities simultaneously, all under the same broad professional appellation of Kumano bikuni.

Closest to the image of what the original Kumano bikuni were probably like is the one shown in figure 3. Here a woman in nun's robes with shaven head covered by the usual nun's *zukin* sits by the roadside performing etoki along a pilgrimage route where many travelers are sure to pass. She hangs on a little stand a kakejiku depicting a *mandala*-like depiction of heavens and hells to which she points with a staff as she delivers her narration. The paintings that Kumano bikuni used as visual props were known as *Kumano e*, *jigoku gokuraku e*, or *rokudō e*.[18] Such paintings existed in hanging form (figure 3) or horizontal emaki form as well as in illustrated book form.

Another special feature of Kumano bikuni is that these women proselytizers could gain access to the secluded female members of exclusive households with an ease no male missionary enjoyed. Depicted in figure 4

---

16. See Takano Tatsuyuki, ed., *Nihon kayō shūsei* (Tokyo, 1928), 5: section on *Kumano sankei;* and Yoshida Tōgo, ed., *Enkyoku zenshū* (Tokyo, 1917).

17. *Kumano gongen no koto*, in *Shintōshū*, ed. Kondō Yoshihiro (Tokyo, 1959). More than forty variant texts are extant which relate the general story of the origin of Kumano deities.

18. From about the time of the Heike defeat in the late twelfth century, paintings of the tortures of hell or of travels through hell became popular. See, for example, *Jigoku zōshi*, in *Nihon emakimono zenshū*, 6 (1960), or *Kitano tenjin engi*, in ibid., 8 (1965).

is a nun visiting a private home and delivering an etoki narrative using a horizontal hand scroll. Her audio-visual performance is an apparent success since it has moved one young lady of the household to tears. No written text is visible in either figure 3 or figure 4, so we must assume that the nun's narratives were either memorized or composed more or less anew at each performance according to principles of extemporizing on a basic theme. Records exist, however, which indicate that at least some of the nuns under certain circumstances read from written texts. Several mid-fifteenth-century notations, for example, describe mendicant nuns engaged in reading aloud from the *Genji monogatari* on request.[19]

Kumano bikuni played an important role in the insertion of love themes into episodes about the Gempei wars. The Kumano bikuni shown in figure 5 is a nun in name only, a young woman with stylish hairdo carrying her scrolls or texts smartly in a small box under one arm, a completely secular figure. The close relation between love (even prostitution) and proselytizing is an intriguing subject. For the courtesan who had become a nun and was wandering the country evangelizing, there was only a short step between telling of the sufferings of heroes who had been saved or apotheosised (*honji*) and telling of the personal suffering that had led to her own salvation. Indeed, the concept of confession (*zange*) permeates medieval fiction, and confessions of the agonies of love that hinder salvation (*iro zange*), if not based on experience, necessitated the invention of stories about the love relationships of famous heroes. Kumano bikuni, as they created and performed episodes of the *Soga monogatari*, changed heroes who were basically hostile to women into men capable of love. They transformed the *Azuma kagami*'s Tora, the lover of Soga Jūrō, into a woman like themselves who, at Jūrō's death, traveled the pilgrimage routes not only to Zenkōji but to Kumano, Tennōji, Kokawa, Yoshino, and Iwaya and whose confessions brought about the salvation of everyone connected with the Soga family.[20] It is easy to imagine the step from iro zange used to convert a listener to iro zange used to arouse prurient interest.

The Kumano nuns sometimes appear in Muromachi literature itself as minor characters. In *Fuseya*, *Bijin kurabe*, and *Akizuki monogatari*, for example, there are references to Kumano nuns as protectors of stepchildren, an extension of the belief that the Kumano deities took special care of such children. It is possible to imagine that these stories originated in the repertory of the Kumano bikuni themselves, or at least were encouraged and

19. *Yasutomiki*, Kyōtoku 2 (1454)/7/5 and Kyōtoku 3 (1455)/1/23, in *Shiryō taisei*, 29–33 (1936).
20. There was actually a group of nuns called *Tora gozen* who told the *Soga monogatari*. Tsukasaki Susumu believes this group was closely related to the Kumano bikuni; *Monogatari no tanjō*, in *Minzoku mingei sōsho* (Tokyo, 1970), 52: 133–155.

conveyed by them.[21] But it is important to realize that in the popular imagination the Kumano nuns, like many other wandering religious agents
in the middle ages, were thought of as extensions of the powers of the
deities they represented. The nuns became the hands, feet, and voice of
Kumano gongen.

Both Kumano faith and life's normal sufferings were introduced into
narratives about Gempei heroes and their families by the Kumano nuns.
Their greatest contribution by far to the history of Japanese literature,
however, can be seen in the role they played in making the picture scroll,
and especially books, a familiar item in the lives of the common people.
More than any other factor prior to the commercialization of printing in
the Edo period, the proselytizing of the Kumano bikuni put books into
the hands of Japanese on all levels of society everywhere in the land.
Numerous Muromachi-period texts conclude with passages that indicate
the stories had been written down and then distributed (i.e., sold, exchanged for a donation, or given away) as part of missionary activity.[22]
The Muromachi story *Kumano no honji* is clearly a product of such efforts
by Kumano nuns: its original source is uncertain—a libretto text perhaps
or a transcription of an item of vocal literature in their repertory or
possibly a written story read aloud and then left with the listener—but it
concludes:

> If you read this story once, it means you have made a pilgrimage to Kumano
> once. If you read it twice, you will have gone twice. If you read it five times, it is
> the same as if you had gone to Kumano so many times. You should read it
> many times. . . . If you put a copy of this story in your home, then the Kumano
> deities will enter your house and protect it. You should read this *honji* to those
> who cannot read and have them listen to it, so that by hearing it they will be
> guided both in this world and the next, and will not go to hell.[23]

Another example comes from *Komachi no sōshi:*

> For people who hear this story, to say nothing of those who read it, it will be the
> same as if they had made thirty-three images of Kannon and worshiped them.[24]

Although passages of this sort have frequently been cited as examples of

21. Matsumoto, pp. 109, 111n.
22. There has always been a close connection between wandering religious agents and wandering peddlers. It was in many ways difficult to distinguish between the religious and the commercial aspects of such pilgrim/peddler/performer activity or to determine which of their roles
carried the greatest weight with the practitioners themselves. For more on the subject, see
Ōshima Tatehiko, *Otogi zōshi to minkan bungei,* in *Minzoku mingei sōsho,* 12 (Tokyo, 1971): 112.
23. Yokoyama Shigeru and Ōda Takeo, eds., *Muromachi jidai monogatari shū,* 1: 79a line-3 to 79b
line 8.
24. Ichiko Teiji, ed., *Otogi zōshi,* in *Nihon koten bungaku taikei* (Tokyo, 1958), 38: 101. Kiyomizu

the religious or didactic nature of Muromachi period literature, a crucial point seems to have been missed. The little books distributed by Kumano nuns, and probably other religious agents as well, must have been *omamori*, or "talismans," to protect or bring benefits to the owner. Such books should not be viewed in the same context as the works read aloud for pleasure in Heian court society. Nor should these works be judged as literature for private reading such as was made possible on a large scale by the rise of the publishing industry in the seventeenth century. The concluding passage of *Monogusa Tarō* exhorts the owner of this short honji-type story to read the book aloud and let others listen to it at least once a day! Even the most brilliant of short classics could not survive that sort of treatment if the aim was aesthetic enjoyment or even simple narrative interest. The magic in reading these stories lay elsewhere.

Although a number of Muromachi narratives have been recorded in magnificent emaki and ehon, scholars have often wondered, and no one has satisfactorily determined, why so many Muromachi narratives are preserved in an ehon form in which the paintings are so primitive, so quickly done, so childish, in a way, and yet clearly not put together by a child. Usually this particular type among Muromachi period ehon are dismissed as a gekokujō phenomenon. They are discussed as if they typify what happens when the semiliterate masses put fumbling hands to an aristocratic art. If, however, we accept the clear fact that the texts of some stories are, more than anything else, talismans or omamori, I wonder why we cannot view this fact in the context of the category of ehon just described and explore what seems an obvious hypothesis: that shrines and temples and other religious agents brought out ehon on a mass-produced scale as omamori and that the people from top to bottom of society took these omamori books home, much as to this day ofuda and omamori of various sorts are purchased as talismans to protect oneself and one's home.

We know that copies of some medieval stories were almost necessities in the home on certain occasions. Probably in the earliest stages of its evolution *Bunshō no sōshi* concerned itself with the benefits of Kashima myōjin and the potency of this deity in answering prayers of childless couples who wanted children. But as jongleurs spread the story around the country, the effectiveness of the book itself as a talisman overshadowed the specific features of its narrative, and *Bunshō no sōshi* became a book that was read aloud by every family at New Year's time as part of the old custom of *yomihajime* (The first reading of the New Year). Evidence of the belief in

---

dera in Kyoto, where Kannon is the central deity, was considered to be under the protection of Kumano gongen. It is therefore natural for Kumano bikuni to encourage faith in Kannon.

benefits or rewards and in sympathetically induced success, such books were kept in the house and read aloud.

On this foundation, a direct line of subsequent secular development can be postulated where the production of these books is no longer exclusively in the hands of religious institutions or agents. There is only a thin line of commercial consciousness that separates religious artifact from souvenir. It is known that some medieval stories in ehon form were sold by commercial shops whose inventories included paper products of various sorts (*shikishi, tanzaku,* papier-mâchè dolls, and fans, as well as picture books and scrolls). Among the seals of producers impressed in ehon and emaki can be found those of fan and doll shops of this sort, some of which in later generations emerged as commercial booksellers and publishers.[25] Already, therefore, a rudimentary form of publisher-bookseller existed during the Muromachi period, forerunners of the industry that was to play such an important role during the Edo period.[26]

The small storylike tracts of Kumano bikuni brought about an important, almost revolutionary, change in Japanese literary history during the course of the fifteenth and sixteenth centuries. Probably not for our twentieth-century reasons, but out of other needs and preferences, books had become a familiar part of Japanese life. Whether devout religious figures with shaven heads and somber robes singing the nembutsu, performing etoki on paintings of hell, and gathering donations for Kumano; whether missionary educators reading aloud from monogatari or performing religious etoki for the ladies of the house; whether stylish secular performers of etoki and singers of ballads; or whether loose companions on the road who had abandoned all pretenses to either religion or literature, Kumano bikuni were familiar and frequent travelers along the main roads of Muromachi Japan. Their repertories, oral and written, religious and secular, traveled the country with them and helped to contribute to a "national literature" known to everyone high and low who heard them perform.

Literature as Magic
In the passage of time from the Kamakura through the Muromachi periods, most magico-religious performers lost their official religious functions and became performers who used their art to earn a living. Some

25. For details on the seals, see Okami, "Machishū no bungaku," pp. 372–373.
26. There are several hypotheses as to who painted and calligraphed the anonymous Muromachi period emaki and ehon. These hypotheses range from painters of court and shogunal *edokoro* to professional temple painters, independent *ebutsushi, eshi* working among the machishū of Kyoto, and on down to amateur ladies and even children. It is important to note that there is no evidence that either etoki hōshi or Kumano bikuni, the carriers of emaki and ehon, were ever the makers (i.e., calligraphers or painters) of these items.

formed guilds, as did the etoki, biwa hōshi, goze, etc., while a great miscellany of others worked independently. One can call this a secularization or a commercialization of religious or semireligious functions; the secularization process, however, had less to do with a shift in religious attitudes than with economics. Secularization was accelerated, if not actually initiated, by the great financial difficulties in which shrines and temples found themselves at different periods throughout the middle ages. We should not imagine that secularization of all religious arts occurred at once. Men and women proselytizers and performers were cut loose from the financial support of their shrines and temples at different times and for different reasons.

Whatever the case, by the end of the Muromachi period most religious proselytizers had been deprived of their official religious functions. Many, however, never lost their magico-religious aura in the eyes of the populace. The image of the Kumano bikuni as the *miko* (priestesses) of Kumano myōjin was never far from people's minds; even when their function had become little more than entertainment, the very presence of a Kumano bikuni was believed to bring good fortune to a house where she visited. Goze too were so closely associated in their origins and in their stories with *aruki miko* and local deities that they seemed to be bearers not only of vocal literature but of a magico-religious power as well.[27]

A conviction behind almost all Japanese vocal arts before their secularization, and one that adhered to a surprising degree even afterward, was a belief that the souls of deities or ancestors descended through the media of the symbolic props used in the oral recitation (fan, stick, branch of *Sakaki* tree, *gohei*, bow, clay doll). Clearly the Kumano bikuni saw the little books that they urged on the people as having such magico-religious quality. Thus this literature, even when secular in content, cannot easily be separated from the magico-religious qualities that imbued the environment in which it developed. The magic quality of voice projection goes back at least to the intoning of Shinto ritual prayers *(norito)* and to the reciters of history *(katari-be)*, with roots in prehistory. It is well known that vocal literature of many types was believed to have magical qualities in performance during the middle ages as well. Instances are recorded of ar-

27. Fanny Hagin Mayer, "Takada Goze: A Living Tradition," *KBS Bulletin* 99 (December 1969-January 1970); Eta Harich-Schneider, "Die Letzten Goze," *Sociologus* (Berlin) 8 (1958): 57–72; Mizuhara Hajime, *Heike monogatari no keisei* (Tokyo, 1971), pp. 364–406. An interesting study of the relation between so-called *marebito* or mysterious visitors (i.e., deities) and *otozurebito* or outcaste groups of the Tokugawa period that is relevant to the point will be found in Ichirō Hori, "Mysterious Visitors from the Harvest to the New Year," in *Studies in Japanese Folklore*, ed. Richard M. Dorson (Bloomington, 1963), pp. 76–103, which discusses the belief that strangers who appear at harvest or New Year's time are life-givers from another world. Medieval jongleurs absorbed such magico-religious qualities.

tists performing nō and dokugin renga before dieties to get them to heal illness. There can be no doubt that performances of *Heikyoku* and *Soga
monogatari* too were believed to have, besides the ability to move the
listener, the power to preserve the honor of the great clans, perpetuate
their genealogies, reveal the personalities of their leaders, expiate their inner agonies, comfort the tormented spirits of the dead whose last moments
were being recounted, comfort those who were left behind, and aid in the
salvation of all who heard. Surely the deities and the spirits of Buddhist
patriarchs were present when the *kōsōden* and engi emaki that constituted
the great temple treasures were unrolled and etoki was performed. Both
biwa hōshi and goze were believed to be blind due to the sins of a former
life, and they were convinced that their sight would be restored, if not in
this world then in the next, by the religious power of their activities. Jōruri,
with its close ties to Yakushi nyorai (the Healing Buddha), also had deep
magical roots.[28]

This was an age when people believed in the wandering of *onryō*
(vengeful ghosts) and a period when those who had suffered and traveled
(deities, remnants of fallen clans, *tonseisha*, pilgrims, and outcastes) were
viewed as having gained special powers. The performers of vocal literature
were firmly in this tradition. Vocal literature, which constitutes the bulk of
Muromachi fiction, cannot therefore be viewed in purely literary terms
either as an aesthetic exercise or as simple entertainment. Such an interpretation will only obscure our research and lead to erroneous and
anachronistic conceptions of the meaning of medieval literature. Muromachi vocal literature was more than entertainment or diversion; it was a
magico-religious and psychotherapeutic ceremony for artist and audience.
In addition to its qualities as entertainment, it calmed destructive demons,
cured the sick, protected the home, asserted one's ties to clan and land,
confirmed the compassion of the deities, saved one's soul, and affected
one's karma.

With the success of commercial activities in the medieval period,
another magical quality of literature emerged: the use of literature to
achieve material wealth. This is not to be confused with literature that
gives practical instruction on how to become a millionaire. Consistent with
the age in which it emerged, it was based not on logic or practicality but
on sympathetic magic, on a belief in good luck symbols and the power of
felicitous words. *Kammon gyoki* tells us that there was not a house in the

---

28. Legendary origins trace the first *jōruri* to a monogatari composed in the manner of *Heikyoku*
by a blind chanter in the mid-fifteenth century out of gratitude to Yakushi Nyorai for the
restoration of his sight. For a discussion of the doubtful nature of this legend, see C. J. Dunn,
Early Japanese Puppet Drama (London, 1966), pp. 11–12.

capital that did not honor Daikokuten and Ebisu, the lucky gods of wealth.[29] The view of wealth as a result of luck or fate, together with the *shūgen* view of literature, must have greatly reinforced the concept of small books as omamori, as we originally observed in reference to the books of the Kumano bikuni.

Conclusion

The missionary efforts and ultimate secularization of both etoki and Kumano bikuni thus exerted two important effects on the development of Japanese literature. First, they built a body of vocal literature, a repertory of heroes and themes that permeated all genre and became Japan's first national literature. This literature was performed for people on all levels of society and served basic needs that were shared by all classes equally: the desire to know about the conflicts and troubles that were afflicting the world, and the need to learn how to come to grips with or how to escape from the fear and depression such calamities brought. Second, as more and more of their stories were transcribed and circulated, books became a familiar part of Japanese life. Thus, long before the Edo period began, commercial production of handmade books had already started and the history of books was established on its future course. By the time Ihara Saikaku decided to seek his livelihood as a professional fiction writer, both format and general concepts of content were predetermined. He initiated no alteration in the former; on the contrary he actually participated in illustrating his own works. As for content, his *Kōshoku ichidai onna*, to give just one example, is a direct descendant of the iro zange of the Kumano bikuni.

Other wandering proselytizers and jongleurs played crucial roles in the making of the national literature: Jishū *hijiri* at Mt. Koya; the *shōdō sekkyō* priests of the Agui school associated with Mt. Hiei; the biwa hōshi, blind dramatic narrators who played the biwa and who were responsible for the final form of such great works of vocal literature as the *Heike monogatari*, *Hōgen monogatari*, *Heiji monogatari*, and *Jōkyūki* (figure 6); and the goze, blind *tsuzumi*-playing women chanters whose repertory included narratives related to Kumano and Hakone deities and whose performances contributed to the final form of the *Soga monogatari* (figure 7). All of these men and women were major contributors to the mainstream of medieval fiction, and the details of their individual roles in the development of the

---

29. Sakurai Yoshirō, *Chūsei Nihonjin no shii to hyōgen* (Tokyo, 1970), p. 317. Ebisu, Bishamon, and Daikokuten (all representatives of the magic of wealth) appear in kyōgen plays; not only professionals but merchants as well performed dances known as Daikoku mai; ibid., p. 318.

specific stories that constitute Japan's national literature deserve full and separate treatment.

The stories that are the heritage of their traditions are not only long episodic works—the *Heike monogatari*, the *Soga monogatari*, and repertory literature such as *Kowaka bukyoku* and *sekkyō jōruri*—but many short independent works as well, works known variously as *chūsei shōsetsu*, *Muromachi jidai monogatari*, *Muromachi jidai tampen shōsetsu*, *otogi zōshi*. All share the basic anonymity that is the almost inevitable characteristic of works produced by, or at least carried by, itinerant jongleurs. These works have come down to us in many forms: handwritten copies from written texts, transcriptions from performances,[30] emaki, ehon, and seventeeth-century printed books. Irrespective of written format, however, it is safe to say that more serious attention given to all these works as *daihon* or *tanebon* rather than as *yomihon* will inevitably shed much needed light in an area where research has not produced any fundamental advancements for some time. Many puzzling aspects of Muromachi fiction can be easily resolved once we accept some (though of course not all) of these works as transcriptions of performances or daihon, whether or not such daihon were later treated as omamori or yomihon.[31]

If, over the past several decades, scholars of medieval Japanese literature have been shackled to a narrow, anachronistic view of the medieval literary world, it has not been for want of liberating evidence; the shackles have been largely self-imposed. An elitism with regard to what genre are worthy of study; a fascination with the role of social class in literary creativity; an imposition on literary history of concepts, terms, and chronologies borrowed from political history; a disinterest in the enormous emotional and imaginative impact of audience-oriented repertory literature on Japanese society as a whole; a blindness to the centricity of vocal literature in Japan; and an unwillingness to relinquish ill-devised and antiquated scholarly vocabulary—these are the self-imposed shackles, technical, conceptual, and factual, that have led us to such fallacies as the

30. See the analysis of *Rokudai gozen monogatari* as a performance transcription in Kenneth Butler, "The Birth of an Epic: A Textual Study of the Heike Monogatari" (Ph.D. diss., Harvard University, 1964).
31. The practice of viewing variant texts of the same story as copies of hypothetical lost written texts in a reading tradition is a widespread but dubious practice and has so far led to no important breakthroughs in the field of Muromachi fiction. If variant texts, where wording is identical in parts and radically different elsewhere, can be seen as transcriptions of different oral performances of the same work, considerable advances can be made in reconstructing the principles behind the formulaic arts of dramatic recitation practiced by medieval jongleurs. Such principles have been established for Yugoslavian and Chinese oral composition and can be usefully applied to Japanese medieval texts. See Alfred B. Lord, *The Singer of Tales* (New York, 1968), and Eoyang, "Word of Mouth," cited above.

"dark age," to such practices as canonical judgment (or even dismissal) of noncanonical literature, and, most disastrously, to the establishment of a scholarly vantage point from which the birth of Japan's first truly national literature has gone almost completely unobserved. There are still some scholars who, oblivious to the maturation of popular literary forms during the middle ages, view Edo literature as if it were a sudden, inexplicable flowering of some new literary flora. We can no longer condone such a view. And if we still suffer from outdated and inappropriate vocabulary to deal with observable medieval phenomena, then we must, without compunction, abandon the old and hone new verbal and conceptual tools.

PART SIX

Religious Life

The religious life of Muromachi Japan is immensely complex and multifaceted. For not only did the esoteric sects of Tendai and Shingon, which had dominated Heian Buddhism, continue to prosper, the newly popular Pure Land, Nichiren, and Zen sects of Kamakura origin also continued to expand and gain new converts. Organized Buddhism took on an ever increasing variety of forms as syncretic tendencies and revivalist movements one after another revitalized the relationship of Buddhism to new groups of believers.

Two manifestations of these tendencies in Muromachi religious life are revealed in the essays which follow. One is the more intimate role the Zen priesthood, particularly of the Gozan temples, began to play in the lives of the military and court aristocracy. The other is the fifteenth-century expansion of the popular appeal of Buddhism, particularly in its Pure Land manifestation.

The story of Gozan Zen reveals the close association between the bakufu and the Zen establishment which led on the one hand to the strong crossover of the Zen priesthood into the cultural life of the military aristocracy and on the other hand to the administrative dominance of the Zen temples by the bakufu or bakufu-oriented priests. Patronage of the military aristocracy and the political support of the bakufu were the main foundations of Gozan prosperity in the early years of the Muromachi era. But that support was gained at the expense of religious compromise and political acquiescence to military authority that eventually robbed Gozan Zen of its spiritual content and artistic creativity. By the end of the fifteenth century Zen was finding what new vitality it could muster in its provincial temples, where new experiments in syncretism with Pure Land Buddhism were being tried.

Professor Weinstein's exploration of the life and teachings of Rennyo deals with one aspect of the massive and sometimes violent popular religious movements which affected the masses of the people. If the Tendai and Shingon monasteries had once armed themselves for political and protective purposes, they did so on what might be called a monkish mercenary basis. The popular religions of the Sengoku era led to the formation of communities of armed followers of Nichiren, Ji, or Jōdo priests, willing to defend their communities against the brutal attacks of daimyo or peasant mobs. Whatever may be said about the purity of their religious beliefs, these communities were welded together by spiritual bonds of extraordinary strength. At the popular level, Buddhism had reached so great a degree of penetration that whole communities were willing to risk their lives for their right to separate existence.

If the Muromachi period saw the appearance of a "national literature" as Professor Ruch has suggested, in the religious sphere Buddhism may be said to have achieved a national penetration and a particularly Japanese style. This was true for both Zen and the popular sects. In Zen, as Professor Yampolsky shows, the original Chinese meditative practices were discarded for reliance on priestly authority, secret transmission, and formalized techniques of training. In the case of Shinshū, the desire for tangible evidence of salvation on the part of believers led to an equally strong "reliance on the priest." And while Rennyo sought to guide his followers back to a purer reliance on faith in Amida, he recognized the need for a more flexible interpretation of such Buddhist practices as polytheistic worship and prayers for material well-being.

Religion was a major part of the lives of the Muromachi Japanese, particularly after the middle of the fifteenth century. The Jesuit missionaries who arrived in Japan only a century later found a country in which the two dominant classes were the warrior aristocracy and the "bonzes," or priests. Much has yet to be revealed of the nature of this religious life, of what life in the Gozan monasteries was actually like, of what actually motivated the Honganji monto, of what role Shinto beliefs played in the spiritual life of the common Japanese. The two essays which follow converge upon these problems from two different directions.

17

Muromachi Zen and the Gozan System

AKAMATSU TOSHIHIDE and PHILIP YAMPOLSKY

INTRODUCTION

Gozan, or "Five Mountains," was the name given to a group of temples and a system of administration for the Rinzai sect of Zen adopted by the Ashikaga shogunate.[1] Modeled after the Wu-shan system of temple organization which came into use under the Southern Sung dynasty in China, it was introduced into Japan during the late Kamakura period and reached its ultimate form during the Muromachi period. Although the Gozan and their associated temples comprised the official Zen establishment of Kyoto and Kamakura as recognized by the shogunate, it should be understood that other schools of Zen existed at the same time. The Sōtō sect, which had been introduced by Dōgen (1200–1253), spread widely in eastern Japan and depended for its support chiefly on the general populace. In Kyoto, Daitokuji and later Myōshinji were both important Rinzai temples patronized by the imperial family, but were not included in the Gozan system. These temples, especially the Myōshinji, established an extensive network of branch temples in the provinces. In the late Ashikaga period a school known as the Genju-ha gained considerable influence, particularly in the provinces.

Gozan Organization and the Muromachi Bakufu
From the beginning of its establishment as an independent sect in Japan, Zen was closely involved with the imperial court and the military shogunal government. The nature of this involvement was determined partly by the historical tendency of the Japanese aristocracy to seek to dominate the Buddhist establishment and to mold it to its own purposes and partly by factional differences within the Zen priesthood which had their origin in China but were later communicated to Japan. When Japanese Zen monks

The first part ("Introduction") was written by Professor Yampolsky, the second ("Some Problems in Gozan History") by Professor Akamatsu with translation by Professor Yampolsky.
1. This summary is based largely on material found in Imaeda Aishin, *Zenshū no rekishi* (Tokyo, 1969); idem, *Chūsei Zenshūshi no kenkyū* (Tokyo, 1970); and Tamamura Takeji, *Gozan bungaku* (Tokyo, 1958).

traveled to China in the early thirteenth century, the dominant Zen school was one that traced itself to Ta-hui Tsung-kao (Daie Sōkō, 1089–1163). A rival school, begun by Hu-ch'iu Shao-lung (Kukyū Jōryū, 1077–1136), was overshadowed by the Ta-hui factior. Nonetheless most Japanese studied under the less popular Hu-ch'iu school. This is explained by the fact that most of the Chinese priests who had gone to Japan in the Kamakura period belonged to the Hu-ch'iu school. When they in turn sent their Japanese students to China, it usually was to work under priests of this school. The Hu-ch'iu tradition itself was divided into two factions, one descended from P'o-an Tsu-hsien (Hoan Sosen, 1136–1211) and the other from Sung-yüan Ch'ung-yüeh (Shōgen Sūgaku, 1132–1202). Fortunately for the Japanese priests who continued to go to China to work in the Hu-ch'iu tradition, a monk of that persuasion, Wu-chun Shih-fan (Mujun Shihan, 1178–1249), had gained renewed recognition from the Southern Sung court.

Chinese factional disputes were carried to Japan and were reflected in certain antagonisms among the various schools which divided the Japanese priesthood. These in turn had certain political overtones. The important Gozan temples to which shogunal patronage was given belonged to the school of P'o-an, whereas Daitokuji and Myōshinji, patronized by the imperial family, traced their descent from the Sung-yüan school. Tension also existed between the temples of Kamakura and those of Kyoto. Whereas at the outset only temples in Kamakura were given the rank of Gozan, the establishment of the Ashikaga shogunate in Kyoto meant in the long run that the Gozan temples of Kyoto took precedence.

Soon after its establishment in Kyoto, the Ashikaga shogunate adopted a system quite different from the Gozan as a means of patronage and control over the Zen establishment. At the behest of Musō Soseki (1275–1351), beginning in 1338 Takauji and Tadayoshi set up official temples in the "sixty-six provinces and two islands." Named Ankokuji (temples of national peace) these temples served to emphasize the political presence of the Ashikaga in the provinces and to lend importance to the shugo. In some instances military strong points were established in the vicinity of these temples. In addition to the Ankokuji, which were all Zen temples, pagodas known as Rishō-tō were also set up in the provinces. These pagodas were ostensibly designed to console the spirits of warriors who had died since the Genkō era (1331–1333), but they too had a political function. Serving to call attention to the power of the Ashikaga, they were located within the grounds of Tendai, Shingon, and Ritsu temples. The impetus for the establishment of these temples and pagodas derived directly from Sung China where official Zen temples of this sort had been established in the provinces. Some have claimed that the Ashikaga used as their model the Kokubunji system of provincial temples which had been adopted in the eighth century, but direct Chinese influence appears more likely. After the death of Takauji, the Ankokuji and Rishō-tō lost their significance. Instead the shogunate took over the Gozan system of temple organization.

The first reference to Gozan in Japan was in 1299, when Jōchiji in Kamakura was accorded this rank. In 1310 three other temples in Kamakura—Kenchōji, Engakuji, and Jufukuji—enjoyed Gozan ranking, indicating a growing involvement of government in temple affairs by the end of the Kamakura period. Frequent disputes marked the ranking of Gozan temples. Many changes in temple ranking were occasioned by shogunal preference for one temple or another or the influence of certain prominent priests.

In the Kemmu period (1334–1335), the Gozan temples in order of rank consisted of: (1) Nanzenji, (2) Tōfukuji, (3) Kenninji, (4) Kenchōji, (5) Engakuji. In this listing the first three ranks went to temples in Kyoto, the last two to Kamakura temples. After the Ashikaga shogunate had become securely established, it reassigned the temples to suit its own purposes. Soseki had persuaded Takauji in 1339 to establish Tenryūji in memory of Emperor Go-Daigo, and it was ranked within the Gozan system. In 1341 Ashikaga Tadayoshi revised the ranking as follows: (1) Kenchōji, Nanzenji; (2) Engakuji, Tenryūji; (3) Jufukuji; (4) Kenninji; (5) Tōfukuji, Jōchiji (provisional). Thus the Chinese system of naming only five temples was abandoned, and the term Gozan became simply a means of indicating temple rank. One reason for the expanded list obviously was the presence in Japan of two major Zen centers, Kamakura and Kyoto. The Kamakura temples still had the capacity to take precedence over the Kyoto temples until the time of the third shogun. When Yoshimitsu established Sōkokuji in 1382 at Gidō Shūshin's (1325–1388) suggestion, Nanzenji was given a rank above that of all other Gozan temples, and the order then became: (1) Tenryūji, Kenchōji; (2) Sōkokuji, Engakuji; (3) Kenninji, Jufukuji; (4) Tōfukuji, Jōchiji; (5) Jōmyōji, Manjūji. In this listing, for the first time all Kyoto temples were ranked above their Kamakura counterparts. In 1401 Yoshimitsu placed Sōkokuji above Tenryūji, but after his death Yoshimochi, in 1410, again reversed the position of these two temples. This was the last change in the Gozan rankings, and they remained as such, if in name only, into the nineteenth century.

Ranking just below the Gozan were the Jissetsu, or "Ten Temples." This designation, also part of the Sung system of organization, was imported to Japan in the late Kamakura period. As with the Gozan temples, the Jissetsu ranking changed frequently during the Muromachi period. An early official ranking was made by Ashikaga Tadayoshi in 1341. A revised list in 1358 divided the temples equally between eastern and western Japan. In 1380 Yoshimitsu revised the ranking drastically, adding six new temples for a total of sixteen. Thus the original Chinese concept of ten temples was abandoned and the Jissetsu became simply a temple rank category. Once this happened, powerful temples in the provinces rushed to claim Jissetsu status, and the number rapidly increased. Around 1486 there were forty-six Jissetsu. Eventually there were some sixty-odd temples of this category.

One further class of official temples introduced from China was the Shozan. Temples of this classification had already appeared by the late Kamakura period. Scattered throughout the provinces, these temples were usually associated with important provincial families. A large number were originally Tendai, Shingon, Ritsu, Jōdo, and Jishū temples that had changed their affiliation to Zen. The increase in temples of this class, which came in the early and mid-Muromachi period, is a clear index of the prestige of the officially sponsored Gozan establishment. This was shown also by the fact that most Shozan were incorporated as branch temples of specific Gozan temples. Ultimately as many as 230 temples were classified as Shozan.

Not only did the shogunal government in Japan have a hand in the hierarchal ordering of Zen temples, it also created the means of direct superintendence of Buddhist temple affairs. From the outset the Muromachi bakufu contained officials known as *tera bugyō* (temple magistrates) whose duty it was to supervise Enryakuji and the chief Nara temples. For Zen, with which the Ashikaga had a much closer connection, special supervisory officials were established. In the early years the office of the *Zenritsu chōrō bugyō* served this purpose under the direction of prominent civil officials. In Yoshiakira's time an office above that of the bugyō, the *Zenritsu katatōnin*, was created, and such figures as Sasaki Takauji (1306–1373) and Akamatsu Norisuke (1314–1371), themselves prominent shugo, served in the position.

As the official temple administration system, from Gozan to Shozan, became more stable, there was less need for the bakufu to assign shugo-level personnel to the task of superintending religious affairs. Under the influence of the priest Shun'oku Myōha (1311–1388), control of Zen affairs was placed in the hands of the priests themselves and vested in the office known as *Sōroku*. The Sōroku was established as the highest administrative official over all the Gozan temples. In fact it was initially intended that the Sōroku control all Zen temples, including the non-Gozan ones of the

Sōtō sect and those associated with Daitokuji and Myōshinji. But these ultimately remained outside its jurisdiction.

The Sōroku was located within the compound of Sōkokuji, which Yoshimitsu had established in 1382 as the official Ashikaga family temple. Originally the Ashikaga family had patronized Jitōji. But Yoshimitsu, desiring a location contiguous to the bakufu compound in Kyoto, sponsored the creation of Sōkokuji. In 1383 a subtemple known as Rokuon-in was established within the Sōkokuji grounds, and Myōha as Sōroku served also as head priest of this temple. The Rokuon Sōroku, as he came to be called, controlled the appointment of chief priests, promotions in rank, ceremonial procedures, in fact all Gozan functions under bakufu authority. In addition, he assisted in the preparation of documents relating to trade and foreign affairs. Following Myōha, noted priests such as Zekkai Chūshin (1336–1406) and Kūkoku Myōō (1328–1407) held the position.

By the time of Yoshinori the post of Sōroku tended to be assigned to priests who came from highly placed aristocratic families. Thus the actual functions of office were conducted by the assistant Sōroku. This official was housed at a small building, the Inryō-ken, within the Rokuon-in compound, and hence the office was known as the Inryōshoku. The incumbent priest developed a very close relationship with the shogun and became privy to all Zen affairs. Priests with administrative ability were appointed to the position, from which they exercised almost complete control over the administrative aspects of the Gozan system.

The Nature of Muromachi Zen

The nature of Zen taught in the Gozan temples is a matter of speculation. As Professor Akamatsu explains below, we can assume that the Zen practices introduced from China in the Kamakura period had been adapted to Japanese conditions. Difficulties in communication between Japanese and Chinese monks had led to a certain dilution of the teachings from the outset. The extreme popularity of esoteric Buddhism in Japan, particularly in aristocratic circles, led to the continuation of many Mikkyō practices by the priests of the Gozan schools. In the early years of the Muromachi period much attention was paid to the doctrinal aspects of Zen, and the prime Gozan priests engaged in a vigorous religious debate. As the political and literary functions of Zen priests increased, however, there was a marked lessening of emphasis on Zen study. Although the Gozan temples remained politically powerful throughout the Muromachi period, the Zen content of monastic life declined markedly. By the Higashiyama period little or no Zen of any variety was being taught in the Gozan.

The same was true for the other Zen schools, although for different reasons. The Sōtō sect taught initially a relatively pure version of Sung Zen. Losing out politically to the Rinzai sect, Sōtō Zen moved into the provinces where it achieved considerable popularity and support. In the process it too adopted many elements of esoteric Buddhism. Thus the Zen content of Sōtō Zen also underwent a rapid decline, at least in terms of its retention of the teachings of Sung Zen Buddhism.

The Zen of Daitokuji and Myōshinji is today referred to as the Ō-Tō-Kan school, after the names of its three founders, Daiō Kokushi (Nampo Jōmyō, 1253-1309), Daitō Kokushi (Shūhō Myōchō, 1283-1338), and Kanzan Egen (1277-1360). This school also practiced, in the early years of the Muromachi period, a form of traditional Sung Zen, avoiding to a certain extent the political and literary activities that preoccupied the Gozan priesthood. But Ō-Tō-Kan Zen too eventually succumbed to the formalizing tendencies which so affected the Gozan establishment. Daitokuji had close connections with the imperial court, so that it rather quickly shared in the aristocratic proclivity toward Mikkyō ritualism. Myōshinji had been founded by Kanzan at Emperor Hanazono's behest and was initially a very small and unpretentious temple that emphasized a Sung style of Zen. In 1399 it incurred the displeasure of the bakufu because of the assistance it gave to the Ōuchi family, and Yoshimitsu had all its buildings removed to another temple. Several attempts to revive Myōshinji were made, and eventually this was accomplished by Nippō Sōshin (1408-1486). The temple grew in influence, sending out branches into the provinces, until it became virtually the largest of the Rinzai Zen organizations.

Gozan Zen in the provinces tended to be isolated from the populace. Its temples were supported by and took orders from central headquarters temples in Kyoto and Kamakura, and so needed no local parishioners. Many served primarily as agencies for the management of the estates of the main temples. The Sōtō sect and those associated with Myōshinji and Daitokuji were independent temples that had to rely on the people for support. Originally the temples in the provinces tended to attract priests who were sincerely interested in Zen as a religious practice. Priests from the Gozan temples who did not take to the bureaucratized organizational structure or the stultifying literary atmosphere frequently moved to provincial temples, often into temples of the Myōshinji branch. At the outset at least, the atmosphere of these temples differed greatly from the Gozan in that their priests were imbued with sincere religious motivation.

Yet by the mid-fifteenth century Zen practice in these provincial temples had also undergone a substantial change. An oral tradition, handed down in secret, came to be emphasized. The *mondō*, or question and answer sessions held between master and disciple, came to have a fixed form. Many of these were written down and passed around among interested monks and laymen. It became known that if, in the assembly of a certain master, a certain answer were given to a specific *kōan* this answer would be accepted. It also made Zen much more readily available to monks and laymen alike. A Zen that no longer required an intensive lifelong devotion to study and meditation was now at hand.

Syncretism, Bureaucratization, and Popularization
The above descriptions of the organizational and religious aspects of Muromachi Zen reveal a certain pattern in the evolution of the Zen sect in Japan. Tendencies toward syncretism were present from the start, and a propensity toward institutionalization manifested itself quite early. Thus from the middle of the Kitayama period on there was a marked decline in the teaching and practice of meditative Zen. As the Gozan administrative structure fell into place and became almost entirely bureaucratic in nature, enthusiasm for Zen study waned. Part of this may have been due to the increase of esoteric practices and the virtual cessation by the end of the fourteenth century of new stimuli from China. With the Gozan system frozen in a bureaucratic mold, priests with administrative talents gained ascendancy. In the headquarters temples men interested in literary pursuits withdrew completely from temple affairs and devoted themselves exclusively to literature. To be sure, priests gave lectures and continued to write commentaries. But the Gozan priests seemed to concern themselves more and more with trivialities. By the mid-fifteenth century Zen teaching had virtually disappeared in the temples, and the priests devoted themselves mainly to ceremonial and administrative duties. Where in the Kitayama period it had still been the practice for novice priests to visit a variety of Zen teachers, to study under them, and to test the content of their teachings, this practice now ceased. In characteristic Japanese style, a secret oral tradition came to be adopted. Thus by the Sengoku period Gozan Zen existed in form only. Provincial Zen, particularly after the Ōnin War, gained in popularity, but it too changed radically in style. It was now a simplified and formalized teaching with numerous extraneous elements derived from other forms of Buddhism, both esoteric and Pure Land.

SOME PROBLEMS IN GOZAN HISTORY

The Question of Transmission
For a religious practice as elusive as Zen, one of the first questions that

must be asked is how accurately Zen was taught and its inner meanings transmitted to the Japanese. The priest Yōsai (1141–1215), the founder of the Rinzai sect who first went to China in 1168, presumably did so without knowledge of spoken Chinese, for it is recounted that his initial inquiries at the temple to which he went for instruction were conducted in writing.[2] Yōsai went a second time to China in 1187. The twenty years that Yōsai passed in northern Kyushu between his first and second visits were spent in preparation for this second trip. One can assume that during this time he learned to speak Chinese. On his second trip he went to study with Hsü-an Huai-ch'ang (Koan Eshō, n.d.) at the Wan-nien ssu at Mount T'ien-t'ai. According to the *Genkō shakusho*, Huai-ch'ang asked Yōsai about Japanese esoteric Buddhism.[3] Yōsai explained the esoteric teaching that holds that at the time that the first aspiration to study Buddhism is formed one has already obtained True Enlightenment and that once one is unmoved by birth and death one has achieved Nirvana. On hearing this Huai-ch'ang replied that Zen and esoteric Buddhism appeared to be one and the same thing. Perhaps Huai-ch'ang's remark was the reason that Yōsai did not stop being a Tendai priest even after he had studied Zen. In addition to the formal sanction of his having completed his Zen training, Yōsai received from Huai-ch'ang the Vinaya in Four Divisions (*Shibunritsu*) and the Bodhisattva Precepts (*Bosatsukai*). Yōsai continued his earnest studies, combining the practice of exoteric and esoteric Buddhism, that is both Zen and Vinaya, that had been advocated by Saichō (767–822), whose teaching Yōsai sought to restore.

Whereas Yōsai maintained the esoteric teaching that "this very body becomes Buddha" at the same time that he studied Zen, the story has it that Dōgen (1200–1253), the founder of Sōtō Zen, shortly after he became a monk began to harbor doubts about some of the basic Tendai teachings. He was unable to understand why, if the body of the dharma nature was from the outset innate as Tendai held, it was necessary to undertake intensive training to obtain awakening. Dōgen, although still very young, devoted himself to an intense practice of Buddhism, but he was bothered by such teachings as "the very passions are themselves bodhi" and "this very body becomes Buddha" that both Tendai and Shingon advocated. Kōin (1145–1216) of Onjōji, under whom he was studying, was at a loss for a way to reconcile his doubts and urged him to visit Yōsai at Kenninji. It was in 1214 when he was only fourteen years of age that Dōgen left the

2. Yōsai's *Kōzen gokoku ron*, written in 1198, makes this clear. See Ichikawa Hakugen et al., *Chūsei Zenke no shishō* (Tokyo, 1972).
3. Kokan Shiren, *Genkō shakusho*, in *Kokushi taikei*, 31 (1930): 42.

Tendai sect to enter a Zen school that both maintained the precepts and practiced meditation.

The matter of monastic regulation must be considered crucial. Before the introduction of Zen into Japan, among the accepted precepts those dealing with regulations concerning eating were the least correctly observed in the Buddhist temples. Evidence for this can be found in the *Zenrinji shiki*[4] of the late ninth century and the *Sammon nijūrokkajō kinsei*[5] of 970, compiled by the Tendai chief abbot Ryōgen (912–985). Yōsai, before he went to China, in all probability followed the customs of Japanese temples of his time and ignored the precepts governing eating and the consumption of alcohol. This attitude on the part of Japanese priests naturally obstructed a true monastic experience. Later, however, Yōsai, having seen that in China priests carried on their monastic life while observing the precepts, realized the defects of Japanese Buddhism. He abruptly reversed his position and began a strict observance of the precepts. In his classic study of monasticism, *Shukke taikō*,[6] which he began writing after his return to Japan, he maintains that the observance of the precepts is the basis of Buddhism. Dōgen, who greatly valued Yōsai's achievement, also demonstrated by his conduct the correct attitude of the monk.

The significance of Kamakura Buddhism lies in the fact that the methods for the subjective experience of Buddhism for monks and for laymen alike became established in this period. In this way the Zen sect was accepted into the society of the Kamakura period as a religion in which the monks were required to actively experience Buddhism within themselves. As is seen in the well-known cases of Hōjō Tokiyori (1227–1263) and Tokimune (1251–1284), the practice of laymen studying Zen under a master was also established in this period.

But the degree to which either priests or laymen actually gained a deep or correct understanding of Zen cannot be precisely determined, even if one examines the preaching *(hōgo)* contained in the records *(goroku)* of the priests under whom they studied. There is some question of how well the Chinese priests who had come to Japan were able to convey their teaching to their Japanese disciples. Certainly one cannot believe that they were particularly fluent in the Japanese language, although there may have been one or two who were.

Kōhō Kennichi (1241–1316), the teacher of Musō Soseki, studied Zen under Wu-hsüeh Tsu-yüan (Mugaku Sogen, 1226–1286) who had come

4. Takeuchi Rizō, ed., *Heian ibun* (Tokyo, 1947), 1, no. 156.
5. Ibid., 2 (1948), no. 298.
6. Facsimile reproduction of text issued by Rokuonji, Kyoto, n.d.

to Japan from China. But it is clear from a document that remains from that time that their conversations were carried out in writing. When a priest had to converse in writing, even with a disciple who was constantly in attendance on him, one may wonder how much of what the Chinese priest taught could be understood. How difficult then the problem for lay students who studied Zen only in the time they could spare from their political and administrative duties. And if one questions the depth to which Tokiyori and Tokimune, both dedicated lay practitioners, understood Zen, one must question even more the degree of correct understanding held by others of the upper level of bakufu officials. Clearly there was a general discrepancy between Chinese teaching and Japanese practice.

The Question of Soseki's Competence

The problem of transmission becomes especially acute in the Muromachi period and particularly with respect to Musō Soseki, the single most important figure in the establishment of the Gozan complex of temples favored by the Ashikaga shogunate. It is significant that Musō never traveled to China to study Zen. Instead he attended on I-shan I-ning (Issan Ichinei, 1247–1317) who had come to Japan from China in 1299. Moreover, although Soseki served as chief monk, he was never able to obtain his master's sanction. Tamamura Takeji ascribes this failure to Soseki's inability to suppress a tendency to become excessively involved with Buddhist scriptural literature and the written records of the patriarchs, a failing that has been constantly inveighed against in Zen literature.[7] In addition, I-ning, being a foreigner, was unable to use Japanese and must have found it difficult adequately to transmit his teaching. Soseki eventually left I-ning and went to study under Kōhō Kennichi, whose written conversations with Wu-hsüeh Tsu-yüan have previously been mentioned. Soseki continued to have difficulty in overcoming his inordinate reliance on scriptural and Zen literature, although Kennichi did his best to lead him away from this tendency. Despairing of his efforts, Soseki set out to lead a life of seclusion and retirement in the distant province of Mutsu, and there to devote himself to intensive self-discipline. After three years, his confidence restored, he returned to Kamakura in 1305. Going again to Kennichi, he expressed to his master his understanding of Zen. Kennichi acknowledged it and gave him formal sanction.

We can gain some idea of the style of Zen that Soseki advocated from the *Hanazono Tennō shinki*.[8] In the account that deals with the tenth month

7. Tamamura Takeji, *Musō kokushi* (Kyoto, 1958), p. 28.
8. In *Shiryō taisei* (Tokyo, 1938), kan 33–34.

of Shōchū 2 (1325), just after Soseki had become chief abbot of Nanzenji at the invitation of Emperor Go-Daigo, we find reference to a severe criticism of Soseki by Shūhō Myōchō (Daitō Kokushi, 1282–1338), the founder of Daitokuji. According to Emperor Hanazono, Myōchō, speaking in reference to a question and answer session that was held between Soseki and Emperor Go-Daigo, pointed out that Soseki did not transcend the doctrines advocated by such "teaching schools" as Shingon, Tendai, and Pure Land. Myōchō maintained that if a Zen priest with Soseki's limited understanding were to become the head of an important temple of the same class as the Gozan temples, then Zen would without doubt collapse.

As Tamamura has pointed out, since Myōchō belonged to the Sung-yüan faction and Soseki to the P'o-an faction of the Sung Zen tradition, it is probable that their conflict derived to a certain extent from their awareness of the conflict between these two schools.[9] Nevertheless, Tamamura believes that Myōchō's contention that Soseki's Zen did not transcend the area of the teaching schools was quite justified. Soseki, who even though he had studied kōan Zen under I-ning had been unable to receive his master's sanction, himself warned his own disciples against the error of trying to obtain satori by depending on phrases and passages from the scriptures and Zen texts. Yet when he lectured Soseki dealt most frequently with the scriptures; his disciples would then present him with questions in reference to them. Tamamura holds that because Soseki did not follow the style of Zen taught by I-ning he sought instead to establish a rapprochement between Zen and the teaching schools (kyōzen itchi) and to set up an ultimate teaching based on a theoretical position in which he justified his own personal approach to Zen. It is quite evident that Soseki sought in his Zen to affirm the mission of esoteric Buddhism, which placed great emphasis on prayers and incantation.

Soseki, at the request of Ashikaga Tadayoshi, answered in detail certain questions relating to Zen. These questions and answers were edited and published as an imaginary dialogue while Tadayoshi and Soseki were both still living and appeared in printed form in 1344 as the famous *Muchū mondō*.[10] The text was written in readily comprehensible Japanese and clearly shows the extent of Soseki's understanding of Zen. From the content of his questions, the interlocutor Tadayoshi reveals his own remarkable understanding of Zen. The focus of his sharp questioning is on what might be considered Soseki's weak points, the validity of incantations and prayers and the dependence on scriptural writings and traditional Zen texts. Thus we must presume that, despite his certification as a Zen priest,

9. Tamamura, *Musō kokushi*, p. 131.
10. Sato Taishun, ed., *Muchū mondō*, Iwanami bunko nos. 1046–1047 (Tokyo, 1971).

Soseki continued to hold an affinity to the teaching of the esoteric schools, and this presumably continued to influence the content of Gozan Zen.

The Question of Monastic Succession
If teaching and monastic life differed in Japan and China, so did practices of temple organization. Take for instance the practice of monastic succession. Originally the custom in Buddhist temples, particularly government-sponsored ones, was to recognize that various schools of Buddhism could be practiced at the same time and that monks of differing schools, while living together in the same monastery, might each study and practice his own particular version of Buddhism. In Japan the practice was different. Temples belonged exclusively to a specific sect and monks of that sect alone lived there. This custom was first established by Kūkai (774–835), the founder of the Shingon sect, when he petitioned the court to make Tōji and Jingoji exclusively Shingon temples. It was not long before this custom spread to other government-sponsored temples. Tendai and Shingon temples selected as head priests only men who belonged to the school and who could claim direct lineal descent from the founder himself. The Zen establishment in Japan succeeded in altering this custom, but only partially.

Gozan temples in Japan from the first adopted the practice of free selection of head priests. The question of succession was raised when Nanzenji petitioned for inclusion among the Gozan. Nanzenji had been founded at the request of Emperor Kameyama. According to instructions written in 1299, Emperor Kameyama stated that the choice of head priest of the temple need not be limited to the spiritual descendants of its founder Mukan Fumon (Daimon Kokushi, 1212–1291) but that any priest of superior talents and wisdom who would encourage Buddhism and see to it that the required services were conducted might be appointed. It is reasonable to assume that because of this fact the decision to rank Nanzenji with the Gozan was quickly arrived at.

The same was not true for Daitokuji. When Emperor Go-Daigo ordered the Daitokuji to be added to the ranks of the Gozan in 1333, objections were immediately raised. Daitokuji had adopted the practice of choosing its chief abbots from the descendants of its founder Shūhō Myōchō. Ultimately a decision had to be made whether Daitokuji would retain its selection practice or become a Gozan temple. It chose the former. The exact date is not known, but in the Gozan rankings determined by the bakufu in 1341 Daitokuji was not included. There is no doubt that Daitokuji had withdrawn from the Gozan by this date.

Toward the end of Emperor Go-Daigo's reign, there had also been a controversy over the ranking of Tōfukuji in the Gozan. At this temple only the priests in the line of its founder Enni Ben'en (Shōitsu Kokushi, 1202–1280) were appointed chief abbot. An argument was presented that, should Tōfukuji be included in the Gozan, then it should, in all reasonableness, be ranked last. The emperor accepted this argument, but the chief abbot of Tōfukuji visited the court and protested to the emperor that his decision was in error. This protest was eventually accepted, and Tōkufuji was given a position as second in the ranking. The arguments used to advance the case that Tōfukuji was qualified for Gozan ranking, as detailed in the *Kaizō-oshō ki'nen roku*,[11] are that a decision should be made on the basis of the social position of the parishioners, the size of the temple complex, and the length of time that had elapsed since the temple had first been established. Founded under the patronage of Kujō Michiie (1193–1252) in the mid-thirteenth century and with a temple complex much grander in scale than other Zen temples, Tōfukuji had impressive credentials. It retained its rank in the Gozan even though its procedure for selection of the head abbot did not conform to the Gozan practice.

Despite the fact that Daitokuji was rejected from the ranks of the Gozan for its refusal to abide by the practice of selecting chief abbots from outside lines, and despite the fact that Tōfukuji was included as an exception, the later tendency among the major Gozan temples was in the opposite direction. Ultimately even at Tenryūji and Sōkokuji the lines descended from Musō Soseki and Shun'oku Myōha (1311–1388) began to monopolize the position of chief abbot. Thus the system of selecting Gozan temple heads from men of outside lines was gradually abandoned. Single line succession was clearly more congenial to the Japanese practice.

The Question of Temple Administration

From contrasts between Japan and China now let us turn to some peculiar organizational features of the Gozan temple complex as these related to Japanese society of the Muromachi era. Let us consider first the number of monks. According to documents of the year 1283 that detail the annual rice and money account record of Engakuji,[12] we find that at that time there were at the temple one hundred monks, one hundred temple assistants *(anja)*, twenty attendants with ceremonial duties, four laundry workers, and six assistants at the abbot's quarters. This was presumably the agreed upon table of organization at the time the temple was first established. After this, however, the number of monks increased dramatically, and in the 1350s we find that there were some four hundred monks at

11. Kamimura Kankō, ed., *Gozan bungaku zenshū* (Tokyo, 1936), 2: 145; Ryosen Reisai, ed., in *Zoku gunsho ruijū* (Tokyo, 1905), 9: 481.
12. *Engakuji monjo*, nos. 13, 14, in *Kamakura shi shi: Shiryō-hen* (Tokyo, 1955), 2.

the temple. Pressure to increase the number of monks apparently continued, for we find in 1464 an order that forbade the admission of new monks until the number had been reduced by attrition to the original limit. Similar restrictions on the number of monks were made in other Zen temples as well.

The need to restrict the number of monks in any given temple could be justified in terms of the peculiar requirements of Zen practice. Yet it must be pointed out that at the same time similar restrictions were placed on the number of assistants and ceremonial attendants who served in the temple, clearly for political reasons. In a prohibition (*seifu*) addressed to Engakuji by Hōjō Sadatoki (1271-1311) in 1303, assistants were forbidden to carry swords, and those who violated this regulation were subject to lifetime banishment from the temple.[13] There is an indication that Kamakura Buddhism still faced the problem of soldier monks which Heian Buddhism had tolerated. At Engakuji the problem seems to have been solved by the strict enforcement of bakufu regulations prohibiting assistants from bearing arms. A prohibition issued by Hōjō Takatoki (1303-1333) in 1327, gave the responsibility for control of monastic communities to bakufu officials known as *jika gyōji*.[14] Thus jurisdiction for disciplinary action over monks was placed in the hands of the bakufu. In later years these officials came to be known as *Zen'in bugyōsha*.

The Ashikaga bakufu took extraordinary precautions to prevent Zen temples from arming themselves. In 1340 Ashikaga Tadayoshi issued a prohibition to Engakuji reiterating the ban against assistants arming themselves. At the same time he announced that because of rumors that arms were being hidden in dormitories inside the temple compound, officials were being sent to investigate the matter.[15] Apparently there was a very real danger at the time that Zen temples might begin to arm themselves. To prevent any tendency in that direction Ashikaga Motouji (1340-1367), the governor general of the Kantō at Kamakura, issued regulations in 1354 directed to all temples, large or small, under his jurisdiction. The regulations contained general instructions relating to temple matters and made clear that anyone who created a disturbance within a temple compound using swords and other weapons would be severely dealt with.[16]

The arming of Zen temples never occurred because of the self-regulation of the temples themselves and the pressures brought to bear by the Kamakura and Ashikaga shogunates. However, at the beginning of the Ashikaga period occasions arose in which monks banded together to pre-

sent demands to the heads of temples. In 1340 Engakuji was issued instructions by the bakufu that urged the head priest and the monks to meet
and discuss any problems that might arise between temple authorities and
monks and to make all efforts to solve them. On occasions when a decision
could not be arrived at it was ordered that an appeal be made to the
bakufu. Thus the bakufu managed to exert considerable political influence
over the Gozan temples.

The reverse of this was also true. Zen priests on occasion were able to
influence Ashikaga politics. For example, the Tenryūji group centered
around Shun'oku Myōha approached the influential general Shiba Yoshimasa (1350–1410) to have the general Hosokawa Yoriyuki (1329–1392)
removed from office.[17] It is important to note that the shogun Yoshimasa
and the priest Myōha worked together to establish the office of Sōroku, or
supervisor of monks, and to bring to completion the administrative
organization between the bakufu and the Zen temples. The result was an
excessive intimacy between the Gozan and bakufu authorities. This
relationship clearly became an obstacle to the Gozan monks in their effort
to train and practice as men of religion. It also meant that the fate of the
Gozan would go hand in hand with the decline and eventual demise of the
Muromachi bakufu.

The Question of Temple Fiscal Management
The relationship between the bakufu and the Gozan was both political
and economic. One of the important reasons that the Gozan flourished
during the Muromachi period was the excellence of temple fiscal management. In Zen temples it was the custom, imported from China, to have
two administrative sections, the Eastern (*Tōhan*) and the Western (*Seihan*),
under the overall supervision of the chief abbot. The Tōhan, referred to as
the *chiji*, had charge of all economic and administrative matters. The
officer in charge of this section was known as the *tsūsu*. The Seihan,
referred to as the *chūshu*, directed the religious training and practice of the
monks. Its chief officer, the *shuso*, had complete authority over this section.

By the end of the eleventh century the vast majority of Japanese temples
depended on shōen for their income. As a result, there were established
within the temples special sections whose sole duty was to handle shōen
administrative affairs. Instead of administering all estates attached to a
temple together, each important unit or small temple complex would have
a priest whose duty was to administer the estates contributing to his particular unit. Thus, while the number and size of the estates controlled by

17. For a detailed discussion of this incident, see Imaeda, *Chūsei zenshūshi no kenkyū*, p. 461.

such temples as Enryakuji, Onjōji, Kōfukuji, and Tōdaiji were great, the number of monks charged with their administration was correspondingly large.

In contrast to this, the Zen temples, especially those associated with the Gozan, each had a single annual account plan which was administered by the Tōhan section. The various officers associated with the section—*tsūsu, kansu,* and *fusu*—each attended to his own specially assigned bureaucratic functions, and these were not separated on the basis of shōen. As an example of how well coordinated the fiscal administration of a Zen temple was we have the annual rice and money account records for Engakuji dated 1283 and contained in the *Engakuji monjo*.[18] At this time the amount of rice required annually by the temple was budgeted at 1,374 koku and 7 to. However, the income from two pieces of temple property was estimated at 1,569 koku and 8 to, leaving a surplus of 195 koku and 1 to. Expenditures for the year in terms of money were estimated to be 1,745 kammon while the annual income from the two properties was calculated at only 1,575 kammon and 451 mon, making a deficit for the year of 169 kammon and 746 mon.[19] If one assumes one koku of rice as the equivalent of one kammon, the extra rice produced and the deficit in temple monies roughly balance out. Thus the annual receipts and expenditures of Engakuji can be seen to have been largely balanced.

It is important to note that on the rice and money account records of Engakuji the various officers of the Tōhan attached their ordinary signatures and added their monograms (*kaō*). In addition, the chief abbot and certain parishioners also affixed their signatures. Of particular significance is the fact that the chief bakufu officials Hōjō Tokimune and Sadatoki also affixed their signatures and kaō. It can be assumed that this strict practice of account records was introduced to Japan with the Gozan system.

Officers in charge of the administration of each of the temple lands followed the strict administrative practices that had been developed at the headquarters temple. The temple did not alternate estate managers too frequently and made every effort to insure that the administration of its estates brought good results. These practices continued into the Ashikaga period. A directive in 1340 from Ashikaga Tadayoshi ordered that specific regulations be established relating to the selection of the officers in charge of temple shōen. The chief abbot and temple officials, possibly including the Tōhan group, were to confer so as to select honest and talented per-

---

18. *Engakuji monjo,* nos. 13, 14.
19. These figures do not add up correctly, but miscalculations of this sort appear frequently in documents of the medieval period and no attempt to reconcile them will be made here.

sons. The appointed official was not to be recalled just because the chief abbotship of the temple was reassigned. But should an official be accused of corruption, both temple and government officials would judge the case. If guilty he would be expelled from the temple. Two years later, Tadayoshi sent a supplementary directive stating that, because corruption was always a possibility when the same person retained office too long, estate managers should be appointed for three-year tenures. Reappointment should be approved only after the official's honesty had been determined.[20] Of particular note was the regulation that provided that persons who held superior positions in the Tōhan section were not eligible for appointment as estate administrators. This would constitute a conflict of interest, since it was the responsibility of the Tōhan to record the number of tax rice deliveries made by each estate administrator. It was attention to details of this sort that assured the financial health of the Zen temples in the early Muromachi period.

Zen temples were particularly noteworthy in their ability to keep up with the general economic development of the country. Very early on, for instance, there appeared among the officials of the Tōhan section certain individuals who conducted moneylending operations. In the supplementary regulations of the third month of Ryakuō 5 (1342) that Ashikaga Tadayoshi sent to the Engakuji, he indicated that rumors had come to his ears that the temple's priests were lending money at high rates of interest. In his directive of 1354, Ashikaga Motouji, the governor general of the Kantō, indicated that he had heard reports of moneylending operations being carried out by Zen temples. He ordered such practices stopped. Despite orders of this kind, bakufu and Zen temples were soon in close cooperation in money matters. The practice of moneylending by Zen monks, particularly by those in the Tōhan section, became quite common under the regimes of Ashikaga Yoshimitsu, Yoshimochi, and Yoshinori. Several monks in the position of *tsubun* at Sōkokuji became intimately involved in bakufu finances. The public moneylender Shōjitsubō had an office within the grounds of Sōkokuji. Operations of this sort offer yet another example of the close relationship between the bakufu and the Gozan temples.

18

Rennyo and the Shinshū Revival

STANLEY WEINSTEIN

Although the intense religious activity that marked the early part of the
Kamakura period has been characterized as a "Buddhist revival," it
would perhaps be more appropriate to apply this term to the Buddhist
movements of the Muromachi period.[1] To the student of Japanese religion
the designation "Kamakura Buddhism" immediately evokes the names of
such eminent religieux as Hōnen, Shinran, Nichiren, and Dōgen, who today are regarded as the founders of Buddhist schools that claim the
nominal adherence of eighty percent of the Japanese people. Although a
certain risk is entailed in any attempt to generalize about so complex a
phenomenon as the religious awakening of the early Kamakura period, it
would seem that the efforts of these religious leaders were directed primarily toward achieving a reformation of Buddhism as it existed at the
close of the Heian period. Despite the apparent success that these men had
in gaining a devoted following, both lay and clerical, during their lifetimes,
their attempts to reform and purify Buddhism did not immediately bear
fruit. To the contrary, we find in most instances that after the death of the
"founder" a common pattern emerged whereby the self-proclaimed followers venerated the founder virtually to the point of deification while ignoring or distorting his teaching and often reverting to the very type of
Buddhist belief or practice that the founder had attempted to reform.

Early in the Muromachi age the so-called Kamakura schools—Jōdo,
Shin, Ji, Nichiren, Rinzai, and Sōtō—were apparently already thriving in
terms of numbers of temples, chapels (dōjō), clergy, and lay supporters,
even if there was a tendency for these schools to subdivide into rival
branches (ryū) based on the different lineages emanating from the founder.
Hence it was no accident that in the course of the fifteenth century a
revivalist movement took place within the ranks of most of the Kamakura
schools to restore or revitalize the original teaching of the founder. Perhaps

1. Edwin O. Reischauer and John K. Fairbank, *East Asia: The Great Tradition* (Boston, 1958),
1: 544.

the most remarkable figure from this period is Rennyo (1415–1499), who not only struggled against widespread heresy among those who claimed to be Shinran's followers but also succeeded in unifying the diverse independent groups of Shinshū adherents (*monto*) under the leadership of the Honganji to which he was heir as Shinran's blood descendant.

Shinran, who had always considered himself a completely faithful follower of Hōnen (whose disciple he had become in 1201), in fact had reinterpreted many of Hōnen's ideas in the light of his own religious experience. When Hōnen began his studies on Hieizan in 1145, the practice of invoking the name of Amida Buddha (*nembutsu*) as a means of acquiring merit that would contribute to rebirth in Pure Land was already widely accepted by Tendai monks as one of their basic religious exercises, along with the performance of esoteric rituals, various types of meditation, and the worship of a host of Buddhas, bodhisattvas, Tantric divinities, and minor gods of Buddhist and Shinto origin. According to the traditional accounts, Hōnen became convinced in the year 1175, after reading a commentary by the famous Chinese Pure Land thinker Shan-tao (613–681), that the only way men living in the *mappō* period could attain rebirth in Pure Land, i.e., salvation, was by the exclusive practice of the nembutsu (*senju nembutsu*).[2] This was, of course, a radical idea, for it demanded the rejection of such traditional Buddhist practices as meditation and the worship of Buddhas other than Amida. Since his advocacy of senju nembutsu implied a fundamental break with the Tendai tradition, Hōnen moved from Hieizan to Ōtani in the Higashiyama section of Kyoto. There his doctrine of salvation through the invocation of the nembutsu attracted a large number of lay followers ranging from leading court nobles to illiterate inhabitants of the capital.

It should be noted that Shinran, though today the best known of Hōnen's disciples, did not at the time occupy a particularly prominent place among them. His relative obscurity during his six-year stay with Hōnen at Ōtani is apparent from the earliest histories of the Jōdo movement—the *Shishū hyakuinnenshū*, compiled in 1257, and the *Jōdo hōmon genrushō*, written in 1311—which contain a description of the various

---

2. The idea that Buddhism would pass through three periods—*shōbō* (the true religion), *zōhō* (the imitated religion), and *mappō* (the declining religion)—goes back to sixth-century China. Although this concept of a progressive decline in man's spiritual capabilities was already known in the Nara period, it was not until the late eleventh and early twelfth centuries, when it was believed that Japan had just entered the mappō age, that the Japanese became seriously concerned about its implications, viz., that man had so degenerated that enlightenment was no longer possible. It should be noted that the preoccupation with mappō occurred in Japan five centuries later than it did in China because each country adopted a different method of reckoning the length of the three periods.

lineages of the Jōdo school but fail to make any reference to Shinran.[3] While Shinran may not have been considered a leading disciple (*jōsoku*), Hōnen evidently had sufficient confidence and trust in him to allow him to copy the *Senchakushū*, which Hōnen had not permitted to circulate freely out of fear that its doctrine of senju nembutsu would antagonize the Tendai authorities.

In 1207, Hieizan was finally successful in persuading the government to issue a ban on the practice of the senju nembutsu, which resulted in the laicization of Hōnen and his banishment to the province of Tosa in Shikoku. Some of his leading disciples—Shōkū and Kōsai, for example —managed to avoid exile by relying on their connections with court families or influential patrons on Hieizan; Shinran, who had been born into the aristocratic Hino family and hence might have been able to escape punishment, accepted banishment to Echigo province, perhaps because he saw the possibility of making Hōnen's teachings known in this relatively backward area of Japan.[4] In any event, Shinran spent four years in Echigo before being pardoned in 1211, the same year that Hōnen was permitted to return to Kyoto. Large groups of Jōdo followers were already beginning to form around Hōnen's more illustrious disciples, but, unlike Hōnen, Shinran did not at this time go back to the capital, moving instead to Inada in Hitachi province in eastern Japan, where he remained for some twenty years. Whatever his motives in choosing Hitachi as the base for his missionary activities, it was here and in the Kantō region in general that Shinran gained his overwhelming following. Around 1234, again for reasons that are not entirely clear, he returned to Kyoto and seems to have devoted himself thereafter largely to writing, maintaining contact through correspondence with his followers in the Kantō.

Hōnen's disciples are sometimes conveniently divided into two groups: the *kigyōha* who placed primary emphasis on the importance of formal devotional practices, viz., the verbal utterance of the nembutsu as the means to achieve rebirth in Pure Land, and the *anjinha* who held that faith (*shinjin*) in Amida was the essential cause for rebirth in the Pure Land rather than the mechanical act of repeating Amida's name.[5] While the precise relationship between faith (*shin*) and religious practice (*gyō*) fac-

3. In the *Shichi-ka-jō seikai*, a document drawn up in 1204 in which Hōnen's disciples undertook to exercise restraint toward the older sects, Shinran's signature occupies the 87th place among the 190 attached signatures. See Ikawa Jōkei, *Hōnen Shōnin-den zenshū* (Kyoto, 1967), pp. 974–975. The first mention of Shinran in a Jōdoshū source occurs in the *Hossui bunruki*, compiled in 1378, which refers to his followers as "Ōtani monto."
    4. Kikuchi Yūjirō, "Jōdoshū," in *Taikei Nihonshi sōsho 18: Shūkyōshi* (Tokyo, 1964), p. 151 (hereafter cited as *Shūkyōshi*).
    5. Mochizuki Shinkō, *Ryakujutsu Jōdo kyōrishi* (Tokyo, 1944), p. 120.

334   STANLEY WEINSTEIN

tions has been one of the most complex questions in Pure Land dogmatics, it might be said in very general terms that the main line of the Jōdoshū (the so-called *Chinzeiha*) that is represented by the Chion'in and the Zōjōji emerged from the kigyōha. In the anjinha group are included such disciples as Shōkū, the founder of the Seizan branch of the Jōdoshū with its center at the Kōmyōji in Kyoto, and Shinran, who in many respects was probably the most radical of Hōnen's disciples.

The basic premise of both Hōnen and Shinran was that salvation in the mappō age could be achieved only through the power of Amida's vow. Shinran carried the implications of mappō thought further than did Hōnen by asserting that in the mappō age man was incapable of doing a single truly selfless deed. Although the possibility of performing good deeds was admitted in a strictly relative sense, such deeds were always tinged with some self-serving purpose. Based on his own sincere but nonetheless futile effort to free himself from lustful thoughts and illusions, Shinran concluded that the burden of accumulated evil karma was so great that man could never acquire sufficient merit through his own actions to achieve salvation. Unlike Hōnen, Shinran rejected as hypocritical any formal statement of adherence to the precepts that constituted the basis of Buddhist morality, for no man in the mappō age could truly uphold the injunctions of the Buddha. These precepts, Shinran argued, had been formulated for men of an earlier period when moral perfection was possible. Thus, whereas Hōnen and his disciples continued to administer the Mahāyāna precepts while proclaiming that Amida's vow would save all men, Shinran held that precepts had no value for men living in his age. In a similar vein he concluded that celibacy was yet another futile exercise for man in the mappō period, since no one could totally rid himself of sexual desires. Shinran, in an open break with Buddhist clerical tradition, himself took a wife and raised a family.

In contrast to Hōnen's view of Amida's compassion as so all-embracing that his vows to save mankind included the evil man as well as the good man, Shinran, convinced there could be no truly "good man," reasoned that Amida must have formulated his vows for the specific purpose of saving evil men (*akunin shōki*). This position seemed to involve a contradiction, for if all men of the mappō age were incapable of good works in an ultimate sense, how then could these same men fulfill the condition of Amida's vow that required them to invoke his name with "sincere faith"? Could the ordinary man whose daily life inevitably forced him to practice dissimulation be capable of reciting the nembutsu with the sincere faith that Shan-tao and other orthodox Pure Land thinkers expected of him? Shinran, who had been tormented by doubts regarding the steadfastness of his own faith, responded to this dilemma by asserting that the faith that provided the key to Pure Land was not something generated by man but rather a gift of Amida to man. Hence salvation was ultimately not the result of frequent repetition of the nenbutsu, for this would suggest man in the mappō age had the potentiality of doing good deeds sufficient to escape his burden of evil karma. Nor was salvation possible through a faith in Amida that originated within oneself, since no man was capable of complete sincerity. Salvation was assured only when one accepted Amida's gift of faith or, to use the conventional Shinshū phrase, when one "heard and accepted the name of Amida" (*monshin myōgō*). The certainty of salvation was attained not through a gradual process but at the very moment that the acceptance of faith occurred (*ichinen hokki*). In Shinran's view, then, the nenbutsu was no longer a meritorious act on the part of the devotee that led him to salvation, as it was conceived of in other Jōdo schools; rather it was seen to be an expression of gratitude to Amida (*hōon shōmyō*) for his compassionate gift of faith which allowed man to enter Amida's Pure Land.

Since salvation depended solely on the grace of Amida, the worship of other Buddhas and bodhisattvas, even those like Kannon and Seishi who figure prominently in Amida's retinue, was deemed unnecessary, if not an act suggesting a lack of faith in the power of Amida's vow. The highly abstract quality of Shinran's concept of faith can be seen in his choice of Amida's name (*myōgō*) inscribed on a scroll to serve as the proper object of veneration (*honzon*) instead of the customary iconographical representation of Amida.[6] Similarly Shinran inveighed against the use of magic, divination, astrology, taboos, and other superstitious practices as well as against the worship of Shinto gods as means to bring about material benefits in this world (*genze riyaku*). The only tangible benefits that faith in Amida brought were the tranquillity and peace of mind that resulted from the assurance that rebirth in Pure Land was certain.

By all indications Shinran was a highly effective proselytizer.[7] The rapid growth in the number of his followers during his own lifetime was no doubt attributable in great part to his teaching that salvation was open to

6. Akamatsu Toshihide and Kasahara Kazuo, eds., *Shinshūshi gaisetsu* (Kyoto, 1963), pp. 81–82. Note also the statement of Jitsugo (1492–1583), the tenth son of Rennyo: "Our school differs from other schools in that we prefer the portrait to the image, and the name [myōgō] to the portrait"; *Jitsugo kyūki*, in *Rennyo Shōnin gyōjitsu*, ed. Inaba Masamaru (Kyoto, 1948), p. 71 (hereafter cited as *Gyōjitsu*).

7. Kasahara Kazuo has estimated that there were perhaps as many as 100,000 followers of Shinran during his lifetime; "Shinran to Shinshū kyōdan no keisei," in *Ajiya Bukkyōshi: Nihon-hen* (Tokyo, 1972), 3: 209–212. Most of these, according to Kasahara, were not converted by Shinran personally but rather by his disciples.

all who would accept Amida's grace. It would be misleading, however, to
ignore the great charismatic influence that Shinran must have exerted on
his followers, who treated him with a degree of respect bordering on
veneration. At least two portraits of him were made while he was still alive
and were treated with the utmost reverence, as were the myōgō honzon
that were inscribed in his own hand. Devout followers made the arduous
journey to Kyoto to seek his guidance or render homage, and there is at
least one instance of an ailing follower coming up to Kyoto from the Kantō
so that he might die by Shinran's side.[8]

Although Shinran spent the last twenty-eight years of his life in Kyoto,
he does not seem to have had much of an impact within the capital itself,
perhaps because Hōnen's more prominent disciples had established
themselves there during Shinran's long stay in the Kantō, which, as
Shinran's letters indicate, was the main base of his movement. Of seventy
followers whose names are known, all but eight came from the Kantō or
Tōhoku areas.[9] In line with his conviction that he, like all other men of the
mappō age, was corrupt and impure, Shinran steadfastly refused to regard
himself as a master or teacher who formally accepted "disciples" (deshi) in
the traditional Buddhist pattern.[10] Amida's grace extended to all men
equally and hence there was no need for a formal hierarchy which implied
different stages of spiritual attainment. Shinran thought of his followers as
friends (dōbō) or companions (dōgyō), i.e., those traveling the same road
with him, but not as disciples.

Unlike most of the Kamakura reformers, Shinran did not found any
temples. Instead, those who accepted his teachings, the so-called monto,
formed local "religious associations" (kō), often headed by one of Shinran's trusted followers, who was designated head of the monto (monto no
otona) or, later, priest (bōzu) and bore responsibility for giving sermons on
the Shinshū doctrine and presiding at religious services at the chapels (dōjō), which in many cases were simply appendages to their own houses.[11]
The idea of a hierarchy being completely alien to his teachings, Shinran
did not designate any successor to wield authority over the monto. It was
inevitable, however, that certain followers of long-standing like Shimbutsu,
Kenchi, and Shōshin who had been held in particularly high regard by
Shinran would come to occupy a leading position among the monto once

8. Akamatsu and Kasahara, Shinshūshi gaisetsu, p. 72.
9. Kasahara Kazuo and Inoue Toshio, "Jōdoshinshū," in Shūkyōshi, pp. 161–162.
10. Tannishō, in Shinshū shōgyō zensho (Kyoto, 1957), 2: 776 (hereafter cited as SSZ). Although
Shinran himself did not refer to his followers as "disciples," we shall, for the sake of convenience,
use the English word "disciple" to describe his immediate followers.
11. For the general survey of early Shinshū history I have relied chiefly on Shinshūshi gaisetsu and
Inoue Toshio, Honganji (Tokyo, 1962).

Shinran was no longer with them physically. By the beginning of the fourteenth century, the monto, whose number had been increasing steadily, formed several well-defined groups, such as the Takada monto in Shimotsuke, the Yokosone monto in Shimōsa, the Kashima monto in Hitachi, and the Ōama monto in Mutsu. These groups, while showing a common, albeit often imprecise, belief in the Shinshū doctrine proclaimed by Shinran, were independent of each other. As time passed, they tended to establish branches in different parts of the country through the movement of priests who would make converts and organize them into kō centering around dōjō and, later, temples that were affiliated with the "mother group." To take one example, there were branches of the Takada monto of Shimotsuke scattered throughout Hitachi, Shimōsa, Mutsu, Musashi, Sagami, Tōtomi, Mikawa, Yamashiro, Tamba, Bingo, and Echizen provinces.[12]

. Although Shinran is said to have had seven children, he clearly had no intention of establishing a church presided over by his descendants, even though, ironically, that is precisely what happened. Of his seven children, only his eldest son, Zenran, and his youngest daughter, Kakushinni, played a significant role in early Shinshū history. Zenran was disowned by his father in 1256, as much for his espousal of heretical doctrines as for his attempt to use his father's prestige to dominate the monto in the Kantō region. Kakushinni, who took care of her father after her mother returned to Echigo in 1254, was at his bedside, along with several followers, when he died in 1262.

Shinran's cremated remains were first buried in an unpretentious grave in Ōtani. Ten years later they were reinterred on a small plot of land, also in Ōtani, which was owned by Kakushinni's second husband, Ononomiya Zennen. With apparently some support from the Kantō monto, a hexagonal chapel, subsequently known as the Goeidō, or Portrait Hall, was erected here to enshrine a portrait of Shinran. On her husband's death in 1275 title to the land passed to Kakushinni, who two years later transferred the ownership of the chapel and land, collectively known as the Ōtani Byōdō (Ōtani Mausoleum), to the "whole monto community" (sōmonto) on condition that her descendants be granted custodial rights (rusushiki).[13] For their part the monto had the obligation to provide financial support for the Ōtani Byōdō and its custodians. Although the rusushiki had to be a descendant of Kakushinni, the monto in the Kantō were given veto rights over the choice of nominee. Before her death in 1283

12. Shinshūshi gaisetsu, p. 77.
13. Most of the important documents relating to the early history of the Shinshū will be found in Honganji-shi (Kyoto, 1961), 1.

STANLEY WEINSTEIN

Kakushinni informed the monto in the Kantō of her decision to name Kakue, her son by her first marriage, as the first rusushiki.

The three generations after Kakushinni were marked by intense squabbling among her descendants, with the various factions or contenders seeking to legitimatize their claims by appealing for support to the Kantō monto, the acknowledged center of the Shinshū. First there was an unseemly quarrel between Kakushinni's two sons, Kakue and his half brother Yuizen, regarding the ownership of the land on which the Ōtani Byōdō stood. Despite Kakue's claim to the rusushiki based on his mother's will, Yuizen, backed by some of the Yokosone monto, seized the Ōtani Byōdō in 1306 and forced Kakue to flee. Before his death in the following year, Kakue named his son, Kakunyo (1270–1351), to be custodian. Kakunyo eventually succeeded in having Yuizen expelled but was able to secure confirmation by the Kantō monto only after submitting a statement in which he undertook to recognize the primacy of the Kantō monto in all matters relating to the Ōtani Byōdō and to affirm their ultimate proprietorship over it.

As soon as Kakunyo was confirmed as rusushiki in 1310 he began taking steps to raise the status of the Ōtani Byōdō, clearly with the intention of asserting its independence from the Kantō monto and making it the nucleus of the diverse, autonomous Shinshū groups. In 1312 an attempt was made to gain recognition for the Ōtani Byōdō as a regular temple under the name "Senjuji." The attempt was unsuccessful owing to the opposition of the abbot of Hieizan, who protested that such a designation would be inappropriate since the senju nembutsu had once been banned. Nevertheless the authorities did agree to grant temple status to the Ōtani Byōdō, which was redesignated "Honganji" sometime before 1321.[14] In an action involving the disinheritance of his own son Zonkaku (1290–1373), Kakunyo finally succeeded in 1334 in persuading the Shōren'in, which had jurisdictional authority over the land on which the Honganji stood, to recognize the Honganji's independence from the control of the Kantō monto.[15]

The establishment of the autonomy of the Honganji did not, in itself, guarantee its paramountcy over the many Shinshū dōjō and temples that existed by now in the home provinces and in most provinces to the east of the capital. As a reliquary for Shinran's remains, the Honganji obviously

14. It is not known precisely when the designation "Honganji" was adopted. It first appears in a petition, in Kakunyo's own hand, addressed to the Myōkōin, requesting that temple to intercede with the authorities on behalf of the Kantō monto who were being mistakenly persecuted as members of the Ikkōshu, i.e., Jishū. For the full text see Tsuji Zennosuke, *Nihon Bukkyōshi, chūseihen* (Tokyo, 1947), 1: 428–429.
15. For the text of the document see *Honganji-shi*, 1: 206–207.

had the potential of attracting monto on pilgrimages. But this did not necessarily confer special spiritual authority on the rusushiki for, in rejecting the traditional pattern of the master-disciple relationship, Shinran had substituted the radical idea of a fellowship whose members would all equally share in Amida's grace.

Although the blood link to Shinran could no doubt prove to be of value to Kakunyo in his pretensions to spiritual leadership over the monto groups, Kakunyo realized that to secure his position his authority—and, by extension, the authority of the Honganji—would have to be based on more than just blood descent. His own relation to Shinran was through his grandmother, Kakushinni, and Kakunyo's uncle, Yuizen, who had established himself in the Kamakura area, could also claim descent through Kakushinni. A potentially greater threat came from the lineage of Shinran's eldest son Zenran, who, despite Shinran's letters to the Kantō monto disowning him, had acquired followers in Mutsu, the Kantō, and especially Echizen.

To establish himself as the sole legitimate spiritual heir to Shinran, Kakunyo asserted in his *Kudenshō,* a work written in 1331, that he alone was the recipient of a direct transmission of Shinran's teachings through Nyoshin, Zenran's eldest son.[16] In so doing Kakunyo was reverting to a traditional Japanese, if not Shinshū, belief that orthodoxy must be based upon an unbroken transmission from master to disciple. Although a contemporary account records that Kakunyo at the age of eighteen received oral instruction in the Pure Land doctrine from Nyoshin, there is no indication that it was anything other than the usual type of sermon.[17] Nor is there any reason to believe that Nyoshin, who last saw his grandfather at the age of nineteen, had received any special doctrine from Shinran. While it is evident that Kakunyo greatly valued his link with Nyoshin, his veneration of Nyoshin probably was based on the fact that Nyoshin provided him with a direct link to Shinran through Zenran. Since primogeniture was an important factor in determining legitimacy in medieval Japan, Kakunyo attached more significance to an alleged transmission of doctrine from his uncle, who, although the son of a heretic, stood as Shinran's most immediate descendant, than he did to the more extensive instruction that he must have received from his own father, who was only a matrilineal descendant of Shinran.[18] Kakunyo no doubt realized that if he could get the monto to accept his claim to be Shinran's sole spiritual successor, it would follow as a matter of course that his own descendants, whose right to administer the Honganji free from monto interference was recognized in 1334, would be able to exercise control over the monto in perpetuity.

16. *Kudenshō,* in *SSZ* (Kyoto, 1964), 3: 36.   17. *Boki ekotoba,* in *SSZ,* 3: 780.
18. Inoue, *Honganji,* p. 66.

Despite Shinran's success in attracting a large number of followers during his lifetime and the rapid spread of the Shinshū in the years after his death, he did not succeed, at least in the short run, in bringing about a basic change in the religious attitudes of many of his followers. After returning to Kyoto around 1234, he felt deep distress over the failure of his followers to maintain the purity of the doctrine he had taught.

Once Shinran had left the Kantō, it became apparent that many of his ideas, if not backed by his charismatic personality, would prove to be too radical to be accepted by his unsophisticated followers. Despite the basically straightforward character of his doctrine of salvation through grace, the more educated monto soon became bogged down in the sort of arguments that divided Hōnen's disciples: whether one invocation of the nembutsu could be taken as proof of one's faith in Amida or whether repeated invocations were necessary (ichinen tanen no igi). Some learned monto questioned whether true faith required some degree of intellectual awareness (unen munen no igi), while other Shinshū adherents of a scholarly bent even went so far as to hold that rebirth in Pure Land could not be considered certain if the sacred texts were not studied (gakuge ōjō no igi).[19] Another false interpretation of Shinran's teachings that was particularly detrimental to the future prospects of the Shinshū was the heresy known as hongan-bokori, literally, "arrogance based on Amida's vow," which referred to the belief that evil deeds could be committed with impunity, since salvation was offered to all men regardless of whether they were good or evil. This distortion of Pure Land teaching, also termed zōaku muge, "freedom to work evil," which was found among some of Hōnen's disciples as well, greatly alarmed the civil authorities, who felt that it threatened the foundations of society.[20] Although Hōnen vehemently rejected the concept of zōaku muge as inconsistent with the Pure Land doctrine and warned that it would be used as a pretext by the traditional Buddhist schools to justify the suppression of the senju nembutsu, the charge that his teachings condoned or encouraged evil was nevertheless repeatedly made by Hōnen's (and Shinran's) adversaries to demonstrate the potentially immoral or subversive character of the Jōdo schools. The frequent accusations that Shinshū adherents placed themselves beyond traditional morality led some of the monto to revert to the position that "cultivation of virtue" (kenzen shōjin) was a necessary ingredient for salvation. Thus they

19. For a useful summary of the various heresies that appeared in the Kantō after Shinran's return to Kyoto, see Umehara Shinryū, "Itan no kokoro to itan-ha," in Gendai goyaku Shinran zenshū (Tokyo, 1958), 3: 188–124.
20. For the historical development of this important heresy, see the study of Ōhara Shōjitsu, Shinshū kyōgakushi kenkyū (Kyoto, 1956), 3: 73–103.

sought to place their school within the traditional pattern of Buddhist ethics and thus mollify their opponents. But their advocacy of the need to cultivate virtue was of course contrary to Shinran's teachings.

Doctrinal issues aside, the greatest obstacle to Shinran's efforts at reformation was the deeply entrenched religious attitudes of the medieval Japanese, which tended to view Amida as a deity who would work miracles, or the nembutsu as a magical formula capable of bringing about the fulfillment of prayers or the elimination of evil karma. There was also the tendency, with deep roots in Japanese tradition, to deify charismatic religious leaders, as in the cases of Shōtoku Taishi and Kōbō Daishi. Portraits of Shinran received adoration, and offerings were made to him by people seeking rebirth in Pure Land, though such practices clearly violated the whole intent of Shinran's teachings.[21] By the Muromachi period Shinran was variously regarded as an incarnation of Amida, Kannon, or the Chinese Pure Land thinker Tao-ch'o (562–645) and was being credited with having rescued the souls of the damned, "hungry ghosts" (gaki), and even snakes![22]

Another major difficulty in bringing about a reformation in the religious attitudes of the monto was the widespread appeal among medieval Japanese of magical formulas and devices such as amulets and charms, the latter illustrated in a story involving Shinran's immediate family. When Kakunyo was taken ill in 1290, he was visited by Zenran and Nyoshin. Zenran presented Kakunyo with an amulet (fu) which was described as having the power not only to cure illness but also to turn away curses and frustrate enemies. Not wishing to give offense, Kakunyo pretended to swallow the amulet, as Zenran had urged, but in fact hid it in his sleeve.[23]

For the simpleminded monto the aspect of Shinran's teachings that was hardest to comprehend was the abstract concept that one's salvation was guaranteed the moment one accepted Amida's grace. In the other Jōdo schools, the devotee could derive some sense of self-satisfaction from the fact that he was contributing in a tangible fashion toward his own salvation by reciting the nembutsu, chanting a Pure Land text, or worshiping an image of Amida. In the Shinshū, however, reciting the nembutsu or chanting sutras were not regarded as means of entering Pure Land, and the use of images of Amida as objects of worship was frowned upon. How,

21. For a specific example of an offering made to Shinran with the object of achieving rebirth in Pure Land, see the temple document dated 1473 in Kitanishi Hiromu, "Chūsei no minkan shūkyō," in Nihon shūkyōshi kōza (Kyoto, 1959), 3: 59.
22. Ibid., pp. 63–65.
23. Saishu kyōjū enokotoba, in SSZ, 3: 840.

then, could unsophisticated believers in Pure Land be certain of their ultimate salvation, since the crucial "awakening of faith" (*shin no ichinen*) was
something so intangible?

One of the first monks in the Jōdo tradition to face this question in a
forthright manner was Ippen, the founder of Jishū, who had studied Pure
Land teachings under Shōtatsu, a monk belonging to the Seizan branch of
the Jōdoshū. In 1271, after some three years of intensive recitation of the
nembutsu, Ippen had a revelation in which he was assured that a single invocation of the nembutsu was sufficient to bring about rebirth in Pure
Land, since all men had fulfilled the potentiality of enlightenment at the
very moment that Amida achieved Buddhahood ten kalpas ago. He
therefore resolved to travel about the country, much in the manner of such
earlier teachers as Kōya (903–972), urging people to recite the nembutsu.
Ippen, however, added a new element: as proof that the devotee had actually uttered the nembutsu and therefore was assured of salvation, he
issued an amulet (*fusan*) bearing the six characters of the nembutsu, which
not only protected the holder from disasters in this life but served to
guarantee his rebirth in Pure Land.[24]

Early in his practice of distributing the nembutsu amulet, Ippen en-
countered a monk who declined to accept one on the grounds that he (the
monk) had not yet experienced "true faith." Ippen finally persuaded the
monk to recite the nembutsu and accept the amulet but then sought
reassurance from the god of Kumano, who subsequently declared in an
oracle that because the salvation of all men was assured at the very moment that Amida attained enlightenment, the nembutsu amulet should be
distributed to all persons, whether or not they had faith. Ippen spent the
remainder of his life traveling the length and breadth of Japan distributing
amulets, possibly as many as 250,000.

A certificate or amulet assuring rebirth in Pure Land was welcomed by
the simpleminded believer as something tangible that dispelled any uncer-
tainties regarding the steadfastness of his own faith and his eligibility for
salvation. At the same time, the right to distribute the amulet conferred on
the priest the authority to determine who in fact was entitled to salvation.
The rapid growth of the Jishū owing to the requirement that its priests
lead peripatetic lives made it inevitable that some of its main ideas would
be picked up by Shinshū monto.[25] In 1320 a priest named Ryōgen
(1295–1335) visited Kakunyo at the Honganji for instruction in Shinshū

24. Ōhashi Toshio, *Ippen: Sono kōdō to shisō* (Tokyo, 1971), p. 50.
25. Akamatsu Toshihide makes a strong case for the likelihood of Jishū influence on the monto
groups, particularly the Bukkōji (in Akamatsu Toshihide, "Ippen Shōnin no Jishū ni tsuite," in
Kamakura Bukkyō no kenkyū [Kyoto, 1957], pp. 192–193), and argues persuasively that the bulk
of the Jishū was absorbed by the Shinshū during the Ashikaga period largely as a result of Rennyo's missionary activities (ibid., pp. 201–202).

doctrine and was subsequently placed under the tutelage of Kakunyo's son, Zonkaku. Before entering the religious life, Ryōgen—as a member of the bushi class which included many enthusiastic supporters of the Jishū—had probably been exposed to the ideas of Ippen. Ryōgen established the Kōshōji at Yamashina near Kyoto in 1324 (apparently with the blessing of Kakunyo who supplied its name) and six years later moved his temple, now renamed Bukkōji, to Shibutani in the Higashiyama section of Kyoto.[26]

Bukkōji, under the abbacy of Ryōgen, was soon recognized by Kakunyo to be a serious threat to the Honganji. Despite Kakunyo's blood link to Shinran through his grandmother and his assertion of the spiritual leadership of the monto on the basis of an alleged transmission of doctrine through Nyoshin, the monto groups, dispersed by now over the Kantō, Hokuriku, and Tōhoku regions, still tended to view Kakunyo as little more than the custodian (rusushiki) of Shinran's mausoleum and certainly not as the sole spokesman for Shinshū orthodoxy. Bukkōji's sudden popularity rested chiefly on the use of the "salvation register" (myōchō), a formal document certifying that the persons whose names appeared therein had experienced "true faith" and were assured of salvation.[27] The similarity in function between the myōchō used by the Bukkōji and the salvation amulet (fuda) distributed by the Jishū is apparent.

Another device resorted to by the Bukkōji was the "portrait lineage" (ekeizu), a scroll bearing the portraits of the priests authorized to enter names in the myōchō.[28] Aside from assuring the devotee that his priest was duly authorized to verify the believer's faith, the ekeizu served as a device for the Bukkōji to exert absolute control over its clergy. It stipulated that any priest who violated the injunctions of the main temple would be compelled to return all objects of worship and sacred texts (shōgyō). Significantly the ekeizu made no mention either of Shinran's blood descendants or of the Honganji but instead traced the lineage from Shinran through his "disciple" Shimbutsu to Ryōgen and hence to the priest of a particular branch temple of the Bukkōji.

Despite Kakunyo's condemnation of the use of myōchō and ekeizu in the Gaijashō—his principal polemical work against the distortion and adulteration of Shinran's teachings—heretical ideas continued to flourish among the monto.[29] Although later generations of Shinshū have held Kakunyo in great esteem as the first defender of Shinshū orthodoxy and as

---

26. Tanishita Ichimu, Zonkaku ichigoki no kenkyū narabini kaisetsu (Kyoto, 1943), pp. 109–117.
27. For the text of a myōchō dated 1343, see Rennyo: Ikkō ikki, pp. 446–447.
28. For the text of an ekeizu dated 1329, see ibid., pp. 448–449.
29. SSZ, 3: 64–67.

a relentless opponent of heresy, he was unable during his own lifetime to dispel the false notions regarding Shinran's teachings that had taken root among the various monto groups and were being exploited by their leaders to secure their own control. In retrospect, his most significant achievement was to raise the status of Shinran's mausoleum to that of a temple which would remain in the hands of his descendants free of monto interference. The antiauthoritarian legacy bequeathed by Shinran was still sufficiently strong to prevent Kakunyo from establishing spiritual and hierarchical authority over the monto.

During the hundred-odd years between the death of Kakunyo in 1351 and Rennyo's assumption of the abbacy (*hossu*) of the Honganji in 1457 the Honganji continued to assert, albeit in a relatively low key, its pretensions to leadership of the monto. Unlike Kakunyo, none of the four hossu who followed him—Zennyo, Shakunyo, Gyōnyo, and Zonnyo—did any theoretical writing on doctrine, nor did they undertake a crusade against heresy, which might have further antagonized the monto leaders. Instead they generally adopted a conciliatory, if somewhat condescending, attitude toward the major monto centers while trying to make their own position more secure through exploitation of their links with the religious and political establishment. Since the Honganji stood on land that was ultimately under the jurisdiction of the powerful Shōren'in, it became the custom for successive hossu to receive some of their religious training there, which offered a measure of protection to the fledgling Honganji when threatened by Hieizan.

The Honganji abbots also relied heavily on their blood ties with the aristocratic Hino family, in which Shinran was born, as is indicated by their regular practice of placing children under the guardianship of the Hino or collateral Hirohashi families as "charges" (*yūshi*). The advantages of Hino patronage were soon evident in an order issued in the name of Hino Tokimitsu in 1357 designating the Honganji as a *Chokuganji*, i.e., a temple accorded imperial recognition at which prayers for the tranquillity of the state could be offered.[30] The hossu further sought to protect their interests by sending their daughters into aristocratic families, if not through marriage, then through concubinage. It is no coincidence that the courtier Kujō Tadamoto, whose father had taken a concubine from "Ōtani," rushed to the defense of the Honganji when it faced an attack from Hieizan in 1388.[31]

While the Honganji gently tried to increase its influence among the

30. *Honganji-shi*, pp. 250–251.
31. In his letter to the regent, Tadamoto makes the patently false assertion that the Honganji was founded by Shinran with the approval of the emperor! See Inoue, *Honganji*, p. 117.

monto groups in the intermediate period between Kakunyo and Rennyo by stressing its direct links to Shinran, it followed the traditional sectarian pattern of founding its own branch temples. Moving out from the Kantō, the main base of Shinshū during Shinran's lifetime, the Honganji made a major effort to establish itself in the Hokuriku region where Shinshū had first been introduced by Shinran's direct disciples in the Takada monto. An important bridgehead was opened in 1390 when Shakunyo founded the Zuisenji in Etchū, which became a key Honganji branch temple. Thirteen years later, Rangei, the son of Shakunyo and younger brother of the then hossu Gyōnyo, established the Chōshōji in Echizen, which in turn controlled a network of smaller temples or chapels in Kaga and neighboring provinces. Although the Honganji rejected the use of ekeizu, it managed to exercise control over its branch temples through the granting of myōgō honzon and scriptures personally inscribed by the hossu. Despite the inroads made in the Hokuriku by immediate members of the hossu's family during the first half of the fifteenth century, the Honganji itself remained a minor temple in Kyoto. Early records mention that the Honganji was virtually unvisited by pilgrims during this period, while "people gathered like clouds" at its rival, the Bukkōji, where such devices as the myōchō and ekeizu were still in use.[32]

Rennyo, who as the eighth Honganji hossu was to realize Kakunyo's goal of making the Honganji the nucleus of Shinshū, spent the first part of his life in extremely difficult circumstances. At the time of his birth in 1415, his father, Zonnyo, who was only eighteen years old, had not yet succeeded to the position of hossu.[33] Rennyo's mother, about whose origins little is known, is believed to have been a servant in the Honganji at the time she entered into a liaison with Zonnyo. She was compelled to return to her home somewhere in western Japan five years later when Zonnyo took a wife from the Ebina family. Rennyo, who never saw his real mother again, was raised by his stepmother, who is depicted as being hostile toward him since, as Zonnyo's eldest son, he was in a strong position to succeed to the abbacy despite his mother's lowly origins.

Rennyo, who lived to the ripe age of eighty-four, married five times and had a total of twenty-seven children. He was first married at the age of twenty-seven to Nyoryō, who gave birth to seven children before her death

32. *Hompukuji atogaki*, reprinted in *Rennyo: Ikkō ikki*, p. 189; *Hompukuji yuraiki*, reprinted in Kasahara Kazuo, *Shinshū ni okeru itan no keifu* (Tokyo, 1962), pp. 296–297.
33. For much of the basic biographical data I have relied on Kasahara Kazuo, *Rennyo* (Tokyo, 1963). I should also like to express my thanks to Professor Michael Solomon of Oakland University for allowing me to read his valuable, but as yet unpublished, doctoral dissertation, "Rennyo and the Rise of Honganji in Muromachi Japan" (Columbia, 1972), to which I am indebted for a number of bibliographical references.

in 1455 in the thirteenth year of their marriage. Rennyo's sons, Jitsunyo and Renjun, have left vivid accounts of the poverty of Rennyo's household—shabby clothes, insufficient food, lack of money to pay their single servant, and, perhaps most humiliating of household—shabby clothes, insufficient food, lack of money after his own children adequately, Rennyo was forced to send six of his first seven children out for adoption, keeping only his eldest son at the Honganji. While there seems little doubt that economic hardship forced him to do this, he was careful to place some of his sons in strategic Shinshū temples in the Hokuriku, e.g., The Zuisenji and Shōkōji. exercise control over the monto in perpetuity. Hokuriku, e.g., the Zuisenji and Shōkōji.

Distressed by the enormous popularity of the Bukkōji and other heretical monto groups while the Honganji languished for lack of support, Rennyo, at least according to the testimony of one of his sons,[35] resolved at the age of fourteen to revive the original reachings of Shinran, then known to the majority of monto only in a distorted way. As his biographies indicate, he undertook an extensive study of the writings of Shinran, Kakunyo, and Zonkaku, extracting from them what he deemed to be the essence of Shinran's teachings and Kakunyo's polemics against heresy. In 1449, Rennyo accompanied his father on a tour of the Hokuriku area, where a number of important temples were in the hands of Zonnyo's relatives. Rennyo left his father in Kaga province to proceed on his own through the Kantō, visiting sites along the way associated with Shinran. The low standing of the Honganji at this time could not but be apparent to Rennyo, who later reported with some bitterness to his children how he had been ignored by the Kantō monto and not offered even a modicum of hospitality.[36]

Rennyo succeeded to the position of hossu in 1457, the year of his father's death, but not without considerable opposition from his stepmother, who had sought to have her only son, Ōgen, confirmed. At first glance the struggle over the right of succession would appear to be similar to the dispute between Kakue and his half brother Yuizen a century and a half earlier. The Rennyo-Ōgen dispute, however, illustrates the degree of independence that the Honganji had already achieved in relation to the monto. It will be recalled that both Kakue and Yuizen sought recognition of their rival claims to the rusushiki from the Kantō monto as well as from the civil authorities. In the Rennyo-Ōgen dispute the issue was resolved in Rennyo's favor solely through the intercession of Zonnyo's brother, Nyojō, who was the abbot of the powerful Zuisenji in Etchū and the Honsenji in Kaga.

34. *Jitsugo kyūki*, in *Gyōjitsu*, p. 89.   35. *Renjun-ki*, ibid., p. 64.
36. *Jitsugo-ki*, ibid., p. 148.

Rennyo began his missionary activities almost immediately after succeeding to the abbacy of the Honganji. Instead of attempting to establish a beachhead in the Kantō, which was still firmly under the control of the Takada Senjuji, Rennyo concentrated his efforts on the provinces of Ōmi, Mikawa, and Settsu where a residue of sympathetic sentiment for the Honganji existed since Zonkaku's activities a century earlier. In 1459 Rennyo presented a ten-character honzon, inscribed in gold, to the leader of the Zenshō monto in Ōmi. The following year a similar honzon was conferred on Hōjū, the head of the Katada monto, who had switched allegiance from the Bukkōji to the Honganji just before Rennyo's birth. In 1461 another honzon was granted to Nyokō, abbot of the Jōgūji in Mikawa. Ōmi and Mikawa were particularly important for purposes of proselytization, since there was a good deal of movement by merchants from these provinces to other parts of Japan.

Aside from his obvious goal of ultimately unifying the various monto groups under the leadership of the Honganji, Rennyo sought to revive and make readily accessible to the ordinary monto the original teachings of Shinran. Dissemination of Shinran's major theoretical work, the *Kyōgyō-shinshō*, written in Chinese, could not serve this purpose since it was far too technical to be understood by someone who did not have formal training in Buddhism. Similarly, commentaries on it such as the *Rokuyōshō* by Zonkaku were also of little value, since they too inevitably dealt with the minutiae of doctrine. Instead of presenting his own—or Shinran's—ideas in formal doctrinal treatises, Rennyo hit upòn the idea of issuing "pastoral letters" (*o-fumi*) in the colloquial language. As Rennyo explained, these o-fumi would be accessible to all people and, because of their straightforward presentation of doctrine, would not be susceptible to misinterpretation.[37] The o-fumi represented the distillation of the *Kyōgyōshinshō* in simple language that would enable the ordinary believer to acquire a true understanding of Shinran's teachings. As Rennyo graphically put it: "You should regard the o-fumi as the utterance of the Buddha—when you see the o-fumi, you are looking at Hōnen; when you hear its words, you are listening to the discourse of Amida."[38]

Rennyo's first o-fumi, addressed to Dōsai, a leader of the Katada monto, was issued in the third month of 1461.[39] Despite its brevity it presents an extraordinarily lucid statement of Shinran's teachings coupled with a refutation of some false notions presumably held by adherents of the

---

37. *Mukashi monogatari-ki,* ibid., p. 252.
38. *Jitsugo kyūki,* p. 85.
39. Inaba Masamaru, ed., *Rennyo Shōnin ibun* (Kyoto, 1972), o-fumi no. 1, pp. 47–48. All citations will be from this edition which contains 221 o-fumi reputed to be genuine and 14 of dubious authenticity.

Jōdoshū. In this o-fumi Rennyo urged the monto to put aside all belief in
the validity of "miscellaneous practices" (zōgyō zōshu) and submit completely to Amida: the moment that such a person relies on Amida
(tanomu), he will be saved by Amida's all-embracing radiance. Rennyo,
following Shinran, went on to declare that faith (shinjin) itself derives from
Amida: when one invokes the nembutsu, it should be thought of as an act
of gratitude and not a call for salvation. Rennyo concluded by pointing out
that the true Shinshū doctrine stresses the idea that salvation is assured
from the first moment of faith (ichinen hokki) and is continually verified
through one's daily experience. The obvious intent of this o-fumi was to
refute two widely held Jōdoshū ideas: first, that salvation depended upon
the utterance of the nembutsu and, second, that the invocation of Amida's
name on one's deathbed had special value.

Rennyo's success in persuading Shinshū temples in Ōmi to affiliate
with the Honganji through the acceptance of honzon that he himself had
personally inscribed provoked the resentment of Hieizan, which tended to
regard the home provinces as its private reserve.[40] In the first month of
1465 monk-warriors (akusō) from the Saitōin on Hieizan attacked the
Honganji and destroyed a number of buildings. The assailants failed to
capture Rennyo, who fled to the Jōhōji, a temple under the wing of the
Shōren'in. In an open letter to the authorities the Saitōin sought to justify
its resort to violence by accusing the Honganji of being an enemy of both
Buddhism and Shinto, in particular of having "burned Buddhist images
and scriptures and held the gods in disdain."[41] A charge was also brought
against the Honganji of "reviving the practice of senju nembutsu"—which
testifies to the influence that Rennyo's o-fumi were beginning to have
among the monto in the provinces. It was further suggested that the
Honganji was encouraging sedition by urging ignorant laymen in the
villages and hamlets to form cliques and groups under the name of
Mugekōshū. After considerable discussion among the Katada and Mikawa
monto whether they should try to expel the intruders by force, it was finally decided to pay the akusō a ransom, when it was determined that the
latter were in fact more interested in monetary rewards than doctrinal
questions. The negotiated settlement did not last long: the Honganji—or
what remained of it—was occupied again two months later.

Hieizan forces moved against the Honganji monto in Ōmi proper in
1466. After suffering some serious defeats, the Ōmi monto agreed in 1467

40. No less than ten jūji songō honzon that were inscribed by Rennyo during the period 1459 to
1464 and presented to the Omi monto survive. For a list, see Honganji-shi, 1: 313- 314. The jūji
songō honzon is a scroll bearing the ten-character formula Kimyō jinjippō Mugekō Nyorai ("I put my
faith in the Tathāgata [Buddha] whose unimpeded light fills the universe").
41. For the original text, see Honganji-shi, 1: 311.

to place themselves under the nominal jurisdiction of Hieizan temples and pay the requisite branch temple fees *(matsujisen)*. Meanwhile Shin'e, the abbot of the Takada Senjuji, which controlled the bulk of the monto in the Kantō, moved the Senjuji to Isshinden in Ise, which was an economically more developed area than Shimotsuke, taking care to dissociate himself from Rennyo's potentially subversive Mugekōshū.[42] No doubt another reason for Shin'e's decision to shift the center of his group closer to the home provinces was his fear of Rennyo's growing influence among the provincial monto, who had traditionally been within the sphere of influence of the Takada Senjuji. Despite Shin'e's probable aristocratic origins, his authority as abbot of the prestigious Senjuji rested on the tradition that he was the sole heir to an oral transmission from Shinran through Shimbutsu, which enabled him to assert that he had attained the "status of Shinran." This claim was now being directly challenged by Rennyo in his efforts to revive Shinran's teachings.

Fearing still another attack by the partisans of Hieizan in the early part of 1468, the leaders of the Katada monto urged Rennyo to move to Ōtsu, where there were already some Honganji supporters. To protect himself from further depredations by Hieizan, Rennyo obtained the permission of Miidera, a longstanding Tendai rival of Hieizan, to build on its grounds a Shinshū temple, the Kenshōji, which would enshrine the sacred portrait of Shinran. Miidera apparently welcomed this move as an opportunity to attract large numbers of pilgrims who would inevitably contribute to its own prosperity. About this time Rennyo paid a second visit to the Kantō, where he was now warmly received by the monto—a clear sign of his growing influence in what had been solid Takada territory.[43]

In the spring of 1471 Rennyo left Ōmi, which had been occupied during the preceding year by the unfriendly forces of the daimyo Rokkaku Takayori.[44] After traveling about the Hokuriku for several months, Rennyo finally settled in Yoshizaki in Echizen. Although Rennyo wrote in an o-fumi dated the ninth month of 1473 that he selected the site for his new residence because of its scenic beauty, his choice of Yoshizaki, as Kasahara Kazuo has shown, was based on more than the attractiveness of the landscape.[45] The area in which Yoshizaki was situated was part of an estate belonging to the Kōfukuji Daijōin, whose abbot, Kyōkaku, was sympathetic to the cause of the Honganji because his mother had come from

42. Shin'e declared that, since the Senjuji was the "head temple" *(honji)* of the Shinshū and faithfully adhered to the injunctions of Shinran, it should be distinguished from the "ignorant followers of the Mugekōshū"; Inoue, *Honganji*, p. 149.

43. *Jitsugo-ki*, p. 149.

44. Inoue, *Honganji*, p. 151.

45. Kasahara Kazuo, *Ikkō ikki no kenkyū* (Tokyo, 1962), pp. 59–82.

"Ōtani," i.e., the family of the hossu. Despite the antipathy of the Kōfukuji toward the monto in general, Kyōkaku maintained a close relationship with Zonnyo and his son, Rennyo, who had studied under him. It seems likely, therefore, that Rennyo selected Yoshizaki rather than some other site in Echizen because he felt that he would be more secure through his connection with Kyōkaku.

Another important factor in Rennyo's decision to move to the Hokuriku region was the network of Honganji-affiliated temples that had already been built throughout the provinces of Echizen, Etchū, and Kaga.[46] Rennyo's uncle, Nyojō, who played a key role in Rennyo's confirmation as hossu, controlled the Honsenji in Kaga and the Zuisenji in Etchū. Rennyo's third son, Rengō, was abbot of the important Shōkōji in Nomi-gun in Kaga. When Rennyo arrived in Echizen, Asakura Toshikage, by then shugo of the province, was prevailed upon by the Hongakuji to make land available for Rennyo's new headquarters.[47] Toshikage is said to have quickly acceded to the request, perhaps partially in the hope of ingratiating himself with the already large number of monto in the region who were adherents of Honganji-affiliated temples.

Despite the large number of temples in the Hokuriku related to the Honganji, the area was generally regarded as a hotbed of heresy with the Sammonto, a group founded by Nyodō, at its center.[48] Although Nyodō had received instruction in the *Kyōgyōshinshō* from Kakunyo and Zonkaku during their visit in 1311 and may even have considered himself a disciple of Kakunyo, he seems to have put forward the claim that he was the recipient of a secret transmission from Shinran through Zenran, which signified that he now held a position "equivalent to that of Shinran" (*Shinran'i*).[49] The belief in a secret transmission was also, as we have noted, held by the Takada Senjuji monto with which Nyodō had been affiliated before his move to Echizen. What is particularly interesting about Nyodō's claim to being Shinran's spiritual heir was his reference to an alleged transmission from Zenran. Nyodō, as the successor to Shinran, appropriated for himself the title *zasu*, which traditionally had been applied to the chief abbot of Hieizan, and in a new interpretation of Shinran's teachings proclaimed that one attains Buddhahood the very moment

46. For a succinct account of the Honganji-affiliated temples in the Hokuriku with a map showing their locations, see Kasahara, *Rennyo*, pp. 127–130.
47. Kasahara, *Ikkō ikki no kenkyū*, pp. 73–74. Kasahara indicates that there is evidence that Toshikage had some dealings with Rennyo as early as 1466.
48. The name Sammonto, which literally means "three monto groups," was probably adopted because the movement was centered in three large temples in Echizen: the Ōmachi Senjuji founded by Nyodō, the Yokogoshi Shōjōji, and the Sabae Jōshōji—the latter two presided over respectively by Nyodō's disciples Dōshō and Nyokaku.
49. *Ōtani Honganji tsūki*, in *Dai-Nihon Bukkyō zensho*, 132: 202.

(*ichinen*) that faith in Amida arises. As a corollary, it was asserted that there was no need to worship any images: if one feels the need to worship, the object of veneration should be one's own person, since the Buddha is none other than oneself. These Sammonto ideas, which bear some similarity to Zen concepts, spread rapidly throughout Echizen. By the middle of the fifteenth century Sammonto-related groups controlled five major temples in Echizen.

While silent on the alleged transmission from Zenran, perhaps because of the hossu's claim to legitimacy through Zenran's son Nyoshin, Rennyo vigorously attacked the Sammonto heresies in his o-fumi. In an undated letter to the monto, Rennyo wrote that "the commonly held belief that one is transformed into a Buddha when faith arises is an outrageous perversion of Shinran's teachings."[50] In another o-fumi dated 1472 Rennyo, following Shinran, said that acceptance of Amida's grace (*ichinen hokki*) had a dual benefit (*niyaku*): in this life it gave assurance that one is destined to be reborn in Pure Land; and in the next life, i.e., in Pure Land, it led to the attainment of Buddhahood.[51] This was a rejection of the Sammonto belief that Buddhahood is realizable in this life.

We have already noted the tendency among Pure Land devotees to seek some tangible evidence of their salvation such as the nembutsu fuda of the Jishū or the inclusion of one's name in a "salvation register," practices which inevitably placed great power in the hands of priest as sole arbiter of who was eligible for salvation. Although the priestly interposition ran counter to Shinshū teachings, it nevertheless was widely accepted by monto in the Muromachi period, as is shown by Rennyo's frequent references to it in his o-fumi. According to this concept, which was technically known as "reliance on the priest" (*zenjishiki-danomi*), salvation was not possible, even though one fully accepted Amida, if one did not place complete faith in one's priest. In an o-fumi written in the fifth month of 1474, Rennyo declared that monto who held this view failed to understand the true meaning of "faith" according to the Shinshū tradition. He defined the role of the priest as that of "a servant who exhorts the monto to put their trust completely in Amida."[52]

Rennyo was equally harsh with those priests who encouraged monto to demonstrate their faith through gifts of money or goods, a heresy known as "reliance on offerings" (*semotsu-danomi*). In an o-fumi written in the ninth month of 1473 he decried the practice by priests of designating those monto who made substantial contributions as "good disciples" (*yoki deshi*) or "men of faith" (*shinjin no hito*).[53] He warned monto not to be misled into

50. O-fumi no. 189, pp. 488–489.
51. O-fumi no. 18, dated 1472/11/27, pp. 89–90. See also Shinran's *Jōdo wasan*, in *SSZ*, 2: 497.
52. O-fumi no. 60, dated 1474/5/20, pp. 193–194.
53. O-fumi no. 31, pp. 121–122.

believing that they could make up for their lack of faith through gifts to a priest. This kind of thinking, he asserted, was a serious blunder, which led not to Pure Land but to hell for both the priest and his parishioner. Salvation came only from Amida, and it was not within the power of the priest to compensate for any deficiencies, regardless of the size of the gift from the monto. As early as the summer of 1471, when Rennyo had just arrived in Yoshizaki, he issued a letter to the Shinshū followers there denouncing the tendency of priests to regard monto as "their own disciples."[54] Rennyo reminded the monto that Shinran had rejected the concept of "disciple" and spoke only in terms of "friends" (*dōbō*) and "companions" (*dōgyō*).

Despite relentless efforts through preaching and o-fumi to lead the monto back to the teachings of Shinran and purge the Shinshū of various heresies, Rennyo scrupulously avoided confrontation with non-Pure Land schools. While his o-fumi faithfully reproduce Shinran's ideas on a popular level, they do not contain a single specific reference to the Nara or Heian schools, nor do they mention even once the Rinzai, Sōtō, or Nichiren schools which were very active during his own lifetime. As the o-fumi clearly indicate, Rennyo's primary concern was directed toward correcting the distortions of Shinran's teachings that were so prevalent among the monto. His o-fumi bristle with phrases liked "warped doctrines" (*higa hōmon*), "eccentric doctrines" (*kuse hōmon*), "pseudodoctrines" (*ese hōmon*), and "unusual doctrines" (*mezurashiki hōmon*) applied to the practices of the non-Honganji monto groups. While treating Hōnen's name with the utmost respect, as did Shinran, Rennyo repeatedly criticized key Jōdoshū doctrines such as the interpretation of the significance of the nembutsu, the importance of invoking Amida's name on one's deathbed, and the conviction that Amida would appear before a person at the moment of death (*raigō*) to conduct him to Pure Land.

In addition to his attack on the Jōdoshū, whose main branches he often cites by name, he wrote at least fourteen o-fumi which condemn Jishū beliefs and practices.[55] He particularly criticized the Jishū concept technically known in Shinshū dogmatics as *jikkō anjin*, the belief that true faith was none other than the knowledge that one's salvation was realized along with Amida's enlightenment ten kalpas ago.[56] In a series of o-fumi written in Ōmi and Yoshizaki, Rennyo spoke out against the pretentious garments worn by Shinshū priests who had been influenced by the

54. O-fumi no. 8, dated 1471/7/15, pp. 62–64.
55. Ishida Mitsuyuki, "Rennyo Shōnin no igi shisō to sono hihan," in *Rennyo Shōnin kenkyū* (Kyoto, 1948), pp. 168–172.
56. O-fumi no. 32, dated the ninth month of 1473, pp. 123–124; o-fumi no. 60; and o-fumi no. 77, dated 1475/2/25, pp. 231–233.

peculiar dress of the Jishū "holy wanderers" (*yugyō shōnin*), reminding the monto of Shinran's injunction to dress like ordinary laymen.[57] In three separate o-fumi, Rennyo stressed that, popular usage notwithstanding, Shinran's school should not be called Ikkōshū, but Shinshū, the name used by Shinran himself. The designation "Ikkōshū," Rennyo pointed out, belonged exclusively to the Jishū, with its chief temple at Bamba in Ōmi, and hence should not be used by Shinran's followers.[58]

If the o-fumi suggest that Rennyo was aiming his criticisms primarily at the rival Pure Land schools and unorthodox monto groups in an effort to win their adherents over to Shinran's doctrine of salvation through grace, his missionary activities nevertheless aroused the enmity of the older schools, even though Rennyo had deliberately avoided reference to them. What the traditional schools found particularly offensive in Rennyo's attempt to revive Shinran's teachings was his uncompromising insistence, especially apparent during his first few years at Yoshizaki, that the monto put aside all religious practices other than the nembutsu and rely solely on Amida to the exclusion of all other Buddhist deities and Shinto gods.[59] In an o-fumi dated the twelfth month of 1473, Rennyo went so far as to refer to the Shinto deities and all Buddhas other than Amida as "useless playthings" and particularly cautioned the monto against the commonplace practice of worshiping other deities in addition to Amida in the hope of acquiring greater merit. Concluding on a Confucian note, Rennyo admonished the monto to remember the maxim: "The loyal subject does not serve two lords; the chaste wife does not minister to two husbands."[60]

Within a year or two of his arrival in Yoshizaki his reputation as a great spiritual leader—and, by implication, successor to Shinran—had spread from the Hokuriku to the home provinces[61] and, in Rennyo's own words, was drawing "tens of thousands of believers—lay and clerical, male and female"—on pilgrimages from Kaga, Echizen, and Etchū.[62] A major road was built to provide easier access to his residence, which soon came to resemble a large traditional temple with its imposing gateways. We can get some indication of the size of the Yoshizaki establishment from Rennyo's statement that well over one hundred separate residences were built

57. Ishida, "Igi shisō," pp. 172–174.
58. O-fumi no. 29, undated, pp. 114–115; o-fumi no. 30, dated the ninth month of 1473, pp. 115–118; o-fumi no. 123, dated 1490, pp. 372–373.
59. O-fumi no. 32, p. 124.
60. O-fumi no. 43, dated 1473/12/13, pp. 150–153.
61. Note Rennyo's reference to priests from Kyoto traveling to Yoshizaki in his o-fumi no. 48, dated the twelfth month of 1473, p. 162.
62. O-fumi no. 24, dated 1473/8/2, pp. 103–105.

to house the priests who had settled there to look after the throng of pilgrims.

It is not difficult to imagine the reaction of the established Tendai temples in Echizen to the sudden influx of large numbers of Shinshū followers who might erode their own hold on the province. Appeals were made to the shugo of Kaga and Echizen to take some action to stem the tide. Rennyo, anxious to avoid a head-on confrontation with the Tendaishū, explained defensively in an o-fumi written in the twelfth month of 1473 that "as a man from the capital" (*kyō-hito*) he found life in Echizen difficult and had hoped to return to Kyoto a year earlier but was prevented from doing so by the local priests (who no doubt realized that his presence was attracting vast numbers of monto, which made the priests a potentially powerful force in the Hokuriku).[63] Rennyo professed to be unhappy with the congregation of monto in Echizen and reported that during the preceding year he had instructed the monto, in deference to the wishes of the shugo and Tendai temples, not to gather in Echizen but had been unable to dissuade them from coming. He concluded by saying that he found the crowds of monto around him so burdensome that several months earlier he had in fact again attempted to return to Kyoto only to be intercepted at Fujishima, the site of the important Honganji-affiliated Chōshōji, by local priests who prevailed upon him to turn back.

The following month Rennyo issued another o-fumi in which he complained that the priests were ignoring his explicit instructions to discourage monto from assembling in Yoshizaki.[64] While sympathizing with those monto who had made the journey to do reverence to the honzon and portrait of Shinran (*goei*), he openly questioned the motives of some of the visitors "who lacked any understanding" of the Shinshū teachings and simply went through the motions of piety. Rennyo was particularly distressed to find a resurgence among his own followers of the *zenjishiki-danomi* heresy (i.e., reliance on the priest for salvation) with paradoxically himself as the object. His caustic advice to those monto who came to venerate him in the hope that he could verify their faith and promise them salvation was to do their worshiping at cemeteries, since that act of piety could at least prevent their falling into hell!

Despite Rennyo's efforts to restrain his followers, it was becoming increasingly evident that the Echizen monto, as a potentially powerful force within the Hokuriku region, could not avoid entanglement in the Ōnin War. The extensive network of Honganji-affiliated temples throughout the Hokuriku permitted the Yoshizaki priests, who themselves came from

63. O-fumi no. 48, pp. 162–164.
64. O-fumi no. 51, dated 1474/1/20, pp. 170–173.

different provinces, to mobilize the monto "in defense of the faith" if they felt that such action might serve their interests. In 1473 Togashi Masachika, the shugo of Kaga, was forced to take refuge in Echizen after suffering a defeat at the hands of his brother, Kōchiyo.[65] Masachika requested support from Asakura Toshikage as well as from the Yoshizaki priests, who were led to think that a victory by Masachika would strengthen their own position in Kaga. Another factor working in Masachika's favor was that Kōchiyo had entered into an alliance with the Takada Senjuji monto, the rival Shinshū group. Even though Rennyo viewed bushi with distaste,[66] increasing numbers of bushi were declaring themselves to be monto,[67] perhaps in the hope that they could exploit the latent strength of the Shinshū movement.

In the tenth month of 1473 the issuance of an o-fumi, signed not by Rennyo but by the Yoshizaki priests and calling on the monto to rise up in defense of their faith, signaled the opening of the *Ikkō ikki* in the Hokuriku.[68] Although apparently sympathetic to the cause of Masachika, which had the support of Asakura Toshikage as well as the bakufu, Rennyo was alarmed by the belligerence of the monto who, incited by their priests, had begun to attack temples of other sects and challenge the civil authorities. The following month he promulgated for the first time in the history of the Shinshū a set of eleven rules incumbent on all monto which included prohibitions against treating Buddhist and Shinto deities with contempt, criticizing other schools, and otherwise engaging in any type of intolerant behavior.[69] Monto were also instructed to show respect to shugo and jitō and to refrain from eating fish and meat, drinking sake, or gambling at religious services.

The excesses of the monto led Rennyo to soften his position noticeably with regard to the traditional Shinshū attitude toward non-Pure Land divinities as well as toward the use of the nembutsu as a means to realize tangible benefits in this world. In a remarkable o-fumi dated the second month of 1474 Rennyo, reverting to a position held by Zonkaku, the twice disinherited son of Kakunyo, asserted that Amida includes within himself all other Buddhas, bodhisattvas, and even the Shinto deities.[70] The implications of this statement were twofold: first, that one need only put one's faith in Amida, who, as Rennyo repeatedly said, had the power to

65. Inoue, *Honganji*, pp. 155 ff.
66. Note his disparaging comments about bushi as "enemies of Buddhism" in *Eigen-ki*, in *Gyōjitsu*, p. 262.
67. *Jitsugo-ki*, p. 150.
68. O-fumi no. 37, pp. 130-131.
69. O-fumi no. 38, pp. 131-133.
70. O-fumi no. 54, dated 1474/2/17, pp. 177-180.

save even the most evil men; and, second, that any disrespect shown toward a Buddhist or Shinto deity was in effect blasphemy toward Amida. Thus, through the worship of Amida the monto could receive the protection of such popular deities as Kannon and Jizō.

In the same o-fumi Rennyo reaffirmed that the primary concern of the monto should be rebirth in Pure Land and that the nembutsu was the appropriate expression of gratitude. However, he added a new interpretation, one that was at variance with Shinran's, when he explained that the desire for rebirth in Pure Land inevitably becomes a prayer for well-being in this world as well. Thus when a person looks to Amida for salvation, he at the same time will gain tangible benefits in this life, "just as the farmer who grows rice gets straw as a by-product."[71] In the very act of placing one's faith in Amida one worships all other deities; by seeking rebirth in Pure Land one prays for prosperity in this life. Fearful that the aggressive activities of the monto would eventually result in the suppression of the burgeoning Shinshū movement, Rennyo cautioned the monto not to try to convert people of other sects or proclaim their own beliefs openly. He ended his o-fumi with the admonition that the monto who has true faith is respectful to the shugo and jitō, pays his taxes in full, and adheres to the code of secular ethics.

Once the battle was joined in the seventh month of 1474 between Masachika and his Yoshizaki monto allies on one side and Kōchiyo on the other, Rennyo sought desperately to restrain the monto who rampaged through Kaga, urging them in a series of o-fumi not to rebel against the legitimate authorities, attack other religious establishments, or attempt to appropriate power for themselves. In the fifth month of 1475 he issued a set of injunctions ordering the monto to refrain from their attacks on established institutions;[72] two months later, another set of six virtually identical regulations appeared, but to no avail.[73] By now the monto were already in conflict with Masachika, their erstwhile ally. Despite Rennyo's extraordinary success in persuading the majority of the Hokuriku monto to accept the hossu as the sole arbiter of Shinshū orthodoxy and as the successor to Shinran, he now found himself caught in the midst of a civil war in which there was an unavoidable conflict between his own image of the Shinshū as a religion compatible with the feudal order and the view of local monto bushi and priests who regarded the uprisings as a chance to extend their own power. Rennyo decided that under these circumstances he had best quit the Hokuriku and return to the capital region, where

71. Ibid., p. 178.
72. O-fumi no. 79, dated 1475/5/7, pp. 236–240.
73. O-fumi no. 83, dated 1475/7/15, pp. 246–250.

he could devote himself to his long-cherished dream of rebuilding the Honganji.

In the eighth month of 1475 Rennyo sailed from Yoshizaki for Wakasa. From there he traveled through Tamba and Settsu to the village of Deguchi in Kawachi, where he established a temporary residence. As his o-fumi indicate, there were already large numbers of people in the home provinces who professed to follow Shinran's teachings.[74] In an o-fumi dated the first month of 1476 he observed that despite the enthusiasm of the local monto for Shinshū, neither they nor their priests had any real knowledge of its teachings. Their understanding, as Rennyo phrased it, consisted of bits and pieces "picked up on the verandah or from the other side of the *shōji*."[75] Although heretical ideas such as the *zenjishiki-danomi*, *jikkō anjin*, and *hiji bōmon* (belief in a secret transmission of doctrine) were all found here, Rennyo had little difficulty in winning the allegiance of the local monto. As in Yoshizaki, he issued a continuous series of o-fumi, including refutations of heresy, straightforward sermons on Shinran's teachings, and exhortations to the monto to abide by secular laws and refrain from intolerant behavior toward other schools.

Rennyo moved in the spring of 1478 from Deguchi to Yamashina, the site he had selected for the new Honganji. It took five years to complete work on the temple, which consisted of a Goeidō in honor of Shinran, an Amida-dō, a Shinden (which would serve as the residence of the hossu), and a number of minor buildings.[76] Monto from surrounding provinces participated in the construction, and Shinshū adherents from Kawachi carried the timber for the pillars of the Goeidō from the forests of Yoshino in Yamato. The Goeidō was formally consecrated in 1481 when the sacred portrait of Shinran that had been enshrined in the Kenshōji was brought to Yamashina over the objections of the Miidera priests, who feared that the loss of the portrait would lead to a decline in the number of monto pilgrims. Contemporary accounts describe the Honganji, which covered six *chō*, in superlative terms, one source likening it to Pure Land itself and another speaking of its "unsurpassed magnificence."[77] As Inoue Toshio has observed, the new Honganji must have been all the more impressive in view of the devastation that Kyoto had suffered during the Ōnin War.

When Rennyo at the age of seventy-four relinquished the abbacy of the Honganji in favor of his fifth son, Jitsunyo, he could look back at his life with a sense of great achievement. At the time of his birth the Honganji

---

74. O-fumi no. 86, dated the third month of 1477, p. 254.

75. O-fumi no. 86, variant version dated 1476/1/27, p. 257.

76. See Kasahara, *Rennyo*, pp. 265–270, for a detailed account of the construction of the various buildings.

77. *Nisui-ki*, quoted in Inoue, *Honganji*, p. 160.

was a small, impoverished temple in Kyoto, albeit with grandiose pretensions, rarely visited by the monto, while the rival Bukkōji flourished.
Although Shinran himself was widely revered, his teachings were grossly
distorted and misunderstood, and despite the large number of monto
scattered throughout the country, there was no universally accepted
nucleus capable of providing leadership. During the thirty-two years of his
tenure as hossu, Rennyo had indisputably succeeded in reviving Shinran's
teachings and making them readily accessible to the masses. Although
heresy remained a problem for the Honganji through the Edo period, and
indeed has remained so down to our own times, credit must be given to
Rennyo for providing the definitive statement of the Shinshū faith. It was
no doubt a matter of great personal satisfaction to Rennyo when in 1481
Kyōgō, the heir to the Bukkōji in whose shadow the Honganji had
languished, formally acknowledged his allegiance to the hossu—along
with forty-two priests including some members of Kyōgō's own family.[78]
Rennyo, who warmly embraced Kyōgō, gave him a new name, Renkyō,
containing a character from his own name and built for him a temple
called Kōshōji. By the time of his death in 1499 Rennyo had realized the
unfulfilled aspiration of Kakunyo in making the Honganji the undisputed
center of the Shinshū.

78. Kasahara, *Rennyo*, pp. 282–283. Yamada Bunshō states in his *Shinshūshi-kō* (p. 126) that 42
of the 48 branch temples that supported the Bukkōji switched allegiance to the Honganji at this
time.

GLOSSARY

ANKOKUJI 安国寺
"Temples of national peace" established by Ashikaga Takauji and Ashikaga Tadayoshi.

BAKUFU 幕府
Literally "tent government," the term applied to the shogun's government.

BASARA 婆娑羅
Extravagance and ostentation.

BIWA 琵琶
A lute.

BIWA HŌSHI 琵琶法師
A lute-playing priest.

BŌZU 坊主
Buddhist priest.

BUGYŌNIN-HŌSHO 奉行人奉書
Administrative directives.

BUGYŌNIN-SHŪ 奉行人衆
Corps of administrators.

BUGYŌSHŪ 奉行衆
See bugyōnin-shū.

BUSHI 武士
Armed fighter; warrior.

CHA-NO-YU 茶の湯
Tea ceremony.

CHIGAI-DANA 違棚
Split-level shelves.

CHIGYŌ 知行
Fief.

CHŌ 町
Unit of land measurement: 2.94

acres until 1594 when Hideyoshi reduced the size to 2.45 acres for his cadastral surveys.

CHŪMONRŌ 中門廊
Covered entrance arcade.

DAIKAN 代官
Deputy or supervisor.

DAIMYŌ 大名
Regional military lord.

DENGAKU NŌ 田楽能
An early form of nō drama.

DŌBŌSHŪ 同朋衆
Individuals who served in the courts of shogun and daimyō as arbiters of taste and practioners of the arts.

DOGŌ 土豪
Powerful peasant chiefs.

DO-IKKI 土一揆
Peasant leagues.

DŌJŌ 道場
Buddhist chapels.

DOSŌ 土倉
Pawnbroker or moneylender.

EGŌSHŪ 会合衆
Elders of city government.

EHON 絵本
An illustrated work or book.

EKEIZU 絵系図
"Portrait lineage" or scroll bearing the portraits of priests authorized to enter names in myōchō

or "salvation registers."

EMAKI 絵巻
An illustrated horizontal scroll.

ENGI 縁起
History of the origins of a shrine or temple.

ENKYOKU 宴曲
A song form usually on Buddhist themes.

ETOKI HŌSHI 絵解法師
"Picture explainer"; men and women who used illustrations as visual props.

FUSHIMONO 賦物
Prescribed themses for *renga*.

FUSUMA 襖
Wall panels.

GEKOKUJŌ 下剋上
The overthrow of superior by subordinate; a term referring to the political upheaval of the Sengoku period.

GENKAN 玄関
Vestibule.

GŌ 郷
In medieval Japan the landholding which had developed out of the ancient unit of village administration called *gō*.

GOKENIN 御家人
Official vassals of the bakufu.

GORYŌ 御料
The shogun's personal estates or directly controlled lands.

GORYŌKOKU 御料国
Shogunal provinces.

GOSHO 御所
Imperial residence.

GŌSON 郷村
Villages.

GOZAN 五山
"Five mountains"; the temples

at the apex of the official hierarchy of the Zen sect.

GOZE 瞽女
Blind women singers of tales.

GOZEN SATA 御前沙汰
Shogunal council.

GUN 郡
Administrative division of a province.

HAIKAI 俳諧
Comic form of *renga*.

HAIKU 俳句
Seventeen-syllable poetry.

HANZEI 半済
System of income division in which *shugo* assigned to his vassals half the produce of centrally owned *shōen*.

HEIKYOKU 平曲
Music for the performance of the *Heike monogatari*.

HIKAN 被官
Personal subordinates of *kokujin* lords.

HIKITSUKE-KATA 引付方
Board of Inquiry; judicial agency of the Muromachi bakufu.

HIKITSUKESHŪ 引付衆
Adjudicators.

HIKITSUKE-TŌNIN 引付頭人
Head of Board of Inquiry.

HOKKU 発句
Term designating first three lines of a *waka* poem.

HŌKŌSHŪ 奉公衆
Shogunal military guard.

HONKE 本家
Patron or protector of a *shōen*.

HONZON 本尊
Scroll with an inscription of Amida's name.

HŌSHI 法師

Priest.

HOSSU 法主
Abbot of the Honganji.

HYAKUSHŌ 百姓
Peasant.

HYŌJŌ 評定
Council of senior vassals.

ICHIZOKU 一族
Lineage (including cadet branches.)

ICHIMON 一門
Kinsmen within a larger vassal organization.

ITAKARADO 板唐戸
Swinging doors of *shinden* architecture.

IKKI 一揆
League; alliance.

IN 院
Retired emperor.

ISSHIKIDEN 一色田
Paddy land belonging to the *shōen* which was distributed to cultivators.

JISSETSU 十利
"Ten temples"; second-echelon temples of the *gozan* system.

JITŌ 地頭
Title of authority used by warrior land steward.

JŌRURI 淨瑠璃
Generic term for narrative *samisen* music; also used to mean puppet theater.

KAISHO 会所
New form of domestic structure of the Muromachi period.

KAKEJIKU 掛軸
Hanging scroll.

KAN 貫
Unit of cash equivalent to 1000 *mon.*

KANDAKASEI 貫高制
"Cash assessment" system.

KANGŌ 勘合
Tallies used in the official licensed trade between Ming China and Japan.

KANMON 貫文
See *kan.*

KANREI 管領
Deputy shogun.

KARAMONO 唐物
Imported works of art and craftmanship.

KATOKU 家督
Household chiefs of cadet branches.

KAWARAMONO 河原者
Base people; outcasts.

KAWASE 為替
Drafts for the transfer of funds.

KEBIISHI 檢非違使
Policing office for Kyoto; also became designation for provincial enforcement official.

KOKU 石
Measure of rice by volume equivalent to 44.8 gallons (180 liters).

KOKUGARYŌ 国衙領
Provincial domains.

KOKUJIN 国人
"Men of the provinces"; semi-independent local proprietors.

KOKUJIN IKKI 国人一揆
Leagues or alliances of *kokujin.*

KUGE 公家
Kyoto court aristocrats of Heian ancestry.

KUMANO E 熊野絵
Paintings used by nuns for proselytizing purposes.

KYŌGEN 狂言
Comic entr'acte plays in *nō*

performances.

MACHI 町
Social and administrative unit of city or town.

MACHIGUMI 町組
Townsmen organization.

MACHISHŪ 町衆
Townsemen.

MAEKU 前句
First verse of a *renga* poem.

MANDOKORO 政所
Administrative office.

MAPPŌ 末法
Buddhist term indicating period of moral decline.

MON 文
Unit of cash; 1000 equal one *kan*.

MONCHŪJO 問注所
Records office.

MONOGATARI 物語
Classical court tale.

MONTO 門徒
Adherents of the Shinshū school of Buddhism.

MUSHIN 無心
"Inelegant" style of *renga*.

MYŌ 名
Unit of the local cultivator's tenure.

MYŌCHŌ 名帳
"Salvation register" of the Bukkōji.

MYŌDEN 名田
Paddy fields named after a cultivator indicating some degree of private ownership.

MYŌGŌ HONZON 名号本尊
Scroll with Amida's name inscribed which served as an object of veneration.

MYŌJIN 明神
A diety.

MYŌSHU 名主
Heads of large households who had *myōden*.

NEMBUTSU 念仏
Invocation of the name of Amida Buddha.

NENGU 年貢
Annual ground rent in kind.

NŌ 能
Dramatic art form combining chanted text, stylized dance, and music.

O-FUMI 御文
"Pastoral letters" which were usually written in colloquial style.

ONSEI BUNGAKU 音声文学
Oral literature of the Muromachi period.

ONSHŌ-KATA 恩賞方
Office of Rewards.

OSHI-ITA 押板
Decorative platform.

RENGA 連歌
Linked verse style of poetry.

RENJI MADO 連子窓
Slatted windows.

RUSUSHIKI 留守職
Custodian.

RYŌKE 領家
Central proprietor of a *shōen*.

RYŌKOKU 領国
Provincial domains; territory under a *shugo*'s jurisdiction.

RYŌSHU 領主
Proprietary lord.

SAKAYA 酒屋
Sake dealers.

SAMISEN 三味線
Three-stringed instrument played with a plectrum.

SAMURAI-DOKORO 侍所
Board of Retainers.

SARUGAKU NŌ 猿楽能
An early form of *nō* drama.
SATODAIRI 里内裏
Unofficial imperial residence.
SEKISHO 関所
Toll barriers.
SEN 銭
Unit of cash.
SENGOKU DAIMYŌ 戦国大名
Type of daimyō characteristic of
the Sengoku period.
SENJU NEMBUTSU 専修念仏
Exclusive practice of the nem-
butsu.
SHIKI 職
A post, appointment, or office
with its accompanying income.
SHIKI-HYŌJŌSHŪ 式評定衆
Counselors.
SHINDEN 寝殿
Palace-style architecture.
SHITOMI 蔀
Hinged wall panels.
SHITSUJI 執事
Chief officer of the *mandokoro*.
SHITSUJIDAI 執事代
Assistant to the *shitsuji*.
SHŌGUN 将軍
Term designating the warrior
leader at the top of the military
class hierarchy; the de facto ruler
of Japan.
SHŌEN 荘園
Private landed estate.
SHOIN-ZUKURI 書院造
Architectural style associated with
the military aristocracy of the Mu-
romachi and Tokugawa periods.
SHŌJI 障子
Sliding door.
SHŌKE IKKI 姓家一揆
Leagues of village communities.

SHOKUNIN 職人
Generic term for occupations out-
side agriculture including artisans,
intellectuals, and entertainers.
SHOMIN 庶民
Common people.
SHORYŪ 庶流
Cadet branches of a lineage.
SHOSHI 所司
Chief officer of the *samurai-dokoro*.
SHOSHIDAI 所司代
Deputy of the *shoshi*.
SHOZAN 諸山
Temples associated with im-
portant provincial families.
SHUGO 守護
Great territorial lord whose area
of jurisdiction extended over
whole provinces.
SHUGODAI 守護代
Local lord who was the deputy of
the *shugo* at the local level.
SHUGO DAIMYŌ 守護大名
Provincial lords of the early Muro-
machi period.
SŌDAI 総代
Representative.
SŌROKU 僧録
Highest administrative official of
the Gozan temple system; chief
Zen prelate of Japan..
SŌRYŌ 惣領
Lineage chief; chief heir.
SŌRYŌSEI 惣領制
Pattern of warrior organization
in which authority over the ex-
tended family was retained by
the senior house.
SŌYŪDEN 総有田
Common lands of a village.
SUIBOKUGA 水墨画
Monochrome paintings.

TAN 段
 Land unit equivalent to approximately one-third acre.

TANSEN 段銭
 Temporary provincial unit tax imposed for palace construction, coronations, etc. which eventually became a tax on the *shugo*.

TATAMI 畳
 Straw matting used as flooring in Japanese houses.

TEIKIICHI 定期市
 Regular market.

TOIMARU 問丸
 Wholesaler.

TOKONOMA 床の間
 Modern-day decorative alcove.

TOKUSEI 徳政
 General term for debt or sale cancellation decree.

TOKO 床
 Raised-floor alcove.

TONSEISHA 遁世者
 Person who has taken Buddhist vows and is leading a "detached" life.

TON'YA 問屋
 Wholesale merchants.

TSUKEKU 付句
 Added verse of a *renga* poem.

TSUKE-SHOIN 付書院
 Writing alcove.

USHIN 有心
 "Elegant" style of *renga* poetry.

WAKA 和歌
 Court poetry; 36-syllable poetry.

WAKŌ 倭寇
 Term used to refer to pirate bands which ravaged the Asian continent in the 14th–16th centuries.

WEN-JEN 文人
 Chinese literati tradition.

YORIAI 寄合
 Assembly or council; Council of Chief Vassals of the Muromachi bakufu.

YORI-UDO 寄人
 Bugyōnin specialized in legal administration.

YŪGEN 幽玄
 Aesthetic term conveying aura of mysteriousness.

YŪHITSUSHŪ 右筆衆
 Corps of Administrators.

ZA 座
 Trade or craft guilds.

LIST OF CONTRIBUTORS

AKAMATSU TOSHIHIDE, Professor Emeritus of Kyoto University is now Professor at Ōtani University. A foremost specialist on the history of Buddhism in medieval Japan, he has published *Kamakura Bukkyō no kenkyū* (2 vol., 1958–66), and *Shinran* (1961).

GEORGE ELISON, Associate Professor in the Department of East Asian Languages and Cultures at Indiana University, has acquired a special interest in medieval Kyoto. He published *Deus Destroyed, the Image of Christianity in Early Modern Japan* (1973), and is now at work on a major study of Oda Nobunaga.

KENNETH A. GROSSBERG, A Junior Fellow of the Society of Fellows, Harvard University, is a Princeton trained political scientist specializing on the political dynamics of the Muromachi bakufu.

JOHN W. HALL, is Alfred Whitney Griswold Professor of History and Chairman of the History Department at Yale University. Among his published works are: *Government and Local Power in Japan, 500–1700: A Study Based on Bizen Province* (1966); *Japan: From Prehistory to Modern Times* (1968), *Studies in the Institutional History of Early Modern Japan* (with Marius B. Jansen, 1968); *Medieval Japan, Essays in Institutional History* (with Jeffrey P. Mass, 1974).

HAYASHIYA TATSUSABURŌ, formerly Professor at Ritsumeikan University is now Professor at Kyoto University. A prolific writer on medieval culture and on the history of Kyoto, he is best known for his *Nambokuchō* (1957); "Higashiyama bunka" in *Iwanami kōza Nihon rekishi* (1963), *Machishū* (1964), *Kyōto* (1967), and his contributions to the multivolume *Kyōto no rekishi* (1967–).

ITŌ TEIJI, Professor, and now President of Kōgakuin University, is a specialist on the history of architecture in Japan. He has written *Chūsei jūkyoshi* (1958).

KANAI MADOKA, Professor at the University of Tokyo, is on the staff of Shiryō Hensanjo. Although his prime specialty is Japan's international affairs during the Sengoku and Tokugawa eras, he has written extensively in the field of early modern political organization. He has published *Hansei* (1962), and *Hansei seiritsuki no kenkyū* (1975). He was also chief Japanese translator of G. B. Sansom's *The Western World and Japan*.

KAWAI MASAHARU, Professor at Hiroshima University has specialized in the study of medieval institutions in western Japan. His publications include *Setonaikai no rekishi; Ashikaga Yoshimasa* (1970); and *Chūsei buke shakai no rekishi* (1973).

365

DONALD KEENE, Professor of Japanese at Columbia University, is the author of numerous books and articles on Japanese literature and theater. Among his outstanding publications are: *Japanese Literature: an Introduction for Western Readers* (1958), and *Landscapes and Portraits: Appreciation of Japanese Culture* (1971). He has translated works of both classical and modern literature, and has edited *Anthology of Japanese Literature* (1955), and *Modern Japanese Literature* (1956).

CORNELIUS J. KILEY, Assistant Professor of East Asian History at Villanova University, is the author of articles on the legal and institutional history of Japan up through the Heian period. His "Estate and Property in the Late Heian Period" is contained in J. W. Hall and J. P. Mass, eds., *Medieval Japan, Essays in Institutional History* (1974).

KUWAYAMA KŌNEN, Research Associate at the University of Tokyo is on the staff of Shiryō Hensanjo and specializes on the political history of the Muromachi era. He has contributed the study "Muromachi bakufu keizai no kōzō" in Nagahara Keiji, ed., *Nihonkeizaishi taikei* (2 vols., 1965).

MIYAGAWA MITSURU, Professor at Ōsaka Kyōiku University, is a leading authority on sixteenth century land systems. He is best known for his *Taikō kenchi ron* (3 vols., 1957–63).

V. DIXON MORRIS, Associate Professor of History at the University of Hawaii, is a specialist on medieval Japanese history and literature. His dissertation is a study of the city of Sakai.

NAGAHARA KEIJI, Professor at Hitotsubashi University, has written extensively on the political and social institutions of medieval Japan. Among his major publications are, *Nihon hōkensei seiritsu katei no kenkyū* (1961), *Nihon chūsei shakai kōzō no kenkyū* (1973), and *Sengoku no dōran* (Nihon no rekishi series, 1975).

PAUL NOVOGRAD, a Ph.D. candidate at Columbia University, is specializing in the study of Japanese gardens.

JOHN M. ROSENFIELD, Professor and Chairman of the Department of Fine Arts, Harvard University, is a specialist in Buddhist art. He is the author of *Japanese Art of the Heian Period* (1967), and co-author of *Traditions of Japanese Art* (1970).

BARBARA RUCH, Associate Professor of Japanese Language and Literature and Director of the Institute for Medieval Japanese Studies at the University of Pennsylvania, is a specialist in medieval Japanese literature. She is the author of several articles and editor of *An Anthology of Medieval Japanese Short Stories.*

ROBERT SAKAI, Professor of History and former Chairman of the Asian Studies Program at the University of Hawaii, is the author of several studies of Satsuma and co-author of *The Status System and Social Organization of Satsuma.* He was editor of *Studies of Asia* from 1960–1966.

SATŌ SHIN'ICHI, Professor at the University of Tokyo, is best known for his studies of medieval legal systems. Among his works are "Muromachi bakufu ron," in *Iwanami kōza, Nihon rekishi* (1963); *Nambokuchō no dōran* (Nihon no rekishi series, 1965); *Chūsei hōsei shiryō shū* (with Ikeuchi Yoshisuke, 2 vols., 1955–57).

RICHARD STAUBITZ, Assistant Professor of History at Yale University, is a specialist on local government in Japan, particularly the nineteenth century.

SUGIYAMA HIROSHI, has recently been appointed Professor at Komozawa University. At the time of the Conference he was on the staff of Shiryō Hensanjo. He has written *Shōen kaitai katei no kenkyū* (1959), "Muromachi bakufu" in *Nihon rekishi kōza* (vol. 3, 1957).

TANAKA TAKEO, is Professor at the University of Tokyo and a member of the staff of Shuyō Hinsanjo. His major works cover Japan's foreign relations during the medieval period: *Chūsei kaigai kōshōshi no kenkyū* (1959) and *Wakō to kango bōeki* (1961).

TOYODA TAKESHI, Professor Emeritus of Tohoku University, is now teaching at Hōsei University. His scholarship has ranged widely over the economic history of medieval Japan. His published works include: *Chūsei Nihon shōgyōshi no kenkyū* (1952), *Sakai* (1957), *Bushidan to sonraku* (1963), *Nihon no hōken toshi* (1964), *Ryūtsūshi* (1969), and *Kōtsūshi* (1970).

H. PAUL VARLEY, Professor of Japanese History at Columbia University, is a specialist on Muromachi cultural history. He is the author of *The Ōnin War* (1967); *Imperial Restoration in Medieval Japan* (1971); *Japanese Culture, a Short History* (1973); and co-author of *Samurai* (1970).

STANLEY WEINSTEIN, Professor of Buddhist Studies at Yale University, is the author of numerous studies on both Japanese and Chinese Buddhism. His publications include: "The Concept of Reformation in Japanese Buddhism," in *Studies in Japanese Buddhism* (P.E.N. Club, 1973); and "The Beginnings of Esoteric Buddhism in Japan: The Neglected Tendai Tradition," in *The Journal of Asian Studies* (1974).

KOZO YAMAMURA, Professor of Asian Studies and Economics at the University of Washington, has published extensively on the economic history of modern and pre-modern Japan, most recently *A Study of Samurai Income and Entrepreneurship* (1974). He is one of the founding editors of *The Journal of Japanese Studies*.

PHILIP YAMPOLSKY, Adjunct Professor of Japanese and East Asian Librarian at Columbia University, is the author of several studies on Japanese Buddhism, including *The Platform Sutra of the Sixth Patriarch* (1967).

INDEX

INDEX

CORNELL EAST ASIA SERIES

To order, please contact the Cornell East Asia Series, East Asia Program, Cornell University, 140 Uris Hall, Ithaca, NY 14853-7601, USA; phone (607) 255-6222, fax (607) 255-1388, ceas@cornell.edu, http://www.einaudi.cornell.edu/bookstore/eap

CPSIA information can be obtained
at www.ICGtesting.com
Printed in the USA
LVHW091917271119
638742LV00008B/38/P